The Theatre of Thomas

CW01665102

'Almost the only question we ask of any piece of theatre is: Is it alive? Thomas Ostermeier's theatre absolutely is. Alongside his 'social vision' of the exterior world is also a profound musicality, which leaps past logic to another deeper human truth. The wordless, the un-sayable, the unreasonable and the instinctive and incidental is always there in his work. There is a poetic dimension which, by definition, cannot be defined by any book. So don't look for answers. Here, perhaps, in this book is a description of a journey that is as much a kind of self-interrogation as the revelation of a "method" '.

—*Simon McBurney*

With *The Theatre of Thomas Ostermeier*, the German director presents his directorial method for the first time. The book provides a toolkit for understanding and enacting the strategies of his advanced contemporary approach to staging dramatic texts. The book includes:

- Ostermeier's seminal essays, lectures and manifestos translated into English for the first time.
- Over 140 photos from the archive of Arno Declair, who has documented Ostermeier's work at the Schaubühne Berlin for many years, and by others.
- In-depth 'casebook' studies of two of his productions: Ibsen's *An Enemy of the People* (2012) and Shakespeare's *Richard III* (2015)
- Contributions from Ostermeier's actors and his closest collaborators to show how his principles are put into practice.

An extraordinary, richly illustrated insight into Ostermeier's working methods, this volume will be of interest to practitioners and scholars of contemporary European theatre alike.

Peter M. Boenisch is Professor of European Theatre at the University of Kent, and a Fellow at the International Research Centre 'Interweaving Performance Cultures' at Berlin. He is the author of *Directing Scenes and Senses: The Thinking of Regie* (2015).

Thomas Ostermeier is the most internationally recognised German theatre director of the present. He is best known for his acclaimed productions of *Hedda Gabler*, *Shopping and Fucking*, and *Hamlet*. Since 1999, he has been Artistic Director of the Schaubühne Berlin, and since 2005, he has also been Professor for *Regie* at Ernst-Busch-Theatre Academy Berlin. He became the youngest ever recipient of the Golden Lion award for his life's work at the 2011 Venice Biennial.

Thomas Ostermeier. © Ute Mahler & Werner Mahler/OSTKREUZ.

THE THEATRE OF THOMAS OSTERMEIER

PETER M. BOENISCH AND THOMAS OSTERMEIER

The Theatre of Thomas Ostermeier

Peter M. Boenisch and
Thomas Ostermeier

For Maria

It all started with your offer to write that chapter on him....

thanks for all your support throughout so many years

London. 26/4/2017

Routledge
Taylor & Francis Group
LONDON AND NEW YORK

First published 2016
by Routledge
2 Park Square, Milton Park, Abingdon, Oxon OX14 4RN

and by Routledge
711 Third Avenue, New York, NY 10017

Routledge is an imprint of the Taylor & Francis Group, an informa business

British Library Cataloguing-in-Publication Data
A catalogue record for this book is available from the British Library

Library of Congress Cataloguing-in-Publication Data
Names: Ostermeier, Thomas, 1968– author. | Boenisch, Peter, author.
Title: The theatre of Thomas Ostermeier / Thomas Ostermeier & Peter Boenisch.
Description: Milton Park, Abingdon, Oxon ; New York, NY : Routledge, 2016.
Identifiers: LCCN 2015039801| ISBN 9781138914469 (hardback) | ISBN 9781138914476 (pbk.) | ISBN 9781315690810 (ebook)
Subjects: LCSH: Ostermeier, Thomas, 1968—Criticism and interpretation. | Theater—Production and direction.
Classification: LCC PN2658.O77 O77 2016 | DDC 792.02/33092—dc23LC record available at http://lccn.loc.gov/2015039801

ISBN: 978-1-138-91446-9 (hbk)
ISBN: 978-1-138-91447-6 (pbk)
ISBN: 978-1-315-69081-0 (ebk)

Typeset in Bembo
by Book Now Ltd, London

MIX
Paper from responsible sources
FSC www.fsc.org FSC® C013604

Printed and bound by CPI Group (UK) Ltd, Croydon, CR0 4YY

Contents

Foreword

Simon McBurney

'Will you write the foreword?'

Thomas Ostermeier looks at me, or more properly looks down at me. Being 6'4", he is eight inches taller. He is always asking questions. This one is unexpectedly specific.

'Foreword' comes from the Latin praefatio, 'to speak before'. If you have picked up this volume, it is the main speaker you are here for. So what to say, before? What is there to say that is not already within the book? I can tell you a little about Thomas.

He is tall. He stoops a bit, perhaps as a consequence of leaning over scripts in darkened theatres. He is restless, and when he laughs, and he laughs a lot, it is infectious, on the in-breath, like a delighted horse.

'I can't keep still ...', he once told me. 'In school I think I had what would now be called ADS, I couldn't stop moving and talking. But when we did theatre I found my energy could suddenly be productive. I did not come to it through literature or art. I mean my family were a very working class Bavarian family. There were at most three books in the whole house. My father was a soldier and my mother a shop assistant. But in the school theatre, all my energy found a place. I could speak, I could move. I could play.'

And before I have answered, we are off down the corridor of the Schaubühne am Lehniner Platz, converted from the Universum cinema designed by Erich Mendelsohn in 1928. This oval modernist building sits like a boat on the Ku-damm. Heavily damaged in World War II, it was rebuilt and re-opened as a cinema, then from 1969 was a dance hall and also used for musical theatre. In the late 1970s, when the Schaubühne was under the artistic direction of Peter Stein, the interior was gutted and changed to allow an infinitely flexible space in which all parts could move and be adjusted. It is a dream space for any theatre maker. Unimaginable in any country other than Germany with its enlightened subsidy of the arts. Currently, Ostermeier and his team have divided the theatre into three spaces. The newest one he wants to show me. It was designed specifically for his production of Shakespeare's *Richard III*, adapted and translated by Marius von Mayenburg.

Thomas flings open the door.

'What do you think?' I see an extremely shallow semi-circular thrust stage, a cylindrical auditorium of three galleries, rising to the ceiling.

'I have built the Globe in our theatre!' He laughs.

This is not so much the Globe as a vertical snow-boarder's half-pipe. The audience is so perilously close to the actors that they will be inseparable from the action. As they were in Shakespeare's Globe which, as we know, addressed an audience not of passive observers but active participants. Everyone was in the same space. Lit, of course, by the same light. One of the most revealing qualities of the reconstructed Globe in Southwark, for example, was to show us that the soliloquies were not private meditations, but public debates. But this 'Globe' in the Schaubühne, while it engages the audience similarly, is no reconstruction. It is a space for now. For the twenty-first century and, as with all of Thomas' work, it addresses the immediate present. It demands (you could almost say forces) the audience to pay attention. There is no possibility of disengagement. Because of how we are seated we will be obliged to be part of whatever takes place on the stage, to interrogate and be interrogated. Which is what Ostermeier does. He interrogates.

> I am mainly used to Germans telling me what to do ... so how does it feel to be welcomed with such warmth in France?

François Hollande leans forward for an answer. Thomas leans his huge frame forward over his plate. For a moment, in front of the French President, he looks uncharacteristically vulnerable. Now it is he who is being interrogated. He frowns.

'Not every German is like Angela Merkel.'

Hollande roars with laughter. The table relaxes. It is only weeks since his election. He is optimistic, razor sharp, and extremely witty. Together with the artistic directors of the 2012 Avignon Festival, and other assorted French directors we, the only two foreign directors at the festival, have been summoned to a dinner to celebrate this fact while he makes his first official visit to the city.

A few days earlier, at the climax of the opening night of Ostermeier's remarkable production of Ibsen's *An Enemy of the People*, a harsher voice screams from the audience: 'What is a German doing telling us how to think about our lives, when you think what you did here, or have you forgotten?!?'

This would be somewhat alarming in the middle of a normal production, but for Ostermeier and his team it is meat and drink. Dismantling the barrier between audience and the stage in the fourth act, they switch the play from a stage bound drama into a public referendum on the current state of political and social culture – and mayhem breaks out in the audience.

Back at the Schaubühne in 2015, I remind Thomas of our dinner with Hollande three years previously. 'You were not so complementary about Cameron either', he laughs. The delighted horse again. 'Listen I have to deal with some stuff to do with *Hamlet*. An actor is sick ...' And he is off.

Thomas Ostermeier's *Hamlet* still runs in rep, and tours globally, even though it was created seven years ago, in 2008. A permanent ensemble of actors ensures this longevity; just one of the remarkable aspects of the work of the Berlin Schaubühne. When Ostermeier was installed as artistic director in 1999, at just thirty-one years old, critics and aficionados were alarmed imagining the hallowed Schaubühne being overrun by barbarians. They needn't have worried. Ostermeier's tenure has been a life force bringing a whole new generation of audiences to the theatre. Actors, dramaturgs and technicians from his previous life in the tiny anarchic Baracke which he ran at Deutsches Theater strengthened the collective atmosphere of the building. 'Making an ensemble is an art', he tells me. 'It is a way of life.' Despite being elected to run one of the most influential theatres in the German-speaking world, and therefore someone who now could legitimately be thought to be firmly 'established', he remains relentlessly questioning. He has changed much in this iconic theatre. For example abandoning some long held traditions such as only using a clique of German directors, and instead inviting ground-breaking theatre-makers from round the world whose work he deeply admires. If he is the worst amongst these directors, he declares, then he would be the best artistic director the theatre could have.

I look back at the vertiginous multi-galleried space before me. There will be no hiding here from being drawn into Richard's world. The world of his consciousness, the world inside his head.

> 'Dive, thoughts down to my soul.'

Richard confides in us just before the entrance of Clarence. Dive thoughts, let's hide together, he says to us, the audience, his fellow collaborators who share in all he thinks and feels – us, his fellow collaborators who laugh at his outrageous behaviour because we know what the other characters in the play are not privy to. It is a monstrous joke of Shakespeare's: placing us in Richard's mind, to delight in his infamy, his brutality, his violence. Like that we become complicit in his every thought. He tells us. Everything. And the visual metaphor of compression that is this vertical snowboarder's half-pipe fits the piece exactly. We are compressed into Richard's mind.

This visual clarity is a striking aspect of Ostermeier's work. Never literal, his settings are kinetic, playful environments in which everything you see reflects meaning. His *Hamlet* was a single rectangular space, earth filled, the dead ever present, a site of rot and corruption in which the characters slipped and stumbled, each gesture revealing the inadequacy of the human condition. In *An Enemy of the People* the walls are blackboards, furniture drawn onto them in chalk, then scrawled over, crossed out, defaced and, brilliantly, just before Stockman's big moment, whitewashed. The sparse simplicity of the space throws the emphasis onto the actors, the text, and the moral question at the heart of the piece.

'I never wanted to do this play, I found the characters too one-dimensional', he tells me. 'But I have had it on the list for a long time, and it came up at weekly meetings with my collaborators, the dramaturgs. All very smart guys, unlike me.' He laughs. '"You cannot wait any longer to do this play", they told me.

"Yah but its not that good ... it's too simple!"

"But this is the moment to do it."

"Yah but I am not a fan ..."

But then I found a few solutions. I made the mother and the daughter into one character ...'

His production of *Enemy* is of course not just a psychological drama about courage and moral rectitude. In it we are forced to consider the urgency of the social context, how people live in a society that privileges economic relations above personal ones. Stockman, brilliantly played as disaffected young political radical who only wants to play in his indie band, discovers there is a serious health problem with the town's baths which are the source of the town's wealth. The water is toxic. The town doesn't want to admit it for fear of impoverishment. But Stockman blows the whistle on it ... 'And then a year after we were touring this show, Snowden blows a slightly bigger whistle ... I guess my dramaturgs were really smart ...', Thomas says.

At every moment I am reminded this is a collective process. Making an ensemble is an art. Ostermeier's insatiable curiosity has its root in genuine uncertainty. He does not know. He uncovers.

Exposing the political and social wounds of plays he directs, touching the actual concerns of the audience and infecting them with the urgency of these issues, is his intent. But, as he says self-deprecatingly, far from being 'in-yer-face', and someone who 'shakes up of the classical repertoire', he considers himself quite conservative: '... I am just trying to be honest with the play, get to the core of the text.'

He acknowledges the early influence of teachers like Einar Schleef and the director Manfred Karge who were '... guys in the East German tradition, with a high estimation of skill, who were not so much interested in the psychological, but looking out at the kind of society you live in'. But that is not to suggest that for him, with his army of dramaturges and thinkers this is an intellectual exercise. Ostermeier's theatre is embodied. The meaning lives through bodily exertion and physical engagement. This brings an immediacy and a challenge.

The half-pipe is packed the night I come to see *Richard*. From the opening the body is centre stage. The clouds have lifted and men are dancing, violently rejoicing, engaged in their 'lascivious' capering, dancing 'nimbly to my lady's chamber', music blasting out in celebration. But Richard will not, as consequence of his bodily shape, get to partake of this Dionysian celebration. And so he reveals to us:

> ... Since I cannot prove a lover
> I am determined to prove a villain ...

Lars Eidinger is on fire. At once mesmeric and grotesque, his demeanor simultaneously repels and sucks you in. It is unrestrained, replete with urgent embodied desires, right in front of you. And within you. His instincts, once confided to us, are there within us, part of what it means to be a human animal. Richard is absolutely conscious of what he is doing. And we enjoy it. Indeed we laugh at it.

And then suddenly the 'playing' stops ...

'I've been watching you throughout the show!' Eidinger suddenly yells at a member of the audience in the second balcony which because of the space is only yards away from his spittle-flecked lips. 'I've been watching you. I can see the light on your iPhone! You're f***ing filming, turn that f***ing thing off!'

If there was any illusion of being an observer it is shattered now. I have no idea if this is intended, but that is irrelevant because in all Ostermeier's productions something like this can happen at any moment. Everyone is alive to what is happening in the here and now. And the point is made in this production of *Richard*. The political and the personal are inseparable. Our inner world determines what happens in the outer world. The journey of *Richard* is about the journey of the dark trails that cross all our souls, a theme the poet returns to time again through his life. We are complicit in that journey not just in *Richard*, but in *Timon*, in *Hamlet*, crucially in *Macbeth* where he chooses to make his bloodiest murderer the most beautiful poet. And so the climax of this *Richard* on the battlefield is him fighting. Desperately. For his life. Against all the odds. And losing. But here the clarity for Ostermeier is absolute. Because he has chosen to show Richard fighting against himself. There is no enemy except within. And the shadows he thrusts and cuts against are those that haunt our generation, our society, our dark culture, our selves. And we recognise once more that this century of violence, corruption, brutality and injustice is also the century of the 'self'. To change without we have to change within ... and to see within we must be confronted with what darkness is there. We have to ask the hard questions. We have to interrogate our own selves.

But alongside this 'social vision' of the exterior world is also a profound musicality in Ostermeier's work. I don't just mean that he uses music, which he does to hilarious effect in *Enemy* when Stockmann and his pals attempt to rehearse the band they have together and play David Bowie's 'Changes'. Rather something deeper that contributes profoundly to the emotional power of the plays he directs.

'One of my first memories', he tells me, 'was that every Sunday we had visits from the family. My uncle, grandfather on the sofa, my mother serving coffee and cake. It was then, aged 7 or 8, that I loved to perform the conductor. Classical music on the stereo, with something like a chopstick, I would stand on a chair and then imagine an orchestra in front of me. They would all roar with laughter. Me, I was completely exposed, but in my own world, completely lost in a musical passion ...'

Music is beyond words. It leaps past logic to another deeper human truth. And the wordless, the un-sayable, the unreasonable and the instinctive and incidental also form part of any work in the theatre. And it is there always in Ostermeier's work. Something happens because it appears just like that. Not because it is worked out. Not because it has an intellectual place, a specific meaning but because it simply is. There is a poetic dimension which, by definition, cannot be defined by any book. So don't look for answers. Here, perhaps, in this book is a description of a journey that is as much to do a kind of self-interrogation as the revelation of a 'method'.

Richard fights with himself. In contradiction to what is there on the page. In this huge and lonely battle, curiously moving, strangely beautiful, meaning is implied but not explicit. This is not what Shakespeare wrote. But it is what he intended. What he intended was for the final moments of Richard's life, in which his tragic fate is exposed, to come alive for us. Almost the only question we ask of any piece of theatre: Is it alive? And here it absolutely is.

Perhaps this book answers how Thomas effects this, or perhaps it does not. But what I do know is that common to all Thomas' work is a simple sense of human exposure. In all the fierce and brutal passion there is also great vulnerability. The effect is both touching and disturbing. The personal and political are inseparably entwined, as are dissonance and musicality, brutality and compassion. His work leaves us in a state of uncertainty. The final judgement is up to us.

Talking about *Enemy of the People* he said, 'this production is about my friends, about myself, about us ... you know, vegetarian, politically informed, online, always a bit angry, upset with political scandals, corruption. But when it truly comes to doing something what do we do? What action do we take? ... So the end of the play in our version is where we are standing politically at the moment ... I mean all of us who think we are politically alive and yet live in the richest so called Democracies in the world ...' Stockman and his wife look at the shares on the table ... they look at each other ... then they look at the shares ... They look at each other ... then they look at the shares ...

Simon McBurney co-founded Complicite in 1983. He is an actor, writer, and director, and was the first British Artiste Associé at the Avignon Festival in 2012. His 2015 solo piece for Complicite, *The Encounter*, was co-produced with Schaubühne Berlin. In 2015, McBurney directed a stage adaptation of Stefan Zweig's novel *Impatience of the Heart* at the Schaubühne – his first production for Thomas Ostermeier's company, and also his first German-language work.

Acknowledgements

Without the opportunities provided by a Small Research Grant awarded by the British Academy and the Leverhulme Trust, I would not have been able to immerse myself so intensely into Thomas Ostermeier's work at the Berlin Schaubühne. These periods of research residence at Berlin were further complemented by study leave provided by the University of Kent during Spring 2014. At Kent, I am particularly indebted to the former Dean of Humanities, Professor Karl Leydecker (now at the University of Dundee), for his most generous personal efforts in re-directing my career as I briefly took to the stage at the wrong theatre, disregarding his sagacious *Regie*-instructions. Above all, though, my thanks are due to Thomas Ostermeier for his unreserved enthusiasm that turned what was once planned as a book about his work into a collaborative effort to articulate and document his methods, craft and technique as well as the intellectual context of his work. Thomas, his actors and colleagues at the Schaubühne, and his students have welcomed me most warmly whenever I intruded on their work in rehearsals, workshops and seminar sessions. As a pure theatre theorist by trade – a 'theatre scientist' even, as they say in Germany – these past few years at and around the Schaubühne have been genuinely transformative not only for my own understanding of *Regie*, but also of the true task of theatre scholarship. At the Schaubühne, I owe particular thanks to Maren Dey, Florian Borchmeyer, Christoph Schletz, Eva Meckbach, Johanna Lühr, Rebecca Berg, Leila Frieling and Carsten Höth for their generous support of this project. To Elisa Leroy, assistant to Thomas Ostermeier, a special thank you for contributing with such great interest, care and curiosity, and with untiring effort and commitment even during your rare holidays! Arno Declair, Florence von Gerkan and Jan Pappelbaum have assisted us by providing images, and Robert Shaughnessy, David Barnett and Clare Finburgh have kindly commented on draft versions, not least helping us out in our at times vague command of the English language. And finally, thanks to Ben Piggott, Kate Edwards and Talia Rodgers at Routledge who have helped us with great patience to bring the seed of an idea to its eventual fruition.

Peter M. Boenisch
London and Berlin, September 2015

This book about my methodological experiences over the last twenty years would never have been possible without the initiative of Peter M. Boenisch. I would never have taken the time, and would not have had the diligence to do this work without him: he deserves my infinite thanks. Without the collaboration, help and patience of my wonderful personal assistant Elisa Leroy, this book would not have seen the light of day. That is why I would also like to thank her profoundly.

This is a book mostly about directing actors: Without the troupe of actors who have accompanied me all these years at Schaubühne, I would not have had the possibility to conduct my research on acting. I would also like to take this opportunity to thank my loyal set designer, Jan Pappelbaum, with whom I've been working for twenty years now; the costume designers Nina Wetzel and Florence von Gerkan; the video artist Sébastien Dupouey; the musicians Nils Ostendorf, Malte Beckenbach and Thomas Witte; the dramaturg Florian Borchmeyer, and the Schaubühne's vice director and my long-term collaborator Tobias Veit. I also thank Jürgen Schitthelm, co-founder and former proprietor of the Schaubühne, as well as Schaubühne's former vice director and nowadays managing director Friedrich Barner, who trusted me with the artistic direction of the Schaubühne; and last but not least: my closest collaborator of all these years, the wonderful playwright Marius von Mayenburg, who also provided me with beautiful translations of Shakespeare and Ibsen. Without these, I would not have been able to delve into the realms of these two writers as deeply as I have.

Thomas Ostermeier
Berlin, September 2015

Chapter 1

Playing with the R(ealism) effect

An introduction to Thomas Ostermeier's theatre work

Peter M. Boenisch

No other German theatre company, and no other contemporary German theatre artist, is as present around the world today as Thomas Ostermeier (b. 1968) and the Berlin Schaubühne am Lehniner Platz, the theatre ensemble he has been leading as Artistic Director since autumn 1999. In addition to servicing the four venues at its Berlin Kurfürstendamm home with a continuous repertoire programme of around 500 performances per season, the company also plays around 100 performances abroad each year. In the course of the 2014/15 theatre season, approximately 68,000 spectators saw Schaubühne works outside Berlin – of course not exclusively, but mostly productions directed by Ostermeier himself. In the twelve months between July 2014 and July 2015, the company travelled to Avignon (where they began and ended the season with performances at the Avignon Festival), Oslo, London, Seoul, Dublin, Moscow (on three occasions with three different productions), Belfast, Cluj Napoca, Amsterdam (with two different productions on two occasions), Lausanne, Delhi, Kolkata and Chennai, São Paolo, Rennes, Montreal, Wiesbaden, Macau, Recklinghausen, Tianjin and Beijing (with two productions), Naples, Athens, Paris, Lisbon and Venice (with two productions at the Biennale). As a result of this global presence, Thomas Ostermeier's theatre, above all his own globally celebrated productions of *Hedda Gabler* (2005), *Die Ehe der Maria Braun* (2007/14), *Hamlet* (2008), *An Enemy of the People* (2012), *Little Foxes* (2014) and *Richard III* (2015), has come to represent German theatre to the wider world, far beyond Europe. In 2011, aged 43, Ostermeier became the youngest ever recipient of the Venice Biennale's Golden Lion for his lifetime achievement in theatre. It was with good reason, therefore, that the German weekly *Zeit Magazin* described him as 'the face of modern German theatre'.[1]

And yet, there could hardly be a director less typical of contemporary German theatre than Ostermeier. In stark contrast to his popularity with audiences abroad and at home (at the Schaubühne, tickets for his productions regularly sell out the day they are released), German theatre critics – after an initial hype around the director's work at the 'Baracke', which he led from 1996 onwards – have rarely been more than lukewarm even about his most celebrated works, such as *Hamlet*. Since taking over the Schaubühne in late 1999, Ostermeier has only received three nominations for the Berlin Theatertreffen, the annual showcase of the season's ten best productions as voted by a jury of theatre critics.[2] Comparing the Berlin reviews of his recent *Richard III* (2015) to the production's critical reception in France (where its Avignon premiere made front page news in the national broadsheet *Le Monde* and two other newspapers) reveals a baffling discrepancy. In his native country, Ostermeier's work seems largely to slip through the net of mainstream critical categories, and German theatre scholarship equally has remained largely silent about his oeuvre.[3] Unlike most other theatre artists from the country that has invented 'directors' theatre', his work cannot easily be summed up by a handful of aesthetic principles that recur with each production. At first sight at least, he seems to lack a trademark 'directorial signature', and despite giving plays by Ibsen, Shakespeare, Lillian Hellman and Tennessee Williams a distinctly contemporary feel, Ostermeier steers clear of idiosyncratic, authorial interpretation; these are, of course, all the hallmarks of German *Regietheater* that most professional as well as academic critics consider as gold standard to measure directorial achievement. The Anglo-American perspective that tends to frame his work as that of a directorial *auteur* likewise misses the crucial tenets and core values of his work, which this introductory chapter seeks to outline.

Ostermeier himself positions his approach to theatre, first and foremost, as outside, after and against postmodern deconstruction and postdramatic performing, German theatre's prevalent aesthetic paradigms in recent decades. Above all, he rejects the aesthetically self-referential theatricality of contemporary theatre-making (in Germany, in particular, and certainly elsewhere, too). In his analysis, much of it has become stuck in epigonic clichés of deconstruction while having long lost most, if not all of the critical impetus that originally drove the post-modern provocations against modern certainties in the wake of the 1968 year of revolt, as exemplarily articulated by Michel Foucault and Jacques Derrida. Ostermeier describes himself as 'the deconstructionists' little brother' who finds himself tidying up after them.[4] For him, theatre is, first and foremost, a forum for critical self-reflection – not an aesthetically secluded self-referentiality, though, but the self-critical interrogation of our selves and of the world around us, of our self-assured positions, of all apparently self-evident truths in and of the society that surrounds and conditions us. His own key writings about theatre, from the late 1990s to today, make this central intention very clear (see Chapters 2, 4 and 8 below). He unites these essentially political core values of his theatre work in the notion of 'realism' that underpins his work, which he understands as something very different from any theatrical 'kitchen-sink realism' or plain naturalism. The original Schaubühne manifesto entitled 'The Mission' (*Der Auftrag*), with which Ostermeier and his then co-director, choreographer Sasha Waltz, launched their joint tenure of the venue in January 2000, succinctly summarised some of these 'neo-realist' essentials:[5]

> Theatre can be one of these places where attempts to comprehend the world in a different way intensify into a shared world-view and into an attitude. Theatre can be a place for society to gain consciousness, thus to be re-politicised.
>
> For this aim, we need a contemporary theatre [...]. We need a new realism, because realism counters a 'false consciousness', which these days is much more a lack of any consciousness. Realism is not the simple depiction of the world as it looks. It is a view on the world with an attitude that demands change.[6]

Ostermeier's idea of realism could not be more distinct from representations of face-value, literal realities which in their recognisability affirm the world as we believe we know it. Against the soap-operatic 'capitalist realism' of mainstream media, yet also against much post-dramatic performance work, his materialist realism uses the feel of 'authenticity' in order to confront audiences with some deep rooted, perhaps even disavowed conflicts and contradictions at the heart of our present-day society. In a stance that appears almost outmoded today, his theatre thereby holds up the original values of bourgeois citizenship – liberty, equality, solidarity – combining them with a belief in an enlightened humanism, and a Brechtian utopia that a recognition triggered by the de-naturalisation of our standard perception may result in reflection, insight, a critical attitude, and potentially even in an act to make a change; in his Baracke-years, Ostermeier proclaimed, 'After the victory of communism, theatre will be redundant'.[7] It is in these terms, far beyond the surface of aesthetics, intentions, and interpretations, that Thomas Ostermeier's theatre indeed reveals a surprisingly consistent pathway that leads straight from his early work at the Baracke, where he staged mainly Anglo-American 'in-yer-face theatre', right down to his recent productions of dramatic classics and modern plays at the Schaubühne.

The main motor to trigger this recognition and the defamiliarisation of a normative perspective in his work is theatral play.[8] Ostermeier's directorial approach, introduced in detail in Chapter 6, still remains true to some fundamental principles which he already articulated way back in 1998. Above all, his *Regie* believes without reservation in the actors as 'original creators':

> [...] the prime function of the director is to describe and communicate with the actor. You discuss a dialogue, you agree on a situation in a play – and then it's up to the actor. [...] When something happens in rehearsals which I don't control, when something is liberated in the actors, then I leave the rehearsal room in bliss. I don't get that from feeling 'fine, my concept works'.[9]

Instead of imposing his vision and concepts on a play, which Ostermeier describes as 'deductive method of directing' (see Chapter 6), he follows the principle of an 'inductive' *Regie*. In this respect, he adds to his Brechtian political commitment an aesthetic approach in the tradition of Max Reinhardt, based on the conviction that each play demands its specific directorial approach and way of producing it, while also taking further Reinhardt's sense for captivating, at times spectacular, and certainly popular and accessible theatrality. Ostermeier's work thereby makes an important contribution to theatre direction as it draws together the two German directing traditions defined by Reinhardt (crudely spoken, the 'German Stanislavsky') and Brecht, with an amalgam of Meyerhold's very concrete psychophysical technique and Artaud's visionary 'cruelty' providing the medium to bring the two together.[10]

'Jumping into people's faces with our bare bottoms': Existential theatre at the Baracke

Thomas Ostermeier's 'meteoric rise'[11] commenced while he was still a directing student at Berlin's Ernst-Busch-Theatre Academy, the leading theatre training institution of former East Germany, which has managed to remain a central and distinct voice in German theatre training to date, following a distinctly 'Eastern European' theatre pedagogy in the traditions of Stanislavsky, Meyerhold, Eisenstein, and Brecht.[12] In 1996, Michael Eberth, the then outgoing head dramaturg at Deutsches Theater (DT), had secured a grant from the patrons' organisation to turn a disused wooden cabin next to the theatre that had variously served as workshop, canteen and storage space into a small auditorium to stage new, experimental work. Having noted Ostermeier's student productions, Eberth appointed him to run this venture, aptly named Baracke (literally, 'the shack'; in German, the word does not carry the English association of military barracks). Eberth, who himself moved on from his DT position at the same time, left Ostermeier a bunch of playscripts and translations whose productions would quickly make the small, improvised and rather dilapidated space famous far beyond Berlin: *Fat Men in Skirts* by New York playwright Nicky Silver opened the Baracke in December 1996, followed by David Harrower's *Knives in Hens*, Mark Ravenhill's *Shopping and Fucking*, plays by Martin Crimp, Enda Walsh, and not least Sarah Kane. Between autumn 1996 and summer 1999, eight productions premiered at the Baracke, seven of which directed by Ostermeier himself, supported by his dramaturg Jens Hillje (with whom he went to school in his Bavarian hometown of Landshut) and architect-stage designer Jan Pappelbaum, who had turned the wooden hut into a flexible, empty space, while adding portacabins as dressing rooms and box office at the rear (see Chapter 3.1 and Figures 3.2 and 3.3). They had only limited financial and technical support from the DT-main house and were constrained by the availability of the DT ensemble actors to a certain number of performances. Therefore, they ran the Baracke more like a subcultural arts centre, hosting in addition to the performances readings, exhibitions, club nights, political discussions, and concerts, including those of Ostermeier's own punk-rock band, where he played the bass. Breaking with the elitism and conservatism associated with most theatres, they envisioned a theatre that was open, inviting, and accessible for everyone. Continuing a trend started a few years before by Frank Castorf's equally alternative and highly successful Volksbühne, the Baracke managed to turn theatre into a 'hip' and 'cool' destination for a young, fashionable crowd, mainly in their twenties. Eventually, the Baracke team was offered the reins of the prestigious Schaubühne, made famous in the 1970s by Peter Stein. He accepted and decided to start out in a joint venture with choreographer Sasha Waltz and her producer-partner Jochen Sandig that would last until 2005.[13] Together they moved from their make-shift quarters in the former East to the impressive Bauhaus-building by architect Erich Mendelsohn at Lehniner Platz in the affluent (Western) district of Charlottenburg in January 2000, precisely coinciding with the new millennium. Ostermeier was thirty-two at the time – the same age as Peter Stein when he took over the original Schaubühne in 1970.

Ostermeier had dedicated the Baracke to 'material that is relevant', and to making 'theatre that interests us'.[14] The affiliation with the Deutsches Theater allowed him to pursue these aims, working from the very start with actors from one of the country's finest theatre ensembles, such as Thomas Bading, who is still in the Schaubühne ensemble today as one of several long-standing members of Ostermeier's company who have followed the director since his early productions.[15] Bading was already in his late thirties when he played the role of Mark in the young director's legendary production of *Shopping and Fucking*, which became the Baracke's signature piece and subsequently remained in the Schaubühne repertoire to celebrate its tenth stage anniversary in 2008. The actor remembered the work with Ostermeier at the Baracke, and the move to the Schaubühne in a recent conversation:

> At the Baracke, Thomas [Ostermeier] was more naive, more aggressive, more existential and much crazier. He was able to do anything, because the Baracke started off as a no-name-theatre and he had no obligation to fill seats. Free from any pressure, he created works that were very socially conscious, and above all, very disturbing. We always played characters on the edge: characters on the fringe of society, on the verge of social decline and destitution, and at times on the brink of their life – at the edge of death. This is what I mean by 'existential'. The early period at the Schaubühne was similar. In Noréns *Personenkreis 3.1* we all played homeless tramps and junkies.
>
> Back then we quite literally jumped into people's faces with our bare bottoms. It was most hard-hitting theatre, which made audience members pass out in every single performance – our record number in *Shopping and Fucking* was eight on a single night, and that amongst an audience of only ninety-nine! When we came over here [to the Schaubühne], we thought that it would not happen in a space with five hundred seats and air conditioning – but it did, and people still fainted during our performances; it was such aggressive, powerful theatre. The theatre's existing audience was of

> course appalled, and they stopped coming. It took us several years to find a new audience, and we had to learn to make work that does not punch our audience right in their face, but instead to seduce and attract them in different ways that suit the circumstances here. Some may say that Thomas' work has become more pleasing and more shallow for this, but no – you just cannot have people running out of the performance or passing out all the time, and so he has found ways for his productions still to go under your skin, but without us putting our arse in people's faces.[16]

What has not changed with Ostermeier's move from hard-hitting, rather literal 'in-yer-face' productions to the formally more contained work of recent years, such as Hellman's *Little Foxes* (2014) and Yasmina Reza's *Bella Figura* (2015), the latter specifically written for the director and his Schaubühne actors, is the realist attitude through which his productions seismographically chronicle German society. As Ostermeier himself moved from the position of 'no name outsider' to the core of Germany's theatre establishment at the helm of the Schaubühne, the emphasis of his theatre shifted from the radical, harrowing 'realism of the outcast' towards a more directly recognisable 'reality of people of this age, of this class', as he expressed it in his 2005 conversation with Catalan director Àlex Rigola (see Chapter 4.1). The almost exclusive focus on new writing of the Baracke years and of the initial Schaubühne period gave way to an exploration of classical texts that continued to supply Ostermeier with reverberations of current, 'relevant' material. This development set in with his production of Büchner's *Danton's Death* in 2001 and culminated in his major cycles of Ibsen and Shakespeare plays (see Chapters 4, 5 and 7).

Ostermeier's turn to classical plays: Telling stories about us and our disavowed abyss

Whether transporting the living rooms of Nora, Hedda Gabler or Thomas Stockmann directly into the regenerated flats of affluent Berlin Mitte, or whether introducing figments of contemporary reality into the open playing fields of his *Hamlet*, *Othello*, *Measure for Measure* and *Richard III*, the canonical drama as staged by Ostermeier prompts our reflection of our selves and the recognition of our own world, rather than empathising with characters in a distant world that we watch from a safe distance. As Ostermeier argues in Chapter 6,

> [T]he fundamental role of theatre in our culture is to tell stories about us, about our lives, about our problems, about our society. That's why theatre exists. The characters on stage are our vicarious representatives who act, take action, make decisions on our behalf.

In Ostermeier's theatre, the playtexts thus provide a (dramatic) narration whose constituent situations are put into theatral play(ing) so that they offer models of the existential conflicts within our societies. These conflicts are multifaceted and cannot be reduced to singular 'issues' that could be dramatised in isolation. Characters are accordingly not seen as psychological entities the audience ought to empathise with, but as agents within these model situations whose capacity to act is simultaneously determined by the situation. I have previously drawn on Raymond Williams's cultural materialist notion of 'structures of feeling' to outline the political as well as ethical realist core of Ostermeier's work.[17] Williams's term emphasises the individuals' bodily and sensory entanglement within their immediate socio-cultural and economic context, thereby highlighting the role of actual experience in the shaping of meaning and of a Marxian 'consciousness'. As a constant of Ostermeier's work – referring here both to his productions and his mode of direction – a shared 'structure of feeling' (rather than a mere *Zeitgeist*) crucially contributes to the R(ealism)-effect of his productions, by establishing immediate affective connections with the audience and thereby triggering the spectators' recognition. At the same time, the shared 'structure of feeling' (rather than any psychological approach) is also evoked in rehearsal to aid his performers to unlock their characters (see exemplarily Chapter 5.2). As a result, Ostermeier's theatre also reflects the emotional sensibilities of his generation, 'the first generation in Germany who with certainty will not be better off than their parents.'[18] His work echoes the trajectory of an energetic, hedonistic post-reunification 'Generation Golf' of the 1990s into a crisis-ridden, stagnant, and conservative 'Generation Angst', even more so in recent years of global (not only) financial unrest.[19] Looking back in a 2014 interview, Ostermeier describes it as his (in his modest words: sole) achievement to have 'given a face' on his stage to his peer-group's new bourgeois mentality:

> This generation is corruptible; everyone is only after money, success, and security. The longing to come home in the evening, to crawl back into the protected nest, this retreat from society, this fear of not being able to master liberty ...[20]

Not at all an end in themselves, the classics – and Ibsen's work in particular – thereby add to the means at the director's disposal in order to scrutinise the 'structures of feeling' of the 'new bourgeoisie' around him. Ostermeier was never after a 'modern' interpretation of a classic, but above all after an interpretation of society and its disavowed abyss, with Shakespeare offering a particular opening to the latter.

In this aesthetico-political pursuit of staging the drama of the German middle-classes on their way through the early twenty-first century, Ostermeier finds artistic allies not so much in fellow stage directors, but in film-makers such as Michael Haneke, Hans-Christian Schmid, or Christian Petzold. In the 2014 interview, he even associated himself with a role model that had been hitherto rarely considered in relation to his work – the US-American art-cinema director John Cassavetes:

> He just gets it right! His films succeed in portraying these bourgeois, petty bourgeois worlds; they document interpersonal controversies, they lead into a deep abyss, but never in a forced way, or just for the sake of the resulting horror.[21]

Unlike numerous other contemporary European directors, Ostermeier however has never shown a penchant for recreating art movies for the theatre stage, with the exception of Fassbinder's *Ehe der Maria Braun*, and even here, Ostermeier worked from the screenplay by Peter Märthesheimer and Pea Fröhlich, and insists that he watched the movie again only after his production's premiere. Far more than just aping cinema's capacity for spectacle on the theatre stage, Ostermeier seeks to offer his audience a spectatorial experience that reflects their viewing habits. His theatre sets out to speak in a formal language audiences are familiar with; the attribute 'pop' has been much overused in reviews and analysis of his work. Yet, while a filmic mode of narration has been influential and aspirational for his way of bringing both new writing and canonical classics to the stage – he uses quick scenic cuts and a fast narrative pace, and intersperses his productions with recognisable, well-known pop- and rock-songs as well as video-projections – Ostermeier importantly employs such contemporary means of expression only in order to emphasise and extend the unique quality of live acting and theatral play. Along with his actors' pronounced play(ing), these means are then carefully woven together into a precisely scored theatral rhythm. His combination of uncompromising contemporaneity with theatral craft and technique was – and still is – Ostermeier's formula for his success; it was precisely this mixture that overcame a younger audience's preconception of theatre as 'conservative', 'elitist' or 'not for them', while it nowadays appeals to a wide audience demographic who frequents the Schaubühne.

A laboratory for methodical enquiry into the craft of theatre direction

Throughout his career, Ostermeier has paid a lot of attention to directing technique. Rehearsing a production, the director concentrates on fine nuances in the way sentences are spoken, or the pitch of an actor's voice, and he composes a meticulously timed pattern of tension and release, speech, action, pauses, outbursts, frantic pace, slowness, deafening noise, silences, huge and tiny gestures. This scenic rhythm finds a crucial inspiration in Sergei Eisenstein's classic idea of the 'montage of attractions' (see also Chapter 6). Even early work at the Baracke already displayed a strong sense for effectively constructed scenic work, for delicate physicalisation and rhythmic scoring. In fact, in addition to the new playwriting, Ostermeier's precise use of acting and scenic technique contributed in an important way not only to the novelty of his work at the time, but even more so to the at times overwhelming affective impact these productions had on their audience, as noted by Thomas Bading in his comment cited earlier. It was an entirely silent, but intensely visceral scene that led audience members to break down in tears or even faint in *Shopping and Fucking*. Where Mark Ravenhill's script has the young rent-boy Gary invite Mark to penetrate him with a knife and then cuts straight to the next scene, Ostermeier's production showed the deadly sex full on and almost in slow-motion. In a way that should remain significant for his work until today, this endless, wordless scene physicalised, instead of psychologised, all the rage, frustration, desperation, and hunger for love, all the 'real' sensibilities that drove the characters' act. Precisely by going beyond empathy and pity and appealing to a pure affective response, this scene became so intense, and so outrageous.[22]

Much of Ostermeier's work over the past two decades can be seen as a continuation of an encompassing methodical enquiry into the craft of theatre direction within a twenty-first century cultural environment. His encounter with Artaud, Stanislavsky and Meyerhold, in particular, during his studies at Ernst-Busch-Theatre Academy in the class of former BE-actor and director Manfred Karge, was a first formative experience in this respect. Ostermeier's initial pitch for the Baracke to DT *Intendant* Thomas Langhoff and head dramaturg Eberth already reflected this interest in practically interrogating theatre theory: rather than a new writing venue, the area in which the small venue eventually found its fame, he had originally proposed to install at the Baracke a 'laboratory for a methodical study of acting', modelled on the studios of the Moscow Art Theatre – an intention Ostermeier pursued during the venue's first season with his 1997 production of Brecht's *Mann ist Mann* (*Man Equals Man*), for which he brought in the Russian biomechanics-teacher Gennadi Bogdanov (for Jan Pappelbaum's memories of this crucial production, see Chapter 3.1).

Over the years, Ostermeier kept further refining the vocal and physical range of his actors' performances as well as their capacity for ensemble work. In the years of co-directing the Schaubühne with Sasha Waltz, his actors and her dancers attended joint training sessions. Later, Argentinian-born choreographer Constanza Macras and playwright-director Falk Richter became regulars at his theatre, the latter creating both Tanztheater-type works with his longtime choreographer-partner Annouk van Dijk while also venturing into contemporary opera with *For the Disconnected Child*, the 2013 co-production between the Schaubühne and the Berlin Staatsoper. In all of these productions, Schaubühne company members performed alongside dancers and singers from Macras' and Van Dijk's companies, or the state opera. Meanwhile, Ostermeier himself kept developing his own exploration of scenic, affective rhythms that characterise his *mises en scène*. As a result, the emphasis of his work as Artistic Director equally shifted, moving on from the earlier concentration on new writing, which he pursued at a time when few other German theatres opened their stages for radical new playwrights and their development. Nowadays, new work has become a staple at most Berlin theatres, from Deutsches Theater to the Maxim Gorki theatre, which is now led by Ostermeier's former associate

Jens Hillje, together with Shermin Langhoff. Ostermeier meanwhile steered his Schaubühne on a course to eventually become what he initially envisioned the Baracke to be: turning the Schaubühne into the place for radical *Regietheater* of the twenty-first century, Ostermeier, instead of employing a group of permanent directors, keeps bringing in internationally renowned directors to work regularly and continuously with the Schaubühne ensemble actors, and to offer them an exposure to a wide range of approaches to test and develop their craft and talent, in addition to his own way of directing. Over recent years, directors such as Katie Mitchell, Romeo Castellucci, Alvis Hermanis, Ivo van Hove, Michael Thalheimer, Nicolas Stemann and – for the first time in 2015 – Simon McBurney have directed his company, while the regular work with long-time collaborators such as Falk Richter, Marius von Mayenburg and Patrick Wengenroth continues, too. The Schaubühne has thus become that laboratory Ostermeier envisaged, yet now neither focusing exclusively on the methodical study of acting or on new writing, but on 'new directions' and more generally on a systematic exploration of various means of theatre-making today.

Complementing Ostermeier's pedagogic commitment to teaching and training students and emerging directors, this book is a further part and preliminary result of this ongoing practical research in fundamental theatre methodology and its application in the present. In addition to selected key texts on realism, on directing Ibsen, Shakespeare and on the political potential of theatre today, which Ostermeier wrote between 1999 and 2014 (many of which have been translated into English for the first time here; see Chapters 2, 4 and 8), his directing practice is introduced and elucidated through original contributions from some of his core collaborators (Chapter 3), and through two exemplary case studies in Chapters 5 and 7: The latter follows his production of Shakespeare's *Richard III* from early thoughts to its Berlin premiere in February 2015, and it is framed by Ostermeier's own plans, preparatory research as well as a retrospective evaluation. Chapter 5, meanwhile, gives insights into the (after-)life of his production of Ibsen's *Ein Volksfeind* (*An Enemy of the People*) from the points of view of the dramaturg, the actors, the assistant director and other artists involved, as it follows the production's trajectory from its Avignon premiere in July 2012 around the world and back to Berlin, through three theatre seasons until its 131st (and by no means last) performance in the summer of 2015. These sources on 'Ostermeier at work' are then further complemented by our attempt to summarise the fundamental principles behind his directorial method in Chapter 6.

Yet, Ostermeier's reflections on and explorations of theatre, its craft, laws, mechanisms, and techniques, have at all times been in the immediate service of the societal and political function of theatre that he aspires to. Not unlike Brecht, their purpose is in assisting his creation of entertaining, accessible, and meaningful theatre art that skilfully entices the theatre spectators to recognise their own situation and to start thinking about their own life. To express this purpose which his theatre work has been pursuing for twenty years now,

Ostermeier, at the beginning of his career, once more looked not least at the cultural role of cinema, or at least, the kind of cinema he attended. In his 1999 text on 'Theatre in the age of its acceleration' (see Chapter 2.1), he stated that at the time not theatre but cinema was

> the place I frequent [...] when I want to learn a thing or two about life. The place where I am able to make experiences which can challenge my way of life, encourage me to think differently, to appreciate things differently, to act differently, to live differently, and to be different – because someone shows me the world in a way I have never seen it before, and reveals an entirely new world to me.

In a nutshell, and somewhat *ex negativo*, because he actually described the effect cinema had on him, Ostermeier expresses in this statement rather precisely the ultimate ideal that he seeks to realise with his theatral realism, whether staging new work or classics from the Western canon, whether putting the actors' behinds in his audience's face, or whether producing what some consider pleasing performances: to turn theatre into a place which – while being 'cool', open and inviting just like the Baracke was in its days – encourages audiences to think differently, and challenges spectators in their way of seeing the world.

Notes

1 Stephan Lebert, 'Thomas Ostermeier: Der Radikale', in *Zeit Magazin* 50, 8 December 2011, pp. 14–25, here 14.
2 He was invited with *Nora – A Doll's House*, *Hedda Gabler*, and for *Die Ehe der Maria Braun*, the latter originally created for Kammerspiele Munich before its transfer to the Schaubühne.
3 The first German-language book publication on the director's work was the interview volume *Backstage Ostermeier* by senior theatre critic Gerhard Jörder (Berlin: Theater der Zeit, 2014). The first two academic monographs on his work were published in French: Jitka Pelechová, *Le Théâtre de Thomas Ostermeier*, Louvain: Études Théâtrales Vol. 58 (2013), and *Le théâtre et la peur*, Actes Sud, 2016.
4 Jörder, *Backstage*, p. 9. Ostermeier describes himself as putting the broken fragments together again, but in a way that leaves the cracks and fractures exposed: 'Japanese culture has a name for this idea: *kintsugi*. A piece of pottery is most beautiful after it has been smashed and reconstructed again. The purpose of this aesthetic is to make the cracks visible' (ibid.).
5 I used the term 'neo(n)realism' in 'Thomas Ostermeier: Mission neo(n)realism and a theatre of actors and authors', in Maria M. Delgado and Dan Rebellato, eds, *Contemporary European Theatre Directors.* Abingdon and New York: Routledge 2010, pp. 339–57. In the present chapter, I revisit and develop some of the arguments and analysis of this earlier text.
6 Schaubühne am Lehniner Platz, 'Der Auftrag', originally published in the inaugural programme brochure for the spring season 2000, and reprinted as 'Wir müssen von vorn anfangen' in *Die Tageszeitung*, 20 January 2000, p. 15. We decided not to include this document in the present volume since Ostermeier's contribution to the co-authored manifesto drew heavily on revised sections from his more detailed 1999 lecture 'Theatre in the age of its acceleration' that had not yet been published in print at the time (see Chapter 2.1 below).

7 Barbara Burckhardt, 'Der Bassist als erste Geige: Ein Meister-Musterschüler will zurück zu den Wurzeln und ganz nach oben – Thomas Ostermeier, Nachwuchsregisseur des Jahres', in *Theater Heute* Yearbook 1998, pp. 96–102, here 102.

8 Drawing on the work of Rudolf Münz and Helmar Schramm, I make a distinction between 'theatrality', pointing to the 'magic play' of theatre, and 'theatricality' that is associated with fake and deception. See Peter M. Boenisch, *Directing Scenes and Senses: The Thinking of Regie*, Chapter 2, 'The restless spirit of *Regie*: Hegel, theatrality and the magic of speculative thinking', Manchester: Manchester University Press 2015, pp. 33–53.

9 Thomas Ostermeier, '"Ich muss es einfach versuchen": Ein Theater Heute-Gespräch mit Thomas Ostermeier', in *Theater Heute* 5 (1998), pp. 26–30, here 30.

10 Considering Ostermeier's 'directorial balance sheet' at the time, I still wondered, writing in 2008, whether 'it may be all too premature to celebrate Ostermeier as Reinhardt's and Brecht's legitimate heir yet' ('Mission neo(n)realism', p. 356). Today, seven years later, such caution may have become redundant.

11 Marvin Carlson, 'Thomas Ostermeier', in *Theatre is more beautiful than war: German stage directing in the late twentieth century*. Iowa City: University of Iowa Press 2009, pp. 160–80, here 161.

12 In a French interview from 2001, Ostermeier corrected the interviewer's association of his work with the (West-)German *Regietheater* tradition of former Schaubühne-leader Peter Stein. Instead he evokes the legacy of some East German theatre makers passed down to him at the Ernst-Busch-Theatre Academy as most formative:

> The comparison with Peter Stein is not at all pertinent – my work is entirely inspired by the tradition of the Berliner Ensemble: by Matthias Langhoff and Manfred Karge, or even Benno Besson.
>
> (Quoted in Pelechová, *Le Théâtre de Thomas Ostermeier*, p. 84; my transl.)

Max Reinhardt, erstwhile director of the Deutsches Theater, which not only launched Ostermeier's Baracke as an offspring, but much earlier also Brecht's Berliner Ensemble, also founded Germany's first theatre training school, and thereby the roots of today's Ernst-Busch-Theatre Academy (that still maintains its traditional close links to the DT).

13 Waltz and Sandig had set up an equally innovative powerhouse of performing arts at their Sophiensäle, a former trade union hall that had played a significant role in the Berlin workers' movement at the turn of the twentieth century.

14 Thomas Ostermeier, 'Auf der Suche nach dem Trojanischen Pferd: Ein Theater Heute-Gespräch', in *Theater Heute* Yearbook 1998, pp. 24–38, here 24.

15 Other than Bading, these are Jule Böwe, Kay Bartholomäus Schulze and Ostermeier's former fellow-students from the Ernst-Busch-Theatre Academy, Robert Beyer and Mark Waschke, while the other fellow 'Busch'-students Ursina Lardi and Nina Hoss (re-)joined the Schaubühne company more recently.

16 Thomas Bading, personal conversation, May 2015.

17 Boenisch, 'Mission neo(n)realism', p. 344.

18 Jörder, *Backstage*, p. 87.

19 The generation of (essentially West-)Germans who had grown up in the 1970s and 1980s and profited from the post-reunification economic boom got its brand name from the book *Generation Golf* by journalist Florian Illies, himself born in 1971; the title referred to his peers' preferred car, not the sport.

20 Jörder, *Backstage*, pp. 9 and 23.

21 Jörder, *Backstage*, p. 127.

22 I develop this point further in 'Mission neo(n)realism', pp. 353–5.

Chapter 2

Ostermeier writings [1]

Towards a new realism

2.1 THEATRE IN THE AGE OF ITS ACCELERATION (1999)

This text was one of Thomas Ostermeier's first prominent public interventions. It originated from a public lecture given Berlin's Hamburger Bahnhof Museum for Contemporary Art, on 20 May 1999, shortly after the announcement of his appointment as new Artistic Director of Schaubühne Berlin. The text was subsequently published in the German theatre monthly Theater der Zeit *(July 1999), and reprinted in the book* 40 Years Schaubühne, 1962–2002, *(eds Harald Müller and Jürgen Schitthelm, Berlin: Theater der Zeit 2002). It is here published, for the first time, in English. The following slightly abridged and annotated translation is based on the original manuscript. While Thomas Ostermeier would express some points differently today, and while he came up with a number of proposed corrections and amendments to this text he had written more than fifteen years ago, we have eventually decided not to intervene in the text (nor in any other document contained in the three 'Writings' sections) and to present translations of the original versions to retain their documentary character. The text was translated by Peter M. Boenisch and authorised by Thomas Ostermeier.*

I

Every significant move by the innovators in twentieth century theatre has attempted to rejoin the umbilical cord between theatre and reality. Most of the time, they turned to the playwrights' uncorrupted, close observation of everyday realities. Each of their battles was fundamentally fought in the name of a new realism for the stage. Chekhov found in Stanislavsky his (rarely really loved) *metteur en scène* of the misery and the boredom of Russian countryfolk, while Meyerhold discovered his authors in Nikolai Erdman and Vladimir Majakovsky, the latter a relentless chronicler of Byzantine Soviet bureaucracy. Brecht's Epic Theatre, and in particular his *Lehrstücke* (the 'learning-plays', to maintain his own controversial translation into English), already pursued more nuanced aims, for instance to instruct individuals about their role in the class struggle. Still, we should not overlook in this context that Brecht also celebrated the anarchic, anti-social artist, and that, time and again, he dissected the petty bourgeois gone wild, thereby articulating early on the very German curse that would eventually drive him into exile. Marieluise Fleisser, meanwhile, gave her voice to ordinary people from the Bavarian provinces, and her heirs Franz Xaver Kroetz and Rainer Werner Fassbinder continued this tradition, while further extending the view to include different aspects of the life-worlds of so-called 'little people'.[1]

Today, we need a new realism.

Who makes theatre today? Who is auditioning for our acting schools? The pampered sons and daughters of the middle class. They look to find in 'show business' something their dull, everyday German life denies them. Year after year, more young people sign up to audition. They are prepared to accept any frustrated tutor's kitchen-sink psychology as a true measure of the art of acting. The feedback, 'Oh, I just couldn't believe you', causes psycho-pathological seizures in the poor, insecure youngsters, and leads to long pauses, pregnant with meaning, during which they are trying desperately to feel something. Where are the blithe spirit of enlightenment and the lively musicality, which are fuelled, at their very core, in every great spirit, by pain and anger? Only contradiction, through the search for counterpoints, makes things representable on stage and allows for real emotional experience. But, after all, one should not heap reproaches on the actors. As the final link in the chain, they have to struggle with the distortions of the German system of funded repertory theatre. Following the ultimate triumph of 'directors' theatre' in the 1970s, this system began to revolve exclusively around itself, with productions citing, quoting, and cross-referencing each other. Detaching itself entirely from the world around it, it lost two layers of foundation from under its feet: firstly and primarily, the grounding in reality 'out there', and secondly, its own grounding. This affected the understanding, or rather, the utter misunderstanding of its own role. Theatre became ever more marginalised in German society while its directing titans overestimated themselves on an ever grander, ever more deluded, and ever more excessive scale. They forgot that they had actually been employed to help out those beyond the theatres' walls (the playwrights), making their voices heard for a wider public, and not at all to stand between these two groups.

II

The predominance of 'directors' theatre' led to the exclusion of playwrights from German theatre. To count as a proper theatre director, one had to stage the classics. Today, a critical review can still utterly annihilate a director by accusing him of 'only illustrating the script', an allegation just recently brought up against Peter Zadek after his German premiere of Sarah Kane's *Cleansed*.[2]

No wonder then that younger German playwrights eked out a shadowy existence. Not called up, not called for. A vicious circle: no one wanted to put (young) writers on stage and no one wanted to write for (young) directors and their actors. This state of affairs could only lead to a crisis. With the death of Werner Schwab and Heiner Müller, and following the withdrawal of Botho Strauss and Peter Handke into somewhat altogether different spheres, this crisis became obvious.[3] And as the old titans of German *Regie* began to run out of steam, the crisis has eventually consumed German theatre, with the exception of Frank Castorf and his Volksbühne. What is to be done?

The crisis of contemporary German drama after Heiner Müller and Werner Schwab is a crisis of content, of form, and of the mission to which it might commit itself. This crisis reflects the wider crisis of our society. The wealthy constituency of communism's Western conquerors no longer sets itself the task of recognising and analysing the misery and the dependencies of many within this society, in order to then address and change this situation. It is a crisis of a politics that merely manages its day-to-day business, unless it happens to be waging a war somewhere. The majority of people are now no longer aware of the misery and of the dependencies that exist within the rich, cold world of global neoliberal capitalism. The individualised human confines him- or herself to being a flexible part-time employee, always ready to serve for fear of losing their place in the community of functioning consumers: the only community that still exists. Freedom is only found in your spare time, and happiness means that you are spared the misfortune of being poor, unemployed, or homeless. Community and solidarity no longer matter as an emancipated individual's ideal. The collective, understood as a community of free, self-determined and responsible human beings, however, lives on as a nostalgic yearning, even where it prostitutes itself in the form of 'teamwork' in the service of enhanced capitalist productivity. The discontented can only aim for a radical change of this society.

Since the early days of the Enlightenment, theatre's mission has been to put itself at the service of the liberation of mankind, of creating and sharpening our awareness of the misfortune of, and the limitations posed to individuals and marginalised groups. In the twentieth century, this was particularly the case in a society, like the erstwhile West Germany, which too often believed to have already reached its final destination, with its 'least worst' political system of representational democracy and capitalist economy. This calls for telling the stories of individuals who fail in society, in the world, and in their lives – today, in the here and now. The eternal return of undead classics does not do this mission justice, and their revival rarely succeeds.

At this moment in history, where an analysis of society and its conditions has lost its clarity and its purpose, where, to put it another way, it appears to have become impossible to even think an alternative, theatre can no longer remain the site of the formerly evident ideological controversies of yesteryear. It drowns in self pity, or in cynicism, or is simply irrelevant. The political theatre of 1968 is dead. The theatre of the well-tempered culinary revival of the classics for educated gourmets who are prepared to stomach even the spiciest and most exotic dishes, will quietly die out along with the liberal, open-minded educated bourgeois of its last generation.

The next generation, unless dragged to the theatre by mum and dad, has long reconvened at the cinema. This is the place I frequent as well when I want to learn a thing or two about life. The place where I am able to make experiences which can challenge my way of life, encourage me to think differently, to appreciate things differently, to act differently, to live differently, and to be different – because someone shows me the world in a way I have never seen it before, and reveals an entirely new world to me. But good movies are a rarity, and the social space of the movie house has been turned into the multiplex. Cinema is subject to the laws of the market, just as any form of pop culture, whose subversive nature is now even doubted by Diedrich Diederichsen, the German pop theorist. He concludes his recent swansong to life in the reunified and equally 're-normalised' Berlin-Mitte district, *Der lange Weg nach Mitte* ('The Long Way to the Middle'), asking 'How can oppositional thinking and an oppositional lifestyle escape the forms of thinking and the data-mining routines associated with conspiracy theories or the observation of trends, and instead arrive at an adequate form of realism?'

Theatre has to leave behind the desire to always stand on the right side, too, and instead it must confront reality. Theatre is the oldest medium for artistic reflection of the world in which we are living, and for articulating our perception of world, of reality. In order to rise to this challenge, it needs to keep connecting its stories and its characters, who speak of the cruelty of this world and its victims, with actual reality. The playwright establishes this connection of theatre to the world. The tradition of committed realism in German drama is clear and strong: Büchner, Toller, Horváth, Brecht, Fleisser, Kroetz, Fassbinder, Strauss, Sperr ....

At a time when the German drama of ideas keeps revolving around the same old exhausted ideologies and plumbs the mired depths of age-old ideas, or when it dozes off in a state of the highest intellectual self-reflection, or gets off on its narcissistic love of language that lacks any idea or concern, or simply remains without any edge, we need playwrights who open their eyes and ears to the world and its incredible stories. Playwrights who find a language for voices that are not heard; who invent characters to represent the people who are never seen; who think up dramatic conflicts to express problems that have yet to be considered; who find a plot to tell stories that have not been told. The explosion of many different realities, of world views and forms of life which results from the collapse of the great ideologies and the old political blocs, can only be reflected by the different ways of seeing and imagining the world offered by a diverse range of different playwrights.

Realism is more than the simple imitation of the world as it seems. It is a view of the world with an attitude that demands change, born of pain and wounds which are the trigger for writing because they demand revenge for the blindness and the stupidity of the world. The attitude of realism attempts to portray the world as it is, and not as it looks. It attempts to comprehend realities and to reconfigure them, to give them a form. This attitude attempts to use the recognisable in order to provoke surprise and astonishment. It shows processes, by which I mean actions that have consequences. This is the grim relentlessness of life, and when this relentlessness is brought onto the stage, drama comes into being. Sarah Kane fought for this relentlessness. Ordinary life is unrelenting – no matter how much it accelerates, evaporates, and splinters. The individual suffers, even though the subject is allegedly no more than a construction without a core. It is pain that makes you feel real, unless you manage to escape into dreams or lie to yourself. The core of realism is the tragedy of ordinary life.

It is a great art to give a voice to that ordinary life. I do not want to hear the playwright's literary skill when I listen to the characters' speech. Rather, the language has to be stringent and necessary, for the characters and for their stories, which the playwright writes down for the actors on stage, who serve the characters and their stories by offering them to the spectators. There are indeed playwrights who succeed in giving a voice to, i.e. who find a language for, people who have never been seen on a stage, without getting bogged down by naturalistic imitation. The characters created by authors like Marius von Mayenburg or David Gieselmann bring very ordinary people to the stage, without losing their poetry: middle-class kids and suburban caretakers, small-town heroes from the provinces, or protesters against nuclear waste from the German countryside. And because this language is credible, their dreams attain grandeur, and their failures, whether tragic or comic, demand to be told.

But theatre must not deny the reality of acceleration either. This might happen by resisting it, using, for instance, extreme deceleration, as it is celebrated masterfully in Christoph Marthaler's work, or alternatively by attempting to increase the speed, in the plays' dramaturgy and in the fast, dense play of the performer. In order to acknowledge our accelerated cognitive abilities, which are trained through film and television, narrative can and must get faster and more complex. The demand for a new realism in a play's subject matter is not a call for conventional forms. Today, we are no longer able to get away with following the blueprints offered by movies, television and video-clips. Spectators have become more intelligent and more competent in understanding narrative. Today's theatre audience is the first generation to have grown up with television. In fact, filmic narration, characterised by montage and ellipsis, has got to be ever more radicalised for the stage, for instance by means of an indiscriminate dramaturgy of entirely unexpected plot twists at high speed, and by rapid entrances and exits, of characters without any backstory, of characters who do not explain themselves. Of people the spectators decode and enjoy because of their knowledge of contemporary pop culture and its genres, and because they are familiar with the city's social mix. A maximum of action – and then a moment of quietness, in which a realistic narrative becomes magical, as it turns into a moment of metaphysical exhilaration.

Enda Walsh's *Disco Pigs*, for instance, in its brisk tempo of plot and play that it demands from the performers, arrives at such a degree of acceleration that at times, some older spectators find it no longer possible to follow, whereas younger audiences begin to relax and recognise themselves. The rhythm of videoclips is transposed into the actors' accelerated performance. Enda Walsh passes the responsibility straight on to the actors. The phenomenon of acceleration demands a new type of actor, and not the introduction of a medium foreign to the stage, such as film, video, or projection. It demands performers who manage to line up, in their confident and virtuosic play, the ruptured staccato of fragmented emotions, and who manage to reproduce them, always distanced and cool but never cold towards the production – performers who, in short, have at their command both the virtuosity and the speed of an American hardcore band. Sarah Kane's last but one play, *Crave*, is an example of this demand for musicality. It is a score for four voices which follows musical principles of composition, in order to speak about the experiences of four human beings, their unfulfilled longing to find love and a place in this world, without any recourse to psychological developments that need to be explained. Her writing plays on the spectators' real experiences like an instrument. It is almost abstract in its form, but exceptionally concrete in its effect – and this, usually, is the prerogative of music. The actors turn directly to the audience. Forms of a very contemporary epic narration are developed, which once more take account of the most basic theatre situation: an actor stands on a stage and, through her or his character, tells a story to the audience. This is a realism which, on stage, no longer needs to be trapped behind a fourth wall, within the illusionism of naturalistic, psychological acting.

The new protagonists of these plays are no longer heroes; they fight without any awareness of the tragic dimension of their own destiny. Their utopia is the moment of true encounter: Ian in *Blasted*, Gary in *Shopping & Fucking*, Kurt in *Fireface*. Their failure is without reproach; they are their own victims, and therefore they are none. The playwrights refuse to give socio-psychological explanations, they refuse motivations as much as socio-pedagogical lessons for overcoming suffering. They only offer a chain of actions, which is light years ahead of any cliché of human psychology. We behave very differently from what is commonly assumed. And the 1990s have seen the capitulation of social work and psychotherapy; for long, they had been branded agents of normalisation, and they were boring after all. The true battle ground of the 1990s was the body – the *physis*, not the *psyche*. The social was the relation of different physical needs to each other. Encounters were the collision of flesh, of bodies who put their own lives at risk. But the body's biggest problem is its desire to unite with other bodies: through conquest and subjugation. The problem is exacerbated when it becomes a matter of life and death – in the age of AIDS, this, once again, is an everyday conflict.

It became a matter of defending the body against abuse, against its misappropriation, injury, its transformation into a commodity. And it was a matter of feeling the body, of finding oneself in the body, even in its injury and destruction. It was a matter of transcending and leaving the body behind (through gender swapping, gender-reassignment operations, or drugs like cocaine, ecstasy or speed). The ideal was as many real bodies as possible, and they should race through life – or die. The body was the last bastion of autonomy and self-determination. The conflict concerning the body always culminates in an act of violence. Rape is the topos of the 1990s: rape as abuse, as liberation, as rightful punishment. Here, the sublime celebrates its return to the theatre: beauty in the ugly, violence without a reason that leaves us speechless.

The 1990s are the decade of shameless public exhibitionism and voyeurism. Everything wants to be shown; everything wants to be seen. The 1990s were vulgar, particularly on stage. Vulgarity is a by-product of acceleration, last seen in the 1970s. Perhaps, the discretion of Greek tragedy will now return, and with it, the pathos of true emotion.

Yet the last luminous reflection of the romantic hero only enters to stride towards his own demise, towards redemption and self-annihilation. Or else, no hero, no potential saviour enters at all – this is where recent playwriting has become even more radical. The hero no longer steps up to face his conflict – he has already decided to disappear, critically ill, or dead. The others stand back, they wait and attempt to put him back together, to describe him, to dream him up. In his absence, the hero becomes a possibility again: he becomes imaginable, as a projection and as a desire. In Lionel Spycher's *Pit Bull*, for instance, Hakim, the play's hero, is already dead at the beginning of the play. He jumped from the top of a skyscraper into another world, leaving his friends on their own with their ever smaller dreams and their ever greater desires. A utopia arises in its negation, on the horizon without taking shape. But utopia thus becomes a possibility again, and with it, the conception of alternatives.

III

'The Sons Die Before The Fathers.'

The hero who no longer appears reflects a generation of men and women who follow an ossified generation of former revolutionaries who focused solely on staying in power – in the West as in the East. We no longer step up in order to take power and the means of productions into our own hands. Instead, we exhaust ourselves in alternative projects, through which we try living a right life in the wrong one. In doing this, we have lost the courage and energy to demand the world. If someone all the same decides to venture out of their own safe area and step up, the 'consciousness industry', as Diedrich Diederichsen calls the media, hurls itself with the full force of acceleration at the new protagonist, telling their stories, inventing their dramas of rise and fall, of hope and despair, which they sell for a living. Here, acceleration catches up with its own protagonists and destroys the very stuff it lives on. The demand for a fresh supply is enormous. We lament this but still remain part of this acceleration: fascinated and intoxicated by the speed and the pressure which makes us feel and experience ourselves so intensely. In order to keep up, we produce faster, we produce more. But this is an illusion.

The success which Die Baracke had with its audience and with the media is the most recent land-speed record in the world of German theatre. At the end of Year 1, we sold out every day; in Year 2 two productions were invited to the Theatertreffen and we were awarded the title 'Theatre of the Year' by *Theater heute*; in Year 3 we had three productions each at the Festival of Avignon and the Vienna Festwochen, while touring our work to Poland, the Czech Republic, Hungary, Italy, the Netherlands, Belgium, Switzerland, Austria, France and Russia. In Year 4, we are going to the Schaubühne! This is spooky. The effect is ambivalent. The quick success pushes you on to produce ever more and ever faster. You are on fire, and on the verge of burning out. But how are you meant to maintain your own rhythm in the face of a rhythm that is exploiting your work in a state of permanent acceleration? Moving to the Schaubühne seems like a retreat to the last bastion of the blessed. This move can only be legitimate if it does not result in an attempt to artistically withdraw from acceleration. It is about offering the opportunities, and the space, to a group of actors, directors, and authors to work on an art of theatre which makes it possible – to paraphrase Meyerhold – to put on pieces in two or two and a half hours which would have lasted four or five hours in the past. It is about following our own rhythm there, independent of the rhythm of our exploitation by the media.

2.2 INSIGHTS INTO THE REALITY OF HUMAN COMMUNITY: A DEFENCE OF REALISM IN THEATRE (2009)

This text was delivered as a lecture to the participants of the 'Körber Studio Junge Regie' on 29 March 2009. The event is an annual gathering of theatre students at Hamburg's Thalia Theater, to which the twelve theatre conservatoires in the German-speaking countries send one selected production each. It is sponsored by the Körber foundation and the Deutscher Bühnenverein, the umbrella organisation of Germany's public theatre institutions. The lecture was subsequently published in the documentary volume of the 2009 festival, Kräfte messen *(Hamburg: Edition Körber Stiftung 2009). It appears here for the first time in English, translated by Peter M. Boenisch and authorised by Thomas Ostermeier, with kind permission of Edition Körber Stiftung.*

The idea of realism, and what it might mean, has stimulated numerous debates in recent years. Moreover, it has fallen entirely into disrepute in a time that hails performative, postdramatic and deconstructionist forms as the only road to pleasure in the theatre. In this context, the permanent use of terms like 'naturalism', 'realism', or 'psychological theatre' to discredit productions, or in order to distinguish the avant-garde from the out-moded, is particularly unpleasant.

What is realism, what is naturalism? Let us turn to Brecht in this context:

> Things have become so complex since the straightforward 'reproduction of reality' has less than ever to say about reality itself. A photograph of the Krupp factory or of AEG reveals hardly anything about these institutions. Actual reality has slipped into the domain of the functional. The reification of human relations, for example in the factory, no longer discloses these relations.[4]

This implies that, roughly speaking, the photograph of the Krupp factory is an example of naturalism, whereas realism deals with the human relations and the power structures within the factory. Hamlet's address to the actors contains another relevant point on this topic:

> suit the action to the word, the
> word to the action; with this special o'erstep not
> the modesty of nature: for any thing so overdone is
> from the purpose of playing, whose end, both at the
> first and now, was and is, to hold, as 'twere, the
> mirror up to nature; to show virtue her own feature,
> scorn her own image, and the very age and body of
> the time his form and pressure.
>
> (*Hamlet*, 3.2, 18–25)

If I may suggest that Hamlet's speech to the actors can be read as Shakespeare's 'Short Organon' that sets out his understanding of theatre, we can see Shakespeare sketching a similar set of problems as does Brecht's comment about the Krupp factory photograph. First, the purpose of the dramatic play is 'to hold the mirror up to nature' and 'to show virtue [...] scorn her own image', which also means to unmask those in power and to reveal power structures. Yet there is more, and this is where it gets really interesting: to show 'the very age and body of the time his form and pressure'. For me, this implies that for Shakespeare, too, there was more at stake than a simple imitation of reality: in fact, it is about grasping the very core of our human community. Of course, Shakespeare is well aware of the contradiction of this intent: as we all know, Hamlet manages to use the play in order to confirm his uncle's guilt in murdering his father, yet the reality at the Danish court is so complex and full of intrigue that Hamlet is eventually unable to fulfil his mission despite the power of his theatre. At the end of the play he stands in front of a mountain of dead bodies.

I would like to suggest that this short gloss on the plot of *Hamlet* contains a lot of the concerns and the truths of a realist approach to theatre, which has come under suspicion not least through twentieth century literary history, its critic György Lukács, and the notion of 'socialist realism'. Let me put it like this: of course there is hope for the power of theatre in the fact that the play-within-a-play in *Hamlet* manages to unmask, and in this case indict, those in power. Nevertheless, Hamlet, the theatre lover, does not manage to set right the political realities at the Danish court. Still, it is a tool to gain insight, without which Hamlet would probably have remained even less able to act.

It is here where I see another parallel to the potential of an engaged, realist theatre. Of course, one may suggest that realism necessarily means political theatre, yet realist theatre should perfect its ability to portray insights in the reality of human relations. This leads us directly to the main point of contention in the debate between the advocates of performative and postdramatic theatre on the one side, and those of a different idea of theatre on the other. Many productions, which I would associate with the former category, reflect a world that, on many layers, functions not only according to theme and content, but equally with respect to formal principles. In the majority of cases, it appears to me as if these shows are used to confirm the impression that reality has become inscrutable, that we can only capitulate in the face of the surge of information, a glut of communicative means, and the impenetrability of political processes or economic responsibility. Such an attitude towards reality and the world has been spreading for at least two decades. I would even use the term 'capitalist realism' in this context, because – similar to the 'socialist realism' of the former East – these forms of art do nothing but affirm the world view of capitalism. It presents no danger for the ruling ideology.

Capitalism has, I believe, no problem with the fact that human beings perceive themselves as objects with neither identity nor a capacity to act, and to see this idea of humanity represented on stage. Or: to represent a capitalist way of organising society where human beings surrender and suffer the cruelty of the system. This certainly reflects an experience of reality which should not be unknown to most of us. Yet, it leads to a sense of being powerless, not to mention one of depression. The experience of the crisis-prone nature of capitalism has certainly changed our view: that we may not have arrived in the best of all possible worlds, after all.

A realist notion of theatre, which I have described in a different context as 'sociological theatre', is based on the assumption that the conduct and behaviour of human beings with each other changes in accordance with societal transformations in their environment. For instance, the boredom of Hedda Gabler in the late nineteenth century presents itself very differently, articulates itself differently, takes different forms, and shows different relations with her fellow human beings than a Hedda in the early twenty-first century. It expresses itself in a different tone, in different movements, in different manners of physicality. The humble ambition of this proposed approach of making theatre is to identify these differences, to have the ability to observe the reality that surrounds us – the reality of human behaviour, in all its ambiguity and contradictions – and to find forms of expressing it on stage.

At the heart of this mode of theatre, we find – as we might have expected – the actor, his and her talent and art. The art lies in the ability to be perceptive and alert to the manifestations of human action and human behaviour that surround him or her: how the body, gestures, how language changes, and how people adapt to different situations (by this term, I also mean the issue of power relations in the situation, and the intentions of the person who acts); and how situations have a different effect on people's behaviour. The actor's talent consists in the ability to understand and to recreate situations from their own experience, and to do so in their full complexity. In order to refer to a very basic dramatic situation: if I feel that my beloved has betrayed me, there are different possibilities to react. Do I still believe that I might be able to save the relationship? Do I want to take revenge for the betrayal, and end the relationship? Am I financially dependent on this other person? Or, have I myself committed a similar betrayal, and see the chance to compensate for this through the betrayal I have experienced?

In my idea of theatre, there is no single, universal form to solve the problems of a scene. The way in which an actor is going to interpret the scene in the production will depend on the reading that is decided upon in the course of the rehearsals. This reading can be based on a number of factors. First, the situation of the scene; second, the actor's personality, and this means his or her experience, what he or she wants to tell, what he or she considers worth representing on stage. What is the actor's relation to their partner, and to the interpretation and the character of their partner? What attitude does he or she have towards the world of the play? The same scene will play out differently with a different partner, because the action taken should always be responsive to the particularity of the partner. When it works, it means that the ensemble has developed a shared view on the world of the play, which directly results from the personalities involved and their experiences. The entire production can thus pose the question: is it really possible that the world is the way we feel it to be? The complexity of the different ingredients of a dramatic situation – the situation of the play, the aesthetic frame, the people involved – results in a very subjective and personal artistic expression.

The actors' talent, furthermore, is their ability to offer different, contradictory responses to a situation. This is what distinguishes an actor from an amateur, or from the 'experts of the everyday' and similar performers we encounter a lot on stage nowadays. The director's and the actors' shared search in rehearsal manifests itself in the exploration of different possibilities for a scenic solution, and to try out, in an extreme and radical way, even the most far-fetched, and most contradictory responses that go against the clichés of human behaviour as a part of this search for different possibilities. Eventually, we will settle together on the one solution, which, in the context of the ensemble's world view, appears to be the most exciting and the least expected. This is how realist theatre distinguishes itself from a simple movie or television realism, which in most cases attempts to portray emotions in such a way that the spectator can empathise: the broken person is sad, the abandoned one unhappy, and the strong one indestructible and resilient. A realist approach to theatre will attempt to challenge such clichéd human behaviour and will instead remember, explore, and put on stage people's remarkable emotional behaviour, which time and again astounds us in the real world. Realism of course does not mean a one-to-one copy. The stage has different laws, and what we observe in reality must become condensed, heightened, and theatricalised, so that this perspective on the experience of reality becomes discernible, and causes, every time anew, our irritation and surprise about the ambiguity and contradictions in the behaviour of modern human beings. All of us know stories, for instance, how, in the workplace, we are confronted with most subtle intrigues and power struggles every day. As I am sure all of us have experienced, these battles are only very rarely fought in the open, so that they could be named openly, responded to, and fought against. Still, they exist and reduce a fair few people to despair. A realist way of making theatre would sharpen our senses to the subtlety of these processes, and it would at the same time make the utter despair of those who are suffering tangible and comprehensible.

The difficulty and the challenge of this approach to theatre is the exploration of all of the hidden causes, sensations, strategies, and interests which shape human behaviour, in all their complexity. To this end, I believe that we need actors who are trained in these problems, and who have the skill to act on different levels, who are able to permeate the complexity of emotional processes, and who, above all, are able to portray how different constellations of power – be they political, economic or emotional – make human beings adapt their behaviour in a very supple way to the situation, in accordance with their own interests in the situation. Such a task, which comes close to that of a researcher in the laboratory of human behaviour, implies, in the constellation of two actors on a stage, an exponential number of possible human actions. The joy of this work is to conduct, together with these experts, the search for all of these possibilities.

Notes

1 German playwright Marie Luise Fleisser (1901–74) is best known for her 1924-play *Purgatory in Ingolstadt*, and for her *Pioneers in Ingolstadt* (1926), whose Berlin premiere was directed by Bertolt Brecht, causing a major theatre scandal in the Weimar Republic. The Nazi regime prohibited her from publishing, and put her plays on the list of 'harmful and unwanted literature'. Bavarian playwright Franz Xaver Kroetz (b. 1946) and theatre- and film-maker Rainer Werner Fassbinder (1945–82) revived interest in Fleisser's work during the 1960s, and revived the tradition of the

critical popular play (*Volksstück*). In 2002, Thomas Ostermeier directed Fleisser's post-World War II play *Der starke Stamm* (*The thick trunk*) at Kammerspiele München, where the play was originally premiered in 1950. He further directed Kroetz' 1974-play *Wunschkonzert* (*Request show*) at Schaubühne (2003), and adapted Fassbinder's movie *Die Ehe der Maria Braun* at Kammerspiele Munich in 2007.

2 Zadek's German version of the play (which had originally opened at the Royal Court in April 1998, directed by James Macdonald) was translated by himself, Elisabeth Plessen and Nils Tabert, premiering on 12 December 1998 at Hamburger Kammerspiele, with Ulrich Mühe as Tinker and Susanne Lothar as Grace. His production was characterised by a stark realism that took even the most extreme of Kane's stage directions at their word; he famously even started, in vain, to train rats. Thomas Ostermeier, who had first met Kane in 1997, produced all five of her plays and thereby established her reputation in Germany as the most important English playwright of the late twentieth century. He cites her as a major influence on his theatre work, including his later take on Ibsen's classics.

3 Austrian playwright Werner Schwab (1958–1994), who invented an altogether artificial language for his characters, was one of the most successful German playwrights of the early 1990s. Soon after his early death, German theatre also lost Heiner Müller (1929–95), its most influential critical author since Brecht. Meanwhile, Botho Strauss (b. 1944) and Peter Handke (b. 1942), the leading dramatic writers associated with the political generation of 1968, by the mid-1990s had entirely changed their political allegiance, Strauss publishing right-leaning critique of post-reunification German society, and Handke defending Serbian politics in the 1990s Yugoslav wars.

4 Bertolt Brecht, 'Der Dreigroschenprozess: Ein soziologisches Experiment', in *Werke, Grosse kommentierte Berliner und Frankfurter Ausgabe*. Eds. W. Hecht, J. Knopf, W. Mittenzwei, K.-D. Muller. Berlin/Frankfurt am Main: Aufbau and Suhrkamp, 1988–2000, Vol. 21, pp. 448–514, here p. 469. See *Brecht on Film and Radio*, ed. and transl. Marc Silberman, London: Bloomsbury, 2000, pp. 164–5. The above translation from the German is by the authors.

Chapter 3

Making theatre with Thomas Ostermeier

3.1 CREATING STAGE SPACES LIKE IT IS NOT POSSIBLE ANYWHERE ELSE: JAN PAPPELBAUM ON TWENTY YEARS OF INVENTING SPACES FOR THOMAS OSTERMEIER

The stage as actor's tool: re-inventing set design at the Baracke

Even though I have an architecture degree from Bauhaus University Weimar, in the end I never pursued my original desire to become an architect. I think that Thomas Ostermeier and the Schaubühne, as a theatre building with unique opportunities, are to blame. There is hardly another theatre space that offers such immense freedom to create sets, stage environments and theatre situations. It is also an ideal theatre because all workshops are directly based in the building itself. The present set-up of three permanent theatre spaces of various sizes allows us to move from the rehearsal space onto the actual stage already two or even three weeks ahead of the opening night, without the need to take down the set every afternoon for another performance in the evening. The set can remain in the theatre throughout, and every day we continue working on it with the help of our colleagues in the workshops next door. We are therefore able to finish and adapt our sets alongside the final phase of the actors' scenic rehearsals, and together with them and the director. To be able to do all this myself, and to enable others to do this and to work here as well, I have now stayed at Schaubühne for such a long time, as Head of the Stage Design department (or 'Stage Décor', *Ausstattung*, as we officially call it); overseeing all of the ten to twelve new productions we bring out every year, two of which I usually design myself.

My work with Thomas Ostermeier, however, dates back much longer. More than twenty years ago, in the summer of 1994, we first met by pure chance while I was still studying in Weimar. Just as other students made some money working as waiters, I had found an opportunity to earn a bit of money by assisting stage designers in the theatre. At the time, Manfred Karge, the famous German actor and director from the Berliner Ensemble, who at the time also taught the directing class at Berlin's Ernst-Busch-Theatre Academy, brought his production of Goethe's *Urfaust* to the Weimar arts festival. I was able to assist with the set, which featured a huge black cube. Karge also brought his directing students of the then second year along, including Thomas. They also had the opportunity to create scenic projects for the Festival, together with students from my university. Their projects were meant to focus on eighteenth century German poet and playwright Jakob Michael Reinhold Lenz. Thomas contributed with Georg Büchner's monologue about Lenz, and he managed to persuade Karge himself to perform. So the famous director ended up sitting in a trough in an outdoor park, reciting Büchner at sunrise. The performance was timed to start at 4.30am, so that the sun would rise exactly at a certain moment in the text.

During the festival, Thomas, myself, and other students found ourselves sitting in the courtyard of the Weimar palace, the main festival venue, and talking about theatre. At the time, I was not even interested in stage design, but far more in fundamental questions about spatial constellations of performance spaces, and in architectural possibilities of positioning audiences and stages in variably concentrated arrangements. Two years later, while Thomas was still in the final year of his studies, he was offered the leadership of a small, new theatre space at Deutsches Theater, called the Baracke, to present new, contemporary plays. This was a typical development in German theatre of the 1990s, which was a very exciting, fabulous time for theatre. On the one hand, as a result of the new political situation after the fall of communism and of the Berlin wall, a lot of new texts and new artists were around. On the other hand, the artistic directors of most German theatres were rather old men who were suddenly afraid to miss out on this new energy, and who

Figures 3.1 and 3.2 The Baracke, the small experimental space of Deutsches Theater Berlin, was led by Thomas Ostermeier between 1996 and 1999. The 99-seat theatre space was housed in a former theatre workshop, canteen and storage space at Berlin's Schumannstrasse (above left); the dressing rooms and box office were set up in make-shift portacabins at the rear of the building (above right). Photographs © Jan Pappelbaum.

feared their theatre would lose touch with the new developments inside and beyond the theatre. Therefore, they created such more or less improvised small spaces, and they brought in young directors like Thomas. He invited me to join him there, first of all to transform the venue into a theatre space. The Baracke was a very simple space, which was all the time on the verge of collapsing. It was very literally just that – a shed, a *baracke*: an old, small, empty wooden hut variably used to house the canteen of the theatre's workshop or as a storage space (see Figures 3.1 and 3.2). In its place, there is now a new, modern office block with a bank on the ground floor. But back then, there was nothing, it was a blank canvas, and this interested me a lot, as an architect. Unlike a normal theatre building, it really offered the opportunity to rethink the space for each production from scratch, and to construct an entirely different relation between performers and audience for each production, experimenting with different set-ups according to the idea of the production and the logic of the text. Sometimes the audience would face the stage, another time they would sit opposite each other, or they were placed in the round with a performance space right in the middle.

In this entirely flexible environment we created what I still consider our most important collaboration to date, Brecht's *Man Equals Man* (*Mann ist Mann*), in 1997 (see Figure 3.3 and Plate 2). It made me most clearly feel the close overlap of Thomas' directorial approach with my own interests in architecture and theatre. The set was, in a typical way, no traditional 'stage image' *(Bühnenbild)* that illustrates time and place, but it was a living, scenic object. It consisted of a vertical wooden wall, such as used in army training, which was put together from used, reclaimed timber, rather than just being built in the workshop to look old. The recycled wood brought its own history into the space, and enveloped the room with its peculiar atmosphere. There was a sliding door as well, and a narrow-gauge railroad track crossed the stage, on which a little trolley could be shunted around. The second, defining point for our collaboration also manifested itself in this design: Everything on stage could be touched, physically used, and handled by the actors, so that the set became a tool for them, or even another partner, another actor. Everything could be quickly dismantled, moved and reassembled. At the beginning of the performance, there was one wall at the front of the stage and another one in the back so that the performers could hide, disappear and exit in constantly changing ways. By the end of the night, the actors had dismantled the wall entirely, and the bare scaffolding and the few stage lights were all that was left on stage. This production was much inspired by Thomas' interest in the work of Russian theatre avant-gardist Vsevolod Meyerhold and the fundamental principles of his biomechanics. Meyerhold did not allow anything on stage that did not directly support the actors, and contribute to their play. For him, a set was not the means to create a stage illusion, but instead a strictly functional, social means to assist the actors and their play. In his productions, Meyerhold therefore created stages that were art installations: the few elements on stage merged into a stage

Figure 3.3 Ostermeier's production of Brecht's *Mann ist Mann* (1997). Scenographer Jan Pappelbaum considers the work 'our most important collaboration to date'. The image shows Tilo Werner in the role of Galy Gay. Photograph © Wolfhard Theile/drama-berlin.de.

body – a space with its own quality, its own narrative, which instead of illusion offered a sensual impression of its material and haptic qualities. And, it provided a sense of the history of the material, similar to the reclaimed wood in our production. It is this aspect I refer to as the 'social' aspect of his theatre stage: it points to the society, and links theatre to the world outside, instead of replicating and representing it. Brecht is certainly not at all the primary material for Meyerholdian biomechanics. This experimental approach – which dates from the same period as Brecht's early play – offered, however, a way to create a machinery for the performers' play that generated, in the small Baracke, all the spaces that *Man Equals Man* demands (and there are a lot of them!), in a very sensory way that invited associations and was not a mere surface for illusion. This project resonated a lot with the spirit that had influenced the teaching I had received during my studies at Bauhaus University Weimar, where the legacy of Oskar Schlemmer and his thinking was certainly one of the things the teachers passed on to the students.

Even though our understanding and our ways of making theatre together has very much evolved since and developed over the years, some of the basic principles have remained the same. At their very core, Thomas' works (with only few exceptions) are based, in architectural terms, on a strictly contemporary aesthetics. Even the dramatic classics he puts on acquire some form of natural contemporaneity; they come to resonate with our own time and our experience of life. Aesthetically, this is supported by the set, the costumes, and the materials present on stage. To start with, there are no historical settings. One aspect that brought Thomas and myself together from early on is that he hates decoration, in the sense of a constructed, built-up visual space – an imagistic container within which the performers act. For him, echoing Meyerhold, nothing should be on stage unless it directly contributes to the performance, and in particular supports the actors' play. There may well be rather conventional, naturalistic objects and props like furniture, doors, and a wall in our sets – but none of these will be there just to define the locality, or to create an atmosphere. These are the two architectural principles that really have characterised our collaboration ever since: that nothing should be on stage that is not contemporary, and that the stage is always a partner and a tool for the actor. One might follow the development of these principles from *Man Equals Man*, with its wooden wall that was dismantled in the Baracke, to *Hamlet*, with the huge space covered in earth, and the movable curtain. At their heart, these works were installations consisting of only two or three elements with which we narrated the play, and which added a materiality to the stage, through the earth or the old wood with its own history, which we used to build the stage in *Man Equals Man*, and now similarly in building the auditorium in the recent *Richard III*.

The Schaubühne's big challenge: making theatre in a gigantic concrete shell

Our shared thinking about how to create and how to use space on stage then also met with another theatre building: the Schaubühne am Lehniner Platz. The Schaubühne company was originally founded in Berlin-Kreuzberg in 1962, and was for many years based in the Theater am Halleschen Ufer, which is now part of the HAU theatres. As the company, under the leadership of Peter Stein, became very successful in the 1970s, they also started creating unique spatial arrangements for each production, which followed their own logic resulting from the text and the idea for the *mise en scène*. They therefore performed many of their renowned productions from the mid-1970s outside the Theater am Halleschen Ufer, for instance at former UFA film studios in Spandau, or open air in the Olympic stadium, and eventually began to look out for a new, bigger space of their own. They found this old cinema on Kurfürstendamm in the Charlottenburg district of Berlin, built by architect Erich Mendelsohn in the 1920s, but destroyed during the war and derelict since. The spaces now housing the foyer, the theatre café and box office, and the bar, had accommodated some shops and venues, including the Berlin Playboy club and a cabaret in the 1960s and 1970s. But in 1980, the city reclaimed and rebuilt the space for Peter Stein, and this exceptional theatre building came into existence: a unique combination of the listed exterior, which once again looks as constructed by Mendelsohn, and a very modern, flexible theatre interior, which more resembles an aircraft hangar than a theatre. The interior theatre space is a 90 metres long, 40 metres wide, and 12 metres high gigantic shell of concrete walls. When you see it empty for the first time, like we did back in 1999, it does not seem immediately inviting to create theatre in. But the architects who had worked with Peter Stein equipped this building in a way that makes it totally flexible (see Figure 3.4). The floor is variable and can be raised or lowered, powered by complex hydraulic machinery in the building's multi-storey basement. There are also various aluminium curtains one may bring down to partition the space, while the metal grid on the ceiling that covers the entire space in place of any conventional rigging can be opened at any particular point in space. The lead architect Jürgen Sawade stated his aims for this flexible space that allows for freely positioning the stage and auditorium areas: 'All classical forms of theatre architecture that I know can be recreated here, and – I dare to say this, not just as a speculation – all forms of theatre that we do not know yet.'

This idea, of course, is fabulous, but there is a big catch: the interior space as such is built from concrete, which is a catastrophe for the acoustics as well as for lighting. In order to use the space for performance, you have to build an entire theatre space from scratch within this shell. This requires enormous amounts of time for the build, and then an *en suite* run of the production. You can only really exploit the technical perfection and all the flexibility of the space if you build a specific space – however large or small you chose it – within this shell, for the duration of an *en suite* run. This worked for the old Schaubühne before 1989, but after the fall of the Berlin Wall there was suddenly much more competition in theatre, and the Schaubühne was no longer able to sell their productions for runs of two or three months. After Peter Stein left, several artistic directors attempted to cope with this situation with varying success, and a different idea for using this space was needed. Eventually the owners of the Schaubühne took a radical decision and asked Thomas if he was interested in this challenge, and he did not reject this once-in-a-lifetime opportunity. He suggested to also bring on board choreographer Sasha Waltz, who had at the time created a new and important dance theatre venue in Berlin with the Sophiensaele. This venue had become internationally known with her production *Allee der Kosmonauten* in 1996, at the same time when Thomas was first noted for his work on new drama at the Baracke. Between 2000 and 2005, Sasha Waltz and Thomas were co-directors of the Schaubühne.

I believe that only this huge challenge which the space of the Schaubühne confronted us with – the need to find ways of dealing with this enormous space, while at the same time designing something that can go on tour and play elsewhere – has enabled us to come up with the specific approaches to creating stage spaces that we have developed over the past fifteen years working here. Our initial attempt to solve the issue was to build little or no traditional 'set' at all and

Figures 3.4–3.6 Moving to the Schaubühne in 2000, Jan Pappelbaum and Thomas Ostermeier faced the challenge to fill the building's huge, concrete shell (above; Photograph © Schaubühne/Siegfried Büker). In the middle, Jan Pappelbaum's model box for the opening production, Lars Norén's *Personenkreis 3.1* (2000); below, Thomas Ostermeier's production of *Die Stadt/Der Schnitt* by Martin Crimp and Mark Ravenhill (2008). Photographs © Jan Pappelbaum.

instead to use the building's technical opportunities in order to concentrate the basic space *(Grundraum)* according to the demands of each play, creating specific spatial structures for each production, furnished with few items and props. As our priority was the performers, the actors and dancers, we hoped this approach would enable them to master the space. We made our first experiences with Sasha Waltz's dance piece *Körper (Bodies)*, and with Thomas' production of Lars Norén's *Personenkreis 3.1* (*The Human Circle 3.1*; see Figure 3.5 and Plates 3 and 4). We also experimented with a 'total', panoramic space, which enveloped the spectators, for instance for Büchner's *Woyzeck* in 2003 (see Plates 9 and 10). It was a huge site, framed by a painted proscenium over a sloped rake, where we worked extremely naturalistically, almost like a film set. If you look at close-up photographs, you could think the whole play was staged in the Berlin *banlieu* with its East German towerblocks and *Plattenbauten*.

But we soon learned that you don't make better theatre just by positioning the spectators elsewhere for every production, sometimes on two, then on three or all four sides of the stage. In fact, it became a bit tiresome for both performers and the technical team. From today's point of view, I would say that we fell into the trap of being too preoccupied with the question of giving form to the space. The actors had little chance to stand their ground within the spaces we created. They were literally lost in space. The spaces looked visually stunning, but one of the biggest problems was that you could barely see and hear the actors. It was difficult to make focused, concentrated play possible. We therefore eventually decided to bring calmness into the Schaubühne space by building, within the big shell of the Schaubühne, three permanent auditoria of various size, which all are, as far as their dimensions are concerned, more intimate 'chamber theatres' *(Kammerbühnen)*. This basic set-up seemed to fit best the manner of playing and the effect desired by Thomas' approach, and that of most other directors who work at the Schaubühne. His emphasis on natural play and realism was simply not commensurate with our earlier attempts within the large spaces. His aesthetic is quite filmic, very intimate, and not at all 'theatrical'. Instead of showing great 'acting', he tries to envelop the audience in the actors' field of energy, and he therefore needs spaces where actors can be heard even in the back row without the need to project their voice in any theatrical way. Over recent years, in 2013 and 2014, we have further adapted these spaces, perfecting their spatial and acoustic concentration without reducing the available stage space. Now, even in the largest space, the audience has a better feeling of sitting in an intimate space, and moreover, we are now able to offer simultaneous performances on the same night in the different spaces, which previously – because of the spill-over of sound – had not been possible.

The space as object: from Shakespeare to realism, and back

From the beginning, we also produced, in addition to the huge stage environments, a lot of smaller scale new writing work, which required a much more intimate setting and a more focused space. For instance, we divided the space into small units, where the audience, perhaps similar to an art exhibition, would move from one space to the next in the course of an evening (see Figure 3.6). The most important and most satisfying form of building a concentrated performance space was not to see the entire theatre space as one spatial entity, nor as a total theatre space, but to conceive of the stage space as an object. This idea links back to the, in addition to the proscenium space or theatre frame, second fundamental architectural manifestation of building a stage: the raised platform. We began by positioning the spectators in a very close and very concentrated way within a larger dark, black and acoustically neutral space around a narrow 'stage body'. The Schaubühne's massive space volume no longer played a defining role within these spaces, for instance in *Nora – A Doll's House* in 2002 and *Hedda Gabler* in 2005 (see Plates 6–8 and 13–14). I used the basic idea of the raised platform (it here measured 7.5 on 7.5 metres), and changed its materiality in a way that supported the play, while also obtaining the quality of a stage installation. In the naturalistic drama of Ibsen, Norén and the American classics of psychological realism, which Thomas directed a lot in the period up to 2008, I created an extremely reduced, almost abstract representation of modern living. In these plays, we encounter the contemporary, affluent middle class, which Thomas is interested in dissecting, and this *milieu* requires a certain quality of the interior and the furniture. My ambition, as architect, was to create an affective attraction to these spaces. I wanted to avoid the effect that as soon as the audience sees the stage it already sees the critique of bourgeois society. As this was also the heyday of the Berlin regeneration fever, with modernisations and conversions happening on every street, I was inspired to show spaces that were appealing and tempting, which you looked at and you wanted to live in too – like a show-flat you fall in love with and aspire to. Only gradually, the harsh reality of these plays and their plots, all of which are driven by similar aspirations and desires, and their failure, catches up with you, and you realise only then how vulgar and tasteless the new rich middle class really is.

In a rather different way, I used this spatial approach in *Midsummer Night's Dream* in 2006. Thomas' 2005 production of Sarah Kane's *Zerbombt* (*Blasted*) then became rather important, as the play began, once again, within this inviting, contemporary architectural aesthetics, yet in the course of the play the space changed into an empty, atmospheric platform within an empty space (see Plates 11 and 12). This 'tabula rasa' offered a new perspective, which we explored further in *Hamlet* (2008). There was little on the minimalistic set for *Hamlet*, the earth that covers the floor and creates a strong atmosphere, the curtain, and the movable rostrum with the table – all these elements are means for the actors to create the world, the situations, and the scenes (see Figure 3.7 and Plates 21–24). I think that we eventually came full circle with the ideas we had once begun exploring in the Baracke, with *Mann ist Mann*. After our move to the Schaubühne, we had not attempted for quite some time such a concentration on one object as the focus of play, on a more or less multifunctional stage. *Hamlet* and *Measure for Measure* were crucial productions in this respect;

they brought us back to our roots – of creating spatial installations that are manipulated and changed solely by the actors' play, and in which the materiality of the timber, the metal sheets, or the earth helps creating different dramatic situations. Certainly, *Die Ehe der Maria Braun* from 2007, which Thomas created at Kammerspiele Munich, was also important for him in this respect. Nina Wetzel's set was at first sight a concrete space with its three arches, the curtains, the various lamps, and furniture, but it actually is a playground which makes it possible to switch from one location to the next without any interruption, similar to a cut in a movie (see Plates 16 and 17).

Having solved the complex challenge of staging a Fassbinder-movie, along with his Shakespeare works, this offered new perspectives of going about naturalism in a more reduced and more abstract way, too. Here, of course, a lot more is defined by the playtext, which demands much more concrete, and more private spaces. From *Nora – A Doll's House* to *Demons* and more recently *Little Foxes*, we keep coming across the same central living room space, where the entire action unfolds. Even if you only put on stage what is necessary, you gradually start to run out of ideas of how to stage these open-plan living spaces with the notorious sofa, and we gradually got a bit weary of these living-room environments ourselves. In our recent work, we have therefore experimented with a different approach. In *Little Foxes*, *The Seagull* and *An Enemy of the People*, we put a kind of cabinet space on the stage: I literally constructed stage boxes whose main function is to concentrate the space on the actor, also acoustically, and to reduce the décor to the bare means pragmatically required to play. From the installation-like 'stage bodies' in *Nora – A Doll's House* and *Hedda Gabler*, where the materiality of the furniture was an important means of expression, we have thus moved on towards an abstraction where you do not even put the material, the furniture on stage – but, as in *Enemy of the People*, it is only painted on the wall. Of course, actors still need something to sit on. At this moment in time, a lot of our work grapples with this very contradiction of, on the one hand, trying to reduce as much as possible, and finding a spatial-installational form for the few things that you cannot do without, on the other.

The attempt to keep developing our aesthetics beyond an identifiable, rather concrete naturalism towards a different, abstract visual narrative was stimulated a lot by our Shakespeare work. Directly before *An Enemy of the People*, we had staged *Measure for Measure*. We put a golden cage on stage, which narrated the world of the play through the fabulous materiality of composition gold on the walls (see Figure 3.8 and Plates 31–33). It was an entirely abstract space; other than getting an impression of a high-class world, in which the action takes place, nothing was localised, but the actors were able to redefine the space in the quick changes of location purely through their play. We then wanted to try to take some of this experience with us into the *Enemy of the People*, which of course does not have as many scene changes as *Measure for Measure*. But for once, it was an Ibsen play that demanded three different locations, and it therefore prompted us to experiment with our Shakespeare-approach in the

Figures 3.7–3.9 Moving beyond the naturalistic living room: Jan Pappelbaum's sets for *Hamlet* (2008), *Measure for Measure* (2011) and *An Enemy of the People* (2012). Photographs © Jan Pappelbaum (3.7 and 3.8) and Katharina Ziemke (3.9).

context of an Ibsen play, just to find out how much might be transferable from Shakespeare into realism. We started from the decision to build an abstract black box that offered a surface to work with, but which was so huge that the audience would not associate it with a house. We then fiddled around a lot to see how the few elements – the door, the necessary furniture – could tell the three locations of the play. At the same time, the space had to support the moment when the situation suddenly flips in the fourth act, and the spectators should feel that they are part of the public assembly. This meant, the same space, the abstract black box, had to turn into a concrete architecture of an assembly hall, resembling a community centre where everyone came together to hear Stockmann. The simple solution was to paint the black space white as part of the performance. Regarding the other consideration, of the furniture, we used tables that almost resemble mock working tables as they are used in rehearsal rooms, tables which you could therefore use in the living room as a dining table, but just as well as an office desk in the newspaper office (see Figure 3.9). As a result, we were no longer able to tell the social status via the quality and materiality of the classic, modern furniture we used to have in previous Ibsen productions. We therefore came up with the idea of painting some of the furniture and present-day status symbols on the walls, and to thereby use the walls in a way that resembles the long window screen in the *Hedda Gabler* pavilion, which is reduced perspectively into the depth of the stage. This time, a chalk artwork narrates the world in which the play is set.

I think the set for *An Enemy of the People* was therefore directly derived from our previous experience with *Measure for Measure*, which I feel was a necessary

Figure 3.10 Towards an abstract Ibsen: Jan Pappelbaum's set for *Ghosts*, which Thomas Ostermeier directed at Toneelgroep Amsterdam (2011). Photograph © Jan Pappelbaum.

production in helping to bring the two major aesthetic threads in Thomas' work together, and also the two playwrights that have occupied him most over the past decade. In *Little Foxes* (2014), the approach via an abstract basic space was then taken further. The social status of the figures, again, was no longer articulated through the quality and materiality of the stage architecture, but only through three pieces of furniture on stage as well as the costumes. The stage is more or less reduced to the central staircase, the one major element that the play demands. We have taken these experiments with using only a handful of concrete objects and a reduced, abstract architectural narrative even further with two designs for Thomas' work outside Schaubühne: with *Ghosts* and *The Seagull*, both of which he staged first in Amsterdam and later in Lausanne. In *Ghosts* (2011), there are even more changes of location than in *Enemy of the People*, all within the same house, though. In our design, we positioned the famous sofa opposite a dinner table, thereby defining a central playing space on the revolve, enveloped by neutral black walls on the side and at the back (see Figure 3.10). A movable wall that measured three by two metres could be shifted by the actors themselves in order to define their playing space, unifying the space, or separating it off. This set also allowed for quite elaborate entries and exits which the audience barely perceived. *The Seagull* (2013) then combined elements of the Ibsen productions and *Little Foxes*; we worked with the same artist, Katharina Ziemke, who had created the *Enemy of the People* chalk paintings. Inspired by the play-within-the-play, here the whole Chekov action takes place on a small rostrum, surrounded by the actors who all sit on stage and just add a few props and stage elements as required. Initially, they were simply sitting there in the neutral stage space, which was not very satisfying because it lacked materiality. We therefore added soil, and as still something was missing, real living chickens. This whole space is then surrounded by very light, translucent material, onto which Katharina Ziemke's drawings – this time of the exterior of the countryside – are painted live, in the course of the performance, from the back.

Bringing Elizabethan theatre to the Schaubühne: building a Berlin 'Globe'

Richard III (2015) opened another chapter. A few years back, we had a debate about our work, and how we make use of our theatre. I suggested to once again try something out that can only be achieved here, by us, in this particular space. We had neglected one of the unique points about the Schaubühne for quite some years: the fact that it is so changeable and flexible. At the same time, we now of course show a sizeable number of plays in repertoire, and most of our larger productions will go on tour, which limits the potential to make spatial experiments. We therefore decided to take one of the spaces only, Saal C, with its unique semi-round layout that mirrors the exterior form of the building, in order to try to create a different spatial situation there. The idea to build a space inspired by an Elizabethan theatre had been around for some time. Shakespeare has become one of the central authors for Thomas' work, and it was therefore clear that he would initially direct a Shakespeare production to open this new space, and we would then also look at staging other productions here. There is, of course, nothing original about an attempt to recreate a Shakespeare stage; many places around the world have a thrust stage, and for some years one has now been able to visit the rebuilt Globe in London as an attempt of an actual reconstruction. What fascinated us about these spaces is their direct impact on the actors' play. It becomes impossible to ignore the presence of the audience; the actors are particularly exposed and entirely at the mercy of the spectators. The spaces of auditorium and stage coalesce in a common space, and a common time, where every single moment becomes a unique joint experience. The basic parameters of the Schaubühne architecture with its hydraulic floor panels, the existing entrances into the space on three levels (most of which had been blocked off for years) and all the opportunities it offers lend themselves to build a very narrow arena space within the concrete semi-circle, creating a unique, concentrated atmosphere. Not only would the audience members feel close to the stage, as if they were sitting above each other rather than behind each other, but we envisaged the atmosphere of a claustrophobic boiler-room – a stage enclosed by a wall of spectators. As we played with initial thoughts, *Richard III* became Thomas' immediate choice. Our ideas for the space made it ideal for presenting this play with its life-threatening atmosphere, where death and murder is constantly in the air.

These were the thoughts when, some two or three years before the actual production, I began to come up with first ideas and initial models of what this space could become, and what it might look like. These considerations, first of all, considered the general 'Globe space' in Saal C, which was developed independently of ideas for a concrete set for *Richard III*. The idea was to build a semi-permanent auditorium with a different spatial layout, which would remain in the space for several months, not only to perform *Richard*, but also for other productions. Exploiting the unique architecture – the curved space of Mendelsohn's building – and the facilities created in the Stein-era allowed us to conceive a spatial extreme that could not be created in this way anywhere else. In order to function as a frame for different productions, it was important that besides the semi-circular spatial arrangement and the resulting concentration and focalisation the space would not push itself into the foreground of attention too much. It was not meant to become almost another actor in the production which the performers have to compete with for attention, as it is the case in the actual Globe reconstruction. Instead, we attempted to enhance the atmosphere by recycling used, industrial materials – and once again wood played an important role: We used reclaimed timber from an old motorcycle arena that used to be part of funfairs, these narrow domes where motorcyclists performed stunts for the spectators. The actual set for *Richard III* was then designed for this space almost like any other set; you always create a set considering the specifics of the space you are going to perform in, and here it just happened to be the new thrust-stage space we had conceived (see Figures 3.11 and 12 and Plate 36).

Figures 3.11–3.14 Recreating the immediacy of Elizabethan theatre at the Schaubühne: Jan Pappelbaum's model box for Thomas Ostermeier's *Richard III*, and the transformed interior of the Schaubühne's Saal C (above). In July 2015, the production travelled to the Festival d'Avignon, where the city's Opéra Grand Avignon was transformed to fit a touring version of the 'Schaubühne Globe'. Photographs © Jan Pappelbaum.

Very typically for our work, a basic draft for how to use the space, and how to relate the stage space with the auditorium, was ready first, but the actual design and build came much later. Whereas most other directors work from an initial dramaturgic concept, based on the set and costume designers, musicians, video and other artists, who all start working in isolation on their contribution, Thomas tends to wait as long as possible before we begin proper discussions, and before we make concrete decisions about a set design. Here, he wanted to know more about Marius von Mayenburg's translation, about how many actors would be in the production, and he wanted to have a clearer idea about the mechanics of the play first. When he eventually approaches you, he has very clear ideas about the direction the production will be taking, and by then, he has analysed the play intensively. This is typical for our collaboration, and perhaps I am therefore indeed more of a 'decorator' than a stage design artist who would put forward very firm and finite ideas and then expect to see them realised on stage to the letter, or not at all. In order to get into a good discussion with Thomas, it has turned out that it makes things much easier when we start working from something concrete. I therefore build models, I don't draw a lot. For *Richard III*, I came up at the outset with two alternative designs which I thought would work best in spatial terms; both of them, in different ways, maximised the claustrophobic atmosphere. They offered a starting point for our discussions, allowing us to put forward and think through ideas which you may discard again. In the same way, we then try finding our way, step by step. From here to the final *Richard* set one sees on the stage now, there were perhaps ten or more steps and versions. Again, I at times brought in two or three alternative models for the next step, offering concrete alternatives which I offered in parallel to each other, well aware that neither will be the final next draft yet. There will be positives and drawbacks in each solution, but trying it out in a model, showing it to Thomas and discussing it helps with arriving at a decision. It is also a way of finding out where Thomas wants to go, and it is my way of interviewing him about his views.

We then took *Richard* to the Avignon Festival 2015 for its first performances outside our 'Globe'. We performed in the comparatively small, horseshoe-shaped space of the baroque Opera house, where we were permitted to build our performance space through the proscenium stage, covering the orchestra pit (see Figures 3.13 and 3.14). At this point in time, it was not clear how we might tour the production to other venues in the future – not least considering the dirt we produce with our clay and sand mixture on stage. As far as the demand is concerned, we could meanwhile easily perform *Richard* as an *en suite* performance in Berlin, but we want to concentrate on bringing in other productions into the space, too. Initially, following soon after the original *Richard* premiere in February 2015, Marius von Mayenburg directed his own new play *Plastic* within the Globe. At the end of the day, the space is not as flexible as we had initially intended: the *Richard* set has become so massive with its scaffolding, side walls and gantry that it cannot be easily removed. We have to therefore put other pieces, like *Plastic*, literally ahead of *Richard*. While we will first try to tempt other directors into the space, and perhaps possibly adapt existing shows from our repertoire, Thomas and I are certainly planning another production in the 'Globe'-space for the future – but how it will look, and which concrete ideas we may come up with then, will in this case only become clear when we eventually start our work towards this production to come.

Figure 3.15 Jan Pappelbaum. Photograph © Susanne Hopf.

Jan Pappelbaum (b. 1966) is very probably Germany's tallest stage designer (6'10") and has been 'Head of Stage Décor' (*Leiter der Ausstattung*) at Schaubühne since 2001. A trained mason and professional volleyball player, he studied architecture at HAB Bauhaus Universität Weimar, where he headed the student theatre stage from 1990 to 1993. Following his studies, he rebuilt the 'Baracke' building into a theatre space with Thomas Ostermeier, before working as stage designer at Schauspiel Frankfurt and the TAT at Bockenheimer Depot in Frankfurt between 1998 and 2001. His stage design was shown in dedicated solo exhibitions in Oslo (2009) and Krakow (2011). Since 1995, he has developed more than 30 productions for Thomas Ostermeier, including most of the director's works premiered at Schaubühne since 2000 as well as Ostermeier's productions created for theatres in Lausanne, Amsterdam, Moscow, Vienna, and elsewhere.

3.2 REVEALING TRUTHS ABOUT HUMAN EXISTENCE: LARS EIDINGER ON 'ACTING OSTERMEIER'

When I think back to the first time I encountered Thomas Ostermeier's work in the late 1990s, I immediately remember some extremely inviting performances. I just wanted to get up on stage and play along. His work had a very different feel to most other theatre that was around at the time, and I believe this is still true today – but of course I can no longer judge this objectively, as I now indeed play along on his stage. There is barely another theatre director who is this attractive for actors. Watching conceptually strong or aesthetically quite interesting productions, as an actor, you may still think that they are not your cup of tea, or you even feel lucky that you do not have to play *that*. With Ostermeier's productions, however, you always get this immediate appetite to join in, and from what I can tell it has a very similar effect on non-actors, too. People who have seen *Hamlet* have told me things like 'if only I was allowed to mess around for a single hour like you can on stage'. Some even say that seeing this production changed their lives and opened up new ways to how they look at their potential as human beings. You come out of Ostermeier's theatre and you immediately start having ideas. You feel thoroughly liberated and inspired. This has something to do with a primordial human desire for expression, for being free from the usual constraints of everyday life and being able to express emotions and moods. Thomas Ostermeier's work meets this desire in a unique and particular way. The delight and pleasure which actors and audiences feel alike result, first and foremost, from the enormous space for expression he allows for in his work. And this brings me to the point I want to talk about in this text. When I started thinking about 'The theatre of Thomas Ostermeier', a lot came to my mind that, on second thought, was rather general – about directing, and about ways of working as a director. It is certainly true, for example, that Ostermeier gets extremely inspired by pop culture, fashion, art, and music – but, I guess, every director does. Therefore, I thought it may be more interesting to look for the things that really set him apart. Also, I did not want to write much about his productions and the plays, as critics do. As an actor, I am far better placed to contribute here with some reflections on what happens and what I experience when I work with Thomas, and when I share the creative process of making theatre with him.

Getting to the bottom of the play

I have noticed that my own work as an actor has been to a great degree shaped by Thomas, and I now function in a very similar way to the way he directs. First and foremost, this means: you always start from an interest in the material *(stoff)*. The intent to communicate this content then provokes the specific aesthetic of a production, and the mode of playing. In contrast, many other directors have their own approach to theatre, or their own aesthetics, which they have developed over a long time and which they therefore impose on any play. Similarly, there are actors who access the material primarily through their own personality. It can certainly be quite interesting to watch how an actor who works this way plays Schiller's Wilhelm Tell one day, and Big Daddy in Tennessee Williams the next. I would not, however, expect this actor to surprise me each and every time I see them on stage; having seen this actor, or the director who works based on his own aesthetics, say, ten times in ten different productions, it can easily get repetitive and boring. Thomas Ostermeier, on the contrary, keeps reinventing himself with every new production. I feel that his works are all extremely different, and this directly results from his characteristic approach: For him, every material demands its own aesthetics, and as director, he subordinates himself to this demand. If you compare his *Midsummer Night's Dream* with *Hedda Gabler*, or *An Enemy of the People* with *Hamlet*, you cannot immediately recognise a directorial signature. I equally do not think that a spectator who encounters an Ostermeier production would immediately be able to identify it as such. For this reason, his work remains fresh and contemporary even after twenty years, and it still maintains this particular feel and energy I described in the beginning. He does not run out of steam, and neither has his work become a matter of fashion, of trends and certain labels, which have their sell-by date and disappear again quickly.

In his work, Ostermeier is less driven by over-arching concepts or by formal thinking that would take its prompts from the space or a visual starting point, or from certain stage aesthetics. There are other directors in whose work everything that happens in rehearsal is subordinate to such concerns, and where as a result their choice of play feels somewhat secondary to such concerns. Ostermeier works exactly the other way round. Working on a Shakespeare with him is very different from playing his Ibsen. His interest in the subject matter and in the content of the play is always at the centre of his work. It is, above all, the story that urges Thomas to direct a play: the demand to pass on the story. It reminds me of the end of *Hamlet*, where Hamlet asks Horatio to tell his story, because if he won't pass it on, it will be lost for ever, it will never have taken place. I believe Thomas follows a similar command. This was, after all, already signalled by the guiding principle at the Baracke in the late 1990s: their expressed interest was in the stories that are told, and not in the way these stories were told. You can also see this in the way Thomas tells jokes with great passion. The pleasure he takes in humour, fun, and comical situations reveals the same fundamental interest that drives his work. What interests him is the opportunity to observe in a play a series of situations that reveal a certain truth about human existence, a truth that may be as embarrassing as a joke. These dramatic situations allow us to observe varying constellations of different characters, and how they act, react, and interact. His *Regie* is, in fact, a search for ways and means to communicate this interest in the story, the situations, and the people.

On this account, Thomas is extremely precise in his work. Thomas is utterly unable to leave anything undecided, unclear, and up in the air. He has an almost compulsive obsession to get to the very bottom of everything, whatever he does. When I am 'acting Ostermeier' I clearly sense a significant difference: there will barely be a situation that is not entirely clear. There is nothing that has not been discussed previously and clarified. With other directors, you sometimes feel that only some time after the premiere, you really understand the play, or their concept and approach. Thomas always puts his cards on the table. He won't tempt an actor into doing something for an effect that may not even be transparent or accessible to the actor. Such psychological games with actors are alien to him. He is always very explicit and states in great detail his intentions for staging something in a certain way. As an actor, you therefore feel very assured and supported. There is always a kind of score, a very finely and precisely composed rhythmic and dynamic structure, underpinned by precise knowledge about what is at stake in the play and in every single scene. Thomas has the utmost interest to carve something out of the material of the play which can be clearly seen and read.

His way of working can therefore almost feel scientific. In fact, I often do not experience it as 'artistic' – in the negative sense of the word as being 'arty', vague and hazy, as something that would remain more of a pure feeling, or that would be entirely abstract. Everything in Thomas' work is, on the contrary, extremely concrete, extremely clear and out in the open, at all times, driven by his unconditional concern to be comprehensible with regards to the content, and to communicate a clear, unequivocal thought. Nothing, in the end, remains left for interpretation either this way or that way, so you would feel that the director wanted to keep something open for the audience to project whatever they want. Thomas certainly is not one of the artists who invite their audience to see whatever they want in the work, and who leave it at having a mere vision that an audience does not necessarily have to understand in the same way. He presents his work as the result of a long process of interrogation and of thorough examination and research; this is what I mean by 'scientific'. He signals very clearly to the audience that what we show on stage is what we have found, and how we have understood what is written in the play, after digging deep into this material for eight weeks.

His negative critics therefore sometimes describe his work as too clever, as imposing a certain reading of the play on the spectators. I would see that as his big talent. Everything that can at times feel overly pedagogic and even pedantic in his work and in his way of working comes out of his relentless and genuine interest in the play and the material. Being interested in something and not having arrived at the point of full comprehension and understanding would for him remain a contradiction that requires resolution. And so he never stops working until he has grasped every fine detail; unless he achieves this, he keeps asking on and on. For him, every remote corner of a space has to be illuminated, so to speak. Thomas once described *Measure for Measure* in exactly this sense as a clear and lucid play. Shakespeare here looks at the theme, at every conflict, at each character from every angle possible. He opens in this play a space of infinite reflection, where even the mirror reflects itself in the mirror. You can truly get lost in this unfathomable space if you try to fully grasp it, you can lose yourself and lose your mind in it – but this is precisely what fascinates Thomas, what motivates and drives him: never to just put forward an idea, never to rest in one's thinking, but to open up ever more, ever deeper spaces for thought, reflection and discovery.

Inviting imagination

Thomas' work also shows his great sense for poetry, for enduring and daring to endure some sincere, genuine pathos. This is the opposite of playing it safe by trying to please everyone. He claims the right for theatre to put forward an idea, a certain vision or utopia of an alternative, of how things could and should be different in this world. I much admire this serious commitment, and the pronounced public stance he takes with productions like *An Enemy of the People*, which puts him in an exposed, tenuous position. I admire and share this understanding of the role of theatre; as an actor, I also want to put out some answers to the audience. It has become much more common today to approach everything from an ironic distance, and to create a kind of 'as if'-theatre that always emphasises the actors' distance to what they play, where actors always only show or exhibit a character, like a puppet, while the puppeteer remains indifferent. Thomas very much appeals to an actor's commitment to their character. This does not mean at all that as an actor, I am being asked to identify at all cost, and to stand behind everything my characters say, or the way they behave. In Thomas' work, the actor, his or her personality, is always present, and becomes a part of what is up for discussion with the audience; the fact, and the effort, of acting the character is a topic, too. This does not inevitably result in breaking through the fourth wall, but it can happen very subtly in the way you play the character.

In fact, Ostermeier's theatre revolves entirely around the actors and their play. I know no other director who puts the actor as much at the very centre of their work. He of course has a great passion for acting himself, and I believe he takes great pleasure in watching someone for whom he has been able to create a space to gain a presence and make an entertaining entrance. He has a great affinity to showbusiness, he adores music and bands, and he takes delight in creating something like a rock star or pop star on stage, and to watch such a figure with all the fascination and glamour that it emanates – and I am quite certain that he projects himself into what happens on stage in front of him, and he imagines how it would be if he was the actor. But there is never any jealousy about not being in the spotlight himself. In fact, his way of directing is all about supporting the actor in delivering as brilliant a performance as possible. He never imposes his idea of a certain way of acting a character, or of a mode of playing, on the actor. He is, much rather, responsive to the individual actor and to their personality, to their approach and response to the play, and also to their needs. For an actor, this means that you are never able to simply say, just play it like this, and that will do for Ostermeier. As a result, the actor's work becomes much more interesting and challenging. Working with Thomas, I feel that I have a much bigger creative influence. It brings out my own creativity in a particular way, more than the work with other directors. By that, I do not mean at all that I am always able to simply do my own thing, and he would let me get away with it. I would even say that our working relationship has been characterised by extreme differences. I would hope he appreciates having in me a quite candid counterpart, an actor who does not just try to please him and someone who never holds back with his own opinion, who even dares to disagree; but always, I hope, in a productive way. I am well aware that sometimes Thomas feels hurt, which is something one would not expect. But things may come to a point when he feels too challenged and questioned, and he therefore begins to protect himself. But at the same time, I have always felt that out of these conflicts, in situations when we quarrelled and when our two imaginations clashed, this confrontation produced an energy which opened up new directions for the work that neither of us had been able to predict.

While there is, thus, not a single, universal rehearsal method that Thomas would apply to every play, every production, and every single actor, his way of rehearsing is characterised by great caution, and by a great awareness for the fragility of the creative process. He creates an atmosphere that allows, invites and enables the actor to follow an impulse and develop things on the spur of a moment, and where one indeed dares to try out anything. In Thomas' rehearsal, you never feel limited or confined. He sets no boundary that would imply in advance it is not worth trying something else out, or that it would not be not worth exploring a particular direction. This is then complemented, and also further enhanced, by his great talent to break down a huge dramatic situation in ways that enable the actor to directly access the scene. He is extremely good in analysing a situation, and thereby able to help you tremendously when you are stuck. He will give you a very short and precise prompt, 'just play this or that', and you immediately solve the deadlock. I remember such a moment from our work on *Nora – A Doll's House*, where I played Dr. Rank. I always felt that the scene when Rank meets Nora and Helmer for the last time, knowing that he is going to die and he won't see this woman again to whom he is quite attracted, is unplayable. It is easy to *know* that your character has HIV, he loves this woman, and he knows he sees her for the last time – but this remains dramaturgic information. You cannot translate any of this into play. You cannot act being terminally ill. Thomas simply said in rehearsal: act like a proper twat. This may sound like a cop-out even – but for me it opened up an immediate way into the scene which was very direct, and which cut right to the chase of this situation. Rank's misdemeanour as 'twat' of course prompted the question, what is wrong with him? – He has nothing to lose. – Why is there nothing to lose for him? – Because he only has a few more days to live. Thomas steers you towards approaching these matters in a playful way, in a way that allows you to access the huge stakes purely by playing – it is not cerebral and you do not have to construct any intellectual superstructures.

Tuning actors in on the wavelength of the play

Another important aspect of rehearsing with Thomas is his exceptionally close attention to even small impulses that emanate from the actor. He is an extremely inspiring counterpart, someone for whom you enjoy playing because he is so incredibly subtle and sensitive in noticing such impulses and ideas, and in then fostering them with equal sensitivity. In a way, Thomas is the perfect audience, even though he is only one person – but he is a person who is able to stimulate me as he watches me. Too often I observe that directors simply do not see these fine impulses, and because of this inability they nip any creativity in the bud. Let me give a concrete example: the famous moment in *Hamlet* when I scratch with the paper plates. Thomas would never say, I know you are a deejay so it would be funny to do this now. If I remember correctly, the moment goes back to a rehearsal break when I was just waiting for things to continue, and began fooling around with props. Thomas immediately showed his appreciation and started laughing. It is this reaction that inspires the actor and that prompts you to go further. Thomas simply starts laughing, and therefore the actor knows, I'll do it again next time to provoke the same reaction. And Thomas keeps making this extra effort to reassure the actor, he keeps laughing at this same point until the actor has gained the confidence to know and be confident that what he does is funny and entertaining. I remember that in another situation, I played something, and he kept laughing and laughing – so much so that I was unable to remain in character and said to him, 'come on, Thomas, it's really not that funny'. He responded, 'I am not laughing because it's funny but because I want to encourage you to go on with what you try out here'.

He has this almost pedagogic awareness of the importance of how to handle an actor in rehearsal, and how to support him. He does many little things that appear in themselves rather unexciting and very simple, but they are incredibly important and effective. For instance, he will always say brief things while a scene is running in rehearsal, like 'nice, very nice, now you got it'. From an early rehearsal to the final dress, you constantly get this feedback from him, almost like a running commentary. Thomas behaves like the coach of a swimmer who keeps running alongside the edge of the pool to encourage the athlete. That coach would never shout 'stop, cut – now get out of the pool, and I give you some notes'. He would never interrupt the process. Thomas has understood that a director similarly needs to comment and give feedback while the actor is, as it were, swimming and trying things out in rehearsal. This enables the actor to go beyond his or her limits, and to invent something new and extraordinary.

Hamlet, for example, originated from an improvisation I did during the work on *Midsummer Night's Dream*, when I played a fat fairy, entering with a fat suit,

Figures 3.16 and 3.17 Lars Eidinger as Angelo in Thomas Ostermeier's production of *Measure for Measure* (with Jenny König as Isabella), and in his most successful role as Hamlet in the 2008-production which is still playing in repertoire at the Schaubühne. Photographs © Arno Declair.

a dress, a long hair wig and big glasses. Thomas saw me and said, we should do Hamlet like this. That was the first seed of this production, and the birth of this character. Another example is the probably most famous image of the production, where Hamlet wears his crown upside down (see Figure 3.17 and Plates 21–24). One would think, Ostermeier sat down at home and thought hard about finding some new and original way to show this prince who plays being mad. But – like most such images and ideas – it originated by sheer accident. During rehearsals, the crown kept falling off my head because it wasn't yet fitted to the right size, so at some point I got annoyed and just turned it the wrong way around so we could finally get on rehearsing without the crown constantly falling from my head. Thomas immediately paid attention, and started asking, what is going on, what are you doing, why are you doing this, I like this. Similarly, the songs I sing in *Hamlet*, like a lot of the music he uses in his productions, seem to fit perfectly the thematic concerns of the plays and the situations in the plays – for instance, the chanson 'Theater', a German Eurovision song from the early 1980s. I once just started singing the chorus of this song everyone of our generation knows as Hamlet invites Rosencrantz and

Guildenstern to come with Claudius and watch the play he was about to stage. And you then look up the lyrics on the internet, and it reads like a thorough philosophical reflection of Hamlet's situation. It is such an incredibly astute and intelligent text that over time I ended up introducing it in its entirety, spread across various scenes throughout the play. Or take 'Krawall and Remmidemmi' ('Fuss and riot'), a German Hip Hop song that was in the charts at the time we began rehearsing *Hamlet*, and therefore simply the next best thing you would start singing. All of a sudden you realise that it just hits the nail on the head in that moment of the play.

None of these ideas had been invented in advance, by thinking through the subject matter of the play and trying to find music that fits. They all came up by accident or intuition, by fooling around during rehearsals and just doing something, or just starting to sing something you had on your mind. Everything else comes after. For Thomas, such an approach never precludes or contradicts the intellectual exploration of the play, in fact I believe for him the two go hand in hand. Pure fun is always part of a thoughtful reflection, it even supports and enables it, while gaining insight and grasping a play in all its depth is a pleasure, and is fun that wants to be celebrated. It is really fascinating that at the end of the rehearsal process, there is never a need to work through an incoherent mess of ideas; strangely, most of the intuitions and spontaneous ideas the actors come up with in Thomas' rehearsals are just spot on. I am convinced that this is no coincidence. For me, this is the direct result of his directorial approach – an approach that tunes the actors into the wavelength of the play, and that departs from a deep comprehension of the material that triggers spontaneous creativity and playful imagination. It has never happened in working with Thomas that halfway through rehearsal you would realise everything is going down the drain, we have been heading into the completely wrong direction and have hit a brick wall, so that we now need to start from scratch all over again. There are productions where you reach this point two days before the premiere. Rarely, if ever, with Ostermeier. It may start slowly, but when it starts you exactly know the direction and you can go there full steam ahead.

Digging for pure and undiluted stage gold

When I speak of a deep comprehension of the play, this does not mean at all that we would start by sitting around a table for three weeks to study the play inside out. On the contrary, one of the very first things Thomas did on the very first day of rehearsing *Hamlet* was asking me to go on stage, straight away, and do the 'To be or not to be' monologue. In the production, it is still one of the first things that happens on stage – the set piece everyone expects, and everyone wants to see how Ostermeier and Eidinger are doing it. We get it out of the way so we can then concentrate on the play. When he throws you in at the deep end like this, on the first day of rehearsal, you of course at first think this is impossible, I have no idea how to do this. But he manages to counter and undermine this fear by simply asking you to confront it head on, in a playful, intuitive manner. He invites you to draw a very rough sketch from which to then continue your work, instead of first thinking through every single stroke of the brush in advance and trying to think out the perfect painting before even touching the brush once. He takes the opposite approach, and in the end – on the basis of the bold, rough, and broad brushstrokes and all the splashes of colour all across the canvas – he still produces a very fine portrait. To get there, Thomas, in the further course of rehearsals, works like a gold digger. He keeps grinding and milling until he eventually has distilled something that is absolutely pure and undiluted. As rehearsals proceed, he gets rid of more and more superfluous layers, of everything that is just a mannerism, theatrical, artificial, exaggerated, or merely vague and undefined. In the end, nothing remains that runs a danger of diluting the clarity of the stage image, there is no dead weight that would prevent you from really getting to the core.

His way of getting to this point can differ a lot as he works with each actor. When he feels that an actor is on the right track, he may just watch their journey; perhaps because he sees an approach that corresponds to his own, he no longer leads and directs. But when he sees that the actor is lost or heads off in the wrong direction, he very carefully puts them on track – and he takes as much time as it takes until the actor feels securely placed on his track, not just roughly or approximately. Only when you are firmly set on the right track, will you be able to speed up to full throttle without having to worry about falling off the tracks at the first turn. This process can be a quite excruciating experience for the actor when it happens, as you faff around attending to a single line or sentence for an hour, even for a whole rehearsal day if needs be. At its extreme, it can make you feel that he takes away any responsibility from you, and you have no more space to play – the exact opposite of what usually distinguishes his way of working with actors. In my work with him, I had both experiences. There were times when I felt he is observing me and seems inspired by my reading of the character and the way I express myself, and I then felt very much left on my own, in a good way. This was true, in particular, with *Hamlet*. The exact opposite happened in *Measure for Measure*, though, where I played Angelo (see Figure 3.16 and Plates 31–33). We were unable to meet in the way I saw Angelo, and his perspective; perhaps unsurprisingly, it was a character I found quite inaccessible and who did not inspire me in the same way as Hamlet and now Richard. This is something Thomas notices immediately, and he then takes you by the hand and leads you through the play step by step. At some point, he showed me how to play every scene, he directed every single move and gesture, and told me how to speak every single line. I would never have expected this to happen again after the many years we had worked together. As the example shows, it is not at all the case that this reveals a failed production, on the contrary; it can happen in interesting and successful productions.

There certainly is some element of compulsion and obsession in his way of working in every production. He starts, in a very pronounced way, from the body in space, and he carefully crafts the relations of bodies in space. He arranges a lot, and he cannot bear when the arrangement is not consistent with his perception. When he sees the slightest imprecision, he will shift actors round, moving you an inch to the back, and a centimetre closer to your partner. He will really tinker with millimetres, even very early in rehearsal. In fact, in his view, you cannot even rehearse a scene in an inconsistent arrangement. For him, it is the prerequisite that the bodies on stage fit together in a proper relation, and in the right constellation. To act in his work, you therefore need to hone your sense for how to behave in space and for how to behave with the space, and with your partner within the space. You then begin to note that when something feels strange spatially, it more often than not indicates that something in the content of the scene has not been developed properly, and remains yet unclear. I have learnt quite a few things from Ostermeier's sensibility for space. For instance, an actor won't necessarily have the greatest presence on stage if he or she stands plane on stage, facing the audience full front. In fact, it can be interesting to watch an actor side-face, or even to only get to see an actor's back. This leaves more space for the audience's imagination to project something onto this back of the actor. Another somewhat surprising insight for me was that the audience won't necessarily understand you better if you stand still and recite your text. In fact, it will be easier for the audience to follow the text, and to follow a thought or argument, if, for example, you say it while tying your shoelaces. Thomas often has actors go through a sequence of actions while saying their lines. Doing these actions prevents the actor from falling into this theatrical speed of speaking, which is much slower than in reality. You realise that speaking on stage often demands greater tempo, more akin to an everyday conversation, a chat on the street where you tend to speak at the speed of thought, and where you are not primarily preoccupied with taking the audience along either, and with making sure they can follow the thoughts. The spectators are indeed able to cope far better than we often assume, and being occupied with physical actions prevents us from focusing too much on the spectators.

'To make theatre, you need no more than a piece of chalk, a metronome, and light'

Perhaps this is the reason why I often hear people describing Thomas' work as very physical, or even acrobatic. I find this quite interesting because I cannot remember any moment in rehearsal where he would have focussed on working on physical expression. For me, this effect results from his ability to create a space – and I here mean both the actual stage space as well as the mental space and atmosphere. The actor's body then has all this space at its disposal, it can fill this space and express itself within this space without any constraints. This is exactly the reason why, as an actor, you go beyond your limits, not least physically, you excel beyond your limitations. You end up finding yourself doing things you did not know you are able to do. Again, it is never really the case that you sit down and plan, now you fall down this staircase, and how are we going to best do this. It just happens. In this respect, Thomas is also a director who invites actors to practise all the skills we have acquired in our training – fencing, falling down without injuring yourself, and other such stunts. You can bring all of these skills to the table in his work. Even being a puppeteer. At Ernst-Busch-Theatre Academy, where I trained, and where Thomas was trained some years earlier, we have lessons in puppetry, and there is a dedicated puppetry department. Thomas uses these skills in his productions, with the puppets in *Richard III*. Elsewhere, actors don't get the chance to apply all these skills for ten, maybe twenty years, so they forget them.

At the same time, personally, I find Thomas is really at his best when he dares to work with extreme reduction. In this respect, *Hedda Gabler* remains one of my favourite sets, because it is not spelled out to the last tiny detail in a naturalistic way. Basically, there is no more than a sofa suite on a rostrum, which expresses a world that I recognise and know immediately. There is no need to write everything out in full; there is no need for a side table, for bottles of drinks or anything that illustrates a *milieu*. The whole play is narrated through the settee. In *Hamlet*, it is the earth. Such reductions have a totally positive effect on the actor's work because they offer many different possibilities for play. Yet, Thomas can be easily tempted by the means that theatre offers and puts at his disposal. I still remember the first occasion I had to observe him in rehearsal, way back at Deutsches Theater, quite some time before we first worked together. He directed Maeterlinck's *Blue Bird* there in 1999. It felt like watching a child who discovers theatre – what, there is a revolve that can be turned? Well, it must be turning. And we can make rain, too? Then of course it will rain! He exploited all theatre tricks imaginable, out of sheer joy to discover and try out what is possible. Sometimes I have the feeling that even in a production like *Hamlet*, with its excessive use of theatre means, of video, light and music, he tends to underestimate how much he is able to achieve with very little if anything. I am convinced that if you asked him to stage *Hamlet* with no more than a chair and table, his true creative potential would really come into its own. He once said, to make theatre, you need no more than a piece of chalk, a metronome, and a light. I wish he would one day do a piece where he follows this dogma! I certainly would love to be in it.

Figure 3.18 Lars Eidinger. Photograph © Heiko Schäfer.

Lars Eidinger (b. 1976) has been part of the Schaubühne-ensemble since the beginning of Thomas Ostermeier's tenure in 2000. He first worked with Ostermeier in his 2002 production of Richard Dresser's *Golden Days*. They continued their collaboration, with Eidinger playing, amongst others, the roles of Dr Rank in *Nora – A Doll's House* (2002), Tesman in *Hedda Gabler* (2005), Demetrius in *Midsummer Night's Dream* (2006), Angelo in *Measure for Measure* (2011), and the title roles in *Hamlet* (2008) and *Richard III* (2015). Other major roles at Schaubühne include the title role in *Tartuffe* (dir. Michael Thalheimer, 2013), Alceste in Molière's *Misanthrope* (dir. Ivo van Hove, 2010), and Stanley Kowalski in *A Streetcar Named Desire* (dir. Benedict Andrews, 2009). In 2011, Rodrigo García directed the solo *I'd Rather Goya Robbed Me Of My Sleep Than Some Other Arsehole* with Eidinger at Schaubühne. He also directed Schiller's *The Robbers* (2008), and Shakespeare's *Romeo and Juliet* (2013). Beyond Schaubühne, Eidinger is internationally noted for his movie work, and has acted in films by Peter Greenaway, Hans-Christian Schmid, Olivier Assayas, and others. He originally trained at Ernst-Busch-Theatre Academy in Berlin, and worked at Deutsches Theater Berlin between 1997 and 1999.

3.3 A WHOLE NEW WORLD TO EXPLORE: SÉBASTIEN DUPOUEY ON HIS VIDEO ARTWORKS FOR THOMAS OSTERMEIER'S THEATRE

When I met Thomas Ostermeier for the first time, I was sitting in a hotel room in Munich, unable to speak a single word of German. I was then a director of music videos and commercials in France and had never worked in theatre. At the time, in 2005, my wife, Nina Wetzel, who is a costume and set designer and used to work mainly with German theatre-maker Christoph Schlingensief, was creating the costumes for Thomas' production of Gerhart Hauptmann's *Before Sunrise* at Kammerspiele München. In the course of the rehearsals, he suddenly decided he wanted to have some video animation, but this had not been planned, so Nina carefully mentioned my work. We met, I showed him the video for an American jazz singer I had just directed back then, where I mixed photo, film and animation. He liked it, and ever since then we have been making theatre together on numerous occasions. Theatre is a very peculiar place in this world of creativity, which I instantly liked back then, and which I still very much like today. Also, encountering Thomas and his precise realism, almost naturalism, offered me, and equally Nina who also came from a very different approach to theatre, a whole new world to explore.

Figure 3.19 Blurred images of West Berlin in *Hedda Gabler* (2005), Sébastien Dupouey's first collaboration with Thomas Ostermeier at the Schaubühne. With Katharina Schüttler as Hedda. Photograph © Arno Declair.

Initially, in *Before Sunrise*, I was not at all involved in any live process with actors, but created cartoon-like animations that were used as transitions. The animation was based on a few excerpts from Naomi Klein's *No Logo*, as Thomas wanted to connect the content of Hauptmann's play with issues of globalisation and its effects. Soon after, he invited me to do *Hedda Gabler* with him at the Schaubühne, where Thomas helped me to feel at home, not least because we spoke in French. I found this very interesting since language is so essential in theatre – and shifting between languages can offer a whole new perspective on a situation, on a character, or on a sentence. For *Hedda* (2005), we created a few elliptical video scenes: Hedda walking in the forest, Hedda driving, Hedda shooting her guns (see Figure 3.19). We created a lot of footage, and at the same time, I was also trying to orientate myself in the visual world of Berlin's chic West End that was entirely new to me. I walked around a lot, took many pictures, and cut them into the video. So sometimes, as the stage revolves, you will recognise an image of West Berlin – but always blurred. This is how I mostly work, probably because I come from a world of postproduction: you shoot only a few takes, but you edit a lot afterwards. Whether I use found images or material I created (in *Richard III*, the proportion is around 80:20), no image stays as it is. I work a lot with compositing, where you combine a lot of different sources into a single image. I tinker a lot with the material; it is a bit like cooking, which by the way both Thomas and I enjoy a lot – and when I first came to Germany, at the time he was one of the few men who did; cooking, eating, and food in general had not yet become a popular or even fashionable hobby. It made things so much easier between us that we were able to communicate an idea or vision by comparing it with a dish or flavour. It may sound funny, but in the beginning of our work, this was an important point for me, and it still is. And of course, we could also share a lot of other references because he is very Francophile and knows a lot of French and Belgian movies, which also allows us to easily exchange ideas with very few words. Even if these references do not directly reflect what he intends on stage, it makes it much easier for both sides to come to the point without much talking, and to understand what the other wants, or does not want, or would like to achieve. Another thing we share: we both do not like clinically beautiful images, even with today's technical options.

In *Hedda Gabler*, I also tried to fit the video movement into the space and the movement of Jan Pappelbaum's set design, and to a degree to animate it with the images, and interact with its materiality. I feel very close to the concerns of set design, and of building spaces: questions that occupy me a lot are how you can add to the set, or reduce it, how to complete it or enter into an exchange and a dialogue with the space, and not just with the plot, the actors, or the director's concept. From the very start, I quickly realised that Thomas is almost fixated on details. He wanted to make tiny aspects of the actors' play large through video, and this was one of his obsessions which we tried to fulfil over the course of several years and numerous productions,

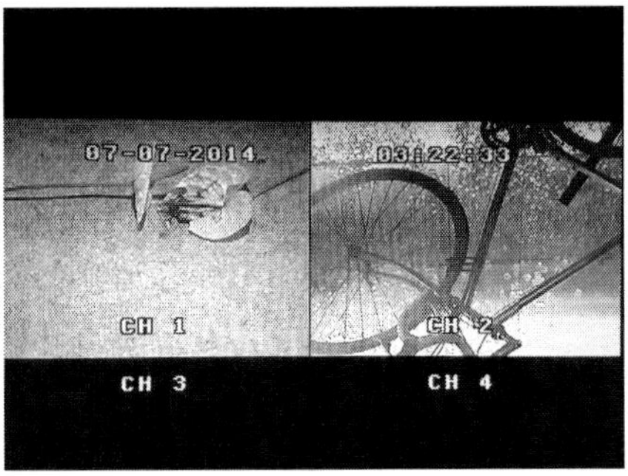

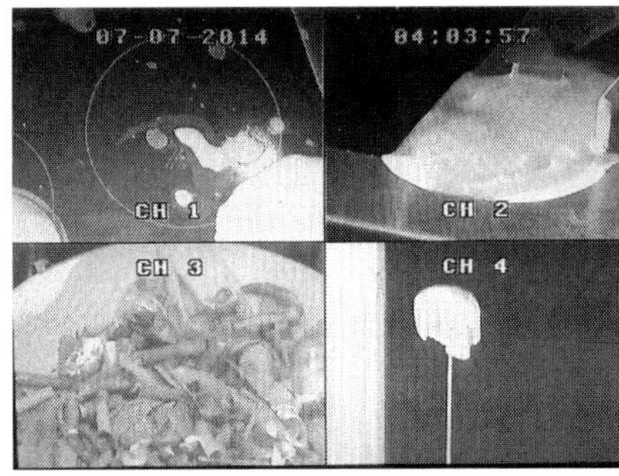

Figures 3.20 and 3.21 Ostermeier's obsession with detail: screenshots from the four CCTV cameras which Sébastien Dupouey installed for the 2010 production of Lars Norén's *Demons* to create complex live close-up projections of actors and objects. Photographs © Sébastien Dupouey.

including *Hedda Gabler* and *Hamlet*. At the time, we tried to capture certain of Tesman's tics, some odd physical movements that you could not necessarily see on stage, on camera – we filmed them in advance and then tried to show the footage in parallel during the production. But because back then we did not have the opportunity of a live signal and of creating a real simultaneity feeling without having cables and cameramen (which would not have fitted on Jan Pappelbaum's uncluttered stage), we eventually left the idea aside. A few years later, this trajectory of our work however culminated in the production of Lars Norén's *Demons* (2010). Thomas' initial reference was the long tracking shot in Godard's *Le Mepris* that follows Michel Piccoli and Brigitte Bardot through the apartment while they are having their argument. Meanwhile, I had been very fascinated by the stage manager's camera, a peculiar form of CCTV, and so instead of working with a big film crew, we settled on playing around with this technology (see Figures 3.20 and 21 and Plate 18).

Thomas is prepared to take such risks and, if necessary, to throw everything overboard. His way of working can be very different, and entirely depends on the project. Sometimes he has an initial discussion and exchange with the entire team about his ideas and conception for a production, while at other times, he prepares things with Jan, and then reveals their ideas for the world of the play to the rest of the team. It is for me and other artists stimulating to work with him as he allows you to make your own suggestions; he then arranges them and you continue to work on your ideas in rehearsal and thereby arrive together at something that sometimes is altogether different. Working with Thomas is therefore very much 'work in progress', probably more for us who work on music and video than for others – I know that some actors consider him as very precise and find it hard to live up to what he wants. With me, as a video artist, however, it is rarely that precise. He brings his ideas to the table, shares some references, and then a proper dialogue starts. At times, this can get frustrating because it can take a long time to find a common path, and to see and really understand whether one's ideas fit in with his vision – also because he talks relatively little about video, and exchanges much more intensely about music. So my work with him can be very free, but at times also very lonely.

What makes working with Thomas so enjoyable is that he keeps looking for new perspectives and is very open to try out new things. He makes different aesthetic attempts to invent dramatic worlds – from the Ibsen chamber plays, to Shakespeare, and productions like *Die Ehe der Maria Braun*. I guess he often looks for a kind of plastic or narrative poetry, he is never interested in video as an effect. It has to add and integrate, and to contribute something relevant without becoming dominant. Video is always an addition, never the main thing, but it adds a certain force and power – and for the video artist, this creates an interesting challenge. *Die Ehe der Maria Braun*, originally created at Kammerspiele München in 2007 just before he started his work on *Hamlet* at the Schaubühne, was, in this and other respects, quite an important landmark for Thomas. It opened for him a whole new perspective on directing, as staging a film presented him with new, different problems. The dramaturg initially did not feel sure about having video in the production, as they were concerned about using a visual medium in the adaptation of a movie. But Thomas wanted

Figure 3.22 Adding a narrative force: projections of Third Reich footage in Thomas Ostermeier's stage adaptation of Rainer Werner Fassbinder's movie *Die Ehe der Maria Braun*, created at Kammerspiele Munich in 2007. Photograph © Sébastien Dupouey.

to show, at the beginning of the play, images of young women who were absolutely fanatic about Hitler (images that, in a strange way, resemble the fanatic enthusiasm for the Beatles, a few decades later). Equally Nina Wetzel, the stage designer, insisted on the potential strength of using live video precisely in order to get rid of the kind of 'movie adaption complex' in this production. So I tried to convey both ideas together and started to work with found material and documentary footage: short fragments, the initial images of the war and the young Hitler women, the later advertisements from *Wirtschaftswunder* Germany. Additionally, there were moments with a live camera that conveyed a sense of the intimacy between Maria and her lovers. I was very intrigued by the delicate and somehow graceful poetry of this production, which took place in a single space, in which he managed to move from one scene to the next with only few, sparse means that opened up dramatic spaces – something that became important for *Hamlet*.

Also at Kammerspiele was another very beautiful experience in our collaboration, *Susn* by the Bavarian author Herbert Achternbusch (2009; see Figure 3.23). It was a particularly interesting challenge to build a world for this play that was so close to Thomas' heart. He was initially somewhat concerned whether I can do this at all; he kept saying, 'Ah, you are not from Bavaria…'. But he took me around, and we spent two or three afternoons where he showed me his family home, the villages where he grew up, some farm buildings, and other places of his early life. I eventually filmed a kind of sad road movie with landscape, driving very slowly through the countryside while filming from the car. These are almost still lives, very quiet and photographic, which then accompanied Susn's monologue. I think most Bavarians did eventually like what I did there.

In addition to his fascination with tiny details, Thomas' second obsession, which has also been occupying us for a number of years, is using the camera as a kind of diary, as a means to create a direct connection with the characters' inner feelings; this leads from *Hamlet* straight to *Richard III*. I found this idea very interesting as he first introduced it in preparations for *Hamlet* (2008). During the rehearsal, other ideas came in, and very soon, Hamlet used the camera as a weapon. He filmed everyone, in particular his mother, and it was his form of witnessing the events (see Figure 3.24). The use of the live video to show Hamlet's perspective in real time added quite a different perspective to the central question whether he is mad or not. Practically, we wanted to use a wireless camera and tested a number of transmission technologies. We eventually very deliberately settled on a transmitter with a bad and noisy, very strange signal. This dark, rough, and dirty video signal perfectly matched the contrast of Jan's dark and cold stage architecture with the living elements that Thomas adds to it. For me, it was an important production, not only because I had just permanently relocated to Berlin. Also, artistically, I tried to go further and position myself between the acting and the stage design, and to negotiate between the two with my video work.

Figures 3.23 and 3.24 The camera as diary: For Herbert Achternbusch's *Susn* (Kammerspiele Munich 2009), Sébastien Dupouey created a slow-motion road movie of Thomas Ostermeier's Bavarian childhood home. In *Hamlet* (2008), they introduced live images, turning the camera into Hamlet's weapon. Photographs © Sébastien Dupouey, Arno Declair.

The golden chain curtain of course lent itself to show abstract video images. An important theme was the idea of chaos, of a post-war world that was out of joint; at the time, all of us were still preoccupied a lot with the aftermath of 9/11 and the images of this day, which certainly raised a lot of questions for us working with media images in the visual arts. Initially, I projected a tiny fragment of footage, just paper and dust flying through the streets, but you could not recognise what it was. I then began taking images of objects that were on stage – old paper, beer cans that remained from the initial wedding party of Gertrude and Claudius – and introduced them, too.

Richard and *Hamlet* are of course very connected, and for me there is a far greater direct link than to the other Shakespeare plays Thomas had directed since. This might have to do with the fact that it is almost the same team, including the same lead actor, Lars, but there are also certain decisions about the set that invite you to make connections between the two productions. With *Richard*, things were more complex than usual, however. I came in three weeks into the production, and by that time, the entire set design and also the music were already very much decided. Thomas had only given me very few prompts. He wanted to build a very dark world that would not immediately evoke contemporary references. He had the imagery of American photographer Joel-Peter Witkin in mind, where you never really know where you are, and where there are many references, to Caravaggio and Renaissance imagery, yet nothing that is pronouncedly 'contemporary'. When I joined the work on the production, I could see on the rehearsal stage a world that was already very

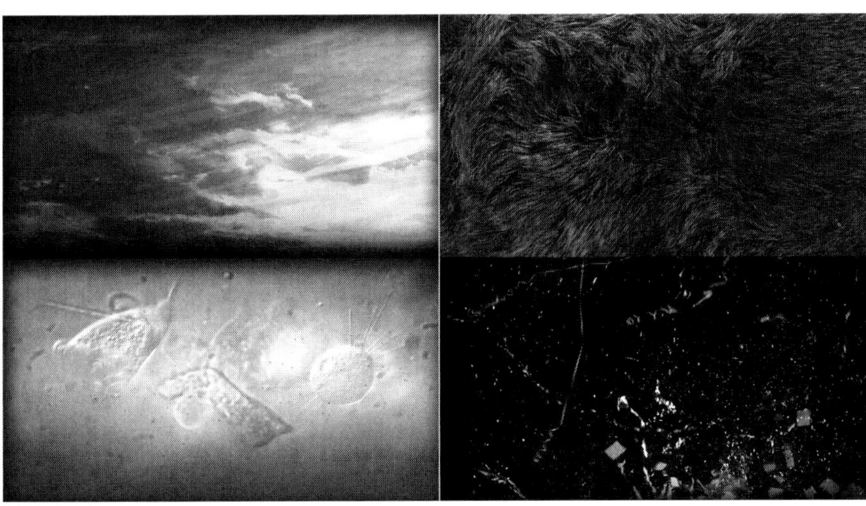

Figures 3.25–3.28 Abstract imagery that does not immediately evoke contemporary references: clouds, a boar's fur, drops in fluid, and golden glitter – some of the imagery Sébastien Dupouey used for his videowork in Ostermeier's *Richard III* (2015). Screenshots: Sébastien Dupouey.

dark with very big music, and in addition there were the acting, the black- and white costumes – there was already so much that I found it hard to get in and to find my own way, and my place. It was also not really clear to me at first why we were using video within this space at all – other than that it was unusual to introduce video into this space, because it was so close, so frontal, and so high. Initially, I thought, if we can get away with it, why not indulge in this very straight 'more is more' approach. We worked on a version of the initial celebration scene, which offered a nice connection with the chaotic world we created for *Hamlet*, and I then suggested working with the set design and experiment with mapping, but it got too much for Thomas. So we eventually went into ever more abstract worlds, using video almost as a source of lighting that adds to the very peculiar plasticity of the stage. It seemed suffice to work with very simple means, and also with only very careful, unobtrusive editing: a world that develops through other forms, the paper streamers, birds, dust, and fog (see Figures 3.25–3.28). The challenge was to connect these images of wide

Figure 3.29 The wide-angle camera, built into the microphone, remains Richard Gloucester's sole friend in the second half of Thomas Ostermeier's *Richard III* (Lars Eidinger as Richard and Sebastian Schwarz as Ratcliff). Photograph © Arno Declair.

landscapes, clouds, heaven, fields, with Richard's inner state, and this is how the idea of illness came up. I started working with microscopic stock-footage, minute things that look huge; images of a cancer cell that looks identical to a satellite image from Google Earth.

In the production, the images are huge, for sure, but it has been a long time since I have been so non-narrative. The live camera only came in later. I found the microphone in the middle of the stage remarkable in the way it created closeness through acoustic means. The actor was able to step back, to retreat into his inner thoughts, and still reach everybody. I therefore suggested adding a camera, not least as I thought it might help those up there on the second balcony. The camera has a very wide angle and is therefore clearly situated within the play's imagery of beauty and deformation, as well as its mirror metaphors (see Figure 3.29). I think it was not at all a bad idea since it solved a lot of questions about the later part of the production that foregrounds Richard's loneliness as soon as he gets into power. With *Richard*, after exactly a decade of working together, we may have now hit a limit, where there is too much on stage, with the music, the acting, the images. I feel we might scale things back again in the future – but the audience certainly seems to like it.

In the course of these ten years, I have also been able to witness how Thomas has developed and refined his own 'school of working' that he shares in this book. Storytelling, in particular, is still a relatively new addition, yet I feel it has noticeably liberated him in his work. Previously, he only had his words and his own acting skills and technique to communicate with his actors, but through this method of improvising, everyone, even we as the creative team, can become references that are shared, and this has made the dialogue between the director and the actors much more interesting, and also brought much more fun into the work. Especially when I know that we will do some films or there will be live video, I am also able to take away a lot from the storytelling and from what I see in these moments. I always take a lot of notes as I do not know yet what I might need in the later work and development of the production.

Coming originally from the world of television and the music industry, I still cherish the luxury of working in the theatre: the fact that you can focus together on a project. In the art world, you usually work alone, or you work for someone else. In this respect, it is also an interesting experience to realise that theatre is to a large degree still a craft, which can be frustrating at times for directors or stage and video designers who consider themselves, first and foremost, as artists. Yet, in theatre, you have got to work with others, you have to build something, you have to tinker and fiddle around with actual, material things and with real people. And there are limits that you must consider in your creative process. Video, in particular, takes time, not least because the technology still continues to develop further, whereas sound and lighting is pretty much where it is, and changes seem far more incremental. Every theatre space is equipped nowadays with sound and lighting, but if you build a new set, like for *Richard III*, you have to install, and mostly that means to buy, new equipment, a new projector, new lenses, other new video technology. The work of a video designer in theatre therefore starts with finding a technical solution that suits both the creative ideas, the space and the budget, and these negotiations, in fact, take up a large part of the work on a production; and at times, it can be a bit frustrating because you eventually cannot but work around the technical means you can afford to have. The payoff, however, is that this collective, shared, and more or less democratic world of making theatre, where you do not have to fulfil expectations or think about audiences and markets, is something very unique. Of course your work should be a success with the audience, but you can still be edgy, and each project has no other purpose than itself. There is such great liberty in theatre, which, when I began, was something entirely unknown to me.

Figure 3.30 Sébastien Dupouey. Photograph © Sébastien Dupouey.

Sébastien Dupouey was born in Paris in 1969 and studied at the École Nationale Supérieure des Arts Décoratifs. He worked as musician and graphic designer, and directed music videos, commercials, and productions for French television. Since 2005, he has worked with Thomas Ostermeier;

they collaborated on *Before Sunrise* (Kammerspiele München, 2005), *Hedda Gabler* (2005), *Cat on a hot tin roof* (2007), *Die Ehe der Maria Braun* (Kammerspiele München, 2007), *Hamlet* (2008), *Susn* (Kammerspiele München, 2009), *Demons* and *Othello* (2010), *Ghosts* (Toneelgroep Amsterdam, 2010), and *Richard III* (2015). He has also worked with directors Falk Richter, Christiane Paulhofer, Lars-Ole Wallburg, Stefan Pucher, Marius von Mayenburg and Mikaël Serre.

Chapter 4

Ostermeier writings [2]

'It's us': Ibsen's plays and contemporary worries

4.1 'THEATRE AGAINST FEAR': THOMAS OSTERMEIER IN CONVERSATION WITH ÀLEX RIGOLA (2005)

Spanish director and dramaturg Àlex Rigola was Artistic Director of the Teatre Lliure in Barcelona from 2003 to 2011, and director of the theatre section of the Venice Biennale since 2010. In January 2005, Rigola brought Thomas Ostermeier's radical production of Ibsen's Nora – A Doll's House *to the Teatre Lliure. Afterwards, he met Ostermeier for the following interview, which was conducted in English and took place in Berlin on 20 February 2005. It was first published in* Documents de Dansa i Teatre *(May 2005, pp. 67–73), and subsequently appeared in* Contemporary Theatre Review *(Vol. 16(2), 2006, pp. 235–250). Following a rehearsed reading in 2010, Rigola recreated his Barcelona stage adaptation of Roberto Bolaño's novel* 2666 *at Schaubühne in 2014. In their 2005 discussion, Ostermeier discusses the place of* Nora – A Doll's House *in his career trajectory, as well as reflecting on the initial years of his work at Schaubühne. It is reprinted by permission of Taylor & Francis Ltd.*

ÀLEX RIGOLA: I think you have said many times that *Nora – A Doll's House* is clearly a sort of step forward for you in your work ...

THOMAS OSTERMEIER: Yes. The big change was that we concentrated on a society that is more upper class than in the plays we did before, like *Shopping and Fucking*. The play's aesthetic value lies in the fact that we built up scenery and an atmosphere of people who came into money in Berlin, and in this performance they are on stage. I suppose this is the big step forward in *Nora – A Doll's House*. But the most interesting point is that we are still talking about fear, the fear of falling down and not being a part of society any more, which is the same fear people have in *Shopping and Fucking* or in *Personenkreis 3.1*. What was so surprising was that bourgeois society and the bourgeois audience came again to our theatre and saw a play about their lives. And by the end of the performance, they were at the same point as the people in *Shopping and Fucking* or in *Personenkreis 3.1*, and so there was the same fear and the same existentialistic point of view on life. To me this was the trick of the performance: I wanted to talk again about the fear of social failure, and in this case we had very high-class characters on stage that were still sharing the same fear.

ÀR: It's funny because, on the other hand, it's a one-hundred-year-old play.

TO: The scandal about this decision to make *Nora* is precisely that it's an old play which describes a society at the end of the nineteenth century, in which the role model of man and woman is nineteenth century, but that if you put it into new modern surroundings, you don't notice any difference. So the thesis was that in the man–woman role model, nothing had changed. For a lot of people this was a big shock: to see a play from the end of the nineteenth century and still have the impression that it's playing in the present. And this tells something of the role of women today in Germany. One evening, a good friend of mine brought his sister to the show and, after the performance, she said, 'ah, you can see there are good contemporary writers'. So she didn't know that it was a classical play, 130 years old. And that's the point.

ÀR: You fill your performance with a lot of signs, which can affect its whole meaning. For example, the shot Nora fires at her husband may have many different origins, since you have given clues to build several explanations. When you start the performance, for instance, with Torvald taking pictures of his children, for just a moment I saw the possibility of a paedophilic relationship between him and his daughter. Maybe a lot of people can't see it ...

TO: Everybody sees it!

ÀR: I don't know if everybody reads it that way. Anyway, that could be a reason for Nora to shoot her husband at the end of the play. Is that one of the reasons? Does it have anything to do with it? Because he likes to think of her as a baby ...

TO: As a baby-doll, yes ...

ÀR: Does she know what he is doing with their children or doesn't she? In the performance you can't see it, but perhaps she imagines a lot of things.

TO: That's really interesting, because I had never thought about it. You are the first person to tell me that there may be a connection between this paedophile thing and the shooting at the end. What is true is that I wanted to show that Torvald wants a wife like a baby, like a doll, and this is clearly seen at the end of the first act, when he takes pictures of Nora. Then the stage revolves and, at the moment he takes the picture, the photo of the girl appears. As a result, this paedophilia thing is in the play, but I had never thought that she shot him because of that. I don't think that she knows what he is doing, but you are right. Some people have told me that they disagree with this first scene of the photo of the girl. They say that she is a child and I shouldn't make her do it because she is not an actress. So I am quite aware of this effect. Anyway, this is a very important point in my *mise en scène*.

ÀR: With the end we can perhaps understand many things about the performance and the play. It generates a lot of questions for me; all the time I am asking why: why they behave in the way they do, why she shoots, if she is bad, if she is ill before she starts living with him, or if living with him has made her ill. Perhaps it started with the relationship or perhaps before ...

TO: The origin of the tension is quite simple: it's a financial question. He is afraid of falling down the ladder, so the real basis of the whole play is financial fear. Nowadays, Berlin and Germany are suffering a major economic depression, and so there is a big fear all around us of the loss of social position, especially among the bourgeois families. This was the original idea of the play and it comes from Ibsen. When the play starts, the first thing people talk about is money, and all through the play they talk about nothing else except money and work. Thus, Kristin Linde, the other woman, is looking for a job, she's very poor and has got nothing; Krogstad is about to lose his job; and Torvald has just got a new position in the bank after years and years of social fighting. This economic awareness is the background for the whole play. In the past, Nora helped him survive under very tough financial pressure. He fell ill and she found the money for him to recover in the south of Europe to go on fighting. So, the whole play is about financial survival, which creates the tension between characters. It is not only the tension between Torvald and Nora, but the tension between characters. It's always about money. The idea was to have a private play with the financial background adding tension and putting pressure on people. And all this tension comes from the fact that they are dreaming of a better life, of a life in which they are part of the high-class bourgeois society.

ÀR: That is made clear in the show, and I like the fact that you do not create an epicentric play around Nora, rather you play with all the actors and all the characters. But there is something about Nora that I don't understand. It's the way she relates to her husband, the lies this kind of bourgeois society lives in. I don't know, but I suppose at your theatre there aren't many people of this sort ...

TO: Yes, there are! And because of *Nora* they are now coming to the Schaubühne. Our normal audience is made up of students, young people, up to 35, very much interested in theatre, and at the beginning of their career. But with Nora there were a lot of people from the old Schaubühne audience coming back because it was a classic, a play they knew, and because of the reputation of the performance.

ÀR: And have they started watching the other shows you perform?

TO: That's a good question. They are also watching the other shows, but I think their favourite is *Nora*. It's a very stimulating experience, because I am very much interested in people who don't usually go to the theatre. As everybody knows, men between 35 and 55 don't go to the theatre at all, because they are so focussed on their jobs they don't have any time. Only from time to time do their wives convince them to go to theatre. But with *Nora*, a lot of these men showed up with their wives and saw a play about their situation, about their lives. A lot of people told me it's not about them, but about friends of theirs, and they know cases of this kind of relationship. I think this social class which is described in *Nora* exists all around the world at the moment. It's us, in fact, the thirty-somethings getting established, having money or not, and often at the peak of their careers. And it's strange for these people to see themselves in theatre. Because theatre is often a strange world, very arty, very avantgarde. So the whole performance again has something to do with realism, which I described in my first text. It's a kind of realism because it's talking about the reality of people of this age, of this class, and it's maybe much more interesting than the realism of the outcast because it is a realism that directly speaks to the people in the audience. When we do *Shopping & Fucking*, we must be aware that the people described in the play don't go to the theatre because they neither have the money nor are interested, but they do go to clubs or concerts. So if you do something like *Nora – A Doll's House*, you get the audience that knows what the play is talking about. And I think this was the big step forward in this production.

ÀR: In *Nora* you suggest that the men and women of today have to be supermen and superwomen. Even Nora goes to the party dressed as Lara Croft.

TO: The whole production talks of different images and pictures we get from the media, which are always providing us with different ideas of how we should be. On stage we have to question these pictures because I think they are very hard and very difficult for people. As a man today you have to be a very good lover, you have to be very successful in your job, you have to be very intelligent, you have to be a very good partner, you have to be a psychotherapist, you have to be very well educated, you have to be a very good father, and so on. You have a whole range of different roles, and this is very demanding. In the nineteenth century, you were a patriarch and that was it: at home you were the boss. But now at home you have to be what I have just said. So the pressure on the individual character is greatly increasing. Torvald is not really fitting into all the roles that are there, while Nora, on the other hand, is trying to be a good wife, a very good friend, a very good mother and also a very sexy woman. I think it's a problem for her to cope with the tension between all these roles, between all these characters. She has to be the baby-doll, as the Ibsen text says. In the Ibsen text Nora herself says, 'you created me after these ideas of yours, so I am a creation, I have to be what you think a woman should be like, I am not myself, but I have to play different roles'. And this is very interesting nowadays because again women in Germany must not only be good mothers or good housewives, but must also be attractive, and they have to be a very beautiful appendage to their men, and they have to have intelligent conversations when they go out, so that their husbands can show off their women. And all these roles are creating very high tension, because women have to act all the time.

ÀR: And the solution is *Wunschkonzert*?[1]

TO: *Wunschkonzert* is the other side of the coin. In Berlin, two thirds of the people receiving social aid are single women. As a result, the provocation with these two shows is that, as a woman in Berlin today, either you've got the solution of being with a terrible man, or you've got the solution of staying alone and not being a part of social life. These are two female biographies at the moment. There is no female biography onstage or in real life where women are really part of society and have power over themselves.

ÀR: There was a great moment in *Wunschkonzert*, when you explain all the play in just one or two minutes: it's the moment when she plays a solitaire on the PC. When I saw it, I was really impressed, I started crying. ... You realize the woman plays every day although she knows the game perfectly well and it's a completely mechanical game. There is something deeply emotional about it. ... For me, it was the best moment of the play.

TO: I was always crying in rehearsals at that moment too. ... And it's funny that the game is called solitaire, eh?

ÀR: Yes. Everybody can play solitaire, but the way she played was so impressive. ... Tell me something, you talk about people in their thirties approximately, our age. I think you are 36 or 37 years old ...

TO: 36.

ÀR: I think we have a different point of view on things. For example, we are the first generation to have been brought up with the TV at home, and that's a difference with the other generations because, for example, we can read a lot of images per minute and that makes us explain things in a very different way. I remember that, when I was a child, in my parents' house there were only five or six LPs. Now, instead, we have a lot of music in our houses and we can use it all. We have another kind of culture, and for me it's easier to communicate with younger generations. But what do you think will happen in twenty years' time? Do you think you will be able to communicate like you do now, or maybe something similar will happen to what happens in advertising? The best professionals in advertising are 20 or 30 years old and when they are 35 they finish their work.

TO: Yes, I know, they can't go on, they can't compete with the younger people.

ÀR: I am saying this because I think communication with the audience is the most important thing. How do you feel about it?

TO: I don't know where I will be in twenty years' time. I think that theatre is a very slow art form, and now I am working on developing my communication with actors. I think that you need maybe ten, fifteen or twenty years' time to be really able to communicate with them and that, only after about twenty years, can you achieve mastery over communication with actors. It's true that we get many effects by using all these images from the media, but still the most important thing in theatre is the actor, and how you can manage to liberate an actor and to have him free from fear on stage. This is my pace, this is my way, this is my future: to work with actors and to find a form of communication where they are not afraid to go on stage anymore. This is my biggest aim: to create a show without fear, in which they are comfortable on stage. But the truth is that I am really not thinking about these questions – is there any future for my work in twenty years' time? – and so on. I am quite OK with the fact that I am working now, but I am also OK with the idea that I might not work in theatre in ten years' time. This is possible. I think Heiner Müller once said that you are only a good drama writer until the age of 30, because drama is about conflict, and only until the age of 30 do you have enough conflict and anger to produce theatre. Afterwards, you are so comfortable and established that there is no need for conflict anymore, and so there is no more anger to produce theatre. Maybe he was right, because all the big plays by the big writers were written before they were 30. Büchner died at the age of 24, Sarah Kane died at 29. Maybe there's a time between 20 and 30 when you are really powerful enough and you may be angry enough to create a world of conflict on stage. And maybe that's why we should be OK with the idea of not doing shows anymore at the age of 40, 45 or 50. My idea is to become a teacher. I am already teaching quite a lot, and I think it's important to conserve the memory of the people who have done theatre between the age of 20 and 40 and then take their knowledge to the younger generations. This is my idea of a biography.

ÀR: I think a lot about the life of a teacher, too, because I think it's important not to always work with the pressure of the theatre. With plays you have a lot of pressure in your work, and I think there will be one day when I'll go and teach too. When I see what some of my masters are doing, I think there is a moment to stop, but I also understand it's very difficult ...

TO: Like Peter Zadek's *Peer Gynt*. ... When something like this happens, I also think you should stop.

ÀR: Yes. You can go to school and teach people a lot.

TO: Well, this is my idea of theatre. Theatre is about conflict and you need to have enough anger inside yourself to provide the two parts of a conflict with a will to win. If you lose your own anger, the two sides do not have enough will to go into conflict, and the tragedy comes from these two points. Tragedy is about two sides which are right in their own way, and so the greater the anger and the will to win, the bigger the tragedy. Everything we see on stage which is boring is done by people who do not have enough anger anymore, who feel comfortable, who agree with the world, and I think only people who don't agree with the world should do theatre. If you agree with the world around you, there is no need to do theatre. It's very important that you don't agree with what is going on, because then you need theatre; you need a way of expressing your feelings of disagreement.

4.2 READING AND STAGING IBSEN (2010)

Originally published in Ibsen Studies, *Vol. X, No. 2 (2010), pp. 68–74. Reprinted by permission of Taylor & Francis Ltd.*

I would like to give you some idea of my approach to Ibsen's plays. These thoughts are based on my work since 2002. Roughly every two years I have directed an Ibsen play: *A Doll's House* in 2002, *The Master Builder* in Vienna in 2004, *Hedda Gabler* in 2005, *John Gabriel Borkman* in 2008, and *Ghosts*, which I shall be directing in Amsterdam at the end of 2010. First of all, I would like to give you some idea of why, in my opinion, Ibsen's work has a special value nowadays. And then I would like to talk in a more general way about the problems you encounter in the dramaturgy, in the writing and in the directing of Ibsen's plays.

Money and soul

In Germany, especially in the German *Regietheater* of the 1970s, 1980s and early 1990s, Ibsen was always known as the writer who revealed the mysteries of the soul. This led to a special tradition in putting Ibsen on stage, and actors often had a typical way of interpreting Ibsen's characters in their mind. It was a way of trying to portray the inner landscape of the character. Ibsen was widely interpreted as the writer who had put the ideas of Freud on stage before Freud himself developed them. The consequence was that the actor would try very hard to make believe that his feelings on stage were sincere, so Ibsen's plays have often been performed with a lot of pauses, emotional seizures and passionate looks out of windows. Presenting Ibsen's work in this way can be very boring, or at least risks being very boring, especially as this belief in feeling completely destroys the play and leads to performances in which the characters no longer act in the sense of taking action. What directors have to face when approaching Ibsen's plays is a problem which every director has to face when approaching a classical writer or a classical play: even before we read the play for the first time we already have lots of clichés of interpretations in our mind, and lots of ideas of how an Ibsen play should be done.

When I first stepped into the world of Ibsen's plays, and now I am talking primarily about the plays I mentioned previously, the ones I directed or am going to direct, I was struck by the fact that the characters are under huge economic pressure and that Ibsen always uses this economic pressure as the motor of the play. And for me this is the very link to the present which makes this writer so contemporary. In Germany – and I suppose this is also transferable to the rest of Europe – since the beginning of the 1990s the dominating neoliberal ideas of our societies have been threatened by growing economic fears. People have become obsessed by the fear of dropping down the social ladder and of losing their social status. This can mainly be seen in the middle class, which until the 1990s was the winner of the so-called glorious 'Wirtschaftswunder', the economic miracle of the 1950s. In the 1980s we had to face mass unemployment for the first time since the Second World War, and in the 1990s and the 2000s the economic crisis meant that the middle class were confronted with the danger of losing their jobs, their wealth, their social status. A society where jobs and money are everything is a society where religion, nation and family have lost their power. Somebody who is unemployed and has no money is faced with being a complete nobody with no reason to go on living. Or they try to find a meaning in life in values which were most important in the golden age of bourgeois society, like family values, in marriage, in Christian religion, in having children and being a good mother to them. This is something which is very popular in Germany at the moment and in our generation has created a new kind of bourgeoisie known as 'die neue Mitte', the new centre of society.

I mentioned two very important topics which I found in Ibsen's plays. First of all, the overall issue of economic pressure and financial worries. Second, the aspect of family, the pressure on the role of a woman in the time of Ibsen and nowadays, especially in the new conservative spirit we have to face now and which impacts on society. I see more parallels in the difficulties of being a couple, having children and trying to solve the problem of having a family life then and now. First of all, let us remind ourselves of some examples concerning the economic pressure:

> *A Doll's House*: Helmer, the bank director, and the loans; the fact that Nora does not want her husband to know about the loans she got from Krogstad.
>
> *Hedda Gabler*: Tesman's career as a professor is put into danger by Løvborg; the house he bought, which he cannot afford if he does not get the job.
>
> *John Gabriel Borkman*: Of course, him speculating and losing everything; the magic belief in the power of money to solve all our problems is the core of the play.

So what we have here – and there are more examples in the other plays, but I would like to concentrate on these examples – is that the characters are completely preoccupied with constant worries about financial or economic issues. This unwavering belief in the power of money destroys every human relationship. Especially the male characters become more or less narrow-minded and blind to other needs around them. Career, social status, money, status symbols like the house in *Hedda Gabler* are more important than the human beings around them, more important than emotional relationships, more important than love, friendship, even family bonds in the example of the two sisters in *Borkman*. For financial reasons Borkman decides to marry the woman he does not love and gives the woman he loves to another man, sacrificing her for his career. He destroys even the tie between the twin sisters, which is traditionally considered the strongest possible tie between human beings.

In contrast to the cliché of characters in Ibsen's plays and the interpretation of them in German theatre from the late 1950s until the beginning of the 1990s, the characters have thus sacrificed their souls, their emotions, their passions, their love or their ability to love to their financial desire. They are living in a rationalised, secularised cold world where some of them still try to maintain other values, but then suffer total shipwrecks in this world, like Elvsted, like Nora, like Mrs Alving. Actually – and this is one of my main points – as you may already have understood, I am fascinated by this writer because he shows how middle-class individuals try to find a way in a completely cold world without abandoning the ideals that the bourgeoisie pretends to have. But as we know since Richard Sennett's *The Corrosion of Character*, this is difficult and becomes more and more difficult, as demonstrated by the characters of Engstrand in *Ghosts* or Brack in *Hedda Gabler* – the cynical and less emotional characters in Ibsen's plays tend to triumph. What is interesting to me as a director is to have a playwright who shows how human beings with all their emotions try to survive with their souls intact in a completely materialistic and rationalised world, where only the power of money rules. And I think these are things which can be observed in our daily life: our physical appearance, what the body expresses or does not express, or the way that what it expresses is no longer readable – all of this is influenced by our brave new world. Very often modern societies, especially Western democracies, have to face physical and mental problems. Physical problems such as not feeling well in our bodies, having problems in our modern system, having to fight diseases like illnesses of the nervous system, burn-out syndrome, the complete loss of the connection to our bodies, depression. We have to face the fact that our materialistic view of the world can be rediscovered as symptoms in our bodies. And this is the very interesting link in staging Ibsen's dramas nowadays, examining how this way of life affects our physical appearance, and what kind of social and physical approach we have to each other.

The writer of the exposition and the two dramas

This leads me to the second part of my thoughts, which are more common points in the drama of Henrik Ibsen and how these are linked to my passion for special sociological views of the human being or of theatre as a sociological laboratory that examines the behaviour of human beings. For 2,500 years, text-based theatre has had the idea that the human being reveals his capacity for being good or bad especially in situations which can be considered dramatic, like after an airplane crash when a few people have survived on an isolated island and they have nothing more to eat or drink. This is more of a Hollywood dramaturgy in which we soon find out through the development of the story that people are capable of sacrificing themselves, giving the last water to others, but also capable of killing someone in order to survive. In Ibsen's plays the dramatic situation is usually much more difficult and complex. This is because of the fact that, after the bloody medieval times in which conflicts until the end of the nineteenth century could be solved by weapons, in duels, bourgeois society is less violent. So the complexity of the conflicts is much more complicated than in a Shakespeare drama where 'I kill in order to become the king'. The conflict of Hedda Gabler for example, is, actually, quite difficult to describe; yet even if we cannot describe it easily, everybody among us can recognise Hedda Gabler's feelings: living the wrong life, being together with the wrong person, not being courageous enough to live an independent life, hating the others around her because they show her, like a mirror, how miserable and small her courage and ideals are.

So in order to tell us about all this, the writer Ibsen often decides to make an exposition out of half of the play (and sometimes even more), which means preparing the drama, which is then done in one long breath of one or one and a half hours. And now I am coming back to the point in my first section: I think this exposition in Ibsen's plays is the biggest danger and a trap every director risks in staging an Ibsen play. Because what mostly happens in this section of the play is that you play the drama and are overdramatic and emotional, while the drama actually is not there yet. Most of the time Ibsen has one character who tells everything that is important for the audience to know to another character, and primarily we have the situation of simple conversations. As a lot of directors don't take this as an opportunity, but try to put something into the scenes that is not there; they are caught in the trap.

And there is my point: I think this part of the play is for the director who is obsessed with sociological observation of human behaviour in daily life. Here lies the chance you can take when you direct Ibsen's plays. Because while directing you can be very nuanced and show how a body moves in space, how a body approaches another, how people shake hands, talk to each other while not watching each other, how they try to perform their happy life and so on. You have a laboratory without drama, and this can be very exciting for directors like me, who are also interested in the appearances of daily life where you can already observe the effects of modern times. What Ibsen himself does in order to improve this situation of simple conversation a little bit is that often the characters tell the stories of the last years to the protagonists. The character confronts the protagonist with things from the past he or she would love not to be confronted with any more. This is true of Hilde Wangel in *The Master Builder*. This is true of Pastor Manders and Mrs. Alving, who confront each other with the love they had. This is true of Løvborg in *Hedda Gabler*, who confronts Hedda with the ideals and the passion of her past. This is true of Christine Linde and Krogstad in *A Doll's House*. And it is certainly true of Ella and her effect on Gunhild in *John Gabriel Borkman*. So what Ibsen does is to confront the main characters of the play with ghosts from the past, to quote the title of one of his plays. And here we are facing the main topic of Ibsen's plays – something which is not a big surprise to anyone who knows Ibsen: that bourgeois society is built on lies and hypocrisy, or, to say it in German, on a *Lebenslüge* – it is built on living a lie. When these characters are confronted with the ghosts from the past, there is anxiety. This transforms the very non-theatrical situation of the conversation into a theatrical situation in which they are confronted with their younger self of the past via the ghosts who 'appear', and the younger self is represented in this 'Genganger', the revenant – confronted with the fact that 'when I was young I never wanted to become like these lying and hypocritical grown-ups'. So it is as if you were meeting your subconscious or as if you were meeting your emotions which are not meant to live in the house, but in the cellar.

Meeting these emotions can, of course, be very painful because it calls your whole life in question. The appearance of these characters is a challenge and at the same time a gift to the director: they can be in your living room and you don't recognize them, just as Nora doesn't notice Linde. They are coming out of the fog, which was what I tried to show in *John Gabriel Borkman*, they appear like chimera behind glass like Løvborg in *Hedda Gabler* or they even fly from the sky, which is what I did with Hilde Wangel in *The Master Builder*. These are all theatrical effects or ways of staging this dramaturgy which improve the on the whole not very dramatic situation of the first half of Ibsen plays. It is as if there were two dramas happening: the drama which took place five, ten, or fifteen years before the play starts, and the drama in the second half of the play. And to create this passage, this sequence at the beginning of the play until the drama can really happen, to make this interesting – this is the true challenge for everybody directing Ibsen's plays.

Note

1 *Wunschkonzert* (Request Show) by Bavarian author Franz Xaver Kroetz is a silent play for an actress, written in 1971, which follows a day in the life of a single woman, taking us through a series of mundane tasks and ending with her suicide. The play is without any dialogue, performed to the soundtrack of a radio music request show. At Schaubühne, Ostermeier directed the play in 2003 as companion piece to *Nora – A Doll's House*, again with Anne Tismer in the lead role.

Plates 1 and 2 Beginnings at the Baracke: Thomas Ostermeier's production of Mark Ravenhill's *Shopping and Fucking*, with Jule Böwe, Thomas Bading and Bruno Cathomas (1998, above, Photograph © Gerlind Clemens), and below, his biomechanics-inspired version of Bertolt Brecht's *Mann ist Mann*, with Tilo Werner (left) and Ronald Kukulies (1997, Photograph © Joachim Fieguth/ drama-berlin.de).

Plates 3–5 The first season at the Schaubühne: Thomas Ostermeier opened his tenure in 2000 with Lars Norén's *Personenkreis 3.1*, followed by Sarah Kane's *Crave* which is still playing in repertoire today, in the 2015/16 season. Photographs © Arno Declair.

Plates 6–8 Ibsen, our contemporary: the 2002 production of *Nora – A Doll's House* was Thomas Ostermeier's first Ibsen. With Lars Eidinger (as Dr Rank), Anne Tismer (Nora) and Jörg Hartmann (Torvald Helmer). Photographs © Arno Declair (top), Jan Pappelbaum (bottom).

Plates 9 and 10 Büchner in cinemascope (top, across both pages): Jan Pappelbaum's set for the 2003 *Woyzeck* enveloped the spectator with a huge contemporary banlieu landscape. Photographs © Jan Pappelbaum (top) and Arno Declair (left).

Plates 11 and 12 Sarah Kane's *Blasted* (2005), with Ulrich Mühe and Katharina Schüttler. Photographs © Arno Declair.

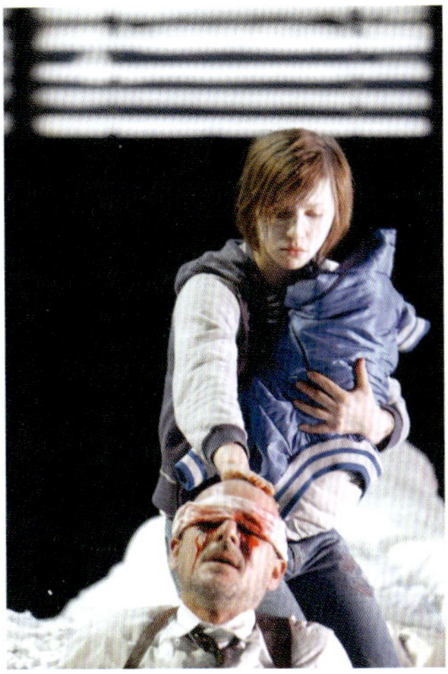

Plates 13–15 Ibsen's *Hedda Gabler* (2005), above, with Katharina Schüttler as Hedda and Annedore Bauer as Ms Elvsted. Below: William Shakespeare's *Midsummer Night's Dream* (2006), with Nabih Amaraoui (left) and Gail Sharrol Skrela. Photographs © Arno Declair.

Plates 16–18 *Die Ehe der Maria Braun*, after Rainer Werner Fassbinder's movie, with Brigitte Hobmeier, Hans Kremer and Steven Scharf (top left) and Jean-Pierre Cornu (top right, 2007, Kammerspiele Munich). Bottom: Brigitte Hobmeier (on video) and Lars Eidinger in the 2010 production of Lars Norén's *Demons* (2010). Photographs © Arno Declair.

Plates 19 and 20 Thomas Ostermeier, backstage, at the 2011 tour of *Hamlet* at Venice (top). *Othello* premiered at the 2010 Epidauros festival in the historic Greek amphitheatre. Photographs © Jan Pappelbaum.

Chapter 5

Ostermeier at work [1]

An Enemy of the People (2012)

Figure 5.1 *Ein Volksfeind* at Schaubühne Saal B in September 2012. Photograph © Arno Declair.

Rehearsals: (studio rehearsals) 2–26 May 2012; (stage rehearsals Berlin) 25 June–12 July 2012; (dress rehearsal Avignon) 17 July 2012; (follow-up rehearsals Berlin) 3–7 September 2012
Premiere: 18 July 2012 at Festival d'Avignon,
8 September 2012, Schaubühne Saal B
Running time: *ca.* 150 minutes, no interval

Adaptation by Florian Borchmeyer and Thomas Ostermeier

(Continued)

(Continued)

Cast:

Dr Thomas Stockmann: Stefan Stern (until March 2014),
Christoph Gawenda (since May 2014)
Peter Stockmann, Mayor: Ingo Hülsmann
Katharina Stockmann: Eva Meckbach
Hovstad: Christoph Gawenda (until March 2014)
Andreas Schröders / Renato Schuch (alternating, since May 2014)
Aslaksen: David Ruland
Billing: Moritz Gottwald
Morten Kiil: Thomas Bading

Creative team

Assistant directors: Sina Flubacher, Hannah Fissenebert; Stage design: Jan Pappelbaum; Stage design assistant: Doreen Back; Costume design: Nina Wetzel; Costume assistant: Marie Abel; Music: Malte Beckenbach, Daniel Freitag; Dramaturgy: Florian Borchmeyer; Light design: Erich Schneider; Wall drawings: Katharina Ziemke; Stage manager: Elske Herrmann; Prompter: Heike Kroemer; Dog trainer: Simone Brunner; Direction interns: Panni Néder, Nicholas Mockridge, Korbinian Schmidt; Stage design intern: Sammy Van den Heuvel; Costume design intern: Désirée Andersch.

Technical team

Technical Director: Daniel Kaiser; Make-up: Helga Petritsch; Props: Wolfgang Reuter; Sound: Sven Poser, Daniel Bolliger; Light: Jörg Hentschel; Head of costume: Dagmar Fabisch, Johanna Ballhausen; Wardrobe mistress (Ladies): Anne-Katrin Haubold; Wardrobe master (Men): Günter Welz; Technical inspector: Helmut Müller; Stage inspector: Max Schirmer; Stage master: Felix Rohde; Construction: Lena Lentz; Head of stage machinery: Stephan Staehle; Head of workshops: Helmut von Arentsschild; Paintshop: Andreas Geißel; Decoration: Thomas Mielenz; Carpenter: Hartmut Rosen; Metalwork: Katja Kentenich

5.1 THE DRAMATURG'S WORK: FLORIAN BORCHMEYER

Prior to starting as a dramaturg at the Schaubühne in 2011, Florian Borchmeyer (b. 1974) was an award winning documentary film-maker. He still is a programme curator for the international programme at the Munich Film Festival. A literary scholar specialising in Latin American studies, Florian received his PhD on sixteenth century chronicles of the discovery of America. For a number of years, he worked as a journalist in Cuba. Following his work on David Marton's Schaubühne production Ulysses' Return, *which premiered in January 2011, he was offered a permanent position at the theatre. Since 2013, he is the Schaubühne's head dramaturg. With Thomas Ostermeier, he translated and adapted* An Enemy of the People, *Lillian Hellman's* Little Foxes, *and Yasmina Reza's* Bella Figura.

After accidentally arriving at the Schaubühne – as Thomas Ostermeier has once described it, as 'something the cat brought in' – my work on *An Enemy of the People* started in early 2012, when some preparations for the production had already begun. Decisions such as to transfer the play into the present and to cut characters like Captain Horster had been made. Some contemporary German playwrights had been approached to create an adaptation, because Marius von Mayenburg, who at the time was Ostermeier's regular dramaturg and who until then had prepared all translations for him, was not available. Yet Ostermeier was dissatisfied with the submitted drafts, which took quite a few liberties with Ibsen. He wanted to stay close to Ibsen's original, while still taking the play out of the confines of its nineteenth century setting. Eventually, we therefore decided to go for it ourselves, and we locked ourselves away for a few days to fix a first draft. One of the first decisions we made was to merge the characters of Stockmann's wife and his adult daughter – a decision that was at first met with some doubt when we discussed it at the Schaubühne's regular dramaturgy meeting. Yet, by this manipulation, we managed to bring down the age of all characters by an entire generation. And whereas Ibsen in his play, which he conceived as a comedic issue play that therefore differs a lot from his well-known psychological realism, relied a lot on types, we managed to create a far more exciting and much more complex modern female character. In Ibsen's play, the two female figures portray two contrasting attitudes. The mother is loyal to her husband but mentally and intellectually completely bound to the confines of the home, and entirely ignorant of any political issue. The rather progressive daughter, meanwhile, is full of idealism and she supports her father intellectually and politically far more than his wife, especially at the moment when the entire town turns against him.

Uniting these contradictory personalities, we invented a young teacher who joins her partner in both their band and their political ideals, but who, at the same time, is a young mother who begins to realise the responsibility of looking after their new offspring, which starts with being able to pay the rent. The contrast becomes a tension within one and the same character; a tension many of us will know from our own lives. The decision required some artful intervention into Ibsen's play, for instance in the relationship of Petra, the daughter, to Hovstad, the newspaper journalists who fancies her and for this reason supports her dad, Doctor Stockmann. Settling for an affair between Hovstad and Katharina Stockmann made the situation more delicate, but the hint at a crisis in the Stockmanns' relationship introduced a further current symptom of our contemporary society: economic processes are emotionalised, whereas emotional processes are assessed in economic categories. Business consultants advise companies about the emotional relation of their employees and clients, while relationship counselling assesses the 'performance' of a relationship, and how to 'add value' to your marriage. We were able to reflect this absolute conflation of different levels, of the personal and private on the one hand, and of the economy and politics on the other, in our production through the relationship triangle between Stockmann, Katharina and Hovstad, which became a crucial dramaturgic arch, and which further supported and added to the 'brother conflict' between Thomas Stockmann and his brother Peter, the mayor. Far beyond the one female character, this decision therefore allowed us to bring a lot of our contemporary world into the play. On a few occasions, we then also updated some details. Petra's moral objections against translating American trash for Hovstad seemed somewhat trivial from a contemporary perspective, and we therefore replaced it with the urgent media issue of the conflation of advertising and news reporting. By suggesting an alternative situation where the engaged journalists require occasional financial input from the same capitalists they then seek to critique and attack in their paper, we added a further dramatic constellation that also contributes to the play's central themes and conflicts.

Overall, the shift of the entire play into the context of a much younger generation of contemporary thirty-somethings worked in a surprisingly straightforward way. The reason behind our decision to reduce the age of the protagonists in our version was neither to cater for a young audience nor to reflect our comparatively young ensemble of actors – the Schaubühne could have equally cast a production that maintains the original age of the Stockmanns in their fifties. For us, it was a very deliberate choice and proposition. We wanted to address the very specific situation of the generation that was politically socialised after 1989: those who had not been brought up any more within the rather strict political categories of previous generations. This generation considers itself to stand politically somewhere on the left, they all feel the urge to be politically conscious and somehow engaged – but it all remains at a vague level of 'doing good'. Few of them join and contribute to political parties, few seek to develop a fuller political understanding, and few truly stand up for true political struggle – the moment a conflict emerges, they retreat because it might impact their career progression. Or, the moment they have a baby, like the Stockmanns, they immediately settle down in a middle-class existence. All too quickly, this generation therefore disappears within the mainstream; their alleged 'political conscience' instantly evaporates, and all of a sudden they even adopt almost reactionary bourgeois attitudes. Symptomatically for this generation, it takes nowadays only a very small step from a rather big-mouthed proclamation of 'political engagement' to the total retreat into private life. And that is what we wanted to talk about with this play. Of course you could have presented *An Enemy of the People* as a story about those in their mid-fifties: the 1968-generation, and the story of those who once shouted communism and then, like our social democratic government of the late 1990s, led Germany into its first war since 1945. This is just as much a possibility for approaching the play, but it did not seem the most pressing and urgent issue for us at this very moment in time.

After the initial period of creating the dramaturgic concept, following to a certain degree a principle of trial and error, we then tried to find the suitable language for our translation. We worked from a range of existing translations, including the Norwegian original, which despite neither of us speaking the language was reasonably easy to make sense of, and in many respects in fact became our major reference. While, notwithstanding certain interventions, the first three acts remain very much original Ibsen, we made more changes in the fourth and fifth acts. Stockmann's speech in Act IV sounded too dated, and at the same time Thomas brought in this political pamphlet called *The Coming Insurrection*. It is brilliantly perceptive and rhetorically masterfully composed, yet in its reductive political argument – which does not for a moment consider the option of political change or revolution but advocates 'eradicating the rotten roots' of society – it seemed to us to perfectly reflect a contemporary, twenty-first century Stockmann. In the fifth act, we changed the dramaturgy, most of all because we found the original very confusing and even distracting from the very direct and even brutal narrative it actually tells. Equally, the ending, where Stockmann says, 'the strongest man in the world is he who stands most alone', and decides not to emigrate but to stay and launch a school in order to disseminate his ideas, seemed rather pathetic and unconvincing, at least for a character situated within a contemporary world. We therefore rewrote this act, unravelling a lot of Ibsen's construction of the shares and the corruption conspiracy; even now, I find that the original Ibsen is not really coherent in his fifth act, and I find our version much clearer. Yet, later during the rehearsals, our new ending was cut, and we decided for the silent, open end, with the couple sitting in front of the company shares. More generally, a lot of the detailed work, if not the actual work on the translation in fact happened during rehearsals. While very little was changed about the scenes, the basic dramaturgy, or even the content of the dialogues, *what* the characters actually said changed quite fundamentally.

Our first version, which we began reading at the outset of the rehearsal period, was deliberately unrefined and not all too premeditated. It was quickly done, and by this aimed for a direct tone that suggested spontaneous contemporary dialogue. It certainly was not perfect, and maybe not even good in places. So we kept working on it with the actors, and I was there, typing away on my laptop on every single day of the rehearsals. We in fact explicitly advised the actors that our translation was not meant to be considered as literature, but as a working draft that we were now putting into their hands. Everyone was asked to rephrase the dialogue in the way they would speak in real-life situations. We simply could not have invented a sentence like Billing's *'Mensch Stockmann Alter, damit wirst du übelst berühmt'* ('Ey, Stockmann dude, this will make you dead famous'); that's simply Moritz Gottwald as he talks and speaks. We have filtered, and on occasions carefully directed, the actors' suggestions, and Marius von Mayenburg also gave us feedback and advice on our efforts. I also spent some more time on *The Coming Insurrection*. Initially, we had used the 'official' German translation that was freely available on the internet, but on consulting the French original, we found that this German version in parts really deviates from it, and Stockmann's speech therefore went through a thorough further edit based on the original source.

From a dramaturgic perspective, Stockmann's speech did present us with the biggest dramaturgic challenge. As in our version, it engages with the actual audience, we had no idea where this scene would lead us to. We in fact envisaged the possibility that the audience would reject and hate Stockmann. We were very conscious during rehearsals to present Stockmann as a highly ambiguous character who, for instance, preaches truth, but the first thing we know about him is that he lies to his family, and keeps his suspicion and his investigation about the polluted water altogether secret. Similarly, we tried to develop a complex and multi-faceted character in Aslaksen. I backed up our discussions during rehearsals about the populist trait in Stockmann by further research, a lot of which is documented in the programme book. This includes research on how Stockmann's discourse of the bacterial contamination of our society, which at the same time idealises the notion of truth, may have influenced Hitler, who in *Mein Kampf* almost verbatim paraphrases certain sections of Stockmann's speech.[1] In theatre history, Stanislavsky, who played Stockmann himself, voiced his concern about his audiences' idolisation and celebration of his character, while he himself saw Stockmann as a rather dubious fellow. Equally, Ibsen made it very clear in some statements that Stockmann is anything but the voice of his author.

Yet, from early try-outs and the Avignon premiere onwards, we became aware of our audience's rather one-sided sympathy pro Stockmann – and this created quite a problem within our dramaturgic conceit. As a matter of fact, it runs counter to Ibsen's scene, whose scripted fictional audience attacks Stockmann, smashes up his house, and virtually throws him out of the city. It is truly a situation of one man against the rest of the world. We therefore had to invent a way to return from the discussion as it takes place in reality, with the actual audiences in their majority taking Stockmann's side and often booing or attacking Aslaksen and the mayor, back into the original dramaturgy. We therefore use Hovstad and in particular Billing to launch the mutiny and to attack Stockmann with paint bombs so that he has to hide behind his lectern, and the scene then cuts into the final act, where in the original Stockmann and his family return to their smashed-up home. We had to work a lot on the text of this scene to make this transition work, motivating the mutiny by some of the original Ibsen-speech with its anti-democratic celebration of the individual, of a truth that is always on the side of the minority, and the right to silence and exterminate opponents. I feel that at least some in the audience now begin to have second thoughts about their solidarity with Stockmann.

While the original is very precisely situated – one can identify a rather concrete South-Norwegian seaside town, and the play references expressly named political offices in the community – we tried the opposite and sought to avoid any resonance with a specific political scandal (something the originally commissioned adaptations totally went for, to their own detriment). In fact, we were particularly intrigued by the exemplary character of the conflict, and by the metaphoric dimension of the waters that pollute our community. We therefore left the basic narrative of the thermal baths and the poisoned water intact, and merely brought Ibsen's bacteriology up to scratch. Instead of a tannery, which no longer is an altogether common sight in our societies, we found we were able to leave the precise nature of Morten Kiil's environmentally unfriendly business quite open. And even the inclusion of *The Coming Insurrection*, a text that was mainly circulated by 'Occupy'-activists to critique the financial system after the 2008 crisis, does not really tie down our version of the play to the current financial crisis. One only needs to watch the repeats of old newscasts that are shown late at night on German public TV: pick any year, and while we may think everything was reasonably good back then, the newscasts are full of 'the present crisis'. There is always unemployment, the breakdown of one market or the other, costs that are too high, and recession looming. 'Crisis' has thus become a rhetorical topos in politics, rather than referring to any current and actual situation. I am therefore convinced that the production would have equally functioned in exactly the same way before the 2008 financial crisis. In fact, it has become one of the most fascinating aspects of working on this production that the play's model character, which we also reflect in the set design, immediately triggers a concrete and very specific interpretation wherever we perform. Right at the production's premiere at Avignon, people referred to a scandal with contaminated blood infusions. After it came out in Berlin, we got a very odd letter from the local tennis association, enquiring who had leaked all the internal details about their recent internal quarrels. And on our arrival at Montreal, the drinking water was actually poisoned all over the city by an actual industrial accident. There is always and everywhere a current case that maps precisely onto the play's scenario.

5.2 THE ACTORS' WORK: THE PATH TOWARDS *AN ENEMY OF THE PEOPLE*

Christoph Gawenda – Hovstad (original cast) / Dr Thomas Stockmann (second cast)

My first encounter with *An Enemy of the People* was at a workshop several months before rehearsals started, in the winter of 2011. Thomas Ostermeier had already

Figure 5.2 Christoph Gawenda (original role: Hovstad; here as Dr Stockmann in the second cast from May 2014). Photograph © Arno Declair.

decided that Stefan Stern should play Thomas Stockmann. I was asked to learn the part of Peter Stockmann in the major scene between the two brothers from the second act, and later we also worked, script in hand, on the scene between Hovstad and Thomas Stockmann. From the start, I had a very good connection with Stefan, and it was clear that the two of us could get on well with each other, as brothers or best friends. After the workshop, I really wanted the part of the brother, but for some time I did not know what was going to happen, and then there was talk that Ingo Hülsmann, who at this point in time had not yet joined the ensemble, would get the part of Peter Stockmann. It was the first time that I encountered such a casting situation within an ensemble company. Usually, you are just cast in a role because you are in the ensemble and the director may have seen you before – and you are just told what you will do next. It was a strange but very useful experience, which I wish would happen more often within the German ensemble system. But of course, there is no time, and it is total luxury.

It does tell a lot though about the way Ostermeier works. The chemistry between the individual cast members – and here, in *An Enemy of the People*, in particular between the actors playing the two brothers, as well as Hovstad and Stockmann – is vital for his approach. His working method really hinges on these dynamics, which you cannot predict in advance, and so he tries things out before making final casting choices. Further, it is important for him that as an actor you are open, and you open up, with all your own personality and your biography, in rehearsal, but then also in every single performance. Ostermeier wants you to play direct, to face the situation of the play in the moment, and never to merely repeat certain arrangements and instructions that had once been devised in a rehearsal. I confront the situations by just throwing myself into it, and therefore – whether I play Hovstad or now Stockmann – it automatically becomes very personal. I can understand both of them very well and recognise aspects of my own behaviour in their actions; and this gives you the key for playing a character. In Thomas' work, it is then okay to follow our instincts and spontaneity, as long as we stay within the framework of the situation and do not start any 'metastatic excess of improvisation', as he once described to me giving notes.

As for Hovstad, the role that I originally created, it was important to me not to reduce him to someone who is just weak and who therefore changes sides at the earliest opportunity. It is very easy to read him like a spineless opportunist who betrays his convictions. But even when I first read the play, I felt that he has no choice, that, on the contrary, Hovstad within his very own logic remains true to his own principles, and that he is after something entirely other. What I found out about him during rehearsals is that he is dissatisfied with his life, where he ended up, and where he is. He knows that the current local government managed to hush up a few scandals, and that Peter Stockmann has a few skeletons in his cupboard. All of a sudden, Hovstad finally gets the chance to do something because his best friend has made this huge discovery. Therefore, it is he who actually talks the doctor into all this, who is initially much more reluctant to stir up a public fuss about it. We all know these moments from our own lives: you get so fired up about something, and you stubbornly work yourself up, and get entirely engrossed, so that the whole thing develops its own dynamics, totally removed from the original cause which gets lost from sight.

But Hovstad's aim has been to attack all those people high-up, and to give them what they deserve. The very moment Peter Stockmann makes clear that the local tax payers would foot the bill for the whole scandal, and not the bigwigs, Hovstad has to realise that the mayor would stay in office, and actually be comfortably off the hook because he could shift the whole costs for the mistake with constructing the bath pipelines in the wrong place to the public purse. At this point, Hovstad does not primarily think about the health of the people using the baths, but he realises that after all the initial euphoria about seeing this door of change opening up a tiny bit, it won't work. Even worse: publishing the story would not remotely affect those in power in any way. As having a go at them was his sole intention to start with, I find that in his own ways, Hovstad remains quite consistent with what he wants, and I therefore do not see him 'switched' in any way. Hovstad still keeps his options, he may still go public with the whole scandal, but he will be waiting for the right moment when the politicians are no longer able to shift the consequences that easily. He is therefore of course very disillusioned, and for me this continues his biography and similar experiences from his past. This is why he is so inherently discontent and why he lacks self-confidence which he then over-compensates for by showing too much self-confidence. This constant dissatisfaction, and constant lack of something, this total disillusion, makes him desert his best friend in this cause.

And I feel that Thomas Stockmann is very much like him. When I began to play his part, I realised that the path he goes down in the course of the play does not at all come out of the blue. There is a lot of injury, of suppressed pain and anguish in him, and that is why he jumps on this chance to stand on the right side – against all odds. This very clear inner action, this anger and rage, which connects these two characters beyond their friendship from university which we hear about is something I had not quite as clearly realised before. What I then discovered by playing Stockmann is that he is not so much driven by honest integrity, but that there is a lot of dark energy in him, which grows proportionally with the resistance he experiences. His reasoning is not always based on objective arguments, but quite decisively influenced by his feud with his brother, the mayor. I realised that playing Stockmann, I am very much fuelled by the energy I get from my brother, and it pushes me to go ever further. It is no longer about truth alone, or about saving people from bacteria – all this spurs me on, but it is even more important that all of this goes very directly against my brother.

Another thing about him that became clearer to me is that his relationship with his wife is extremely fraught; of course, in our version, the close relationship between Hovstad and Katharina indicates this, but playing Stockmann I realised that he knows that his marriage is totally screwed up – quite a lot in his life is actually pretty messed up, and this pushes him on. If he was only a good guy, without all this dark energy, he would have simply given up long ago. Right and wrong are not at all clearly distributed in this play, and throughout, you become ever more doubtful and uncertain. Whether the mayor in his suit, or the others in their leisurely chequered shirts, it is not as clear cut as these external impressions at first suggest. At the end of the day, no one in the play is one-hundred per cent right, and everyone is to a degree off the mark.

Christoph Gawenda (b. 1979) joined the Schaubühne in 2010, after working for five years at Staatsschauspiel Stuttgart. He trained at Hochschule für Musik und Theater Hannover, where, as part of his training, he spent time at St Petersburg State Theatre Arts Academy and with the Lee Strasberg School. At Schaubühne, he performed in works directed by Ivo van Hove (Gaveston in Marlowe's *Edward II*), Katie Mitchell (Duncan Macmillan's *Lungs*), as well as by Àlex Rigola and Michael Thalheimer. His original role as Hovstad was his first time working with Thomas Ostermeier, with whom he also worked on *Richard III.*

Eva Meckbach – Katharina Stockmann

Thomas regularly invites actors to read together through plays he considers doing, and to discuss our opinions. We first read *An Enemy of the People*

Figure 5.3 Eva Meckbach (Katharina Stockmann). Photograph © Arno Declair.

around three years before the play was eventually staged, and discussing its strengths and weaknesses, my own character of Mrs Stockmann was definitely on the weakness-side. She portrays such an outdated idea of a naïve and outright stupid wife, and of a woman's place in the world that it became painful even to read. But I was confident that Thomas would produce an adaptation of the play that would work. It is a particular strength of his to be able to unlock a play's full potential for the present. He carefully thinks through every single character and their relations, and through the situations of each scene, and on this basis he arrives at some very deliberate, powerful and also bold interventions – such as inserting 'The Coming Insurrection' into the fourth act. My own role now combines Stockmann's wife and his daughter into one character.

In rehearsal, Thomas always asks, 'how is it in real life, how would you behave in this situation?' For me, as Katharina Stockmann, this meant – within the framework proposed by the adaptation – to explore how you react as a young mother, with your responsibility for a baby, when all of a sudden your entire existence is put on the line. In rehearsals, Thomas kept reminding me – 'look again, read again what she is actually saying here: would you really do this, or say it this way, with a baby in mind?' He starts from your own honesty, as a human being and as an actor. I believe he wants to rid his productions of anything 'artificial', and instead to be as close to real life as possible – and we, the actors, are this real life; it's me as I am, with my thoughts, my attitude, and my physical appearance. That's why our work gets so personal. But it is also important to see that even though I investigate the play and my character on the basis of my own personal experiences, it is not about me, not at all. I am always in the situation of the play, which is enhanced with my own life and my observations of every-day life. But the situation of the play is always clear and in the foreground, otherwise we would be merely wallowing in private stuff, and that's utterly not interesting.

For Thomas, it was important to show a young, hip, cosmopolitan couple from present-day Berlin, at whose place friends hang around to make music together – and how all of a sudden this small ideal world starts disintegrating, and eventually collapses. In rehearsals, we improvised a lot about the relationship of Thomas Stockmann and Katharina. Much later, when we had already moved from the rehearsal studio to doing runs on the actual stage, Thomas sat down next to me during a lunchbreak and asked me, 'what do you want to show about this marriage? I could imagine that she is actually quite unhappy'. I totally went for this idea. It became much more interesting to show a couple where, for Thomas Stockmann, even home is not the safe haven to return to, but where everything is at stake – for him, and also for Katharina. They both reach their limits, a point where everything is on the line. So this one remark opened up a whole new dimension, it enriched our production, and made it so much more real. Only the other day, I read in a magazine that, statistically, more couples separate *after* having children. It seemed so dull to play a happy relationship – precisely because it is somehow the standard assumption that a young mother is 'naturally happy', with the children and all.

Once we had agreed on this, Thomas just let me get on with it. Something else we came up with is that it is me who kisses Hovstad. In the script, he kisses me, I back off and say 'don't you think of Thomas?' He would reply something like 'all the time, but I love you', and so on. In the second or third rehearsal of this scene, I just went for it and initiated the kiss – and everyone in the rehearsal room went, wow, wicked, what are you up to? But Christoph Gawenda who played Hovstad just went with it, he spoke my next lines, I spoke his, and we just turned this scene around. I think it tells even more about Katharina, and also feels much more modern. I read it that here she takes what she wants. For once she doesn't feel like limiting herself to 'what is done' and what is expected of her, because she already feels nothing but limits around her in her life. It has actually become the one moment in the production most people mention and ask me about. I don't think it would cause any indignation if he kissed her – but because she takes the initiative, it causes quite a scandal even.

Overall, I like a lot about Katharina, but there are also some aspects which I would have liked to do differently. In the end, for instance, I would have loved to have had more space to explore what it does to the marriage, but also to Katharina as a person, that her father literally exploits her and abuses her for his own capitalist ends, to save his factory. I'd still like to find out. It had, however, become quite clear very early on when we were still reading the text that the pathetic ending which still was in our first adaptation, too, wouldn't work. All of us agreed it needs to be an open end. So we came up with this action of looking at each other, we don't know what to do next – and then it's over.

Continuing to give notes and calling rehearsals long after the premiere, Ostermeier can appear at times somewhat obstinate – when he keeps telling you to say a line differently, and you start thinking, oh come off it, let me say it my way. But then, *Ein Volksfeind* was broadcast on television and I was able to watch myself playing 'my version' – and suddenly I realised that Thomas was absolutely right about those sentences he went on about. Seeing it from the outside, it became ever so clear why he wanted the different emphasis, that tiny nuance of shifting a stress from one word to another. Of course I wouldn't say he's *always* right, but he certainly has a special talent for carving out tiny, minute details, whether in Ibsen or in Shakespeare. His grasp of the text is so precise and his perception sharp as a razor, so that he is able to get across in a single phrase, in a single 'How are you?' an entire marital tragedy.

Eva Meckbach (b. 1981) trained at the University of the Arts Berlin before joining the Schaubühne ensemble in 2006. Directed by Thomas Ostermeier, she played Hermia in *Midsummer Night's Dream* (2006), Desdemona in *Othello* (2010), Jenna in Lars Noren's *Demons* (2010), and Elizabeth in *Richard III* (2015). At Schaubühne, she also performed in productions by Benedict Andrews, Romeo Castellucci, Alvis Hermanis, Àlex Rigola, and others.

David Ruland – Aslaksen

Initially I found it quite hard to get a handle on this character. But one day we all went to a guest lecture at the Ernst-Busch-Theatre Academy by a German politician from the liberal democratic FDP-party, who had been invited to talk about the Euro crisis. While he was giving his talk and then answering questions by the theatre students, in his suit, his tie and his glasses, I suddenly heard Thomas, who sat next to me, whispering, 'Look! That's him, there sits Aslaksen!' Later that day we were back in the rehearsal room, and Thomas gave me a note that eventually, for me, unlocked the entire character. He said, just try playing a fella who smiles everything away, who is very eloquent, and who always aims for broad consensus. These hints for me at once cracked that

Figure 5.4 David Ruland (Aslaksen). Photograph © Arno Declair.

tough nut of Aslaksen's character. This is always a special moment during the rehearsal process – not knowing for ages what to do and then, almost in a single instant, everything becomes clear, all the way up to the first night and beyond. For me, I call it the 'key rehearsal'.

That's how Aslaksen became this rather unpleasant consensus-type politician who always smiles at everyone, 'oh of course I listen to your view, and please do contribute with your opinions.' It is interesting that this type of person seems to be recognised immediately, not only in Europe, but almost anywhere in the world. Sometimes, I get a laugh straight away when I first enter the stage – the clothes he wears, the way he moves: people instantly know perfectly well who is entering here. Politically, he is a spineless coward who turns against Stockmann at the first moment. But, to be honest, in his defence of our democracy against Stockmann's utopian vision, 'I am totally with him', as he would say. I indeed would rather live in our bourgeois, middle-class democracy than in the simplistic socialist utopia, which we find in Stockmann's speech, based on the text of 'The Coming Insurrection'. I once said this in a rehearsal, and Thomas turned to me and replied: 'And that's exactly why you are playing Aslaksen.'

And it is true: Aslaksen really has quite a lot of me, and I could subscribe to many of the positions he puts forward in the play. I find it hard to say where the actor stops and where the character begins. It is also because in his recent works, and really for the first time in *Volksfeind*, Thomas encouraged us to use our own words. It's always the most awkward moment as an actor when you recite a text in a realistic play that you'd simply never say that way in real life; that's always going to come across as stilted. It was really liberating that the words weren't sacrosanct – for sure, the sense and the meaning was, but not the choice of words. It is only the words that have been changed into modern language I would use myself, but always exactly in the sense of Ibsen. And once I say it in my words, it's to the point, and Aslaksen indeed totally is *me*, and everything comes from me. *Ein Volksfeind* is by now totally permeated by our own words. For example, when Stockmann empties the bucket of paint over my head at the end, I say, 'Yes, that's exactly who you are, Doctor Stockmann!'. That was my suggestion.

Then, there is of course the fourth act. In the beginning, I was incredibly nervous. We premiered in Avignon at the Festival. I've grown up bilingually in Saarbrücken, but I still wasn't sure whether I would cope leading the debate spontaneously all in French. It was like driving a car through the dark without headlights. But of course, from an actor's point of view, I actually also loved this challenge, because you really go off and soar if you no longer have firm ground under your feet, as in this moment. And, I just love improvising. So for this scene, I quickly added all sorts of responses, and began to ask questions of the audience. I think Thomas and I still don't quite agree here. He says that I mustn't bury the spectators and their will to speak with my opinions, and he says, the clearly important thing for the evening is what *they* say. But I find I can't just be a neutral host saying 'what do you want to say, and now you'. I need to tickle them a bit, especially if the discussion is somewhat reserved to begin with. I see it as my job to trigger dissent and opposition, and I do think it works quite well most of the time.

After a while of performing the play, I then noticed that I had developed my own toolkit of arguments, with which I was able to steer and control the discussion. I know that as soon as someone makes this point, I can respond so and so, and so on. I was absolutely terrified when I realised, playing this role, that as a politician, you don't even need to really listen in order to survive a public debate; you can simply respond with a counter question, or turn to another argument. All politicians do that, but it's something else when you become one of these politicians, too, and experience for yourself how this really works – and it does work! It's most astonishing abroad. I do the discussion in French or English, but we always ask people to respond in their local language. We have translators for us on stage, but even so at times I don't entirely get what is being said at every single moment – but I am still able to respond simply by countering with a different topic, and the discussion still goes on! My most harrowing realisation was that it even works in German, here at Berlin. A spectator makes an elaborate and worthwhile point, maybe even for two or three minutes, and I simply counter, 'Oh well, but look, the issue is actually a bit different ...'. I basically totally ignore the question and manoeuvre around the topic. I can really control everything with my toolkit of responses.

David Ruland (b. 1979) trained at Ernst-Busch-Theatre Academy Berlin and worked at Deutsches Theater Berlin before joining the Schaubühne ensemble in 2003. Here, he played under directors Luk Perceval (Schiller's *Mary Stuart*, 2006; Chekhov's *Platonov*, 2006), Benedict Andrews (Sarah Kane's *Cleansed*, 2004; Debbie Tucker Green's *Stoning Mary*, 2007; Tennessee Williams' *Streetcar*, 2009; Edward Bond's *Saved*, 2010) and Ivo van Hove (Molière's *Misanthrope*, 2010; Marlowe's *Edward II*, 2011), as well as performing in around ten productions by Thomas Ostermeier, including Wedekind's *Lulu* (2004), Williams' *Cat on a hot tin roof* (2007), Mark Ravenhill's *The Cut* (2008), and Lillian Hellman's *Little Foxes* (2014).

Ingo Hülsmann – Peter Stockmann

Ein Volksfeind was my first time working with Thomas Ostermeier. Having worked at many theatres and with many directors over the past twenty-five years, I found it very interesting to see how Ostermeier creates an effect through precision, and through close work on the most minute details of a character. Most other directors approach a character by establishing some fundamental categories and psychology. Ostermeier's very exact work on individual sentences and single actions, which then eventually come together as a whole, as a character, and as a theatre evening, is a remarkable and impressive

Figure 5.5 Ingo Hülsmann (Peter Stockmann, the mayor), with Stefan Stern as his brother Thomas. Photograph © Arno Declair.

method. I had never before encountered such close and rigorous precision, with which he attends to the play and to each character. It reminds me of the almost forgotten German director Rudolf Noelte and the notorious exactitude he became famous for in the 1960s.

You could therefore say that I arrived at Peter Stockmann by putting this politician together from many different small pieces, very much like a jigsaw puzzle. Initially, very little was fixed and given, and most of the mayor's character emerged, bit by bit, from the work in the rehearsal room. I initially offered Ostermeier my own vision, my picture of Peter Stockmann. He then dismantled it into myriad jigsaw pieces, which he then reassembled to form a very different image of this politician. This was a great and most interesting experience. Ostermeier gradually approaches and carefully builds up a character. His way of intervening in rehearsals is quite remarkable and unique; at times, he just lets everything run and just observes what the actors do and offer, to then give a single note and a short lead at exactly the right moment. For instance, my initial take on Peter Stockmann was to play a politician in the tradition of Helmut Kohl, full of passion and emotions, who at times happens to just let loose on a poor protester who is standing at the roadside throwing eggs, and simply punches him square-face. In Britain, it would be a John Prescott. My idea of this politician in the small town was exactly this shirtsleeve guy who does local politics on the side, and perhaps owns his sausage factory as a main job, while also organising with his buddies the local party branch. But eventually, we came up with quite a different picture of Stockmann. Thomas proposed a much more cautious, restrained and deliberate character, someone who carefully observes and then pulls the strings, manipulating and exploiting the flaws of others. Of course, he would still have exactly the same aims, but the way of pursuing his objectives has dramatically changed in this vision of the character. I was more than happy to follow this lead, not least since it is an exciting thing for an actor to try out such a radically different angle on a character. I found it a truly exciting process.

And that's how we eventually put together our new jigsaw image of Peter Stockmann: his specific physical behaviour, his cunning and thoughtfulness, the emotional reservation and his quiet smoothness – someone who maintains a deliberate, weighing restraint, and who never is really simply straight out and direct. We didn't really talk about any specific, real-life politicians as role models. However, some people were invited in, for instance a political adviser from the German Social Democrats who coaches some famous politicians. She observed our rehearsals, and then said to me, the guy you are playing is very much someone in local politics or in one of the German *Länder*. She then explained how politicians who step up to the national level and are elected to the federal *Bundestag* parliament change in their demeanour and behaviour. They would wear a more expensive suit, they wouldn't be 'matey' and get too intimate with the public, instead they prefer to remain behind the lectern, and above all they would always control their affects. That was very interesting.

For me, the crucial thing as an actor is to get the right note at the right time and the right place. That's what a director must be able to give, and Ostermeier indeed finds the right words – not always, but certainly often enough to produce a really good show. For example, in the first scene, he suggested I be more playful, to hide my true intentions when I visit my brother at home and barge into this strange band rehearsal. He said, 'Never forget that you have to conceal something in this moment.' Or, in the second act, when I again visit my brother Thomas to dissuade him from going public with his findings, Ostermeier emphasised the stakes for my character. He said, always remember: if the baths go down the drain now, if you don't succeed in persuading your brother, your character will lose everything. So Ostermeier indicates actions which I can use and work with as an actor. He raises the stakes, and intensifies the situation. Of course we also worked with language, with tone and emphasis, but I found this more secondary. Once we had thus found the character, we only changed perhaps one or two pieces in that jigsaw, trying to emphasise this moment, or tone down that one. But the main challenge for playing Peter Stockmann now is to find the right state, to produce the right temperature for this character. This is something Ostermeier observes very carefully: whether the temperature of a character is right, whether the stakes are right, and that's how he develops the rhythm of his productions, which is crucial for his work.

The audience discussion in the fourth act was certainly a further challenge. I find it beautifully crafted how the fourth wall is gradually opened up, how the play, bit by bit, creeps into the auditorium. The discussion, then, is always new and different. My character of course sets everything up with his short speech to the public, but then I let Aslaksen do the dirty work of stirring up the people. This scene produces some remarkable and also some bizarre moments. It is a very satisfying moment in this acting profession when the boundaries get blurred, and theatre begins to listen in to the real world.

> Ingo Hülsmann (b. 1963) is a German actor and director who has received numerous national and international awards for his work. In the 1980s, he became noted as an actor in productions by acclaimed directors Hans Neuenfels and Ruth Berghaus, and was awarded the prize as best young actor in German theatre in 1988. He has since worked in the ensembles of major German theatres such as Freie Volksbühne and Schillertheater Berlin, Schauspielhaus Hamburg, Burgtheater Vienna, and from 2001 at Deutsches Theater Berlin, most notably leading productions by director Michael Thalheimer. In 2012, both Thalheimer and Hülsmann moved on to join Schaubühne.

Moritz Gottwald – Billing

I absolutely love Billing, and I absolutely love playing him. He is totally laid back and just up for any revolution to get under way, without really having a clue what is really going on. For him, it doesn't really matter that it's about

Figure 5.6 Moritz Gottwald (Billing). Photograph © Arno Declair.

poisoned water from the baths; a collapsed bridge or anything else would have done for him just as well. He finds the excitement of the situation wicked, the prospect of change and of something happening. This exactly mirrored my own life back then. While we were rehearsing, there were big student protests at the Ernst-Busch-Theatre Academy going on, where I was still in my final year at the time. For many years, it had been planned to bring the School's different departments and spaces which are scattered all across Berlin, outdated, and outgrown by the School, together in a new, central space. Then suddenly the politicians decided they don't have the money. So the entire school took to the streets, we did street theatre, stormed and interrupted performances, and we occupied and camped on the site where the new building has now actually been built, as in the end we succeeded. So during the first rehearsal weeks, I camped outdoors overnight, and I felt as if I was part of a real insurrection. I was, probably for the first time in my life, politically active and totally engaged. Thomas of course noticed this, we talked about it in rehearsals, and he said, 'just like you talk about this protest now, I want to see Billing on stage. Remember how you are feeling now, all this rage, this energy, this determination to camp outside in the cold for a week, remember this for the third act.'

That's of course the act when Billing gets upset, but also where he flips from one moment to the next. Before, in the first act, he just sits on the couch, smokes Stockmann's fags, drinks Stockmann's wine, and even pinches his lighter. When Katharina gets worked up, he just blows smoke rings in the air and says, 'yeah, it's a shit system' – his typical attitude. That's such great fun to play! But then it gets out in the third act that two weeks earlier, he has applied in the city hall for this job. It is here where his vehemence in getting behind the whole revolution becomes clear on another level: we realise that, at the very bottom, Billing is trying to fight turning into another Aslaksen. Between them, there is almost a father–son relationship. Billing's two central relations are: Hovstad, of course – that's how I want to be, and Aslaksen – that's how I don't want to be. But at the same time, Billing begins to realise that at best he will be like Aslaksen one day, which is the very reason he rejects Aslaksen so aggressively. He knows that twenty years from now he will say exactly the same things, and that's why he doesn't want to hear these sentences – even more so as Aslaksen at the same time totally unmasks and embarrasses him in front of his great role model Hovstad by mentioning his application to city hall.

And then, of course, Billing totally switches, and not even on stage. Fifteen real-time minutes ago, I screamed at the top of my lungs about bringing down the system, and after three minutes off stage with the mayor, I come back and say, well, Thomas, after everything the mayor has just told me ... There isn't even a proper turning point. It's so easy to give energy out of pure activism when no serious consequences are attached, and so I'm just as easily off again, because again there is no consequence for me at all. I think Billing, who is not a central character nor even moving the plot, here still offers a link for people in the audience: it's this coming of age, where you'd only just sat in the park with your torn jeans, drinking beer from the bottle and listening to punk music, but then you realise that you actually would like to wear a pair of jeans that aren't all torn, and apply for a job because you want to rent your own place, and want to buy this old car – this transition, that's Billing, and that's perhaps what at least some in the audience somehow painfully recognise in him: it's not pleasant, it has something of treason and surrender.

All this is already in Ibsen's original very beautifully crafted, although it's taken me a while to come to terms with some of the sentences that Billing belts out: 'Well it wasn't about getting the job, but about getting the rejection. That will give me the power to continue fighting the system.' What utter bollocks! I really struggled saying this without finding it totally awkward, until in one rehearsal I was so enraged and in fury that I stopped questioning what Billing says. And that's where the penny dropped – yes, this is totally stupid bullshit, but Billing is absolutely serious, it's this fervour when you say something and only afterwards you think, oh God, what nonsense have I just said – but Billing wouldn't even do that, that's how he is and how he feels. That helped me a lot to get my head around quite a few such unbelievable platitudes he comes up with throughout. They aren't at all simple, wooden, bad playwriting.

Looking back, I very much remember thinking to myself, I'm here rehearsing Ibsen with Thomas Ostermeier, the great director, and I had heard from colleagues how intense his rehearsals can get – and I am running around with yellow skinny jeans, headphones and hipster glasses – surely it can't be that simple? That surely isn't a dramatic character from Ibsen? I had not encountered this way of working through situations before. It was such free and liberating work, and I don't think I've ever had that much fun working. Take the beatboxing thing, for instance. During rehearsal breaks, I am incredibly hyperactive and have to do something. So I go outside, walk around in circles, or just grab a guitar. One day there was the microphone there, for the speech in the fourth act, and I just started beatboxing – during a break, not during rehearsals. But Thomas said all of sudden, okay, let's do that. I panicked a bit, because I'm not a good beatboxer, I'm actually no beatboxer at all. But Thomas turned it into an action in the play. And that's why I'm now setting up the microphone for the big speech, do the mike-check, which technically of course is totally redundant, and then I beatbox. That's typical for Ostermeier's work: always trying things out, and keeping things which are good fun and entertaining.

What is really unique about his work – you don't work with him on the character. That simply happens. So as an actor, in his productions, it's not my task to feel the character in a Stanislavskian sense and to become the water that fills the vessel of the role. It's the reverse: I, Moritz Gottwald, offer myself and my experiences, with all the masks and disguises I have at my disposal as an actor, and Thomas lets me get on with my decisions and my vision of Billing and what he does. He only interferes when the situation is no longer correct, when the stakes are too low, when the timing and rhythm is wrong, and he says, this must happen tighter, or leaner, or he'd say, don't make your sentence smaller. I have not once heard him say, 'Billing wouldn't do this' – that's more how we think, these typical actor thoughts. Thomas speaks, above all, about the situation and the objective, about the energy in the space, and about the stakes. In contrast to other directors, you don't really feel that he's directing you and you never have the feeling that you're doing something just to serve the director's idea. Working with him, you know the situation, you know your task in a situation, and you know where you have to play the ball, but within these limits of the situation you are free to play how and what you want.

> Moritz Gottwald (b. 1988) performed in youth theatre productions in his hometown of Halle prior to training at Ernst-Busch-Theatre Academy Berlin. He joined the Schaubühne ensemble in 2012, while still in his final year at the school. Since then, he played Claudio in *Much Ado About Nothing* (dir. Marius von Mayenburg), Spencer in Marlowe's *Edward II* (dir. Ivo van Hove), and Romeo in Lars Eidinger's production of Shakespeare's *Romeo & Juliet*. Directed by Thomas Ostermeier, he also played Leo in Lillian Hellman's *Little Foxes* and, as Buckingham, in *Richard III*.

Thomas Bading – Morten Kiil

At the very first rehearsal, Thomas briefly hinted at how he imagines Morten Kiil – and I agreed one-hundred per cent. It has rarely happened to me that

Figure 5.7 Thomas Bading (Morten Kiil) and Xenia (the dog). Photograph © Arno Declair.

I knew from the beginning where the journey was going. Sometimes, it can take six or eight weeks to get to that point, but here, that was it, and I had my character. Thomas demonstrated how he envisioned Morten Kiil: his quiet serenity and almost dispassionate equanimity, the understated play, with the very low voice, to which I gradually added hints of an alcohol problem. As he enters only a couple of times for short scenes before his big entrance towards the end, he had to have a certain aplomb mixed with some mystery about him: you should never really be sure whether he is for or against Stockmann, and whether he is his friend, or will bring him into prison. As we learn that he is Katharina's father, it should always remain a possibility that he is honest and serious.

Building on such considerations, I then developed this character, as I usually do, 'from the feet up', as the saying goes. It is very important to me to show a gestus – and gestus starts in the feet: how a character walks, how he moves, what kind of human being he is. The social position and status of the character are of great importance to me: is he a king, murderer, or factory owner? I then have some strategies that help me to try things out and find the character in rehearsal. For instance, at first, I won't speak the lines too articulately, I won't project, or I'll even speak in my dialect. All this helps me to make things very concrete for me and to discover what kind of person he is. I don't follow a certain plan there, I just do this automatically. In my acting,

I often get a bit generic, and too driven by emotions. This is where Thomas becomes an important counterpart: he adds the thought that goes through my character's head and expresses it in a very clear and most precise way. This clarity leads me to find very concrete actions and attitudes, and I try to combine it and add to it my emotion. For me, out of this mixture, the most interesting things emerge.

With Morten Kiil, I had not immediately realised that he is quite a rich fellow, and this became an important background for the character. Then, it was important to imagine his life: how does he live? What does he do when he is not on stage, when he is at home, or in his factory? I concluded that he must be a very lonely person. His wife has left him because he smells, as he spends his entire day in his bog hole of a factory. And that was the reason why Thomas gave me a dog. He is Morten Kiil's only friend, and they belong together like pot and lid. First, I was shocked. I have an enormous respect for dogs. I have never had a dog at home, and I therefore was really worried. We began trying out different stage-trained dogs. They first brought a Rottweiler. It scared the shit out of me. The next one was too lively. Then came the German Shepherd. We initially did not consider it a possibility because, as a sign, it seemed far too clear, explicit and 'German'. But it turned out that Xenia, the shepherd dog, and I had an immediate connection. We somehow became instant friends, and so it still is Xenia with me on stage today. It was a very nice thing for me personally to eventually get over a fear that was entirely unrelated to the play, and that I had the opportunity to learn and understand more about animals. But Xenia is a difficult colleague, too, and it was quite a challenge. We had to go through a long training process to learn to get on with each other. We usually met an hour or so before rehearsals, and I took her for a walk. It took some effort so that our being together became natural, and that I act with her, and react to her when she looks at me.

The rehearsals, though ... the famous saying goes 'never act with animals or children' as you will become invisible. It was true in rehearsals too: when we were on stage, Thomas directed the dog, not me. 'She must look straight ahead!' – 'Why isn't she looking straight ahead?' He is a very meticulous director, and everything has to function like clockwork, actors included. He cannot understand if someone does something he expressly asked them not to do, and it threw him that the dog did not look straight ahead when she was supposed to look straight ahead. So the rehearsal was stopped and everything was organised to make the dog look straight ahead. In the end, the dog owners were placed in front of the stage so the dog looked straight ahead. And she did. As long as they sat down there.

Of course after a long training, we got to the point – by repeating things often, over and over again, and by making sure that Xenia knows that if she does it well, she will get a treat – and that she will get it from me, and not from her owners. But I have to respond to the dog. Of course I cannot make her look in a certain direction. But there were performances when we kept looking into the same direction, and our heads turned synchronously from left to right. Sometimes such nice things happen by sheer accident.

> Thomas Bading (b. 1959) trained at Theatre Academy Hans Otto in Leipzig and was an ensemble actor at Neues Theater Halle and later Deutsches Theater Berlin, where his path crossed with Thomas Ostermeier. He played the role of Mark in Ostermeier's celebrated production of Mark Ravenhill's *Shopping and Fucking*, and followed Ostermeier to the Schaubühne. There, he performed in Ostermeier's productions of Lars Norén's *Personenkreis 3.1* (2000), Caryll Churchill's *This is a chair* and Büchner's Danton's *Death* (2001), Wedekind's *Lulu* (2004), in John Murray and Allen Boretz' *Room Service* (2007), in *The City/The Cut* by Martin Crimp and Mark Ravenhill (2008), *Othello* (2010), Lillian Hellman's *Little Foxes* (2014), the revival of *Die Ehe der Maria Braun* (2014), and *Richard III* (2015). During Luk Perceval's tenure as associate director at Schaubühne, he created numerous roles with the Flemish director, including the title role in Chekhov's *Platonov* (2006). He also played in several Schaubühne productions by Falk Richter, Jossi Wieler and Benedikt Andrews, and has played roles in numerous TV and movie productions.

5.3 *EIN VOLKSFEIND* AROUND THE WORLD: THE ACTORS' DIARY

Season 2012/13

Premiere – Avignon (France), Festival d'Avignon, 18–25 July 2012 (7 performances)

MORITZ GOTTWALD: I was honestly afraid of the first performance. It was entirely unpredictable how the spectators would react to the fourth act. I was worried that we'd open up the debate – and no one says anything. Of course we had done some try-outs and had a certain sense, but still we were not sure at all what would get across from 'The Coming Insurrection', and whom the audience would support. It is a super-complex text, with its long sentences and garbled arguments. It is impossible to really comprehend it, hearing it only once and very quickly. What you pick up are some slogans and buzz phrases. But if you take a step back and really think through the speech, it is impossible to agree, as it invites us to abandon democracy and humanism. So the question with which David, as Aslaksen, opens up the forum, inviting those who support Stockmann to show their hands, was really an honest, open question – we simply didn't know.

CHRISTOPH GAWENDA: But this heavy burden was then lifted from our shoulders, and we realised that people really are up for it – for the play, for the discussion, and beyond. I don't think I have ever experienced such a lively and vibrant response from a theatre audience.

EVA MECKBACH: People just go for the opportunity to voice their opinions no end, they seem so hungry to speak their minds. So Thomas had the right instinct about producing this piece.

DAVID RULAND: The reaction has been unbelievable, right from the first night. Maybe it is a matter of temperament, but the French audience is totally exuberant. For a moment I thought that's how it must have felt during the French Revolution!

MORITZ GOTTWALD: It seems like the Avignon audiences watch theatre in a far more naïve and uninhibited way, almost like a Punch and Judy show or a pantomime – 'look who's behind you!' They got up and tried to stop Christoph and me throwing the paint-bombs, they took our bombs away and pushed us out of the door. Someone else jumped up on the stage and attempted to protect Stockmann, and he tried to get others to join him and help. And then, after the attack, when Stockmann emerges again from behind his lectern, someone shouted 'Le petite journaliste baise ta femme!' ('The little journalist shags your wife!'). Well, we had invited them, so now we have to be prepared to deal with all that. It was just wonderful!

DAVID RULAND: In the end, the boundaries between the fiction of the play and the reality get totally blurred, and the spectators turn into a community discussing an argument, and they do so with quite some furore. They became so involved here because they connected the topic of the play in ways we could not foresee to a scandal about contaminated blood preservations from the 1980s, where thousands of people had been infected with HIV, and many died. Just recently, a court had finally rejected a case by survivors and relatives of those who died, so this topic was up in the air again. People connected it with the play, saying, it was like this, no one wanted to warn the public, and a lobby of politicians and big business talked down the danger.

EVA MECKBACH: It was really intense how the blood scandal mapped very directly onto the play. I was deeply moved when an older gentleman got up to make a statement. He was visibly upset and shaking, and with tears in his eyes he spoke about his daughter who nearly died because of these infected blood transfusions. He was so upset, he shouted at us, that it was precisely these machinations and deceptions out of greed for profit and for power that nearly killed his daughter. It became so personal. Honestly, I won't forget his face.

DAVID RULAND: There was so much anger and frustration in the room. It got very close and people really insulted and attacked us as politicians. Any sense for the difference of acting, for the 'as if' of the theatre, simply vanished, and they just went after us.

INGO HÜLSMANN: People got so excited and were so close to the topic that suddenly they indeed began to blame me personally, 'You did this back then, and you were responsible'. I just thought to myself, 'it wasn't my fault, and to start with I have no idea at all what you are talking about!' As Moritz said, this is something that only happens in France and in no other country! But all this was even topped the next day as I walked down the streets through Avignon, and suddenly someone begins shouting, totally agitated, 'there he is, look, there he is, Monsieur Le Maire, come here!' So this complete stranger who apparently was in the performance walked towards me, stopped me in the middle of the street, and he then he rang his wife at home on his mobile! He said, 'I got the mayor on the phone' and passed the mobile to me, forcing me to talk on the phone with his wife, in my poor French, and to answer some questions she still had. He was not to be convinced that I wasn't 'Monsieur Le Maire' but only the actor playing the mayor! So I said, 'Bonjour Madame. Oui, je suis l'acteur Ingo Hülsmann, le role du maire …'. What was really funny was that she at once kept complimenting our performance, but then again she asked me about the water and gave me advice on how to solve the problem of the poisoned water, only to then again stress that it was such a good show. It was unbelievable how she exemplified this total blurring of the borders which we experienced here. This was so bizarre, my daughter who was with me just watched what happened totally flabbergasted. It was the weirdest moment – in the middle of the street, imagine that! Really extraordinary!

Berlin (Germany), Schaubühne, Saal B, Premiere 8 September 2012 (54 performances by July 2015)

EVA MECKBACH: After Avignon, we knew the Berlin premiere would be really difficult, so we braced ourselves. The discussion in the fourth act lasted about a minute, one person said something rather irrelevant, and that was it.

MORITZ GOTTWALD: But then, in the premiere you have all theatre critics and journalists in the audience, and they aren't really allowed to participate, are they? It's their job to sit there cross-legged, furrowing their brows, scratching their chins and wondering what nonsense Ostermeier has come up with this time. It was clear that nothing would happen.

DAVID RULAND: But generally the audience's attitude in Berlin is rather cool. The spectators here in the German capital are quite saturated, they have seen so much theatre, so my feeling is that for them it's just another participation piece. They say, OK, I say something now because I have to. But I am very angry with the Berlin critics who wrote that Ostermeier's participation theatre failed – Avignon had already proven the opposite! That really upset me. If the reaction from the audience is lukewarm and tired, it's no problem for us, we just go on, which works just as well within the frame of the production.

EVA MECKBACH: Though, honestly, if I was in the audience, I would need to bring myself to speak up as well. And after that very first night, it certainly got much better than I expected. I would say the majority of the audience, here at Berlin too, connects with the theme of the production. There are always people who want to speak up and vent their anger. It seems to me that the production has come at just the right moment to provide a forum. People say, finally someone is showing it like it really is with these politicians and their attempts of staying in power and pushing through their agenda at all cost. You can feel their frustration about politicians, after the banking crisis and austerity politics. One of the strengths of the play is to show how politics is all about spinning news and concealing facts. Whether it's the Fukushima disaster, the NSA spying affair, environmental issues or the global weapons industry – you always have your Peter Stockmann who already has got the alternative report in his pocket. Everyone shares this sentiment to a degree, and that's why people start debating. The play shows what we all think about politicians.

MORITZ GOTTWALD: Of course it's not always good when we are abroad, and always boring in Berlin. There are good and not so good discussions everywhere. Yet, what I need to mention about this first stretch of performances here at Berlin – the paint issue! The discussions and problems this has caused once we started performing here are beyond belief. Yes, we do throw paint-bombs, and it can happen that the bomb bursts in your hand. You can practise it, and we did even have specifically scheduled 'paint bomb throwing rehearsals', and you need to concentrate that you don't squeeze it too much. But it can go wrong. Initially, we were throwing the bombs from quite far back in the Schaubühne space, maybe from behind the sixth or seventh row, over the heads of the audience. And then it happened: one of my bombs burst. The front rows are obviously the most expensive tickets – gents in their suits, ladies in their evening dresses who get all dressed up because they go and see Ostermeier theatre. And they got full of paint. It's of course water-colour, but still a woman claimed her Chanel-bag had been irretrievably ruined, and she demanded the theatre buys her a new one, for some 2,500 Euros. A teacher who was there with his class wrote to the theatre direction saying he would never again come to the Schaubühne after he'd been thrown at with paint. Some people behaved as if Ostermeier had staged some 'offending the audience' paint bomb attack against the Berlin theatre-going public on the expensive seats. So in the end, after only twelve performances at Berlin, it was decided that we were only allowed to throw right from in front of the stage, and people in the front get protective sheets they can use. We also partly use pump-guns now rather than paint-bombs. It is a pity – the effect when the first bomb hit out of the dark from the depth of the auditorium has simply been lost. It was such a strong theatre moment that made people jump from their seats. Now it's become obvious and predictable. I really regret this decision very much.

Melbourne (Australia), Melbourne Festival, Arts Centre Melbourne, 21–27 October 2012 (7 performances)

INGO HÜLSMANN: A very far away place, not only geographically. Australians seem to look at our European problems with some amazement, and many reactions are, 'well you over there in Europe ...'

EVA MECKBACH: It has been interesting, very cultured and civilised, but it made me understand that there is an entirely different perspective on things that preoccupy us, in Western Europe, so much.

DAVID RULAND: They also had a local election going on, but the debate always remained very factual. And then there was the matinee performance when someone raised his hand to say, 'well the discussion is quite interesting, but when are we allowed to go to lunch?'

CHRISTOPH GAWENDA: I begin to notice that because of the play, because of the discussion in the play, but then also because of the discussions we have after the play, which are partly stimulated by the play, you experience something very special about each city where we play. These are not just performances that could take place anywhere, but we really take away something from each city, from the people who are there, who watch us, and who talk to us. Each journey so far has created its own unique story, and its own special memories.

Lyon (France), Théâtre National Populaire Villeurbanne, 29 January–2 February 2013 (5 performances)

DAVID RULAND: Lyon was very lively again. But it was also the first time that someone had a go at us because we come from Germany. When I offered my stock argument in the discussion, 'well, isn't Stockmann dangerous for democracy', someone replied, 'what you Germans think about democracy, you have shown the world in 1933'. The only way to counter such remarks is to just leave them without getting too emotional, and not to engage in a discussion. I just replied, that neither I nor him can be held personally responsible for the deeds and crimes of previous generations, and that today, we all benefit from our present-day democracy. You have to stay sober and matter of fact dealing with such attacks.

EVA MECKBACH: When people brought up the Nazi crimes, it was a very strange, personal experience for me. I rarely feel 'German' in my everyday life, and all of sudden, after being confronted with these comments, I started to feel in an odd and uncomfortable way that I really am German. I realised that these borders between nations and people exist, and that there is this historic responsibility. Of course you know this intellectually, but I've never before felt it and experienced it so viscerally and truly emotionally as here.

Montreal (Canada), Festival Transamériques, Théâtre Jean-Duceppe, 22–24 May 2013 (3 performances) and Quebec (Canada), Carrefour International de Théâtre, Grand Théâtre de Québec, 27 May 2013 (1 performance)

INGO HÜLSMANN: Now this was truly something absolutely beyond belief! On the day we arrived, some sewage works had been cleaned, but some workmen made a mistake and the entire rubbish has gone straight into the fresh water supply. Imagine: a city of millions without clean tap water! Some brown dirty brew came out of my shower in the hotel room. What properly freaked me out, though: they have little loudspeakers in each hotel room, and just as I got up to have a shower and go to our rehearsal, some alarm announcement went off right in my hotel room: 'Attention! Attention! The city of Montreal advises you not to use the water until further notice.' I first thought our team must be playing some prank on me! For us, for this production, this was hitting the jackpot. The discussion with the audience – sorted, no problem here to find something to talk about! Someone even asked whether we had arranged this to get publicity, which was of course a most absurd suggestion!

DAVID RULAND: But what an incredible coincidence, it seemed sent to us by the theatre gods! It was simply surreal. In the performance, the simplest reference to the water supply, let alone that the water is poisoned, brought the whole house down with laughter.

INGO HÜLSMANN: But I was quite surprised and very puzzled to see how calm and even indifferent some people reacted outside the theatre. An older lady I spoke to in the supermarket, where all the water bottles had of course sold out, just said, 'ah well, we're used to that, it could be worse.' Such an altruistic attitude is very foreign to me – what then does it take to get Montreal into protest mode – an atomic plant exploding outside the city walls? Surely, they all laugh about the water thing in the play, and they all connect it to local politics and the privatisation of what was previously a public service, but they generally seem more than sceptical about the idea of starting a revolution because of something like this.

DAVID RULAND: It does show though that this play, with its very concrete political topic, written in the nineteenth century, actually offers a model conflict for each and every political conflict, and that's why wherever we go, people connect to it. In Quebec, there was a student or young lecturer in the audience who said in the discussion, this is exactly the same thing that happens at our University now, and he started to talk about a current case that again exactly mirrored the basic conflict of Ibsen's play, even without the water. Many people, and also many who don't go to the theatre a lot and who don't know much about Ibsen, immediately recognise how the play reflects the politicians they know from their own life and from the news. The production offers a unique opportunity to articulate this recognition. It is a particular quality of the production, but also the ultimate confirmation for Ibsen, that his play is contemporary without much effort, without forcing some idea onto it. It seems so organic how this conflict from 1882 still works, and how everyone, anywhere around the world, perceives it as *their* conflict.

I also need to admit that I slapped Christoph Gawenda. When I, as Aslaksen, passed the buck to Hovstad and told him in the third act, 'well you brought the article in', he got up from his chair, starting yelling at me and came so close that, before I knew what was happening, I landed him one in the face, and Ingo had to hold him back as he was going after me. We put the matter to rest afterwards; it's a lively and living production where extreme things can happen, and where you also defend yourself against an extreme play of your fellow actors.

Athens (Greece), Hellenic Festival, 3–5 July 2013 (3 performances)

MORITZ GOTTWALD: We had come with great expectations, and we were braced for everything: the current political situation, the Greek protests, Angela Merkel, and now some German actors turn up in Athens to discuss democracy. We thought they must be going to storm the stage and tar and feather us. But nothing. Absolutely nothing. They were in no way whatsoever keen to engage in the discussion scene. We really screwed up badly.

CHRISTOPH GAWENDA: I guess we were a year late. I could imagine that a year earlier, everything may have been different.

EVA MECKBACH: They just seemed beyond that point of outrage, and everyone seemed just depressed and lethargic. The discussion never got beyond a strange meta-level of debate, absolutely generic, with people making points about truth, and what does truth really mean, and so on. Speaking to some Greeks, they said, 'we are so desperate, we simply can't get upset anymore. We have seen that even people setting themselves alight in front of the parliament building do not change anything, and if at all, things get worse.' This really scared me.

MORITZ GOTTWALD: But it was also the first performance where people did not speak English or French, and where they participated in the discussion in a language none of us speaks. We have a translator, whom David very actively introduces, but it took us the trial and error here to find out how this works best. The first thing we learnt is that it is more important to have someone translating who is from the theatre world, or who at least is used to being on a stage. We had professional translators, but some of them were all of sudden totally out of their depths standing on a big stage and being in this performance situation. Then, we also had the interpreter translating the audience's comments into German for us aloud and through the mike. This just slowed everything down and disrupted the flow, and perhaps this was another reason, at least in parts, why Athens just did not work. At later performances abroad, the translators translated quietly just for David, and then David made his comments, which were then translated for the spectators. This works brilliantly – except that we, the others, who stand in the auditorium and run around passing the microphone, no longer hear the German translation and at times have no clue what is going on.

Season 2013/14

Venice (Italy), Teatro Goldoni, Biennale di Venezia, 10 August 2013 (1 performance)

Figure 5.8 *An Enemy of the People* at Teatro Goldoni in Venice on 10 August 2013. Photograph © Jan Pappelbaum.

São Paolo (Brazil), Teatro Paulo Autran, 27–29 September 2013 (3 performances)

DAVID RULAND: For the first time, someone actually jumped on the stage to go after me. It started with this guy shouting abuse from the upper gallery, in German ...

MORITZ GOTTWALD: Which was unfortunate. It is already hard enough to get across to audiences everywhere that these aren't actors but people who also simply bought their ticket like everyone else. Then this guy started shouting at us in German, 'you corrupt asshole, you politician swine, you are screwing us all' and all that. I'm sure most in the audience thought he was an actor whom we had planted, simply because he spoke German, which many of them wouldn't have understood. I was really impressed how David handled this situation very confidently, and responded: 'First of all, we don't shout at each other. We have a discussion culture, so if you want to discuss with me, please come down and we can talk.' And well, that dude did come down! He stormed past me through the auditorium doors, red-faced and short of exploding, it seemed you could see the steam coming out of his ears like in a Disney cartoon ...

DAVID RULAND: So he jumped on the stage, came towards me, grabbed my tie and pulled me towards him. I thought, hmm, this *is* getting a bit delicate now ...

MORITZ GOTTWALD: Meanwhile, without coordinating us, Christoph and I had come back down from the aisles and simultaneously arrived on the sides of the stage – so Thomas' directing mantra No. 1 is true after all: if the situation is right, you just act accordingly! We really didn't fancy a fight, but we were ready to intervene and go between. Man, that level of adrenaline pumping through your body, and also the tension in the space when the situation is at the tipping point of a fight! You just think – Dude, relax, this is only theatre! But how wicked!

DAVID RULAND: I just kept saying, 'calm down, we can talk', and indeed he did calm down after a while, and at some point he went off the stage again. Later on he was around for a beer, and everything was okay again. But it was a very unsettling and menacing moment, for which I am now at least somewhat prepared should it happen again in the future.

INGO HÜLSMANN: But it's not only because of this drastic singular expression of opinion by a German emigrant that I shall remember São Paolo. What an extreme city! On the evening of our premiere, inhabitants of a favela stormed and blocked the main highway in the city, and the entire traffic in the city collapsed. It was beyond comprehension to experience a city of twenty millions coming to total standstill. There was a legendary traffic jam of more than 200 kilometres all through the city, which made the news across the world. So our coach couldn't get through to the hotel, and we had to walk to the theatre. Half of the audience came late. It was such an absurd situation, one of the most absurd interruptions of reality into our production. You realise that you will never be able to capture these incredible real-life stakes and translate them into art. Even if you'd manage to get this actual reality into a piece, it would inevitably be obsolete again.

CHRISTOPH GAWENDA: I found the intensity of the performances in São Paolo, the engagement of the spectators in the debate, and the way the debate went, to be one of the most intensive discussions we've had in the production: it was suddenly at an altogether different level of immediate relevance than anywhere else.

Buenos Aires (Argentinia), Festival Internacional de Buenos Aires, Teatro General San Martín, 6–9 October 2013 (3 performances)

INGO HÜLSMANN: Buenos Aires in short: 25 minutes of class struggle live, and proper riot in the house!

DAVID RULAND: The reaction was crass, incredible, absolutely overwhelming. I had barely nudged people a little bit, and then I didn't need to do anything for the next half hour. People raised their hands to signal their wish to speak, but all of a sudden everyone just started speaking and discussing. Some jumped on their seats, there were various groups in the auditorium all shouting at each other, waves of discussion and shouting surged through the theatre, and we had absolutely no control anymore.

EVA MECKBACH: The mood got so explosive that no one in the room bothered any longer about controlling their emotions. For the first time it actually happened what Thomas had always envisaged: that people start a debate with and among each other, and not just between some individuals and us on stage, as a list of singular expressions of opinions one after the other. Then someone shouted, 'if there are politicians in the room, do get up and make yourself known!' And Darío Lopérfido, the director of the theatre festival, did stand up. He was sitting right in the very centre of the theatre. He was minister for culture in the de la Rua government around 2000, which had left the country in quite a financial mess. He tried to make a statement defending himself, he said, 'if I really were a bastard like these politicians, would I have invited this show?' But he was shouted down. It got tumultuous. There was so much anger, rage and desperation in the air, you just expected them to get at each other's throats any moment.

MORITZ GOTTWALD: Truly unbelievable! I was in the audience trying to pass around the microphone, but there was no point anymore. You begin to feel totally euphoric and somehow even illuminated once you realise you have kicked something off over which you no longer have any control whatsoever; that you have created a vent for so much retained energy and need for debate, which suddenly finds its space and outlet. I guess you could see that I was really lost and didn't quite know what to do, and suddenly some complete stranger waved his hand and called me over to him, and he said, 'do you speak English? Shall I translate for you what happens?' So he told me what people were debating, and I could just stay with him, as no one needed the microphone any more anyway. I think we could have just gone home at this point, and scrap the final act. For an event like this I would have been more than happy not to take a curtain call.

DAVID RULAND: You realise that the poorer a country is, the more politically minded people are, and the more productive the discussion in the play gets. I was shocked to see poverty and homelessness to a degree I had never seen before with my own eyes. Also, you constantly ran into some little demonstration and protest march wherever and whenever you went. At every corner someone had a megaphone with ten people around him debating. It has become such a strong experience for me to encounter this strong political consciousness, this charged energy where politics really matters, very existentially, for your own life.

New York (USA), Brooklyn Academy of Music, Next Wave Festival, 6–10 November 2013 (6 performances)

Figure 5.9 An Enemy at the Brooklyn Academy of Music in November 2013. Photograph © Katharina Ziemke.

EVA MECKBACH: To be honest, I was a bit shocked and frightened. You could really physically feel neoliberalism, even though it's such a cool city. No one spoke up for Stockmann, everyone supported Aslaksen and the politicians. It was scary.

MORITZ GOTTWALD: But actually, I don't think they were necessarily siding with the politicians, nor of course with Stockmann's cause. It was a very cool, reflected, unemotional debate, perhaps also because there is a different culture of debate in the States. The discussion is more mannered, and restrained. They understand what happens, what our point is, they think about it, come to their conclusion, and then they articulate it very well and thoroughly. Not everyone, but a few people really made some very intelligent remarks, which impressed me a lot. When David asks people to raise their hand for Stockmann, some people do, perhaps only just about the majority, not the usual 99.9% we get pro Stockmann in most of the performances. But as he then asks further why, there was this young spectator in his twenties, not much older than I. He said, 'I have raised my hand because what Stockmann describes is true right here as well: Everyone feels comfortable in a majority, but then we go home, have a shower and watch our HD-LCD-TV to fall asleep. This is wrong, yet you will not be able to do anything against it. And that's why I have raised my hand.' I stood there and thought, blimey. New York produced a few of these very serious, very unemotional, or differently emotional, statements, where even David, who is usually always at hand with a quick and witty remark, remained silent for a moment.

CHRISTOPH GAWENDA: As you say, they were a tough nut to crack, and it was very slow in the beginning. But how this young guy started articulating off the top of his head his own system-critical theory, which was no less complex than the Coming Insurrection-manifesto, about how individuation is used to silence people and make us controllable – I was absolutely stunned, and I think we all were.

Paris (France), Théâtre de la Ville, 27 January–2 February 2014 (7 performances)

DAVID RULAND: The reaction in Paris was very different to Avignon and Lyon. It was remarkably sober, and somewhat cerebral, very similar to New York.

EVA MECKBACH: It was interesting, though, that some people were very familiar with the *Coming Insurrection*, and therefore it was one of the very rare cases when a whole fraction of the audience expressly stated that they do not support Stockmann's position. It was interesting to hear some people really engaging with some of the positions of this text.

Rennes (France), Théâtre National de Bretagne, 20–22 March 2014 (3 performances)

DAVID RULAND: After almost two years, we can be quite sure that the production works virtually everywhere. All over the West, and Rennes is a typical example, similar standard arguments come up, against democracy and the political system I advocate and defend. There is a certain fundamental critique of the political system. When I try to defend democracy, the standard response from the floor is that all politicians are corrupt and they cover up the truth. I try to challenge them, suggesting that a general bashing of politicians is very simple, but if people had the choice today, they most likely would not vote for Stockmann.

Berlin (Germany), 2 May 2014 – premiere of second cast

CHRISTOPH GAWENDA: I had never experienced a re-cast within the same production. I got the call in late March, and it was tremendously exciting after more than eighty performances as Hovstad to see the play from another angle. Stockmann's character has quite a different temperature, and he is somewhat more complex. And the feeling of being hit by paint-bombs is also quite intense! At the same time, it is quite peculiar, not to say absurd, to encounter my own former character Hovstad in two totally different permutations, with Andreas Schröders and Renato Schuch alternating in the role. Andreas brings in his entire biography as old-style rock'n'roll rebel for whom the ship has almost sailed, whereas Renato – who is some fifteen years younger – is desperate to board the same ship in the first place. He approaches the role with the youthful fervour that I recognise, but with Andreas I have gained a whole new perspective onto this character.

DAVID RULAND: They are two totally different types who paint the character in very different colours – but both perfectly fit into Aslaksen's social-democratic newspaper: the ageing rebel in his leather jacket as much as the young eager journalist with a migration background. As Aslaksen, I would employ both. And Christoph, meanwhile, brought his own fervour, and a rather more aggressive side into Stockmann's personality.

MORITZ GOTTWALD: The reason why it worked out so effortlessly is that the situations, which we had developed together, also with Christoph, remain the same. Christoph therefore does not need to try and copy Stefan's approach to the role; he has a very different personality which he can bring in to fill the clearly defined dramatic situations and play the processes we have agreed in his way. After almost ninety performances, you start to hear the text in a fresh way because a different person articulates with the same words a differently nuanced thought. The only thing we did not change was the tight choreography of the scene changes.

Siegen (Germany), Apollo Theater, 4 May 2014 (1 performance)

EVA MECKBACH: Our only ever performance in Germany outside the Schaubühne. There is no denying that most of us had reservations about travelling to a regional theatre. Yet – it was fantastic! The spectators were very different from Berlin, they participated in the debate with great enthusiasm, some local politicians were in the audience, made themselves known and took part, there was spontaneous applause, and afterwards all of us sat together for a meal. A most positive surprise, and a great evening.

DAVID RULAND: You can indeed become a bit spoiled, having travelled around the world with this production. Over the years, though, even the debates in Berlin have become a bit livelier, even though they still usually remain on a very straightforward level, concerning fundamental aspects of the play, or of politics as such. People still only rarely bring in concrete issues or personal matters, and things seem somewhat remote from urgent political matters. The Siegen audience, even though it was a notably older audience than at the Schaubühne, was remarkably alert, and they really took part, especially once I started jumping in with my counter-arguments, the debate really got going there.

Istanbul (Turkey), H. Muhsin Ertuğrul Stage (Istanbul Theatre Festival), 27–29 May 2014 (3 performances)

Figure 5.10 The only performance Thomas Ostermeier changed to reflect local politics: *An Enemy* at Istanbul's Muhsin Ertuğrul Stage in May 2014. Photograph © Jan Pappelbaum.

MORITZ GOTTWALD: The one where I missed the plane which didn't go down well at all ... It was bound to happen one day. But luckily I still got there by the evening and did not miss a performance.

DAVID RULAND: Our visit was only a few days ahead of the first anniversary of the Gezi Park protests. Our hotel was just around the corner from Taksim Square, so we walked across the square a couple of times. It was spooky: when we were there, it was quiet, but the day we arrived back home, images of police beating protesters and spraying them with tear gas were all over the news, and you recognised the same square you had walked across just the previous day.

It was also the first and only performance where Thomas changed the production to reflect the local political situation. He integrated the story of Erdoğan's adviser Yusuf Yerkel kicking a protestor following the Soma coalmine disaster. This was a brilliant coup, and very delicately done. There was a great response.

CHRISTOPH GAWENDA: Although on the first night in Istanbul, Ingo Hülsmann, who was meant to kick me as the two brothers have their argument in Stockmann's flat at the end of the second act, virtually forgot it. He was so perplexed that at the moment when I boxed his ears, huge applause roared through the auditorium. Instead of kicking me, he only looked at me in utter surprise, and then the moment was gone. We only found out afterwards that the Turkish surtitles had translated the phrase 'brainless agitator', for which I slap him in the face, with the term 'çapulcu', the word Erdoğan had used to discredit the Gezi Park protesters. In the second and third performance, the kick did take place, and people recognised it immediately. I found it the right decision to respond to these current events, but some people I talked to thought it was too provocative and laying it on a bit too thick.

EVA MECKBACH: One of the large Turkish newspapers even ran a story titled 'German game', describing the production as German anti-Erdoğan propaganda and suggesting that our performance was an example of how the entire Gezi protests were spurred on from abroad. I found this very telling for the climate in the country, where freedom of speech, especially in public, is notably restricted. People do not talk much about politics, and they never refer to Erdoğan by name, they just speak of 'him'. In this context, the play really hit home. A female spectator said in the discussion, we have one like him – and she pointed to Ingo – as our president. I found her courage and the courage of others who talked very frankly in the discussion remarkable.

DAVID RULAND: It was an extremely charged atmosphere with some incredibly open critical statements against the repression and the government. There was great interest in taking part in the debate, and particularly young, politically engaged audience members spoke up.

EVA MECKBACH: In retrospect, I found the Istanbul visit perhaps the most amazing, and most touching performances. It made us feel like we were not just producing entertainment, but like we were in the right place at the right time with a most relevant play. You really got the feeling that you can achieve something by making theatre, and you can express issues that are on the minds of a lot of people.

Season 2014/15

Oslo (Norway), Nationaltheatret, Ibsen Festival, 12–13 September 2014 (2 performances)

CHRISTOPH GAWENDA: It was quite impressive to perform the piece in the theatre where Ibsen premiered his play. Some of the greenrooms backstage still look like they come straight out of Ibsen's time. The discussion was a bit halting, though, and the response of the audience more reserved than elsewhere.

DAVID RULAND: I suppose they see so much Ibsen, in so many different interpretations and approaches that they have seen it all.

London (UK), Barbican Theatre, 24–28 September 2014 (5 performances)

CHRISTOPH GAWENDA: Once more you could realise that people in Anglo-American countries are most accomplished in public speaking. They have no inhibition grabbing the microphone and making a coherent, articulate statement in front of other people, speaking elaborately over several minutes without hyperventilating or getting panic attacks. Even in London, where because of the peculiar seating arrangements in the Barbican theatre we were barely able to pass microphones around – they just speak up.

DAVID RULAND: It is indeed a very rhetorically adept nation with a long tradition of public speaking – the motherland of parliamentary representation of the people. We had some very enjoyable debates that covered a wide range of topics. It was loud and lively, and many people talked at the same time. One night, the Scottish independence referendum that had taken place the week before caused a lot of discussion, and in the audience the controversy of the yes-voters against the no-voters continued with great passion. Another very heartfelt statement came from a gentleman in the upper circle who described the growing poverty in the UK, the attacks against the poor, and the ignorance of the very few who possess most of the country's wealth. A rather awkward statement turned out to fit exactly into this category: a young girl in the audience commented that freedom had already stopped as she was eating crisps during the performance, and someone next to her told her off. Thomas later invited her to have a beer, and it turned out it was the only thing she had to eat for dinner, and that she was otherwise not able to afford a beer in a Central London pub.

CHRISTOPH GAWENDA: Ever since London, I have become very conscious about the final scene. After one of the performances, someone asked me why we were taking the money. For this guy it had been perfectly evident that we took the stocks and gave up all our political convictions. It may have reflected this one person's own point of view, but if we really indicated either of the two possible outcomes of the final scene, I would be very disappointed with myself. As I see it, the audience must not know at any cost what is going to happen after the final black. The more ambiguous it feels, the more it is what we want to tell. In an ideal performance, it would really be a fifty-fifty option. It was the very first scene that, after some weeks of storytelling and improvisation, we had rehearsed – and perhaps the only scene that has never changed a bit over all the time. And even I have no answer, and I don't think I should have one: as Stockmann, I may feel an inclination to take the money one night, and then again I am certain that we won't do it, it really depends on the emotional trajectory of every single performance that has led up to this point.

Moscow (Russia), Theatre of Nations, Territory Festival, 5–6 October 2014 (2 performances)

DAVID RULAND: The response to the first performance was very restrained. The discussion was slow, and we had to work really hard to get anyone making a statement. We were very unsure how the production went down, but afterwards people spoke very positively about the show. But then, on the second night, people stood up and entered the stage ...

EVA MECKBACH: That was very strange. David asked those who are pro-Stockmann to raise their hand. Someone from the second circle asked what to do and implied that he would rather come down but he was stuck up there on the balcony; a short while later a female spectator in the stalls picked up his comment and said, well, we can stand up for you, and within a minute, there were maybe 200 spectators on the stage. Afterwards, some of us doubted whether this was spontaneous at all, especially after the lame response the day before – but of course we'll never find out.

CHRISTOPH GAWENDA: As I remember the situation, it at least felt pretty spontaneous. Initially, only few people got up, I then encouraged them and said 'do come', and at some point there may have been just peer pressure to join in. But isn't it ultimately futile to ponder whether this was secretly staged? The response was so strong that people decided to join in, and you cannot ask for more. The energy on stage had the quality of an uprising. People had followed the play and its themes with such commitment that at this point they felt they had to do something, that they must act – so they did what had the maximum impact in the situation they were in: they entered the stage, the very place they had been watching up to that point.

Afterwards, that moment kept resonating within me for a long time. When it happened, I was however entirely overwhelmed and very confused. The only thought that kept coming to my mind was how are we practically able to continue? Are we going to leave out the paint bombs? Or, are they going to throw them into the crowd? So, in the end, like a little boy, I just took a seat right on top of the lectern and just waited to see what would happen. I felt entirely out of my depth and at a loss what to do, not just in a bad way. At some point, I got up again, grabbed the microphone and asked whether we should stop playing and form some working groups to continue the discussion, or whether people wanted to see the fifth act instead.

DAVID RULAND: It was a great experience. It wasn't a riot at all, though. Everything happened very calmly. I also agree that it is totally irrelevant whether it was premeditated, since participation in the debate is what counts for us, and this certainly happened. Overall, however, the debate was less overtly critical than in Istanbul. There was one hidden Putin-reference, as someone said to me, 'We don't trust people with no hair on their head', which got a big laugh, but there was no explicit political critique.

CHRISTOPH GAWENDA: Before the performances, we had a discussion with Thomas about the ongoing Ukraine crisis and the Russian military action. We agreed not to raise the situation from our end, in order to avoid a confrontation of us Germans with the Russian audience, which we felt was out of place and would also prevent us from really finding out what is on the minds of these people. So we left it entirely open to them to set the topics, which I feel was the correct decision.

Then, there was also a pretty uncanny, very personal moment. A young female spectator asked me how we, as Stockmanns, manage our situation with the little one. At the time, my own daughter was nine months old, and her question all of a sudden threw me back onto my own private situation, where my partner and I, in a typical way, felt stressed and found it difficult to cope, not the least because I was touring a lot and relied very much on my partner. So all of a sudden, all the different layers collapsed because of this question, and in my response, it was one-hundred per cent me, Christoph Gawenda, speaking about my own family situation. I thought about this for a long time, and afterwards talked many times with my partner about this very touching moment.

Belfast (Northern Ireland), Grand Opera House (Ulster Bank Festival), 23–25 October 2014 (3 performances)

DAVID RULAND: I have taken some very intense impressions from this city. Walking along the 'peace walls', seeing the many memorial plates to victims of bomb explosions or assassinations, and talking to a lot of people, almost all of whom had lost someone in the times of the troubles, not to mention these artful political murals – I had never experienced something as intense and upsetting so close to home. The context did not, however, impact greatly on the debate in the performances; yet it did not matter, as once again, a fundamental debate about the state of contemporary democracy always got the discussion going.

Cluj-Napoca (Romania), Hungarian National Theatre, Interferences International Theatre Festival, 26–27 November 2014 (2 performances)

THOMAS BADING: It all felt very personal here. I grew up in East Germany, and a lot of the issues brought up in the discussion reminded me of the past in the GDR. The place looked like time had stood still, and it brought back many personal memories. The debate was not about 'art', but about very existential topics, including poverty.

CHRISTOPH GAWENDA: And once more, there was a situation that seemed to mirror the play. Very close by, a foreign Western company wanted to open a huge opencast goldmine, after previous mines had already polluted the groundwater with uranium and other poison. There were ongoing protests in Romania against the government that had passed special legislation which allowed this large-scale mining operation, planning to relocate entire villages.

DAVID RULAND: We did expect that these things would surface in the discussion. We were very much briefed on the issue because the film-makers who did a documentary about our touring to Moscow, London and India had previously made a film about these mining plans that we had all watched. But when I tried stirring this specific topic in the discussion, it did not take off at all, which came as a bit of a surprise.

EVA MECKBACH: But overall I felt that the performance was very well received. The discussion was a bit slow because we were translated into three languages – English, Romanian, and Hungarian, which is the second language in this part of Romania. I found the people very welcoming, and we had a lot of contact with students from a local acting academy, who looked after us the whole time.

Lausanne (Switzerland), Théâtre Kléber-Méleau, 11–15 February 2015 (5 performances)

EVA MECKBACH: My major memory of Lausanne is the incredibly beautiful theatre. The audience there was a proper theatre audience, who are all aesthetic aficionados. The debate was not particularly political, and not too many memorable comments were made, but from an aesthetic perspective, I felt that we very much connected with the audience on that level.

Delhi, Bharat Rang Mahotsav Festival, National School of Drama, Kolkata, Kala Mandir, and Chennai, Sir Mutha Venkatasubba Rao Concert Hall (India), 18, 21 and 24 February 2015 (3 performances)

CHRISTOPH GAWENDA: The journey through India was for all of us an outright culture shock, and a proper sensory overload. After we arrived, we took a long walk through Delhi, including some of its more remote areas, and it really took a while to process and come to terms with what I saw and experienced there. In the evening, we were then invited to a dinner with the people from the Goethe Institute, in a different part of the city, in a luxurious villa, which could have been in Berlin. I had never experienced such a stark contrast between rich and poor, neither in Europe, nor in Latin America, where I have spent some time.

DAVID RULAND: Politically, it was fascinating, too. Only a few days earlier, the Aam Admi Party, a new anti-corruption party, had a landslide victory in local elections in Delhi. The audience was politically hyper-aware and alert, and the discussions in all three cities were fantastic. The audience members participated fully and contributed a lot. They talked a lot about environmental problems in a very controversial way; some said, better

Figure 5.11 'An outright culture shock': *An Enemy of the People* touring India, here at Kolkata's Kala Mandir on 21 February 2015. Photograph © Jan Pappelbaum.

be ill than poor, and they suggested pollution is the price they have to pay in order to survive. There were also lively discussions about democracy, political representation, corruption, the fighting between different religions, and postcolonial issues. In all three cities, the admission to the performance was free, and there were long queues in front of the theatre – a mainly young, student audience, and many artists and intellectuals, who all contributed in a very engaged and passionate way. I didn't have to do anything to get some impressively lively debates going.

CHRISTOPH GAWENDA: The energy in the room was charged as hardly anywhere else. People were extremely on my side, and vocally supported me. Even during my speech, a woman yelled at the mayor, Aslaksen, and the others, that they should go and leave me along – this may have been a bit much, but the power that was around was extremely infectious for me as well, and I don't think I ever gave as much emotion into Stockmann's speech as I did in India. In the debate, then, they did not stick to the topic of the play, as it often happens, but they immediately applied it to their own situation. Barely any one mentioned the poisoned baths, they all talked about their own issues, so we learnt a lot about what is going on. There was so much hope, but also cautious scepticism about the possibility of any change in the room. I think it worked extremely well, and in particular in Chennai.

EVA MECKBACH: And everyone knew the play! There was a very popular Indian movie adaptation from the 1990s, *Ganashatru*, by Satyajit Ray. And it felt a bit like in the cinema, too: the audience is anything but quiet, people keep going in and out, they answer the telephones, and they also have a different way of applauding – the moment you leave the stage, they stop. We didn't know that in Delhi, and only afterwards someone told us to just remain on stage, which we did in Kolkata and Chennai.

But for me, the performances were the minor aspect of this journey – even though they were, of course, the reason why we had come to India in the first place. But all these other impressions were so strong that for me, they touched me far more than the three performances – all these impressions that were so difficult to absorb and come to terms with, and which caused a mixture of overbearing, shame, helplessness, and also gratitude for all the privileges, even decadence, that we enjoy in our Western lives. It is difficult to put in words, but I must say that this experience has changed my life, in a way. I found it almost impossible to connect the play, and our production, with this context; Stockmann's unconditional idealism, his determination not to give up, was perhaps the only link I was able to make between the play and the people I met.

THOMAS BADING: I also felt in an odd way alien and totally out of place, and began to ask myself some ethical questions: should we be here at all, and play our theatre, in India, in this totally different culture, and very different every-day life? The contradiction between what you saw and experienced, and the hotels we stayed in, and equally the artists and intellectuals we met, was so great.

And, it did not work out at all with the dog. I should mention that whenever we are overseas, beyond Europe, I am given a local dog, which is very unnerving for me. The Indian dog I was given, allegedly an experienced stage dog, was so nervous in the afternoon rehearsal that he relieved himself on stage, twice, and he constantly pulled the leash. It just did not work, and so I eventually went out on stage in the evening with only the leash and the collar, and Eva said, 'look, he thinks he has a dog'. My character acquired a whole new level of absurdity; he now properly seemed to be an egg short of a waffle. Some spectators commented that no one had expected him to be so sharp and crystal-clear in the end, when he gives Stockmann the shares to do something with them. That was a curious experience.

Naples (Italy), Teatro Politeama, Napoli Teatro festival, 12–13 June 2015 (2 performances)

CHRISTOPH GAWENDA: I always take a walk through the cities we perform in, mostly on my own, and here I got lost and ended up in very strange parts of the town. Naples therefore left quite an uncanny impression on me. We were not sure how an Italian audience would respond to the production. They did not overtly respond to the comedic aspects in the play, there were hardly any laughs, even in the places where they always come. Still, people turned out to be pretty involved in the story, and the discussion, especially on the second night, got extremely lively, loud and very much as you imagine Italians discussing, and one audience member in particular got properly worked up. The main topics, though, concerned the one common denominator that most people, wherever we play, seem to subscribe to: Western democracy has sold out the very values which it once fought for and stood for. On this baseline, the discussion then develops according to the individuals who stand up and speak out, based on their own biographical experience and personal circumstance.

> *An Enemy of the People* = total number of performances July 2012–July 2015: 131

5.4 THE ARTIST'S WORK: KATHARINA ZIEMKE

Katharina Ziemke (b. 1979) is a visual artist whose paintings, wax and ink drawings are internationally exhibited. She studied in Paris at the École Nationale Supérieure des

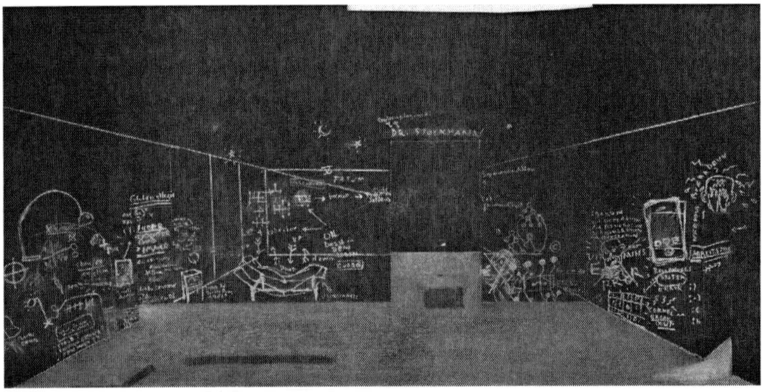

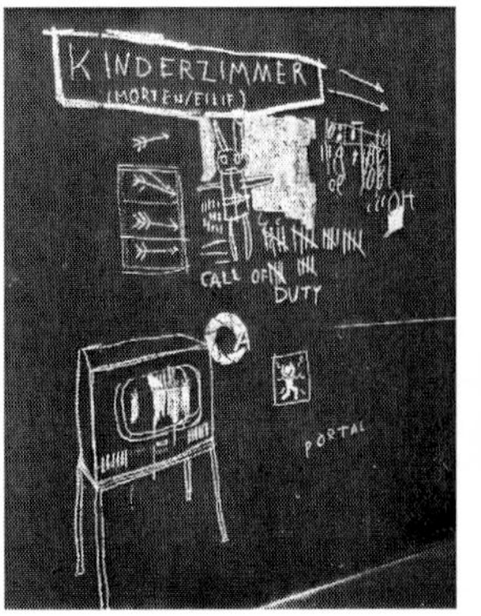

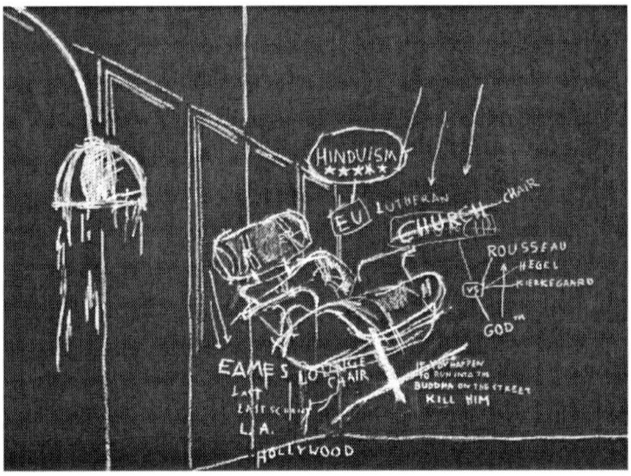

Figures 5.12–5.16 'Like an actor who had to find a way into a character': Painter Katharina Ziemke's model-box for her chalk drawings (top left), an initial draft sketch (middle left), details from her spontaneous life-size draft in the rehearsal studio in June 2012, which with few amendments became the final artwork (top right, middle right), and the backdrop added for the Berlin premiere in September 2012. Photographs © Katharina Ziemke.

Beaux-Arts, and has been living in Berlin for several years. Her drawings for the set of An Enemy of the People *were her first work in theatre. In 2013, she also contributed to Ostermeier's* Seagull *which he directed for Toneelgroep Amsterdam.*

I first met Thomas Ostermeier when an art collector brought him into my studio and introduced us. He was interested in my work, even bought a painting, and sometime later he contacted me about his idea to have drawings on the wall. I liked his passion about trying out something different, and his eagerness not to stand still and instead to challenge the spectators' expectations raised by his earlier, very realist Ibsen settings, which he seemed to experience more and more as a limitation and burden. Up to that point, I had never collaborated with another artist; and, what I did for *An Enemy of the People* has very little to do with my own work and style. First, I usually work on paper and had never gone into a three-dimensional medium; so this presented a fascinating challenge. Second, my own style as an artist is very different from these drawings. Not least, I am much interested in colour – something that is entirely absent from these drawings. Some people who know my work and saw the production told me they did not recognise me at all in these paintings – but that was very much the challenge. They are all from Stockmann's perspective. So I felt a bit like an actor who had to find a way into a character.

We started having our conversations in March 2012, when the rehearsals for the play had already started. Initially, Jan Pappelbaum had made some drawings of his own. Thomas' vision was of some awkward visuals, as if someone expressed very directly, and in quite a brute way, his confused thoughts – like a scatterbrained mind-map that was painted on the wall, a mirror of Stockmann's

Figure 5.17 Thomas Ostermeier and Katharina Ziemke discussing her drafts at the Schaubühne's rehearsal stage in North Berlin. Photograph © Winfried Veil.

soul. I had read the play, though not the adaptation Thomas and Florian made for the production, but the standard paperback edition from the bookshop. Even there, Stockmann seemed to me like a very contradictory character who also has a lot of dislikeable character traits, for instance that he considers himself as a kind of saviour. It was important to me to reflect this fanaticism in the artwork. Thomas and Jan had already decided that it should be chalk drawings on the black wall. Thomas was not altogether explicit in his brief, but he referred to the work of Jean-Michel Basquiat, which he had seen in a Paris exhibition; his works were characterised by immediacy and spontaneity, and he often switched on several radios at once in his studio, responding in his paintings to what he heard – something that, in a way, fits with Stockmann. Chalk also emphasises the preliminary, provisional character; you can just erase it again. And it rubs off onto the actors' costumes and becomes part of the play. Then, Thomas and Jan wanted to have some designer furniture and other status symbols to show his contradictory personality: on the one hand, he rejects the whole capitalist consumer society, but then he wants to have the latest gadgets such as an iPhone and a Nespresso machine, and certain status symbols, like the Le Corbusier lounger or a designer floorlamp. It therefore was fitting that they were just painted on the wall, perhaps more as an aspiration than a material reality. I looked for quite a few of these design objects, and tried to adapt them into this awkward, naïve style. I had to look for a balance where you still recognise them, but it looks like the sketch of someone who can't really draw; some reviews spoke of children's drawings. I thought of the notes and drawings of a physics teacher on the blackboard at school: the universe on a blackboard, with a lot of formulas.

Most of the objects are called into question straight away by some words or symbols, revealing Stockmann's confused and inharmonious personality. It was clear from the beginning that the painting would include words and writing. This mixture aesthetically expresses the many intellectual concepts that are running through Stockmann's mind. Thomas liked it that there were some words you notice and which you can read very clearly, certain buzzwords that catch the spectators' eyes straightaway, whereas other words are crossed out, or remain indecipherable scribble. I think if you watch the artwork carefully you can discover a lot of details. There is, for example, a skull right on top of the Le Corbusier lounger, bringing in an air of morbidity, and emphasising how Stockmann is really at odds with himself. Around the children's bedroom, you can find symbols from contemporary computer games; in the version I had read, Stockmann's children are older, so I envisioned them playing *World of Warcraft*, but there is also a cuddly bunny toy, which then actually fits the baby in the Schaubühne adaptation. In the beginning, I also had some allusions to a lawsuit, but Thomas found this too explicit, and too much of an illustration and commentary of the play and of what you see on stage. It was a very new experience for me that I had to stand back, and negotiate my place alongside the play. But it is certainly justified that Thomas made sure that my artwork was no distraction or stood out, but that it contributed to a whole where all elements are in balance.

When I showed my first drafts to Thomas, for quite some time it was not clear at all whether we would eventually find coherence together, and whether this would work out at all. I tried out a lot of different things until we arrived at something that he liked, and which I liked, too, and where our ideas eventually met. I also think Thomas and Jan were initially not quite yet on the same page. Jan had built this perspectival black-box space, and I think he envisaged the drawings of the furniture to fit this perspective space, whereas Thomas found my attempts in that direction far too tidy, and wanted something much more naïve. So I made a lot of drafts that were rejected, until we settled on something far more non-illusionistic. It also seemed like Thomas found it hard, at first, to envisage the effect of my drawings just by looking at my A3-drafts, so at some point he simply invited me to come to the rehearsal space, where he was already working with the actors, and to actually take the chalk and put things up on the walls. So I entirely spontaneously positioned things like the sofa and the lamp on the wall. Thomas suggested a few changes and wiped off a few things he found too concrete; for instance, the words '100% renewable energy' next to the lamp, and around the chair, the names of Hegel, Kierkegaard and Rousseau, and allusions to various religions. I quite liked to show this guy who constructs his own world-view, who is searching for something (he would probably say, 'truth'), and borrows something from many different concepts. The only thing Thomas left was the phrase, 'If you happen to run into Buddha in the street, kill him', which he liked very much. But after not too much time, we had very quickly created the drawing you still see in the production today. At the end of the day, Jan photographed it in detail, and now an old-fashioned overhead transparency is used to project these photographs onto the set, and a stage painter recreates my drawings from that day.

There was only one later change and addition. Initially, at Avignon, there was a background painting with the words 'Sun King', based on an internet image Jan had found and created. You still see it in some of the production photographs made in the initial period. I really disliked it, and found it did not gel with my artwork at all, but Thomas very much liked it. So a few days ahead of the Berlin premiere of the play in September 2012, I showed him my version, and eventually he bought in. So there is now a kind of pronged sun, inspired by the 'bargain offer'-signs in the supermarkets; Stockmann's critique of our consumer society thus even includes the sun. And also there are what most people see as mountains; this is actually a stock market-graph of share prices, but you have to look twice to realise it, and then you can follow through this association. Overall, it was a most interesting challenge, and a very enjoyable experience to get into Stockmann's head and to reflect and express some of his characteristics, which you realise in the play, too, on an entirely different level of the production.

5.5 THE ASSISTANT'S WORK: CHRISTOPH SCHLETZ

Christoph Schletz (b. 1976) joined Schaubühne in 2009 and was Thomas Ostermeier's permanent Assistant Director until 2013. After performing in school productions, he studied at the École Philippe Gaulier while it was still based in London, and later worked as a personal assistant to the US-American director Robert Wilson, before returning to Germany to read European Studies at Passau University. Since leaving his permanent position at Schaubühne (where he continues to work on a freelance-basis, mainly for international touring), he has been production manager of an interdisciplinary performance project, sponsored by the German Ministry for International Development, that aims to promote awareness of the risk of deforestation and climate change in Columbia, as well as directing an opera in Munich.

Few people know what an Assistant Director actually does. Half of the job involves organisational and administrative tasks, such as planning and organising rehearsals, and – especially when assisting a director who does not permanently work at the theatre – acting as liaison between the freelance director and the theatre where you are employed. The 'AD' is the central interface for *everything* the director wants, the actors want, for getting information they want, passing on information to the director, and coordinating with the entire technical team and the theatre's craftspeople. A large part of the job involves diplomacy, and acting as a buffer for everything that does not work, in particular. This mostly means passing on with somewhat restricted force the feedback and notes of the

Figure 5.18 Christoph Schletz, Thomas Ostermeier's assistant from 2010 to 2013.

director, which are usually articulated with merciless intensity in pursuit of the cause, and to thereby mediate between the director and everyone else; equally, mediating in the other direction, and at times also between some of the actors, if necessary. As AD, you need to be able to foresee problems days before they occur, and you need to sense what the director needs before he tells you. Above all, you need a very thick skin, in particular in the rehearsal period, in order to have a chance to withstand the pressure. You are the target for the full shitstorm, from all corners imaginable. The most invidious aspect of the job is that you know you will never succeed, do it well, or make it right; in a way, you always fail, something always goes wrong, happens too slowly, or a mistake is being made. Especially at the beginning of our work, Thomas kept calling me his lightning rod; on the one hand, this did not help with all the stress and the frustration, but on the other hand, it made clear that all the thundering was never personal. As Assistant, you just happen to be sitting closest to the director. You are the Sisyphus rolling the stones up the hill, and there will always be two or three which roll down the hill again.

Working on *An Enemy of the People* at Berlin and on its international tours, a production that was quite noticeably very important to Thomas, it was my task to keep an eye on the production, especially the mode of playing and the discussion scene, and to see that it is performed in his sense, even when he was not present at a performance (and he attended a lot of them). It starts before the performance with some rather simple and mundane tasks – checking if everyone has arrived in the theatre and if everything is where it is meant to be. Also, having another look at the stage, and here especially checking the chalk painting. And if the play hasn't been performed for a while, running lines before the performance, and just having another chat with everyone involved, the actors, the technical crew, the stage manager. The AD is the person everyone approaches with their issues. You might think that after so many performances, things ought to run without you, but there is always the one thing that's not quite right, or not quite in its place. So you always have to make a few decisions on the spot. When we are on tour abroad, I am also liaising between our own crew and the local team, and here in particular there will always be things that have to be solved differently than at home.

Then, you watch the performance, ideally through Thomas' rigorous eyes, even though you will never be able to replace him, and one should rightly not overestimate one's own position as AD when giving notes and feedback. In *An Enemy of the People*, it all worked rather well and smoothly, as everyone was very much on the same page, and as I knew quite well what Thomas wanted for the production, especially in the discussion scene – how much to engage in the discussion, who intervenes, and at what point Thomas Stockmann begins guiding the scene back into the scripted act. I believe I had a fairly good sense for the balance Thomas tried to achieve between stimulating a discussion, ideally among members of the audience, and directly intervening with own

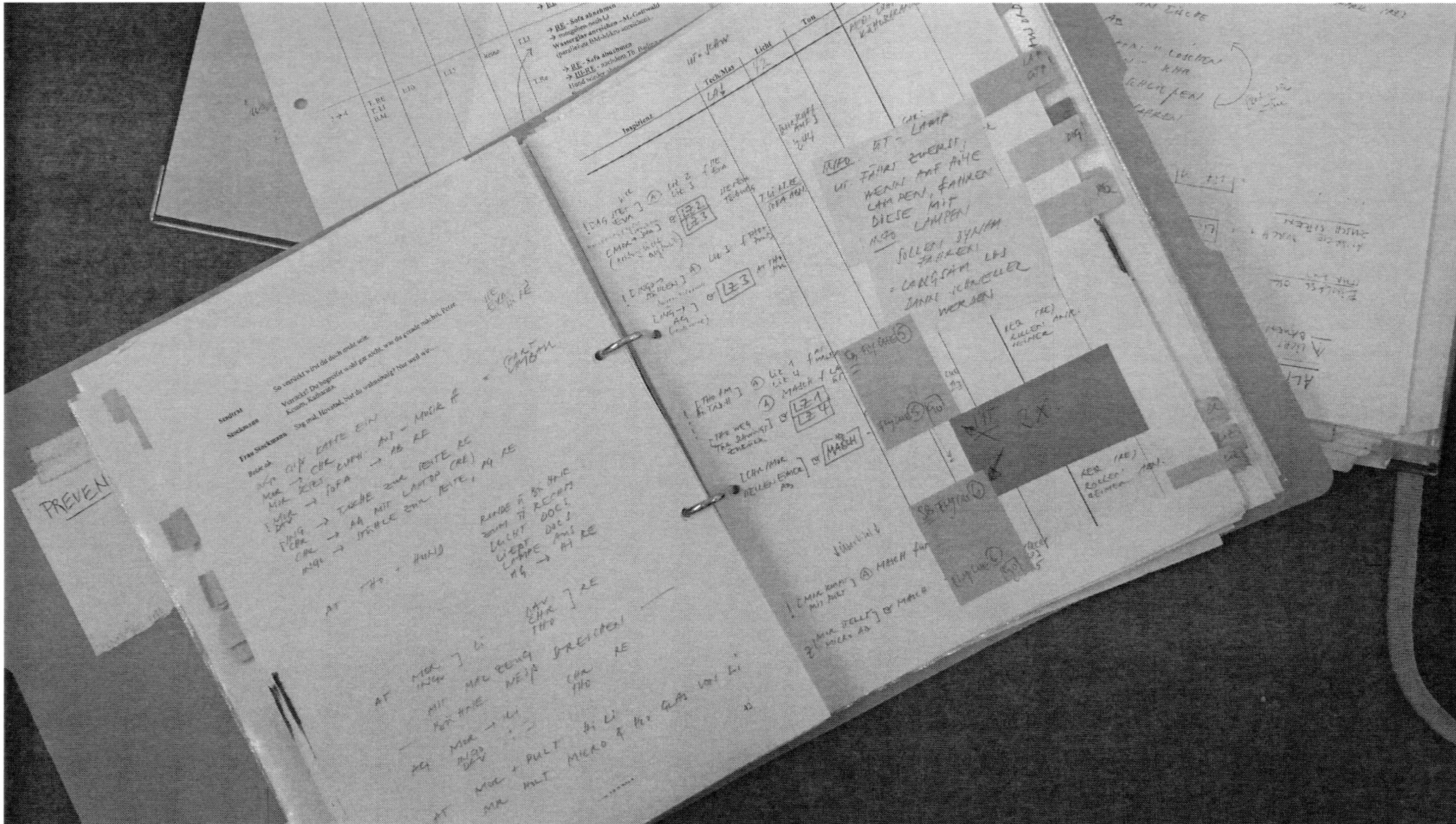

Figure 5.19 The promptbook of *An Enemy at the People* on the stage manager's desk (end of Act III). Photograph © Peter M. Boenisch.

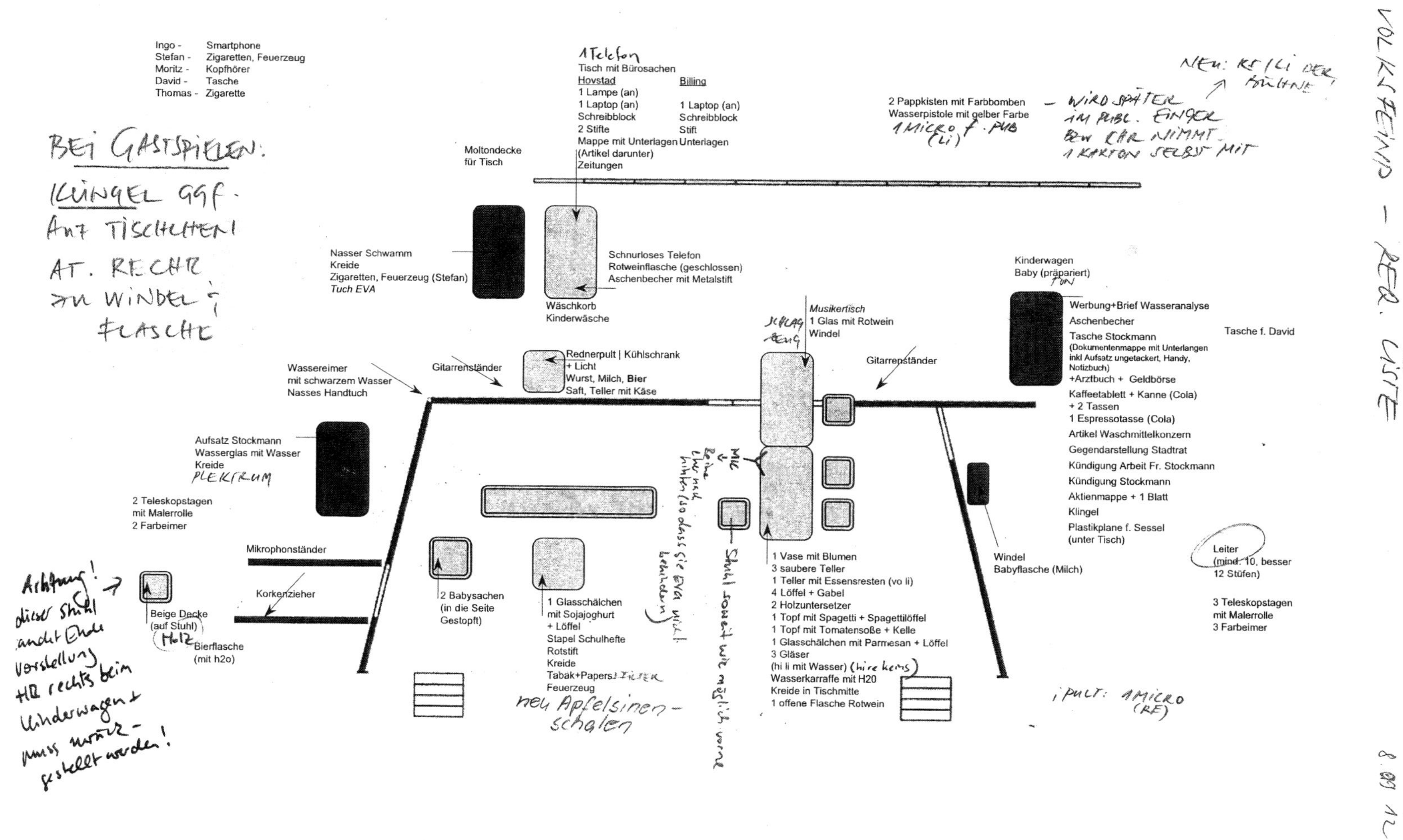

Figure 5.20 The prop list for the set-up of An Enemy of the People. © Schaubühne.

political statements. These issues were usually discussed in a notes and feedback session following a performance, as the actors were naturally too immersed in the performance to have a clear sense of how everything resonated with the audience. I have developed a quite close relationship with some of the actors, and some approach me to get an honest and open opinion about their performance, while others don't.

While I have also worked on other productions by Thomas for a longer period, such as *Hamlet* and *Demons*, *An Enemy of the People* was undoubtedly the liveliest production, and the one that kept transforming and developing all the time. Much changed, after around eighty performances, with the change in cast. The new combination, with Christoph Gawenda moving from Hovstad into the lead role, and Andreas Schröders and Renato Schuch alternating as Hovstad, released new energies and created very different dynamics, as if reassembling the pieces of the production in a new and different way again after so many performances. Also, Thomas kept rehearsing the play, in particular as we went abroad. He tried new things, and at times adapted scenes, depending on the location, and responding to local situations and reactions, which simply is not possible in most other productions. For me, it was one of the most exciting and instructive aspects of working on this production to see what you can still do with a production after the premiere, and how playing a production can remain a process that evolves and keeps developing. Thomas has an impressive sensitivity to see how the production might be tweaked depending on where it was performed, and only very rarely, he got it wrong, in hindsight. He has an inexhaustible determination to keep the standard of a production at the highest level imaginable, whereas other directors step away from a production, or quite openly pass the production over to the actors after the premiere. At times, you start wondering whether this is a desirable virtue of Thomas at all – at one point or the other, we all got annoyed when he called *yet another* rehearsal even though we had only just played *Enemy of the People* two weeks ago. But every time, he found out something new, and actors realised this, too, and they found new things after the fiftieth or so performance – quite naturally, perhaps, because our perception and understanding of situations, emotions and relations had changed and moved on, and we ended up turning entire scenes around for this reason. As Assistant Director, you could never have the same impact on maintaining the quality of a production. This was an exquisite learning curve for me, and I give Thomas much credit for the determination and the energy to keep rehearsing his productions long after their premiere, and to never slacken the reins. I firmly believe his work is so successful because he keeps watching them himself, and he looks after them, and as a result also our local Berlin audience never tires of a production like *Hamlet*, which we have now been performing for more than seven years.

Overall, I have been able to learn a lot during my years as Thomas' Assistant Director, more than any of his students he teaches at Ernst-Busch-Theatre Academy. We did five productions, and a number of revivals, countless rehearsals and travels around the globe. After a while, I had tuned into his biorhythm, and I had learned how best to assist him in the rehearsal room: when to ask him something, when to speak to him, or when not to speak at all, what to communicate verbally, and what information to send in a text message. Over the years, we spent a lot of time together, and we shared a lot, in rehearsals, performances, and travelling, and there were certainly some hard and difficult times. We somehow like each other, and if it was up to him, I would just continue to work as his assistant for ever. The reason why, quite unusually, I did spend such a long time as his Assistant Director (working with other directors, I moved on after one or a few productions, as is usual, and few directors have a permanent Assistant Director at all) is that you never tire of observing and listening to him; you learn so much. Also, my own theatre background, from training with Gaulier to working with Wilson, was not at all grounded in a character-based realistic aesthetic. Wilson, for instance, realises his visual concept, whereas his assistants take care of the play. It was an incredibly enriching experience to learn how to approach a play through the characters, their motivations, and generally through the most minute knowledge of every single detail. And not only is Thomas able to dissect the plays and their characters exactly for himself, but he manages to communicate and pass on this insight in an engaging way that is beyond description. I have experienced other productions with him, where actors had different ideas, or were simply unable to find a proper handle on their character, where he patiently explained, hour after hour, day after day, what the character wants, and where the character is within the play. And even if it bugs you that he tends to intervene a lot (and actors comment on that *a lot* and some *hate* it) – you have to admit that in almost all cases, it changes your performance for the better, and really makes a difference. If he wasn't almost always right, it would be annoying, but as it is, in the end, you simply have to respect his talent, imagination, and astute perception. You probably have to have both this rigour and this energy to succeed as a director; Wilson equally asks for one-hundred per cent concentration, and unconditional commitment and dedication, but Thomas is still the most demanding director I have met. In fact, I began to realise that I miss his strict regime when working with other directors, where you may experience less pressure and rehearsals are far more laid-back and easy going – but then, there rarely emerges a production that is artistically so satisfying and really draws on your full potential as his are. I feel, though, that Thomas' real ideal might be working like Nicolas Stemann, who is on stage himself in most of his productions, not playing a character, but present as a director who directs things on stage while they are happening, much like the conductor of an orchestra. Sometimes Ostermeier seems to lack such an opportunity to go wild and to properly indulge himself in all his creativity energy.

Note

1 See Steven F. Sage, *Ibsen and Hitler: The Playwright, The Plagiarist, and the Plot for the Third Reich*, New York: Carroll & Graf, 2006.

Chapter 6

Ostermeier on directing

6.1 THE ART OF COMMUNICATING: THOMAS OSTERMEIER'S 'INDUCTIVE METHOD' OF *REGIE*

Based on his two decades' experience of directing theatre, Thomas Ostermeier has arrived at a set of core principles that underpin his Regie *work. In this collaboratively written chapter, we attempt to bring together these techniques and to summarise, for the first time, his methodical approach to directing. The following text results from several years' worth of intensive observation and from numerous conversations – on occasion of rehearsals and meetings at the Schaubühne and elsewhere, of various workshops, and around the teaching of directing students at Berlin's Ernst-Busch-Theatre Academy. Working through and writing up many notes, we have opted for a first-person narrative, since it feels to be the most helpful and most natural mode for both authors and readers in this endeavour to articulate and explain a personal method. At times, we will address you directly – imagining you, our reader, as a fellow director, theatre artist, or as someone seeking to gain a deeper insight into the craft of making theatre behind Thomas Ostermeier's productions, which you may have seen on stage. Importantly, though, we have no intention of offering tried-and-tested recipes for how to cook up a production that tastes exactly like Ostermeier's theatre. What follows is not a manual intended to be applied and executed to the letter. On the contrary. In his teaching and in his workshops, Ostermeier refers frequently to the famous dictum by French film director François Truffaut, 'You will never overtake someone if you merely keep treading in their footsteps'. In the same vein, Thomas Ostermeier, the 'I' of this narrative, reveals his footprints, in order to enable you to overtake them.*

The director and the *Stoff*: bringing dramatic situations to (our) life

There are two major approaches to theatre direction: the inductive and the deductive method, as seen from the perspective of the director. Bertolt Brecht introduced this useful distinction in various typescripts dating from his exile period in the late 1930s and early 1940s, most notably in a 1939 essay on 'The Attitude of the Rehearsal Director (in the Inductive Process)'.[1] My own work as a director is based on what he termed 'the inductive method': this means that the production's form is entirely developed on the basis of the playtext. The play provides the *Stoff* (material). In a very useful way, this German word combines a whole range of different meanings. *Stoff* describes the material, the texture, the substance, the fabric and the subject matter. The term immediately makes clear that the playtext, as the starting point of directing work, is far more than words on a page. It has a substance, a texture, a tangible fabric-like materiality that you can sense, touch, see, feel, and smell. This materiality of the *Stoff* becomes the true point of departure for the inductive director, in contrast to those directors who work deductively – who impose on the play's *Stoff* their own themes, their own forms, and their own aesthetics. Their work tends to look very similar in each production, and it is therefore far easier to describe, as it follows a certain set of aesthetic features that return in most, if not all, of their productions. The distinction between 'inductive' and 'deductive' direction does not, however, imply a value judgement. There are some good, even very good directors who follow a deductive approach to *Regie*, and certainly some of the directors who have worked at the Schaubühne since 2000 clearly fall under this category.

The inductive approach, which I follow in my work, is a way of working that, in its very essence, *communicates* with the material. As a theatre director, you are in communication with two essential materials: the *Stoff* of the playtext, and the present – the present and the presence of your actors, your artistic team, and your audiences. The very purpose of *Regie* is to stage the play in the present – and that means, staging it in a way no one ever has done it before, and like no one ever had been able to stage it before, and no one will ever be able to stage it again. The reason for this is obvious: our production is *our* production – it confronts the reality of the playtext with the reality of life experience and the personality of the actors and the other artists who have come together to stage the play at this particular moment in time. It therefore tells *our* story, of us, today, of the group of people working on this production, and why we have to tell this drama to our audiences today. We tell our story, which is always also still the playwright's story because we fill the dramatic situation (*Spielsituation*) that he or she has created with our life and our actions, and we animate the circumstances they have given us. The production therefore becomes a mirror of our own time in history. Presenting *Hamlet* as anarchic, spoilt brat, as we did it in our production, is only possible on the back of our own time, and our immediate circumstances. Staging a play thus means translating literature into a dramatic process (*Vorgang*) that happens in the here and now. Staging *Richard III*, as German director Jürgen Fehling did, in 1937, in Nazi Germany, shortly before the Second World War, must inevitably strike different chords in the play compared to our production created in 2015. Having been influenced by the Brechtian tradition which I experienced during my own training at Ernst-Busch-Theatre Academy, I am particularly interested in the social circumstances. The method introduced here therefore generates, when it works, via a personal approach to the play's dramaturgy (via techniques such a storytelling and family portraits) studies of human behaviour within a certain historical, political and social context – the context of our time, not an imagined historical context as in a hypothetical production of *Richard III* that would merely invent a Nazi-scenario and portray Richard as a Hitler-like dictator, in stark contrast to Fehling's production that was actually created in 1937 Germany.

Based on these considerations, we can define the director's task in clear and simple terms: first, *Regie* is the communication with the playtext, with the *Stoff*, with the space, and with the actors and their possibilities. It is the communication between all these diverse elements, and out of this interplay something new will emerge, which neither the one part (the actor, the playwright, etc.) nor the other part (the director, the spectator, etc.) is able to know beforehand. This third, unnameable something cannot be calculated, designed, or directed solely on your own; it can only result from a genuine encounter. Taking this basic principle of communication seriously must mean that you allow yourself to be influenced by your partner – whether the actor, the playtext, the space, or the *Stoff*. Communication only functions if you take your counterpart seriously and accept her or him as your partner in a dialogue of equals – even if you do not necessarily agree, or if you do not understand. A basic rule in my work is therefore: I take the play seriously. What the characters say, what they do, is going to take place on stage; in my work, there are never these invisible quotation marks around the play, its characters, or the plot, which have been so typical for some postmodern approaches to staging plays, in particular classical works. Irony is something that the audience might feel as a result of watching a scene on stage; however, starting from not taking the play seriously and from adopting an 'ironic distance' towards the work, are not approaches that I would choose in creating theatre.

This takes us directly to the second core task of *Regie*, which is to comprehend and to bring to life the dramatic situations scripted by the playwright in a way that addresses, engages and entertains the audience. These well-known, basic Stanislavskian ideas of situations and circumstances are a crucial tool for the director, to which we will refer over and over again; they are the director's alphabet (see Box 6.1, 'Dramatic situations and dramatic conflicts'). According to Stanislavsky, a dramatic situation is defined by its 'given circumstances' – and as the term suggests, they are given by the play, and we may therefore also think of them as the playwright's gift to the director. I am rather irritated by people (for the main part academics and critics rather than audiences) who are obsessed solely with the scripted word. The 'play' as such does not exist in any meaningful way; it is not simply the words on the page which you just put on stage. These words are no more than the medium with which playwrights express the circumstances and situations they imagine. The written/spoken text of a play constitutes, let's say, twenty per cent of the story they tell; it is only a fraction of the rich life and of the many dimensions engendered by the

Box 6.1 Dramatic situations and dramatic conflicts

The situation is defined by the 'sum of all circumstances' or, in Stanislavsky's terminology, the 'given circumstances' – all the facts and conditions that shape and impact on the present situation, which are explicitly or implicitly stated in the playtext. The situation then generates responses that eventually result in actions that bear the intention to change that situation; it thus opens up possibilities to act. A dramatic figure, within a given situation, does not 'speak': she or he *acts through language*. She or he performs a speech act, using speech as a means to act and thereby to change the situation, for example by influencing and persuading others. Not every situation, however, is dramatic. Drama is a cultural form in which we recreate situations and human behaviour (in its simplest form: a speech act) in order to come to terms with the complexities of human existence and to reflect on our lives. A dramatic situation therefore articulates and embodies, in an exemplary way, some fundamental conflict in our society. The basic components of a dramatic situation, from this perspective, are thus: a conflict of intentions (antagonism, opposition), an object that they focus on (which may be a material object or an objective), and the two conflicting parties who are locked in a shared world, which demands that their conflict be resolved.

In a dramatic situation, personal intentions and societal pressures and contradictions are therefore closely interlocked: a character never acts out of a single motivation, but is driven by a multi-faceted motive that unfolds on two or even more layers, responding both to personal ('inner') intentions and the ('external') demands of society. For Hegel, the conflict between Antigone and Creon offered the most exemplary illustration of a dramatic situation. Abstractly speaking, their conflict expresses different perspectives on society, politics, and the public sphere: it gives dramatic form to a fundamental contradiction within society. At the same time, Creon's and Antigone's positions cannot coexist within the single (political) world that the protagonist and the antagonist share: their conflict must be resolved. Only one, not both positions, can be upheld in a shared world. Therefore, conversely, if Hamlet had decided to keep hanging out in Wittenberg, *no* dramatic conflict between him and Claudius (about the legitimacy of the latter's rule) would have arisen, since the two dramatic figures would not have shared the same world. And, in *Measure for Measure*, if Isabella's brother's life had not been in Angelo's hands, she would not be locked in one world with him, and thus not be exposed to his lust and desire.

(Continued)

(Continued)

A dramatic situation is therefore far more than a one-dimensional difference of personal points of view, of opposing interests or intentions, or of a clash of (psychological) characters. The conflict when I say, 'Let's get some coffee', but you say, 'No, I want to finish reading this book', is therefore not a dramatic conflict. It might, however, become a dramatic conflict if the 'I' and the 'you', for example, are in love, have just had a fight, and came close to the point of splitting up. The different, contradictory aims (motives) only turn into a dramatic conflict when both characters share a single world – in this last example, the world in which they are in love – and therefore have to solve the conflict one way or the other in order to stay together in this one world that they share. The fact that the conflict is then much bigger than having a coffee or not, and that the two parties have to act within a shared world, makes the conflict dramatic.

Less simplistically, Thomas Stockmann's situation in *An Enemy of the People* is clearly dramatic. He has found out the truth about the poisoned water and attempts to make this truth public, against the wishes of those who have an interest in suppressing this truth. Both parties, though, claim to act in the best interest of the community. This complexity of sharing the same intention while pursuing entirely opposing aims or means is characteristic of a genuinely dramatic situation. Moreover, Ibsen also makes clear the characters' personal motives that equally underpin the conflict on another level, for instance the rivalry and different lifestyles of the two brothers, the bond between the doctor and his friends at the newspaper office, and Hovstad's amorous interest in Stockmann's daughter (in our version, his wife). These multi-faceted contradictions express in an exemplary way the equally ambiguous fundamental conflicts that are at the core of our society. And, within the shared world of the characters, these conflicts have to be solved: this is what makes the conflict dramatic.

circumstances and situations that the playwright has invented. As a director, I am committed to the full one-hundred per cent of his or her imagination, and I view my task as engaging with the full complexity and the profound depths of the dramatic situations they have created. Somewhat paradoxically, this might result in changing the actual words the playwright has chosen. If an actor comes up with a different and better way to express and convey the dramatic situation and its key circumstances to the audience, why not use it? Why stick to an old-fashioned word on the page that for today's audience obscures the comprehension of the play's situation? Of course, I speak here from a position where I am able to re-work Ibsen's language, and even to change Shakespeare's language, simply because we always have to translate their plays into German in the first place before we can start producing their plays. However, I am at the very same time always mindful of the anecdote according to which Helene Weigel once told an actor: 'If you have an idea, forget it!' The same is actually true for the director, most of the time: forget your idea, and instead look closely at what the text tells you. Of course, you can be different and alter the text that the playwright wrote, and you can tweak and intensify the dramatic situations, in the way outlined below. But if you want to be different from the text, you have to be better than the text. If the director wants to do something different from the situation defined by the circumstances, he or she must be able to explain exactly why. And one ought to be very critical: Do these changes add anything? Are they really better than what Shakespeare or Ibsen wrote? Or, are you perhaps better off forgetting them?

When I work with contemporary playwrights like Marius von Mayenburg on Shakespeare, or with dramaturg Florian Borchmeyer on a new translation of Ibsen or Lillian Hellman, we never intend to peddle the idea of 'modernising a classic'. Our aim is simply to ensure that the playwright's words are understood, so that these authors remain what they were in their own time: contemporary playwrights whose work spoke immediately to their contemporary audiences about pressing issues of the day, and who told stories that everyone in the theatre was able to relate to. Shakespeare used verse, but in a way that was popular, that resonated with his audiences, and that worked on his audiences. When his plays were performed at the Globe, the audience was not separated from the text they heard and from the story they saw performed by a hiatus of more than four hundred years. Shakespeare's language was as contemporary for his audience as Ibsen's was when his plays premiered in the latter decades of the nineteenth century. In London, someone asked us how we dare to abuse Shakespeare's name by putting it on the bill of our Schaubühne production of *Hamlet*. I can only respond by saying that we are absolutely committed to Shakespeare, and we have not altered the gift of the circumstances and the dramatic situations which he offers us in *Hamlet*. Everything that happens in our production is a realisation of these circumstances, of the dramatic situations and of the *Stoff* that Shakespeare created, put on stage in such a way that it speaks to a twenty-first century audience with the same urgency and immediacy that *Hamlet* related to the audience at the Globe in 1602. If this then does not conform to the ideas that a certain cultural elite has about *Hamlet*, it may tell us more about this elite, than about Shakespeare and his play.

The director prepares: 'concepts', decisions, and human life

Jan Kott aptly described that *Hamlet* can easily be 'three different plays, though all three have been written by Shakespeare'. He referred to *Hamlet,* the historical chronicle; *Hamlet*, the thriller; and *Hamlet*, the philosophical drama – and there may be more, such as *Hamlet*, the family drama. Kott went on to remind us that, 'One can only perform one of several *Hamlets* potentially existing in this arch-play. [...] One can select at will. But one must know what one selects, and why.'[2] Accordingly, there are many plays in every single play – this is true, at least, for the great classics; in much bad contemporary writing, unfortunately, there isn't even a single play – but let's leave this aside here. It is simply impossible to tell all the many possible stories that a single playtext contains. If a director attempts to stage 'the play' 'objectively', and tries to play all the different layers and melodies of a text, nothing but a confused cacophony will be heard; the production will appear random, empty and meaningless. Without opting for a point on which to anchor the production, you run the risk of drifting about aimlessly, and to thereby lose the respect of the performers, who will doubtlessly find you wavering and indecisive in rehearsal. And for the audience, there is nothing worse than watching seven actors all playing their own version of a play. Directing, therefore, rather obviously means: to give a *direction*. It means, first and foremost, making a decision. Unless you have the privilege of running your own theatre or company, or you have a lot of money to produce your own show, you won't necessarily be in a position to make the decision as to what play you are going to direct. But there is an even more important decision that each director needs to make: why must we stage this particular play right now, at any cost, at this present point in time? You need to be absolutely clear about this, even though you may not have chosen the play in the first place. What hits you about the play? What is the 'feel' of the play (and its *Stoff*)? How do you respond emotionally to it? What tempted you to read on? And crucially, I repeat, why do we have to tell this drama to our audiences now?

Theatre is the art of conflict: a drama is caused by a certain fundamental conflict (*Grundkonflikt*), and a theatre-maker should emotionally relate to this conflict – not by taking sides, but by adopting an emotional attitude towards the conflict as such, and by being emotionally engaged with the conflict. If you are unable to find any such personal resonances with the play and the basic conflict that it offers; if you simply cannot come up with any reason why to do the play right now – then it may be better not to do it, even if this means losing money you may need urgently to earn. But, at least you won't lose your artistic credibility with a failing production, and won't risk having actors tell horror stories about their bad experience with you for years to come. The director's clarity regarding the main topic of the play and the focus of her or his production, energises and motivates the actors and the entire artistic team, for four, six, or even eight weeks in the rehearsal room, let alone during the run, and the time in which the production will be performed in a theatre's repertoire. There will always be times when the energy dissipates, when everything seems to fall apart. Then, the shared 'mission' behind staging that play will come to the rescue. It will become the common vision that brings everyone back on board again. This principal reason for wanting to stage a play, this very personal mission to tell a story to the audience, is therefore far more important than having a concept, if by 'concept' we mean a pre-conceived masterplan that the director came up with in advance. On the very first day of rehearsals with the actors, I never know what will come out of the weeks ahead. I do know, however, which chords in my own life resonate with the play. And this is what I talk about on the first day of rehearsals when I meet the actors and the creative team: What happens in the play? What is interesting to us, today? How does what Ibsen, Shakespeare, or another playwright wrote many years, many centuries ago, strike a chord in our own contemporary lives?

Is not the personal, emotional resonance with our own lives the primary reason for making theatre? Theatre is pointless if it does not capture this relevance and relation with our lives today, in the twenty-first century. Whatever your personal, individual approach and directing style is, whether you are an inductive or a deductive director, whether you prefer to see historical period costumes on your stage, whether you subscribe one-hundred per cent to stage realism, or whether yours is an entirely abstract stage – the fundamental role of theatre in our culture is to tell stories about us, about our lives, about our problems, about our society. That's why theatre exists. The characters on stage are our vicarious representatives who act, take action, make decisions on our behalf. At the end of the day, the unique and singular quality of theatre does not reside in virtuoso performances, in slick, attractive aesthetics, nor in spectacular design and special effects. Instead, it results from being able to find something of our own lives in what happens on stage, from being able to recognise ourselves, even if – and I would say, in particular when – we did not know that we were like this, or even capable of that. In fact, theatre is at its best when it becomes a journey into our own human abyss, where we – as actors, directors, and audiences – discover things about ourselves that we did not know, and that we had not been able to imagine; things that, perhaps, we did not even want to know or to imagine about ourselves.

Theatre is a unique way of exploring what lies behind the masks of our human civilisation. In a dramatic situation that puts at risk our very existence, we are unable to keep up these masks, and they drop. As a result, theatre points towards the fundamental contradictions of our society. This is what Hegel meant when he proposed that drama has the ability to enlarge and escalate a situation in such a way that it becomes existential. To give a simple example: a society in the midst of an economic crisis, which is under constant pressure for ever more austerity measures, and which is constantly told that there is not enough money for everyone, will bring to the fore hostility, prejudices and racism which were always present, but which do not erupt in an affluent, wealthy community. The circumstances of the dramatic situation, however, brought to the fore our dark sides. This is also the main attraction of *Richard III*. The major frustration I feel about much present-day theatre, but equally cinema, television and even journalism, is that all around, we are only being told and shown what we *want to see*, and we are only ever affirmed in what we already (believe to) know. All around, we are being satisfied, and hardly ever confronted, with our selves and with the other, foreign, dark side within us. Serious artists, in my opinion, are interested in such far deeper layers of human behaviour, and they will therefore find their own way of telling a story. Their work will offer a highly personal, a new and engaged expression of an experience of life that guides their perspective on an age-old play by Shakespeare, or even a Greek tragedy. They are driven by the need to talk about their life and their experiences of living in this world and in this society. If you do not have a problem, you probably should not be on stage, or direct for the stage. To make theatre, you have to have a life, and have questions about all of life's contradictions.

Everyone who writes a poem or a book, everyone who composes a symphony or paints a painting, attempts to find an original expression for a situation he or she has experienced in life. Prior to the drama, prior to literature, there is thus always human life. Behind each play, there is a living human being who attempts to articulate, via the play, conflicts and contradictions from her or his own life, based on her or his very specific experience of life, and the contradictions they faced. My own interest in plays, for the main part, is driven by the desire to show via a play some of the contradictions that exist within our contemporary society. Ibsen put it beautifully when he said, 'in my writing I preside at judgment day over myself'. This is particularly important, since it counters the misunderstanding that in my productions of Ibsen I might attack others, or point the finger, for instance, at Berlin's bourgeois, hedonistic middle class. But I have become a part of this class too. My productions are therefore much rather, in Ibsen's sense, a judgment day for myself and my peers.

At its core, my method attempts to retrieve the core of human life within the play. And here, most importantly, I do not mean the life of the playwright, and her or his individual biography; nor do I mean 'the truth' or 'the reality' behind the fiction of the text. Rather, what is important is to understand that before the text existed, there was a fellow human being who had certain experiences with other human beings, who lived certain contradictions, and who attempted to articulate these experiences in an artistic way. Any serious director shares with any playwright a deep dissatisfaction with the way things are. It is this anger that motivates the writer to sit down and write; and as a director working in the twenty-first century, I can take my own experience, and my critique of myself and of today's society, and establish a parallel with the experience and the critique that Henrik Ibsen articulated 130 years ago. I try to sound out the congruence between his and my own dissatisfaction with the respective worlds around us, and therefore try to ensure to work from a similar, congruent impetus – an impetus that is prompted by an experience in life, and not by purely aesthetic experience, or by the desire to create art. By way of an example, my reading of Ibsen's *An Enemy of the People* revolves around the question of what chance truth still has within a society that is entirely defined by economic imperatives. I wanted to investigate the question of whether the economy, the interest of capitalism might impose its own dominance, and whether it might be able to maintain its primacy even in the face of truth, and of rational argument. This was my whole starting point, my 'concept', if you wish to insist on this word. You do not need more than such a single sentence or two to express it, for example on the first day of rehearsals. This brief sentence becomes something akin to Stanislavsky's 'super-objective', on the level of your production. A short, clear sentence that summarises this personal resonance and motivation will suffice, since you want to inspire the actors and your team, rather than making them feel that they have to conform and fulfil your expectations (which, undoubtedly, you will and must have). This central 'story' you want to tell with the play which, according to the inductive method of direction, always originates in a clear understanding of the play and its dramaturgy, will then guide your work on the play, and your conversations with the other members of the creative team, and with the producers. It determines how the main character looks; which actors you choose, if you are fortunate enough to influence casting choices; how the stage space looks and where everything on stage takes place; what the characters wear, and how they talk. At the very same time, what emerges during rehearsals, and what may even evolve over several years of performing a play like *Hamlet*, which is the best example in my own work, could not be more remote from that one sentence about the play that I expressed when we started rehearsing *Hamlet*.

Researching, knowing, and un-knowing the play

Your first approach towards the play you are going to stage was necessarily emotional and spontaneous: you feel, you resonate, you respond affectively. But it is indispensable for a director to be thoroughly prepared before the production begins. Reading the play again (and again, and again ...), you then try to comprehend the play in its entirety: its dramaturgic structure, how it works and functions as a play, and how it has managed to trigger all these initial reactions and feelings you had. I don't think that it is particularly helpful to turn to books, academic writing and all the 'secondary literature' about a play before you have arrived at your own, clear understanding. There is a danger that you might lose sight of your initial gut reaction and begin instead to see only what the books or the scholars tell you. At the same time, you cannot afford to be ignorant about the play, the playwright, about the society they lived in, and especially about the theatre they wrote their play for. I believe that the architectural realities of theatre buildings, and of spatial arrangements, define the way in which plays are written for the stage, and likewise, the ways in which plays are staged, and theatre is made and experienced. This conviction has underpinned my work from the early productions at the Baracke to our decision to build a Globe-like theatre for *Richard III* in 2015. Furthermore, you need to know something about the history of the play, and about famous productions in the past. Therefore, instead of seeking interpretations of the play, I prefer to look for research that will help me to access and grasp the world of the playwright, the experience she or he wrote about, and the society in which they lived, especially if it seems so distant (and yet so close) as Shakespeare's. Quality scholarship – for instance, the research on Shakespeare by Stephen Greenblatt, Jan Kott, Robert Weimann, André Müller and numerous others – certainly helps a director to understand the dramaturgic form of the play and its dramatic situations. Most notably if you are directing a certain playwright for the first time – whether a classic or a contemporary writer – it is useful to read other – perhaps even all – of their plays in order to get a feel for how they think and what makes them tick, and for how the particular play sits within their *oeuvre*. There might also be further writing by the author – about her or his play(s), about their work for the theatre, about the world they lived in. When, for instance, I read how proud Ibsen was, how important it was for him that his characters spoke everyday language like everyday people, how could I possibly ignore this crucial command and not feel obliged to have characters who speak everyday language like everyday people, in my own Ibsen productions – and not characters who speak in the language of 1882? Ibsen clearly spoke about his own present time, and not about a time 130 years before he wrote and staged his plays.

We can now begin to connect all these insights with the central 'kick' we got from first reading the play. We become clearer about the congruencies between the playwright's life experience and their critical impulse and our own, thereby clarifying further the reason why we have to bring this play to our stage today, and which story we want to tell our own audiences of today. I would think that any director should have a list of, say, five to ten plays in mind, for which they have done this kind of preparatory work, which they have researched and thought through, and which they could therefore start rehearsing tomorrow, if necessary. I have such a list, and I know these plays more or less inside out, and have thought about them for a long time. I am perplexed when I meet directing students, and even professional directors, who are unable to name and discuss in detail even a single play they want to stage.

And yet, all the research, all the certainties and all the answers about the play are immediately challenged from the very first moment you truly begin to examine the play in rehearsal. The deeper you immerse yourself in the play during rehearsals, the more you will lose your earlier sense of certainty, and of 'knowing'. Once you start truly to communicate with the *Stoff* of the play, it will likely give you an entirely different set of responses from the ones you initially believed to discover in the play. The experience of reading the play and conducting further research can only be a first step of the director's communication with the play. Once the scenic work starts in rehearsal, you often arrive at a completely different perspective on the material, if you remain open and permeable for impulses that may suddenly arise. More often than not, you will discover the most vital and central questions only while rehearsing, almost (but never actually) by accident. When rehearsing a play, one gets inevitably lost in the jungle of concrete problems, and the tiny branches and ramifications of the material; one inevitably loses sight of the super-objective. Ninety per cent of a director's experience during rehearsals is thus rather painful and depressing: you get completely lost in the forest of the play, you lose any sense of direction, you cannot see any way out. This is at the same time the exhilarating frenzy of rehearsing, the thrill, which requires, as a counterweight, the reservoir of detailed knowledge and the in-depth understanding that the director has gained from her or his substantial research, and the intense preparation that is necessary before rehearsals can begin. It is now that this preparation will become useful, in order to find orientation again, because it enables you to make this genuinely disorienting encounter with the material productive. As important as it is to have a clear motivation, perspective and thesis about the play in the first place, it is also essential not to accept solely what confirms your initial thesis, and never to shut down one's channels of experience. One must never be afraid of getting lost. If you close in too rigidly and narrowly on your own point, if you stubbornly insist that 'the play is about this and that', then you have begun reducing the play by imposing a deductive vision on it. You will no doubt spare yourself sleepless nights, but rehearsals will become a boring one-way road. The director's approach should be never to know, never to preempt what will happen next. It is most important that directing work remains an open (yet never random) process throughout, otherwise you are no longer communicating with the play.

Enabling the actors to flourish: exploring situations and processes

So, you have arrived at your crucial directorial decision about the story you want to tell your audience, and about the play's resonance with your, and our, own life. From your experience of reading the play, along with your research, study, and reflection, you have accumulated a considerable amount of knowledge. Of course, you will be tempted to turn the first day(s) of rehearsal into a university seminar where you fill your actors' heads with all this information. Don't! As the director, you must know absolutely everything, but you must forget it the moment you go into rehearsal. Or rather, you must put it to the back of your mind, so that you have this knowledge at your disposal at any minute, since you never know when you may need it. You will have all these firm and very specific ideas in your mind; you will know, and you need to know, a lot about every scene, about each character, and every single line of the play, because you will have thought it through thoroughly. You know very precisely the big picture of the play's dramaturgic cohesion. Yet, actors cannot play ideas, dramaturgies and concepts. It simply won't work to present them with all these great big chunks of background information, and to then say, 'now go on stage and play this'. In rehearsal, it does not help to talk about concepts, or to attempt to analyse a play or a particular scene from a purely rational perspective. This may, at worst, stall the momentum and kill the power of scenic play. For the performers, it is far more important to be in the very moment, to play the situation, to make experiences, and then to organise these experiences with your help. The director needs to have all the details and all the knowledge ready at hand at any moment, but purely in order to help the actors to play – and not as instruction or prescription.

Within the inductive method, there are always several ways of staging the play, and many alternative pathways for approaching a particular scene; and all of them are equally viable. The actors can explore these paths in rehearsal, and they are encouraged to do so, following their own instincts and their personal experiences. Technique can never replace these two vital aspects of their communication with the text: personality, and life experience. Working towards a production, there is never only the one 'right' or 'correct' path that I would lay down and dictate. And this is indeed the biggest misconception about the director's work, which I encounter time and again: the idea that the director is the person who tells everyone else what to do. As far as I'm concerned, I do not consider it the director's job to turn the actors into drilled monkeys who perform the tricks you have trained them. The director is not an animal tamer, or a dictator, and is anything but the master of the rehearsal room. Rather, I prefer to think of the director as a gardener whose task it is to enable the actors to flourish. An actor, for me, is not a service provider who can simply be replaced, and who produces on command. Actors are equal participants in the process of direction. I never ask an actor to do something outrageous – to scream, to get naked (in fact, I quite often have to stop them taking off their clothes). Actors are artists, and if all goes well in a rehearsal, they will make you an offer. Why, then, should a director interfere with their work by coming into the rehearsal room with her or his own ready-made ideas, concepts, and exact instructions? This would only ever allow the actors merely to execute and reproduce more or less badly what the director had already decided in advance. How do you want to invent new forms and arrive at an amazing, mind-blowing way of staging a scene if you come into the rehearsal room already knowing exactly what you want to see, and how a particular scene 'must look' and how it 'ought to be played'? At the very same time, it is a particular strength of the inductive approach that, through the analysis of situations and processes, it is very clear when the performers, or when the director, lose track and go 'off-piste'. It is another of the director's principal tasks to keep the production on course, and to make sure that everyone is heading together towards the same target.

One of the most important skills of a director is therefore the ability to translate the abstract dramaturgic ideas of the playtext into sensuous and vivid prompts that ignite the actors' imagination and initiate the actors' play: this moment when the playtext turns into the actors' human play (*Spiel*) is crucial. There are entire schools of theatre directing that rely for these prompts entirely on the characters, and on exploring their psychology and their backstories. This is, however, not the material that I give to my actors. Of course, actors want to know, and they have to know, why a character speaks, and what prompts a particular line or action. And rightly so: in order to act (and in most drama, this means, to speak), one needs a cause that prompts us to act and to speak. In our rehearsals, we therefore spend a lot of time, too, talking about what a character wants, and what motivates them (although I prefer the term 'motive' instead of the psychological term 'motivation'). Yet, we only rarely, if ever, discuss *who* a character *is*. There is a more productive route to clarifying a character's motivation than psychology. In our rehearsals, we explore together the dramatic situations, their main circumstances, and the stakes at play, and we try thereby to arrive at a shared understanding of the scene in a way that stimulates the actors' artistic imagination. Most of the time, characters find themselves in a dramatic situation, they are faced with it, and react to it. Playwrights tend to put their characters into a situation they have to master, or which they are even unable to cope with; therefore, they cannot have a predetermined motivation or strategy for dealing with this situation. In naturalistic drama, characters rely on their instinct and on culturally acquired patterns of behaviour to respond to the situation.

This brings us to the most central building blocks of my method: the *dramatic situation* (*Spielsituation*), which is the sum of the given *circumstances* (*Umstände*, see Box 6.1, 'The dramatic situation', above). Among these circumstances which define the dramatic situation at hand, we can identify a main, or central, circumstance (*Hauptumstand*), which triggers a *process* (*Vorgang*; see Box 6.2, 'The dramatic process'). At its heart, the process is the direct response to the situation that wants to effect a change of this situation; it is what drives the dramatic figure to act in order to try to change and overcome the present situation. Such a change of the situation is marked by the turning point (*Drehpunkt*).[3] Or, looked at from the actor's point of view, the main circumstance is what directly prompts the actor's play; it generates concrete actions (*Handlungen*) in the pursuit of the process. In order to fully stimulate the actor's imagination, this cause that forces the dramatic figure to act has to be as drastic and as big as possible. The director can assist the actor by making the main circumstance so large that it becomes such a tremendous enormity that the actor is prompted to get up right away, because she or he cannot but take action now and start to play. I call this intensifying, or 'sharpening' the circumstances (*die Umstände verschärfen*): I attempt to amplify the main circumstance that prompts the situation, and thereby to raise the dramatic stakes (*Beträge*). In theatre, we don't want to see flat situations. Instead, we want to see something extraordinary, even in Ibsen's living rooms. Especially the conversational dialogue in realist drama tends to lead actors readily to speak and play with an energy, or rather, a lack thereof, as if they were discussing whether to order a pizza or Chinese for dinner. Intensifying the circumstances makes the process more dramatic, and hence more interesting for the actor to play, and for the audience to watch. The same simple process – drinking a bottle of coke, for instance – can become radically different depending on the situation. It is quite obvious that you will drink that bottle differently when you just go into a café and order a coke, from when you are sitting trapped in an underground war bunker thinking that you've run out of anything to drink, and then suddenly find one more bottle of coke at the bottom of your rucksack.

Box 6.2 The dramatic process

The dramatic process (*Vorgang*) is the 'headline' that each figure has in a scene. It results directly from the situation, is triggered by the main circumstance, and is focused on the stage partner. The process aims at changing the situation, at creating new and different circumstances. It is therefore genuinely dramatic; if you stop wanting to change the situation, drama stops, as there is no more dramatic conflict. To achieve this goal, one can apply different strategies, and one may adapt and change one's strategy in the pursuit of the same process; the idea of a process is therefore not prescribing a certain action to the player. Further, the process can be active (Richard), or reactive (Lady Anne: she has to react to Richard's outrageous proposal of marrying her, given that he has killed her husband and father-in-law). The goal of a process is thus the turning point, where the situation changes. One can therefore almost mathematically analyse scenes: a process starts with a turning point, and at the next turning point a dramatic figure's process changes again.

The process can always be captured by a verb – following Brecht, you can express the process with the formula, '*in order to ..., I ...*'. For instance, 'In order **to get Lady Anne** (= process), Richard charms her (= strategy/action in order to achieve the aim).' The process is something active, something you do to your partner, and not a mere psychological feeling. Examples include 'to persuade someone', 'to calm someone down', 'to seduce someone', 'to impress someone', 'to convince someone', 'to curse someone'. 'To say', however, is not a process: language is always already an action, and thus a means to effecting change. The process, meanwhile, prompts and urges the actor to play – and not just to 'act out' an action, to pretend to do something, to demonstrate some activity. This is where the approach to a scene via the process offers a different emphasis from the widespread method of 'actioning'. I find this concept of an 'action' imprecise and misleading; it is too general. Anything is an action. For me, actioning as a method leads the actor to remain occupied with her- or himself, instead of inviting the actor to communicate with her or his partner, which the approach via the process does.

The process should be expressed in a sensuous, palpable and immediately playable way, so that the actor is enabled to give it a form and shape. In the pursuit of this process, one can then apply different strategies, in direct response to the partner and their reaction. By way of an example, Richard constantly adapts and changes his strategies, based on Lady Anne's responses. But equally, an actor can and should adapt their

strategies according to the response they get from their partner, and not just the verbal responses – there is far more than the spoken text. In this way, they can truly play in each and every performance anew, instead of just reproducing rehearsed words, blocking and gestures.

We therefore do not think of rehearsing in terms of 'building characters'. The goal we share in rehearsals is to transform language into action. Language is the actor's primary tool. Shakespeare teaches us that language is action, and that it shapes reality. We hint at this when we try to see the playtext not just as description or expression, but as an active process. In sum, for an actor, there are three basic 'motivations' to act that are contained in a dramatic situation, and none of them is psychological:

1. the (main) circumstance that causes you to act or speak;
2. the addressee of your speech or action (even if there is no one else on stage, there is always the audience; think, for instance, of Richard's monologues);
3. the process you play, which is the attempt to achieve a certain change of the present situation (usually by means of words, hence with your speech act).

The actors' play hinges almost entirely on the process. The best assistance that a director can offer the actors in order to enable them to invent concrete physical actions (*Handlungen*), is to agree with them on the processes they play, how far in the playtext a particular process stretches, when exactly a new process commences (in other words, a turning point), or when the figure changes her or his strategy (*Strategiewechsel*) in the pursuit of their aim to change the situation – and thereby to distinguish and not to mix up changes of strategy from turning points. Physical actions, gestures and movement, are all part of the process. Playing the process through the way a figure walks, or the way they talk, can be a more effective and more truthful way to show a character than trying to 'act' a psychological motivation or emotion. Fully exploiting a physical action (for example, putting on a jacket or handling a certain prop) is often the best way to express an inner psychological state. This approach to building a character through the process allows the actor, for instance, to find their character in the way they walk across the stage in a given scene. The actor can thus build the character, quite literally, from the feet upwards (which is, by the way, the reason why I find it essential to rehearse in the shoes you will wear on stage, as the experience of the way you connect to the floor is a crucial foundation for playing). I would even say that an actor should not play a character at all, but that she or he should primarily play a process. Instead of being the starting point for the actor, the character should be what comes together, for the spectator, through the speech, physical action, and behaviour that they hear and see. The dramatic figure appears on stage as the sum of all the situations she or he is confronted with in the play, and their behaviour in these situations.

Time and again I see directors who prevent their actors from playing clear and concrete actions: they seek to express a certain state; they try to describe something with what they do. But they have not found and defined the process that results from the dramatic situation, and that prompted the action in the first place. The task of the director is, instead, to help the actors to grasp the text as an active process which they can play, and not as a description of the character that they would have to 'action', express or illustrate. As much as possible, I try to get the actors away from thinking too much about the character whom they play and whom they want to show, as this only causes them to 'emote' and overact. When an actor attempts to feel, and simulates an emotion, the audience no longer has their own space to sense and feel something. If the actor already acts out how bad something feels, the spectators will no longer feel the pain. If, instead, the actor concentrates on the situation and the process, if she or he plays the clear thought of the text, the audience will be able to feel. Moreover, actors should never have to worry about having, showing or feeling the 'right' emotion. I am absolutely convinced that it is utterly unproductive to steer the actors into psychological pathology. 'Show me some anger', 'Get into a frenzy', 'Show me more', 'Work yourself up properly', 'Give me proper grief' – these are instructions you hear all the time in the rehearsal room. But they leave the actor no other choice but to 'emote' and to act out emotional states according to the director's taste. Directing actors by means of describing psychological states, or any other states, predetermines what the actors have to do. As a result, they are forced to fulfil a certain expectation. They are put under pressure because they have to 'feel properly', and have to show the 'right signs' of the state which the director wants them to 'show'. Such a way of working as a director does not tap into the true, original potential that theatre has: to understand the world through play, and to make discoveries about human behaviour.

You will not be able to make discoveries with your actors if you anticipate, dictate, or preempt their play. In fact, for me, the ideal way of making theatre – which, I am well aware, I do not manage to put into practice myself one hundred per cent all of the time – is not to direct at all, not to dictate, not to order, prescribe, tell or instruct: but instead, to clarify in your work with the actors the dramatic situations within the play in such a way that the performers are enabled to act authentically, and that you therefore through their action gain an insight into human behaviour and into our society. I am absolutely convinced that if you unpack a dramatic situation in all its depth, in its entire dimensionality and complexity, everything will naturally and organically happen just by using the clearly defined dramatic situation as a springboard. This is especially true for

Shakespeare, whose plays have ultimately taught me this lesson: forget all the unnecessary worry about characters, their psychology and motivations, and just focus on the dramatic situation and on the play to which it gives rise. By articulating the situation in a clear, perspicacious and evident way, the ideal director will lead the actors to the point where they simply have to act – where the circumstances of the situation provoke them so much that they cannot but play and offer their ideas. Together, the director and the actors gradually sneak up to this point, by clarifying the situation in ever more meticulous detail. If you have all the ingredients of the dramatic situation (in other words, the circumstances) very clearly in your mind, you will almost automatically come up with a verb that corresponds to the process that you want to show. You never have to make it up or invent it. I would go as far as to suggest that the only thing a director can really learn about making theatre is how to get the situation right. If you find the right dramatic situation, everything else will follow and come together by itself. Conversely, whenever I sense that something is not right in what I see on stage in front of me, the first and best thing to do is to get back to work on the situation.

Engaging with the other: everything is possible

Within my materialist, concrete approach to theatre direction, I do not conceive of the motive that incites the dramatic figure to want something and to act in terms of an individual's psychological motivation. It is no character trait. For me, it is always the situation that determines the behaviour and the action, and not the (psychological) character. For this reason, the scenic play in my theatre emerges at all times from the dramatic situation: a figure is not motivated to perform an action because the character has this or that psychological trait, but *because a certain situation exists, something happens as a result*. What provokes or 'motivates' the process, is from this perspective always concrete: it is a concrete circumstance in the particular situation, never an abstract psychological state. A figure does not do something simply because she or he is evil, not even Richard Gloucester. Much rather, every human being is capable of *anything*, and the situation – the social situation – determines the behaviour.

I often try to get this point across to theatre students with an improvisation exercise that I do for an hour or even an hour and a half. I introduce it as an illustration of the principle of 'intensifying the situation'. All participants are invited on stage, playing a group of people waiting in an airport lounge for the departure of their plane. The instruction is to behave authentically in this situation, and not to 'act', not to be funny or clever. After a while, there is an announcement that the aeroplane is delayed by half an hour. Then, a further delay is announced, until finally the flight is cancelled. This situation is intensified ever more: after a while, the next announcement indicates that the terminal has been sectioned off because of a terrorist threat. Then a bomb explodes outside, and no one can leave, as the outside has been radioactively contaminated. Next, there is no more water, and so on and so forth. In an alternative scenario, with fewer participants, you can also set a similar task, asking them to be a group travelling in a lift that gets stuck, and it's the weekend. The electricity is out, and no one hears the alarm. These situations become dramatic because there is no way out; everyone has to organise her- or himself with everyone else, as there is only this one shared world, where there is not enough water for everyone. The point of these exercises is: in such an extreme situation, every one of us has to decide. Do I harm the other, do I even kill the other so that I can have the last remaining water bottle for myself and survive another day, or do I sacrifice myself and give the last litre of water to the pregnant woman? Every human being has both options within them, and that is what interests me, what I want to explore and examine as a director. Unless we are in such a dramatic situation, we will never find out what we are capable of – in good and in bad ways. In everyday life, we get along with each other in more or less friendly and amenable ways because we adhere to civilised manners. The playwright, however, pushes a figure into a dramatic situation in order to find out what is hidden beneath the conformity of everyday life, beneath the varnish of civilisation. And here, each and every one of us is capable of both: of sacrifice, and of murder, for and against rational, civilised humanity.

I am therefore unable to believe in the approach of writing out character biographies, as is still common amongst Stanislavsky followers. From my point of view, spending your rehearsal time exploring the character's back history prior to the story of the play, gets in the way of the actor's play, rather than enabling and inspiring it. This approach fosters a type of attention that bears no relevance in a dramatic situation, nor even in a banal, everyday situation. As you read this text, we try to explain and get across a point. Imagine a situation where I try to make something clear (my 'process'). My only means of making sure that I achieve this goal is to be attentive to your reaction, to observe whether you become restless, show resistance, or nod off. I can then react by being as lucid, pertinent and rhetorically persuasive as possible. My attention is thus fully focused on the situation, and in particular on my partner and their response – but not at all, I would suggest, on my biography. I have rarely been in a situation where I tried to remind myself, Who is this Thomas Ostermeier? What is his biography and his back history? What is his character like? All such details would be useless in a real-life situation. They equally cloud the actor's attention, as they prevent her or him from being in, and responding to, the very situation right in front of their eyes. I also frequently realise that the psychological approach to acting – and to playwriting – results in oversimplification. It reduces the potential of a dramatic figure, and thereby reduces the actor's possibilities to play. Many theatre schools provide future actors with a simple and reassuring thought: once you find your character, you know how to act in the play. This prompts actors to speak their character in a certain manner. Bad actors believe that this 'speaking the voice' *is* the character. Some more advanced actors will at least attempt to invent a physical approach to their character. But still, the idea of 'character' becomes like a hammock to comfortably rest in for the duration of the evening. But true theatre is the exact opposite of any certainty. It only begins when you leave behind the idea that you 'have found your character', and that you know what to do. *Playing* is much more difficult than 'acting': it requires you to be fully alert and present in the very moment, at all times. Otherwise, it becomes 'dead theatre', as Peter Brook called it – the shifting around of lifeless characters. A truthful dramatic process is all about wanting to reach a certain outcome, and about achieving a goal. Watching it will be most beautiful and engaging if the characters show us persistent changes in their strategies for getting there, in response to the moment, just like Richard does in his dialogue with Lady Anne over the dead body of her father-in-law. Only a bad scriptwriter invents one single, consistent process, and a single turning point for a character. Shakespeare's characters constantly change their strategies, and that is why they are complex, full of different layers, and full of contradictions – like a person in real life, and not like a character in a third-rate Hollywood movie.

As an actor, you cannot meet this challenge by studying the character's biography. Instead, you need to be in the situation and attentive to the reaction of your partner. In order to train this awareness of one's partner, which many actors lack, I have made myself familiar with Sanford Meisner's 'repetition exercises', and introduced them as a regular feature in my rehearsal process (see Box 6.3, 'Repetition exercise'). I find that his exercises constitute an ingenious way of bringing actors together. They develop our ability to observe and perceive our partner in ways that enable true communication. Being able to feel empathy, and to put oneself into the mind of one's partner, is a most vital aspect of human intelligence: the better I am able to empathise with and to understand my partner, the better I can influence her or him, without necessarily manipulating her or him in a negative way. This sensibility perfectly supports my method, which is based on the articulation of a process through which the protagonist makes the attempt to change the situation. Above all, the partner, as the antagonist, is usually the protagonist's first encounter with the reality of this situation. Acting then becomes so much more than expressing emotions or a character's psychology; it becomes about shaping the reality of the situation in such a way that my partner follows my own principles. Therefore, the unconditional attention for, and awareness of, the partner should always guide the actors' play. It is indispensable that their attention be fully attuned to the other who shares their world. This is the skill that Meisner's exercise helps to develop. There is an important political, if not ethical, aspect to this. In our present time, we increasingly lose our sense for the other. It is a major disease of our times that we have stopped seeing the other's capacity to enrich our lives, to make it possible to reach and realise that third 'term' described earlier, through the combined sum of myself and the other. Our world spins solely around our own individual self, and if we consider the other at all, it is in terms of our own personal gain and profit, or as a danger, an enemy or an intruder who needs to be kept out and away, if needs be by brute force and violence. This context is an extremely important concern for what I attempt to do with my method, and goes far beyond the interpretation of a play.

Box 6.3 Repetition exercise (adapted from Sanford Meisner)

The objective of the exercise is to divert the primary attention away from the standard focus on the self (on expressing, acting, emoting) towards what is in front of me (first and foremost, my partner), and to use this as a source of inspiration and as input for my own actions. The participants sit in pairs, facing each other, on two opposite rows of chairs. Initially, the partners watch each other in silence, studying with great attention the emotional information they receive from their partner. They scan down the other's body, concentrating attentively on each part. Moving from the eyes to the nose to the hair and on to the rest of the partner's face, you can already read a lot about your partner in their face: are they tired, nervous, engaged, hungover, in love? You may even read something about their age and their life in their face. Scanning the upper part of the partner's body further – their shoulders, the way they are dressed, the way they are sitting on the chair, how they are holding their hands – you should not interpret, but continue to concentrate solely on the emotional message you receive. Moreover, try not to get distracted by being observed yourself at the same time, and by wanting to project something onto the other who observes you. Instead focus fully on the other person.

In this way, the exercise trains you in one of the most important, yet all too often most neglected skills for both directors and actors: the ability to pay close attention, to see, and to 'read' the partner. Every detail becomes interesting, everything becomes a message you can receive and react to when you play. Just by watching your partner, you are already watching physical theatre in its most basic form. As you continue to scan down the body, via the legs towards the feet, you should try to arrive at an overall impression of the emotional message (not the outward appearance!) of your partner. Now, participants in one row begin to express their observations about their partners in the form *'You are x'*. So, for instance, *'You are nervous'*. The partner then repeats an affirmative *'Yes, I am nervous'*. The first person then asserts again, *'You are nervous'*, and so forth. The repetition should be fast, without thinking; there must be no pauses in the continuous chain of repetition that ping-pongs between the partners. The participants should simply accept what they may otherwise not accept, and rather focus on what and how their partner says something, and derive their own response – its energy, force, and direction – from their partner's response, instead of just projecting themselves and their own emotions. It is therefore important that both partners engage seriously in the exercise: this is not the place to be funny or creative, and one should not be too laid back and easy, but should properly focus and be attentive to the energetic information received from the partner.

The main objective in this continuous interchange is to reach out and properly connect to and communicate with your partner. The exercise can then be repeated, and partners switched, by moving round to the next chair in the row. Every new partner will offer an entirely new set of information, and you can immediately appreciate the difference between partners, while also becoming ever more adept at quickly scanning and responding to the unspoken information you receive from your different partners. The answer, at some point, will also switch to a *'No, I am not x'*. In this exchange, it is particularly important to concentrate on responding to and engaging with your partner, rather than just insisting on your own position by becoming louder and more aggressive in your insistence or rejection – which is most participants' initial, almost natural response to the rejection scenario before properly engaging in the energetic exchange with their partner as a basic prerequisite for true communication. The 'No' response in particular can thus be used to gain your awareness for false theatrical emotion such as aggression and screaming. Simply encourage your actors to try out and play with various nuances of denial, while also meeting rejection and contradiction with attention and respect. The exercise can be an invaluable tool to boost the actors' confidence in drawing their way of speaking and playing entirely from the emotional information they receive, instead of projecting and reproducing clichés of 'false drama'.

Further variations of the exercise include: noting and articulating the changes in the perceived emotional information; changing acceptance (*'I am x…'*) and denial (*'I am not x…'*); putting chairs aside and standing or moving with the partner in the space. Instead of their analysis of the partner, the participants might later introduce a line from their role in the play that comes to mind, and the partner can respond with one of her or his lines – it does not matter if this 'dialogue' does not make sense at this stage. Instead, the participants should again focus on the energetic exchange rather than on the semantic information only, as they continuously repeat these two lines. As participants become more adept at the exercise, you might also expand the spatial attention span, allowing them to engage with others next to them, and thus to create and keep up a repetition dialogue with several people at the same time. An even more advanced version of the exercise one can use during the rehearsal phase is running lines while at the same time remaining engaged in repetition with your partner, so that the actors' attention and radar of concentration is cued into several planes at the same time.

Meisner's exercises make the actor aware of the additional energetic prompt which each turn in a dialogue offers, in addition to the exchange of semantic information. One's own response, and the process one plays, will therefore be not only the response to what has just been said, but also the reaction and response to the dynamic energy one has received from one's partner. An actor will then never have an issue with their 'motivation': they can simply play their line as a direct energetic answer. To do this, the actor really needs to listen, rather than simply wait for their cue, and it is this skill of being present which the Meisner exercises rehearse. As a result, the scene will develop a 'flow': the dialogue will flow like a billiard ball that bounces off the banks of the table and off the other balls. Each response becomes another impulse that keeps the ball in motion. As with Meisner, answering and thereby continuing this chain, does not mean agreeing; you can cooperate or contradict, and thereby provoke your partner, as it were, playing the ball at them with a challenge to see if they can catch it. When the actors respond to and truly engage with this dynamic complexity of the dramatic situation and the play of their fellow actors, they invariably don't simply reproduce learnt words, rehearsed blocking and patterns of gestures. Instead, they are, at best, catapulted into a situation as if they didn't know beforehand what will happen next, and where everything could go either way. When we are in the middle of a situation in real life, we also never know what will happen next, and how everything is eventually going to end, and whether the problem will be resolved. This openness inspires the actors' play, and not only of the central characters, but of all the actors. Even when they do not have lines, the actors will be fully engaged in the situation, rather than waiting for their next cue; their action, for instance the way they watch or engage with the central action of the scene, will support the scene's central focus. If every actor is fully engaged, a spectator watching the minor character on the side of the stage will, through her or his eyes, still be connected to the central moment of the situation, rather than getting distracted and missing out.

Rehearsals: making and organising experiences

Theatre is all about 'play': it is a play (the playtext) turned into human play (*Spiel*) on stage. True play emerges from genuinely relating to, and behaving in, the dramatic situation of the play(-text), as if it were real life. This is crucial in my theatre because I want to speak to our audience about our lives, our society and its issues and contradictions, through the perspective of the play. To make this really happen, knowing and understanding the dramatic situations and processes is not enough. Otherwise, it would be sufficient simply to talk through a play and then start performing it on stage straight away. I have already mentioned briefly that a major tool for the actor is her or his own experience. The purpose of rehearsing is therefore, for me, not to drill and learn by heart words and patterns of behaviour to be reproduced night after night in each performance. Rather, rehearsals are a unique opportunity to make experiences in a safe and secure space, and then to organise these experiences in accordance with the framework offered by the dramatic situations and relations of the play. The actors will then have these experiences at their disposal in order to assist their art and imagination. Thanks to this foundation, they can invent and sustain scenic solutions which will turn the play into a theatre experience that grabs the audience's attention night after night. They will be able to forget everything again and to invest their play in each and every performance, even after months or years of performing a play, with a quality of ignorance regarding what is going to happen next.

It is for this very reason that in my rehearsals, I do not usually start immediately with the scenic work. After the initial read-through, where we work through the entire play, scene by scene, and take time to discuss questions and to clarify situations, circumstances, and processes, a phase follows that consists of essentially two units: the repetition exercises after Meisner, which I have introduced in the previous section, and storytelling exercises (see Box 6.4, 'Storytelling'). The latter are a distinct methodic stage in my work, which at first seems independent from the play. Of course, as I prepare storytelling tasks for the actors, I use key situations and constellations from the play, and I am quite certain that, now that my actors have become familiar with my storytelling method, they try to figure out which scene from the play we are actually working on. It is, however, crucial not to steer the actors' imagination into a particular direction by already telling them, 'now we are improvising about Act II Scene 2'.

Storytelling is a powerful tool with which to ground dramatic situations, and to help actors further in going beyond 'emoting' and reproducing clichés of behaviour. These exercises are very different from standard 'improvisation' scenes, which are mostly driven (and ruined) by the actors' urge to be clever, funny, and entertaining. Conforming with the founding principles of my method, storytelling does not revolve around the (psychological) character, but instead introduces elements of personal experience from the actors' real life. To give a simple example: while many actors may be tempted to act 'being angry' by shouting at each other, a storytelling task about anger will bring authentic behaviour and observations from real life into the rehearsal room. Asked to show and tell us 'a situation when you were really angry with your best friend', they will use words they felt when they were angry in the way they would really say them, and would do what they did or experienced in such a situation. This is more often than not, rather different from what they would do as actors on stage if asked to play or improvise a scene on being angry. When they are not focusing on 'acting', they will show us authentic behaviour: they behave as they would in real life, informed by their own life experience – something few actors will do when rehearsing a scene because of their concerns with 'acting properly' and all considerations and the stress of performing. These factors obscure this truth, which the storytelling exercises attempt to unlock and

Box 6.4 Storytelling

The task given in the storytelling exercises takes the form of a basic dramatic situation, for instance, 'a situation where you persuade someone to do something forbidden'; 'you try finishing something but you are constantly interrupted'; 'you prevent someone from making a big mistake'; 'you have an idea, but everyone turns against you', and so on. The director carefully prepares the exercise, as all of the tasks directly correspond to situations from the play. The examples here are just some of the storytelling tasks used in rehearsing *An Enemy of the People*, where the first two weeks of the six-week rehearsal period were spent entirely on storytelling. The tasks may also be designed to mirror important character relations of the play, for instance situations between brothers, between a couple, between father and son, or mother and son, etc. One task that is very productive for many plays is 'receiving the news of someone's death', or even 'having witnessed someone dying'. These tasks in particular reveal the starkest contrast with a clichéd approach to portraying such situations on stage.

Once the task has been set, any actor can volunteer to tell her or his story. The main agreement is that theirs must be a true story, a situation as it has presented itself at some point of the storyteller's life. At the start, the actor who tells her or his story selects the number of actors they need to show their story; the storytellers do not usually perform in their own story, and normally do not play themselves. The group gets a few moments in an adjacent room, or in a corner, or backstage, to prepare. This should take no longer than two or three minutes, otherwise the scene will become too 'staged' and will lose its vital sense of spontaneity. In a version of the exercise, the storyteller can function as a narrator of the story they are presenting to the group, while the actors in the scene perform it, but this may not always be necessary or useful, depending on the story. Usually, several responses to the same task will be developed simultaneously and then presented, followed by a discussion. Every participant should thus be involved either as storyteller, or performer, in one of the stories; if in a rehearsal there aren't enough actors, other by-standers, assistants or technicians, will quite happily fill in numbers; these untrained performers often offer the most interesting insights.

When watching and discussing the scenes, particular attention is afforded to physical actions, tones of voices, ways of behaving and speaking, and equally to spatial proxemics between the actors in the storytelling scenes. The spectators of and actors in the storytelling scene are then also asked to identify what is similar to the corresponding situation in the play, and what is different.

The next step then brings the situation of the story closer to the play itself. The director selects one or two of the presented storytelling scenes that responded to the original task in particularly productive ways. At this stage, the randomly chosen performers of the storytelling scene will be replaced by the actors who will play the characters in the corresponding scene from the play. But instead of this scene and its dialogue as scripted in the playtext, the actors are asked to re-play once again the storytelling scene as exactly as possible, copying precisely the behaviour, remembering the ways of speaking, the positions in space, etc. Next, more elements of the actual dramatic situation of the play are introduced, starting with some words and sentences from the actual play's dialogue, while still trying to repeat exactly the initial storytelling scene with all the observed behaviour, actions, and gestures. Finally, the actors are asked to repeat the storytelling scene while now using the original dialogue from the playtext. In this way, the real-life story and the scene from the play become merged.

The stories that participants reveal may be very personal and intimate at times, yet the emphasis of the exercise is never on the exposure and revelation of personal biographical events. The rule that other performers act out the storyteller's private experience adds an initial, crucial layer of distancing; it both encourages the storyteller to share experiences comfortably, while also preventing the exercise from becoming too private or indeed voyeuristic. The overall principle of the storytelling approach is similar to Stanislavsky's 'emotion memory'. Here, though, the storyteller is involved and distanced at the same time, this constituting the main aspect of Brecht's move from 'dramatic' towards 'epic' theatre. His 'Street Scene' provides a blueprint for the aims and purposes of the exercise.[4] As a further variation and development of the exercise, the director may also ask an actor to tell the story of her or his character with the same engagement, the same precision and attention to detail (and the same clarity about situations and circumstances) that was applied when real stories from the actors' own lives were being told. This allows the actor to introduce the storyteller's perspective – of being both involved and outside the story – into their play, and into their ongoing exploration of the dramatic situation, the circumstances, and the processes that make up the foundations of the production.

make available. Within the story, however, actors allow themselves to behave authentically, i.e. as they would in their own life, because the parameters of the situation are those of everyday experience. They show certain physical actions, a tone of voice, certain gestures, without trying to 'act' a particular motivation, to demonstrate a character, or to go through the motions of what a supposedly good actor should do. Storytelling aims at eliminating this curious discrepancy between what we usually see on stage and what we see in our real lives, helping the director, and above all the actors, to get rid of all the fake behaviour that is just theatre and has nothing to do with life.

These short scenes that are performed more or less spontaneously allow us to observe (or, playing the scenes, to directly experience) material on which we can then draw in order to enrich the scenes in the play, and to avoid fake theatricality. The actors directly sense the behaviour, gestures and physical relationships in space, absorb the specific dynamics in space, and equally, they can study the characters' overall *Gestus*. They are thus enabled to experience and explore aspects of dramatic situations in the play through the lens of the real-life situations and experience introduced by the storyteller. Of course, no story will map exactly onto the set of circumstances and processes in the play. Still, without getting bogged down into thinking about motivations or the emotional journey of their character, actors are enabled in the process of personalising the situation of the play by drawing on their own life experience as human beings. In addition, noting the differences between the real-life story and the situation in the play allows the actors to find out more about the situation in the play. The exercise becomes a very practical means for showing and analysing processes and situations, and often reveals the most precise and truthful nature of the situation and the process we want to show. The director can then reactivate this experience at the appropriate moment, when rehearsing the corresponding scene in the play. Whether one is 'in' the storytelling scene, or watching, everyone observes the scene closely, and as such the storytelling tasks also help the actors to practise further their skills of watching and observing their partners, which was one of the main aspects of the Meisner exercise.

Watching these storytelling scenes will also make clear very quickly the fact that life is never without ambiguity, and that every situation involves different layers and levels. Even very simple and improvised storytelling scenes remind us that in a social situation, human beings show a full range of behaviour, on which they draw, which they mix, match and refine in response to the situation and to their partner. Real-life situations thus contain the core of a dramatic situation, which oddly, is often lacking in performances of dramatic plays. Not only is it of little interest to put on stage an actor who is angry and therefore yells in the face of her or his partner; it has, above all, very little to do with our lives. In a storytelling exercise, you are far more likely to encounter a multidimensional process where someone is very angry indeed, but may be inclined to hide the anger and, rather than erupting, they stay calm. And because they are internally so angry, they will probably remain markedly calm and composed. Their focus is not the anger, but the motive that underpins the process they are going through – and just yelling out the anger may not be the best strategy to achieve this goal. Once actors begin to add such multiple resonances to their play, the relationships we see on stage become closer to the complexities we see in real life. I often talk of the first, second and third level. If you only ever show an audience the first level ('anger', in our example), nothing on stage will be of any interest because life rarely has just one level. The main aim of rehearsing a play, which the storytelling exercises prepare in particular, is to seek out how the complexities of all these many levels may manifest themselves. On stage, I want to see an actor physically playing the third level, while with his text and dialogue he acts on the first level. Working on these different levels, framed by the basic concepts of situation and process, thus further adds to the intensification of the situation. Watching a multidimensional, complex, and ambiguous situation on stage resonates with life.

Finally, storytelling also helps to bring the actor and her or his partner with whom she or he is acting and playing, and even the entire ensemble, together in a shared dramatic situation – not by everyone playing and showing the same thing, but precisely by connecting with the situation on all different levels. At the same time, being a storyteller implies, without needing even to think about it, that you are telling a story to an audience, that you attract, intrigue, and engage an audience with the story you tell. This is an attitude that is also crucial for my vision of theatre, which is always a dialogue with the audience who is present. The storytelling exercise helps actors to explore this rapport with the spectators, and to discover a much more engaging way of putting the audience under their spell than showing off with their acting skills – namely, telling a story about all our lives. The exercise thereby activates all aspects of the actors' intelligence, their skills, and their experience in the service of their play, as well as the play(-text), and our production.

Storytelling brings together both personal, real-life experience (the storyteller), and pure, spontaneous play (those who show the story) – the main elements of my theatre. We thus transfer the biographic energy that drives the storytelling (and which we often see and enjoy in forms of devised theatre) into the production of the playtext, without making a play about our private lives, which would be of little interest to the audience, and probably not all that dramatic anyway. I first used storytelling exercises in a systematic way when rehearsing for *An Enemy of the People*. For years, I had found the breaks, the small-talk over coffee or lunch, at times more inspiring than the rehearsals. It was here that I often found the keys that eventually unlocked a dramatic figure for the actor, and I told them, 'Why don't you bring this attitude, when you talked about this personal experience, or the way you behaved just now, into your character and that particular moment in the play?' The storytelling exercises produce these chance moments in a rather more structured and concentrated way. They are yet another attempt to enrich the actors' play by fuelling their imagination and by enabling them to make experiences, so that all the channels of creativity which the actors have at their disposal are stimulated and opened.

Getting started with the scenic work: exploring and energising character relations

Following the initial rehearsal phase which comprises the repetition exercises and storytelling scenes, we begin with the actual scenic work on the play. When properly exploring the scenes of the play now, the actors can therefore draw on the experiences they have made during the exercises. By this point, I expect them to be fully text-ready. We start at the beginning, with the first scene of the play, and then work through the text, scene by scene, with all actors present in the rehearsal room all of the time, or at least most of the time. I refuse and reject a rehearsal schedule where you work on a bit of Act I, then a scene in Act IV, and back in the afternoon to Act II and later the finale in Act V, because this is where the same people are on stage together, and actors come and go all the time as they are called in only when needed. Such a purely pragmatic, supposedly efficient managerial agenda goes against the collaborative nature of making theatre, and forces the director to become the worst kind of dictatorial *auteur* because there is no other way to function within such an uncreative framework that turns theatre-making into work on an industrial production line.

Before we can really commence with our work on the rehearsal stage, though, another crucial preparatory step needs to be taken. It is necessary to clarify two aspects of vital importance, both of which concern the 'birth of the scene' at the very outset of the play: how this situation arises out of the circumstances; and how they engender certain processes that set the play in motion. First, everyone involved therefore must be perfectly clear about the situation at the very beginning of the play (*Ausgangssituation*), and which main circumstance triggers the overall dynamics of the play. If this remains unclear to the director, to the actors, or to both, it will be very hard to get rehearsals off the ground in a productive way. Equally, if this point of departure is not clearly and carefully articulated in the production itself, it certainly won't be clear to the audience, who will only see the play once, and perhaps for the very first time, possibly after a day at work and whilst being distracted by other things going on in their lives. If a production does not manage to take the spectators with it at this crucial moment, it runs the danger of losing them before the play has even started. Similarly, a director will lose the actors' attention if they have no idea what is going on in the play. Often, too big a focus on objectives and super-objectives can obliterate a sense for what has put things in motion in the first place; even worse, it may produce a form of acting that reveals its knowledge of how the play will end. Of course, we all know that Romeo and Juliet, Hamlet, and Richard are going to die at the end – but why bother watching the production if the actor shows this from the first entrance onwards?

The second, related point at this crucial starting point of scenic rehearsals concerns the relations between the dramatic figures. Knowing exactly how one's own character relates to the others can prompt and inspire the actors' play in highly productive ways. As a further pathway towards building a character that is not based on psychology, a clear awareness of one's own character's relation with everyone else provides a fertile ground for the processes that will be developed in the course of the scenic experimentation. Our behaviour towards a partner is always influenced by our relation to that person. I would be ill-advised to talk in exactly the same way to a directing student, and to an actor from the company, and to the executive manager of the theatre. In order to explore further both the initial situation and these important relations between the dramatic figures at the outset of the play, I use a variation of the well-known 'family photo' or 'family portrait' exercise (see Box 6.5, 'Family portrait'). The actors create a *tableau vivant* that offers them a physical, embodied experience of the character relations and of the constellations between the figures in the play. They get a direct sensory, as well as spatial, experience of their own character in its relation to the other figures, feeling whom they are close to, what hierarchies in relation exist to others, and where there are tensions and frictions that may become explosive. It is here that the characters' 'back story' comes in, and that the actors learn about the emotional state of their character at the start of the play, but again in an entirely practical, concrete and non-psychologising way. In *Hamlet* workshops, I use the contrast between two constellations: the portrait before the murder of Hamlet's father, and the portrait after the murder. Hamlet is moved from the very centre of the family portrait to the margin, and his ties to the family as well as his central position in the political network of relations are severed; he becomes a threat to the new power, and Polonius and Ophelia have to distance themselves from him for political reasons. Claudius, on the other hand, moves from an outside position to the very centre of the portrait and of power, where he has to negotiate his new relation with the empty seat of power.

The chief purpose is, once more, to stimulate the actors' play, and to charge them with a sensory, visceral, and corporeal memory of this moment of experiencing their character's relation with other figures. It is interesting to observe that without much intellectual analysis (or intervention from the director), the actors in the portrait can sense physically when things do not yet make sense in their proposed constellation in the tableau. This process of refining and clarifying their sense of their own figure in relation to the others is an important experiential aspect of the exercise, and should therefore not be cut short by the director. It appears that this tableau exercise shares some energetic dynamics with the therapy method of family constellations used in psychotherapy. The very position one occupies within the portrait generates an emotional charge, and thereby allows the actors to draw their characters' emotions from this place within the web of personal and political relations

Box 6.5 'Family portrait'

This exercise gradually builds up a portrait photograph that contains all the characters in the play within a single frame. Starting with the main character, the actors, one by one, position their character in a spatial and gestural relation to both the main character, and to the other characters. Distance and proximity are as important here as where and how someone looks, turns, stands, or sits, whom they touch, or whom they ignore and turn away from. Encourage the actors not to use too many (if any) words at this point, but have them focus fully on their experience of their relations with other characters in spatial and kinaesthetic terms, through their looks, posture, gestures or physical connections with others, for example, touching someone, holding hands, placing a hand on someone else's shoulder, etc. You can use chairs, or even a table, to introduce different spatial levels – standing, sitting on a chair, or on the floor – in order to refine further the opportunities to articulate and to play with these relations through the performers' bodies and their positions in space. The director should try not to interfere nor to rearrange the portrait if it happens to differ from their research and their view. Instead, let the actors explore their ideas and come up with alternative versions, even if they do not seem to agree initially with your own analysis. The director, as well as all the participants, should rather ask questions, thereby stimulating further clarification of the relations expressed in the tableau. Furthermore, any absent characters – those who feature prominently in the play but who are never on stage – should also be integrated into the portrait and find their place within this physical manifestation of the story – there will always be someone in the rehearsal room who will be able to stand in.

You can use a series of such portraits to work through the part of the story that has already happened prior to the start of the play, or to clarify what happens between acts as dramatic time passes, and relationships change. Instead of having to invent a back story, the actors can directly understand and experience the relations and emotions out of which their figures act by feeling them while being in the portrait. Do not forget to document these portraits. You can come back to these tableaus when later during the rehearsal period relations become imprecise, and actors may benefit from a reminder of their visceral experience of these relations in the Family Portrait exercise.

they are put in. None of this is really an 'interpretation' of the play and its characters; it is more of a playful exploration, which allows for a profound experience of the play's dramaturgic constellation – the very thing that you want to communicate to the audience equally instinctively in order to keep them on board even in plays with a large cast.

Box 6.6 Status (adapted from Keith Johnstone)

The improvisation game scenarios that Johnstone introduces are a useful tool for developing the actors' awareness of the importance of status.[5] In a memorable and easily adaptable improvisation scenario, an employee enters a meeting with her or his manager, expecting a pay rise and promotion. Status here reflects social hierarchies and power structures – the classic 'high–low' dichotomy, in this case of employee vs. manager. The nature of the situation – the employee expects a promotion – allows the employee to assume a higher status, as she or he believes that her or his value to the company is so high that the manager needs to put more money on the table in order to reward and retain the employee. The twist in Johnstone's scenario is, however, that the manager, meanwhile, has called the employee in to break the news that she or he is being made redundant. Their encounter will reveal that status also reflects social conventions, since the manager is very likely initially to adopt a lower status, for example of a buddy who is seeing eye-to-eye with the employee, by engaging in small talk, enquiring how the situation is at home, with the wife, the kids, the mortgage, etc. However, this is only in order to find out how best to break the news of the redundancy, and to prepare the ground for the bad news. It is unlikely, at least within standard conventions of social interaction, that the manager will immediately assert his superior power status and ruthlessly break the news directly. Instead, he initially *plays* a different status hierarchy. Ultimately, his 'true' status is of course reasserted. This scene, at the point of realisation, thus involves a complete change of status between the two actors. The employee drops from his high of expecting a promotion to the rock-bottom of being made redundant. One may then continue the improvisation, introducing the employee's knowledge of the manager's secret extra-marital affair with his secretary, which results in another reversal and change of status. Exploring the status relations in a dramatic situation will clarify and refine the dramatic process.

In order to explore and to clarify character relations further, it might also be useful to bring in some of Keith Johnstone's astute reflections on 'status', which reveal another indispensable ingredient of character relations and dramatic situations (see Box 6.6, 'Status'). In addition to a hierarchically superior status afforded to certain characters owing to their social or professional function (the king, the boss, the father ...), Johnstone reminds us that there can be a different hierarchy of status that results from the situation. Social hierarchies will rarely translate directly into the status hierarchies in a concrete situation. One can detect what I call (situational) 'internal status', in addition to the (social) 'external status', and once more, a fascinating three-dimensional web of relations emerges: the hierarchically 'lower' player may be able to assert a higher status, or the superior player might strategically adopt a 'lower' status. The discrepancies between the played situational and the social status can result in dramatic tension. The shifts between the social status, the played status, and the status of the situation (where the employee from the example may, for instance, initially assume a higher status, as he expects a pay rise), and the resulting reversals in status hierarchies, thereby become a most useful addition to the work on character relations.

My obsession with status results from the fact that it feeds into a sociological, rather than psychological, approach to human behaviour. It makes the hierarchical power relations between characters available to the actors, refining their awareness and behaviour, as most of them will have been trained to be present, visible, strong, and self-confident on stage. This is fine for the actor, but often gets in the way of their portrayal of a weak, self-conscious and insecure character. Many situations in life, and many if not most dramatic situations in plays, are defined by the interaction between lower- and higher-status players. I would venture the claim that if an actor takes the character's self-confidence for granted (because she or he simply projects their own self-confidence as an actor onto their character), she or he will not be able to tap into eighty per cent of dramatic characters as these characters have a lower status to someone else, if not everyone else, as this is the very dramatic driver of their behaviour and their dramatic process. Such characters cannot be played without awareness and sensibility for social hierarchies. And above all, a lot of the joy, fun, and entertainment of scenes are derived precisely from the comedic quality gained from a clash of different social statuses. Again, we need only look at Shakespeare's plays. Whether we take the famous porter scene from *Macbeth*, or the two hired murderers facing Clarence in *Richard III* (where the comedy is entirely derived from the confusion of status, as the murderers respect the social status and are polite and apologetic to Clarence about having to kill him), these situations cannot be understood without an awareness that Shakespeare's dramatic world is predicated on a reality defined by a rigorously hierarchical social order. The same lack of awareness makes performances of lower-class characters and servants in naturalistic plays problematic, at least according to my taste and conscience. I have often found it remarkable that this important aspect of status relations remains so underexplored within most actor training schools, which seem to assume a rather stable notion of 'character'. Clarifying status relations has become an important aspect of my directorial work in the rehearsal room, and I find most actors very responsive to the potential that this perspective offers. And again, I have found that the clarification of status relations has been far more productive for actors attempting to unlock their character than discussions of psychological moods, back stories, and motivations. When the actors start playing their characters' status, including all the complexities and contradictions of the various levels which they engender, the sensory quality of a scene will be exponentially augmented.

Combined, the Meisner repetition exercises, the 'family portrait', and the status exercises, lay the ground for telling the relations between dramatic figures in a clear and captivating way that avoids fake emotions and clichés. In conjunction with the design of the stage space as a dynamic 'playing field' rather than an illusionist 'slice of life', these exercises also facilitate a much more dynamic way of blocking scenes. In fact, in my productions there is little, if any, 'blocking', if this means a pre-determined, ornamental arrangement of positions, steps, movement and gestures according to the director's own (good or bad) taste. Actors have a very good sense for appropriate proxemic relations, which the experience of the portraits, the status games, and the other preparatory exercises, appeals to and enhances. Without having constantly to worry about 'being in the right spot' – the place predetermined by the director – actors are invited to rely on their own sense of being in the right place, of sensing when they are too close to their partner, or too far away, in similar ways to our very instinctive sense for proxemics in every-day life, which helps us effortlessly to shift between situations with our boss, with colleagues, strangers, lovers, or with an important politician whom we suddenly find ourselves in a room with. This everyday intuition is also very productively at odds, again, with many theatrical impulses, such as the idea of playing an intense confrontation by going very close to a partner and shouting. The actors will soon discover that distance, just like a low voice, can in fact add far more tension to a situation than being in someone's face and yelling. The director can then make use of what happens naturally as actors begin to invent and explore their own genuinely dramatic spatial arrangements, movements, and behaviour in space in order to tell the play's story and its dramaturgic constellation on a physical, spatial, and very visceral level.

Above all, these rehearsal exercises prepare the ground so that the director can delegate this work to the actors, to their art, to their imagination and their expertise. It will simply become unnecessary to sit down and to think up blocking and scenic configurations in advance. Instead, the most crucial part of the director's work happens in the rehearsal room. Here, the director needs to be fully alert and present in the very moment, as both director and actors try to figure out the depths and details of the situation in a direct scenic encounter with the playtext. It is one of the hardest things to communicate, and very difficult to teach. I see the director's primary role in the rehearsal room as producing and regulating a dynamic flow which eventually makes the actors forget that they are working. We can tie this task and skill directly back to the earlier considerations on communication: as director, you not only communicate with the text, but you also need to be in direct communication with the actors in order to focus and channel their creative energies. If you feel that an actor loses their energetic flow, you need to provide an impulse so that the actor maintains her or his creative orbit. You throw in something that stimulates their response, and that makes them act. It is precisely this urge to react and respond to a prompt that stops an actor thinking all these stupid and entirely unproductive thoughts: Am I good? Do I know my lines? Do I feel the right emotion? Have I got my character? What does my stage partner think? Does the audience like it? Actors cannot be free to play if all these thoughts are going through their heads. As director, you cannot simply tell the actors to forget these thoughts and to stop thinking. The only way to ban these worries from the rehearsal room is to create a flow that is so strong that it puts the actor into a different physical state, like a chemical element that may need a certain energy level to react. An actor is unable to be creative if she or he cannot get into this dynamic flow, or if this flow is interrupted. As a consequence, I can therefore be very demanding because I set a very hard and strict rhythm. If needed, I might literally corner the actors in such an aggressive way that they stop worrying and start playing. I am then very much leading and driving our communication by constantly posing brief questions and by pushing the actors on and making new demands. I create a form of pressure, which in the best sense will be erotic: it will stimulate the actors' creative membrane, which responds both to pressure and, of course, to positive feedback, encouragement and praise. I exploit this, and in this sense I am playing with the actors in rehearsal – in a shared agreement that this is play, and never personal. This means that I can then tell the actors that what they do is awful, or boring, or that it will send the audience to sleep if this is the reality of what I see on the rehearsal stage. Both parties will understand this as part of the need for maintaining the energy levels, for creating that state of creative arousal that stimulates the actors. Personally, I think that a balance of praise and challenge works best; I don't think that a director who builds his approach to the actors exclusively on either harmony or terror, will succeed.

Attending rehearsals attentively: the director's skills in observing and describing

At this point in rehearsals, where actors immerse themselves in the scenic exploration of the play, emotions necessarily become highly charged, since so much energy is invested. The director must therefore demonstrate what I consider to be another very important, and all too often much underestimated quality: the ability not just to stare romantically – to paraphrase Brecht – but to observe accurately. In addition, the director must demonstrate her or his talent of being able to describe precisely, using words which are both exact and to the point, but which are also very sensuous and appeal to the imagination, while not being judgemental. This ability is an all-important prerequisite in order to communicate effectively and productively with actors in the rehearsal room. It will make it easier to arrive at a shared understanding, without being confrontational, of whether what the actors offer and what happens on the rehearsal stage really corresponds to the story we together want to tell with our production. The director should first of all look at and take in what the actors have to offer. There is no need to kill off their artistic instinct by interrupting or interfering too much giving 'directions'. Any aesthetic judgement – whether or not you like what you see – is at this stage not only secondary, but actually entirely irrelevant, and in fact even counterproductive. Much more important is to watch and observe carefully and to articulate and describe clearly what you see and what happens, as well as what you don't see, what does *not* happen, which can be just as important for creating the dramatic situation on stage. When I ask students to describe what we have just rehearsed, many will articulate their personal emotional impression of what they have seen, but they are not yet able to perceive the concrete details of physical actions and dramatic processes that have just taken place right there in front of their eyes, and what narrative message these actions and processes manifestly engender. After more than a decade of training directors, I dare to claim that this is a central touchstone that discerns directorial talent. My key advice to any young director is therefore that they must train and develop their ability to observe. Do this by observing people in real-life situations, by observing their behaviour on a train, in a café, in public, in private situations. Sit down and observe for an hour, and write down in as much detail as possible what people do, and see how their actions reveal their relations, and perhaps even their situations and the conflicts between people you observe. The ability to observe and analyse others in only a fraction of a second is also one of the important abilities playfully explored in the repetition exercise described above.

The director's most important skill, task and quality in the rehearsal room can be illustrated by thinking of rehearsing as a simple three-step process:

1 A scenic process happens on stage. Each movement, each gesture, each step, and every object on stage conveys meaning to the audience.
2 Together, we think about the meaning generated by what we have observed, and for this purpose the director describes every detail very precisely.
3 We then ask, do we actually want what it causes and means? – 'Wanting', again, has nothing to do with an aesthetic decision, nor with an artistic intention, nor with the director's personal taste, but it means: does what we have seen on stage correspond with the story that the ensemble of artists in the room has agreed to tell, and with the focus agreed upon within the given dramatic situation?

The litmus test for any scenic solution invented and tried out in rehearsal is therefore: Does the situation, as it is defined as the sum of the circumstances in the text, correspond to the situation that we see in front of us on the rehearsal stage? Does the physical and scenic action on stage correspond to the situation, and does it correspond to the relations between the characters? Are the relations between the characters and their status clearly articulated, and are they in accordance with the situation and the circumstances in the particular scene of the play? It will be quite normal if you note a (perhaps even considerable) discrepancy between your analysis of the dramatic situation and what happens on the rehearsal stage. If the scene suddenly drifts off in an entirely different direction, always return to a close interrogation of the situation: Why has this happened in the way it just did? Which aspect of the circumstances of the situation has caused the scene to develop in a different way from what you had expected? The ability to describe and verbalise precisely, to express yourself in a sensuous language, is indispensable. Discussing mistakes, things that go wrong, or problems, should then cause neither offence nor intimidation; on the contrary, these discussions become a central reason for rehearsing, as they offer the opportunity to learn together by working together on the clarity and precision of the scene, and on everyone's understanding of the dramatic situation in the text.

Using the dramatic situation as the common reference point to communicate avoids the need to become personal and to suggest to an actor that they have done something wrong or inappropriate. Such personal blame is the ultimate killer of any creative energy in the room, as actors will then only be concerned with 'doing it right', and not with being in, and responding to, the situation. This in no way means that a director should not offer critique. On the contrary, actors are intelligent enough to know perfectly well when something is really awful. I have more than once observed that young, emerging directors lose the respect of actors because they only give positive feedback. In this case, actors don't feel that they're being taken seriously. It seems at first glance bizarre that it is the famously quick-tempered and harsh directors – in German theatre we may think of Frank Castorf or the late Peter Zadek – who have or had the most loyal and dedicated ensemble of actors working with them. In my experience, actors appreciate direct, honest feedback because it shows the director's genuine interest in the actors, and her or his appreciation of their creative ability and their artistic intelligence. Even while it may hurt for a moment, brutal but accurate honesty pushes actors on and stimulates them far more than fake harmony, whereby the emphasis here should be, in particular in the case of young directors working with seasoned actors, placed on the accuracy and precision of the analysis and feedback, not on its brutality!

And if you find yourself stuck in doubt or disagreement – the answer will always be in the playtext in front of you. It is the best mediator. Instead of arguing about points of view, go back to the text together, and at some point the answer will appear clearly in front of your eyes, right there on the page. It is so easy to begin theorising in the rehearsal room, guessing and fantasising about what Shakespeare or Ibsen may have wanted – but you only find the real answer by reading, analysing the dramatic situation, and on this basis, deciding what story you, as a team of artists, want to tell. Of course you may agree on telling the dramatic situation in a different way, with a different twist or focus of attention. My *Hamlet* is a clear example for this: we agreed to focus on Hamlet as a spoilt brat who goes off the rails, messes with everyone at court, and walks all over everyone else. Meanwhile, we decided to relegate to the background the aspect of the situation which involves him being afraid that his knowledge of his father's murder will be discovered. Both aspects – ridiculing Claudius, and fearing him – are part of the situation, for instance in the famous encounter between Claudius and Hamlet after Hamlet kills Polonius ('he is at supper – not where he eats but where he is eaten', *Hamlet* 4.3). It is impossible to pin down, once and for all, *the* one, definitive dramatic situation of any particular scene: you can only ever approach it anew with each new production of a play. As we said at the outset, the situation for Hamlet will be very different if he is confronted, as in the examples from Jan Kott's famous chapter, with 'real existing socialism' and its stagnation and aberrations, or with the hedonistic, pre-financial crash pleasure society of the early twenty-first century that was the background for our production.

Plasticity and chains of action: building up the scenic arrangement

The exploration of the circumstances, processes, and relations provides an impetus for the actors' play. As you begin to arrange the scene based on the material they offer, the dialogue will provide the basic dramatic action that takes place on stage. With their words, the characters position themselves in the world and in relation to the world, and intervene in this world. The actors' clarity about the dramatic situations and processes enables them to make the crucial move from expressing emotions or psychological motivation to putting forward a clearly articulated thought where the words themselves are the action. But, what to do with their bodies? Precisely because speech is action, the actor does not need to illustrate physically what she or he has already expressed in words. Merely redoubling the text does not make for exciting theatre. And moreover, it shows that you do not trust the text, as you assume that you need to translate and amplify it through other means in order to make it understood. This is where one of the foundational building blocks of my method comes in: the psychophysical chain of actions (see Box 6.7). I already explored this important principle of scenic composition, where Stanislavsky meets Meyerhold (the latter famously spoke of a 'movement score'), in early productions during my studies, and at the Baracke. For a long time, I taught a class on psychophysical actions at the Ernst-Busch-Theatre Academy. The most elaborated realisation of this principle can probably be seen in my production of Lars Norén's *Demons* (2010).

Box 6.7 The psychophysical chain of actions (after Stanislavsky and Meyerhold)

The psychophysical chain of actions expresses the inner, psychological life of a character through a physical action. In a classic exercise, Stanislavsky had his students act out the content of a letter their character receives, purely through their physical play. If, for example, the character receives a letter containing the message that their lover has died, she or he might suddenly drop the cup of tea they have been holding in their hand. As the cup drops to the floor, this action also introduces a rhythmical structure to the scene; the cup breaks into a thousand pieces, and this strong rhythmical accent communicates to the spectators in a simple, yet most sensuous and visceral way the content of the letter. The concrete psychophysical action thus takes any pressure off the actor that she or he may feel about responding 'properly' and having to authenticate the content of the letter with acted emotions.

Based on this first element of the movement score, the director can then work with the actor towards developing a proper 'chain of psychophysical actions'. The next process they may want to tell could be that, after the initial news, the dropping of the cup has destabilised the character's body even further. She or he begins to stagger, and as the letter almost literally pulls the rug from under their feet, the character loses their physical balance entirely. From a technical point of view, such play with a shifting physical centre of gravity in the body is a basic tenet of Meyerholdian biomechanics. We may therefore introduce the next action: the character who loses their balance tries to hold on to the table, attempting not to fall to the floor, but as a result pulls the tablecloth off the table. All the china and other objects on the table fall to the floor, giving another sharp rhythmic accent to the scene. To build the chain up further, we may now introduce an accelerating, faster rhythm. Having fallen to the floor, the character finds her- or himself in a state of confusion, recomposes her- or himself briefly, and then attempts very quickly to pick up everything that has fallen down, and to rearrange it all on the table, as if to do undo the mishap. Finally, this brief imagined chain of actions might conclude, after the earlier intense rhythmic moments, with the character sitting down, trying to take a breath, to calm down, and to regain their senses.

Rather than reiterating the spoken word, the psychophysical chain of action expresses the dramatic process physically by developing a series of physical actions that tell the spectators something more about the relations of this dramatic figure, about her or his attitude (*Haltung*) and emotional state, and not least about the dramatic situation itself. In other words, the psychophysical chain of action tells the spectator about the other eighty per cent of the play we considered at the very beginning of this chapter. The idea of expressing a character's inner state through outer, physical action emerged, of course, in the era of stage naturalism. On Stanislavsky's stage, there were sufficient props and objects that the actors were able to use and play with. Over time, this approach to acting – of playing with objects, with the space, and with movement in space – has been lost almost entirely. It has been challenged as much by the advent of performance art and postdramatic theatre, as by blunt and cliché-ridden soap opera naturalism. When, in the 1980s, Peter Stein used Stanislavsky's director's notes for his own Chekhov productions, he again revived some of this old-fashioned art of acting. And there are no reasons why the basic principles of psychophysical acting could not be productively applied nowadays to different, more advanced and even more abstract stage aesthetics, too. Meyerhold's biomechanical experiments, and the 'movement scores' in his famous productions, gave an early indication of the potential of this approach beyond outright naturalism. Regardless of the stage aesthetic, psychophysical actions are an approach that helps actors to tune into the scenic rhythm, instead of just waiting for their cue and firing off their line as soon as they hear their cue, without actually listening and perhaps taking the time to pause and respond. At the same time, the chain of actions keeps the actor engaged with concrete, playable actions, rather than the intangible expression of emotion that other approaches prioritise.

As we use psychophysical chains of action as a first step towards the arrangement of a scene, we also need to find out how to organise these very actions within the available stage space, while, in most scenes, also coordinating the actions of several actors. Another one of Meyerhold's concepts, which he described with the term 'plasticity', is very useful in this respect. Meyerhold conceived of 'plasticity' far more as an energetic, than a purely visual effect. Plasticity means arranging the scenic space so that a multidimensional, dynamic forcefield of dramatic energies emerges. This starts with simply using the full available potential of the stage; above all, using its full depth, and not just the width. Actors tend quite happily to line up on a single parallel line facing the auditorium. This is the opposite of theatral plasticity, and a good sign that they are not in the situation, but concerned with being seen and being on stage. The classic masters of visual art may offer us some instructive insights into basic laws of 'plastic' scenic composition; after all, the term *mise en scène* originated in the context of painting, to describe the composition of figures on a canvas. Whereas actors tend to love to work with parallel lines, painters work with triangles. The triangle is one of the most stable universal forms, and it generates a peculiar dynamic force. Looking at iconic paintings, for instance Géricault's *Raft of the Medusa* or Delacroix' *Marianne*, you can see a spatial peak emerging from the pictorial composition, facing a wide side or line that emphasises the effect. The peak of the triangular form thus highlights a certain point, and the contrast to the straight line not only adds dimensionality, but also creates tension for the observer, purely via the means of spatial arrangement. Furthermore, the triangle offers a clear and concentrated focal point. It might be at the peak of the triangle, or at its centre, but one can sense a point towards which the energetic pull of the composition gravitates. Correspondingly, in every scene, at every moment of the production, there should be a clear focus of energy within the space, a centre which markedly concentrates the scenic energy. The 'milieu' around this centre may then reinforce the plasticity by channelling and supporting these energetic lines, for instance through a certain arrangement of looks and gazes, or through proximity and distance. It may thereby also clarify and intensify central qualities of the situations and relations on stage, again by energetic means, and not just by pictorial illustration and representation.

Consequently, when considering the production's overall *mise en scène* and all its component elements, it is not so much painting at all, but music which for me offers the richest analogies for effectively composing scenic arrangements on stage. In short, the best guideline for the theatre director seems to me: Try to make music with the processes and situations that the play offers. I would even suggest that the main task of the director can best be described as composing and orchestrating a rhythmic sequence of sounds, and by that I do not only mean the sounds that result from the spoken word and dialogues of the text. On the contrary, movement, physical action, and scenic processes all contribute to the scenic sound that the audience perceives. A rhythm is a structure in time; the complete opposite to images. For me, notwithstanding some lessons one can indeed learn from analysing the composition of paintings, theatre is not the art of images. It follows very different rules. Theatre is the art of processes, of rhythms, and therefore, the art of organising time. As a theatre director, I do not need to invent and stage images; they will emerge by themselves, as a result of orchestrating the rhythm of the dramatic situations and their flow. I do not think of the *mise en scène* in terms of a visual arrangement, thus as the 'illustration' of the playtext, but, rather, as a well-orchestrated composition in time, where each instrument – each element of the stage and each medium of theatre – contributes with its own sound to the overall multi-dimensional melody of the play.

As in a musical composition, the different instruments in the orchestra won't all play the same one note; there will be contrasts, echoes, reflections, mirrorings and oppositions. Only if these exist, the notes on the sheet will become sounds, and the sounds will form a melody. Likewise, only the corresponding multi-dimensional quality of the scenic arrangement is going to turn a theatre production into an interesting event and into an at best truly captivating experience for the audience. The principles at the director's disposal correspond in many respects to what a composer has at hand. As with a musical composition, in order to intensify the scenic energy or sharpen the rhythm, one may accelerate the rhythm, and build up the noise. Yet, it might create an even more intense and interesting experience for the audience if one reverses one of the elements: one could, for instance, start with a very loud environment, and reduce the noise to total silence at the very point of maximum energy. The musical principle of counterpoint also works on stage. The opening scene of my production of *Richard III* gives a clear example. The performance starts with a loud party celebrating the glorious post-war summer. The party continues in the background, as Richard begins his initial monologue, 'Now the winter of our discontent ...', where he goes on to describe the 'merry moments' in the lady's chambers and the other aspects of the new peacetime that he deplores. Shakespeare moves the monologue towards a climax: Richard's 'But I that am not shaped for sportive tricks', and the subsequent repetition of this opposition 'but I', with which he sets himself apart from the others, as an outsider. In my production, the scene is arranged so that as the monologue begins, the loud party music decreases and gradually reverts to a single tone. From the moment that Richard utters 'but I', there is silence.

The art of organising time: composing the scenic rhythm

Expanding the musical metaphors, one might compare the best rehearsals with a huge jam session. Everyone involved in the production – actors, and also musicians, set and costume designers, dramaturgs, video artists – should be invited to join in and play along, thus being given the opportunity veritably to respond and contribute by communicating with what they see and experience in the way outlined earlier. In my directorial work, I try not to determine the contribution of the other members of the artistic team, for instance, by commissioning music from the composer that would then be used as a soundtrack in the production. If the physical and scenic dynamics of theatre work resemble a musical composition, as is my aspiration, a composer will rather be delighted to follow the rehearsals and become a part of it, responding to the emerging rhythmic structure of the production with her or his ideas. Working together, in this way, through the whole of the playtext, scene by scene, with the entire creative and technical team, the focus of attention will shift more and more to the composition of the theatre event at large, as it begins to take shape on stage before our eyes.

There is not much to say about the aspect of transitions between the individual scenes you have developed. In brief, don't waste any time on transitions! My advice could not be any simpler and more to the point: try to start the next scene as soon as possible. A transition is best when the following scene organically emerges from the preceding one, instead of a scene finishing, having a scene change, and then starting the next scene. In an ideal production, as I conceive it, you would not need to break the rhythmic flow through scene changes. As far as I can judge myself, I managed to achieve this rather well in *Measure for Measure*, and also in some sections of *Hamlet*, where we arranged the initial scenes, which in the playtext are set in different places, all around a long table. Scene changes and scene transitions are, however, only a minor challenge in the director's work on the scenic composition. As I have indicated, a theatre production is, at its core, not the intellectual interpretation of a play, but an unfolding scenic rhythm. The flow and groove, the melody of the performance, and equally the dissonances and disharmonies you create and work with, are the means with which the story you want to tell with your production is carried and conveyed. Yet, I find that the organisation of time through rhythm remains one of the most underexplored and least understood aspects of the art of directing.[6] All too often, I observe students and fellow directors who only attend to this important element in the very last phase of rehearsals, where they then instruct their actors, 'Play faster!', 'Make it more dense!', or 'Tighten this scene up!', etc. They underestimate the crucial role of the scenic rhythm as an integral part of theatre-making, and of composing the theatre event.

As the previous section suggested, the psychophysical chain of action underpins the actors' play with a certain rhythmic structure. This organic scenic rhythm can then become the basis for composing, as the next step, an overall rhythmic flow for the entire production. On the most basic level, the director's task of orchestrating the scenic sound begins with making sure that the main melody can be heard clearly. When staging a play, this means that the audience must be able to follow the plot, and does not miss major plot-points. The psychophysical example of the letter that causes the cup to be dropped introduces another useful idea in relation to the rhythmic structure, which productively complements the line of physical action: this is the notion of the 'montage of attractions', as proposed by Soviet film and theatre director Sergei Eisenstein.[7] Like his contemporary Meyerhold, he drew much inspiration from popular entertainment. For Eisenstein, theatre and film should consist of an aligned series of intense moments, which he called 'attractions', as in a circus performance. The latter offers a whole variety of attractions, so that one minute, the spectator might be mesmerised by the danger of the animal tamer who puts his head into the lion's mouth – will the lion bite his head off? Is the circus artist going to be injured? The next moment, the audience holds their breath when watching the aerial acrobats – are they going to manage to catch each other mid-air? Will they fall from the trapeze?

Eisenstein's ideal cinema and theatre performances would likewise keep the audience on the very edge of their seats, as they follow the attractions presented by the actors with a sense of awe, anxiety, and excitement. The theatre director can apply Eisenstein's principle literally by introducing acrobatics, spectacular stunts or fight scenes into the production. Yet, one may also apply the idea of the sharpened, intensified situation and exploit affective 'attractions' in order rhythmically to structure the scenic composition: by constructing a montage of similar peaks and accents. In the earlier example of the letter scene, the shattering of the tea cup, the actor's staggering and tripping, the table-cloth being pulled down ... each of these physical actions also produces the effect of an affective attraction in the spectators. Or, to give an example from the *Richard III* production, in the Lady Anne scene, Richard extends his verbal seduction of Anne (where mentioning the bedchamber he performed a rhetoric stunt, an attraction scripted in Shakespeare's text) not only by offering her his sword, but in our production, he gets undressed and then puts the naked blade of the sword onto his naked body. The next moment, he kisses Lady Anne over her father-in-law's coffin. These are some small examples of 'attractions' in the sense Eisenstein had in mind. From a dramaturgical point of view, one may certainly suggest that Richard's bold, outrageous actions contribute to the 'attraction' with which he manages to seduce Anne.

The wave of scenic action: rhythm is variety

It is, however, very important to get the idea of attractions right. Eisenstein's principle does not suggest performing the entire play at maximum volume. Choreographer William Forsythe once emphasised, most aptly, that 'rhythm is variety'. Very often, and particularly in Anglo-American theatre, one is confronted with the misconception that theatre has got to be fast. So everything is performed at high speed, with no time for anyone to catch their breath. Yet, the attraction of a sequence of processes played relentlessly at a break-neck pace and at peak-level, very much like a piece of music that is continuously fast-paced without any variation in tempo, will eventually wear off, and it will become tedious, if not unbearable for the spectator. Similarly, a persistently slow rhythm, anything but unusual in the long-winded variations of European theatre, will also at some point lose its attraction. Only a varied rhythmic pattern can maintain the audience's engagement and, likewise, remain sustainable for the performers. However, Forsythe's principle is easier said than done, and is actually very difficult to put into practice in theatre-making. It is very hard to strike the right balance between fast-paced and slower scenic moments, and one can only learn from practical experience, and from trial and inevitable error.

There is, however, a very useful guiding principle that I introduce to my students in workshops. In Japanese Noh theatre, the thirteenth-century Master Zeami developed the notion of 'jo-ha-kyu' (see Box 6.8). This refers to the universal principle of a slow beginning (jo) and the subsequent rise in energy towards a climax (ha), at which point the energy is released and dissipates (kyu), so that the process of 'jo-ha-kyu' can begin again.[8] It becomes really interesting as the idea goes even further, suggesting that each such wave of 'jo-ha-kyu' is itself built up from smaller waves, and each of these waves can again be broken down into even smaller waves, and so on. A similar idea of basic 'natural', reiterative patterns is proven in contemporary physics by fractal theory. One can therefore propose that such a wave-like rise and fall of energies is also the most natural rhythm for a theatre production. From a beginning, you head towards a peak, and then take the foot off the pedal again. This principle can be applied to the overall structure of the play or production, where it meets the classic model of a dramatic play, with its

Box 6.8 Jo-Ha-Kyu (after Yoshi Oida and Lorna Marshall)

The Noh-principle of 'jo-ha-kyu' can be introduced by means of a simple exercise. All participants are asked to sit in a circle, facing outwards, their backs to the centre of the circle. Everyone closes their eyes. The instruction is to clap as soon as you hear a noise in the room. In the exercise, as the others' clapping also becomes a noise to which to respond, a similar rhythmic pattern will develop each time you do this exercise: out of silence (yo), the clapping builds up towards a certain form of order and organisation (ha), and when energy and rhythmicalisation are at their most intensive, the order breaks down into a frenetic explosion, after which silence resumes (kyu). Then, the cycle begins to build up again. This wave-like principle of a slow beginning, followed by intensification and release, underpins many phenomena in our world: the seasons, life, sex, human cultures and civilisations ... They all follow this universal pattern. It therefore offers a useful guide for structuring a theatre production, too.

beginning, climax, and the ensuing deceleration towards the final catastrophe. A production needs some form of 'jo': if you skip the beginning (and perhaps even the build-up moment of the 'ha'), and instead directly start at the peak, things can only go downhill from there. Such a break from the expected pattern may of course create an intense effect, but the execution of any deviation needs to be particularly carefully mastered. All too often, I observe directing students investing incredible energy in the opening moments of a production, which then go up in a puff, with a big bang, and after that their production never manages to pick up the same force again.

Starting from this macro-level in the production, one can then pursue the 'wave'-principle of scenic energy in each scene. Again, it may be organised in accordance with this principle of concentration and intensification, aiming towards a climax that also serves as the focal point towards which the scene gravitates (such as Richard's 'but I ...', to return to the earlier example). One can even continue to look for this rhythmic movement on the micro-levels of a scene: each process, from one turning point to the next, can equally be thought of as such an energetic wave, and similarly each sentence, every single breath: they all rise to a climax and then decrease in intensity and stress, before building up to the next peak again. I find this idea very useful in order to put the 'montage of attractions' into practice. A clear awareness of the difference between intensification and release, and of the dynamic interplay between acceleration and pause, is an important skill that a director can glean from compositional principles in music. A directly connected matter is the question of the pause. One does not create a rhythmic structure simply by inserting frequent pauses; this would only create an interrupted rhythm, fragmenting the line of action, and producing a stuttering dynamic. As deliberate effects, they might be used to create some form of rhythmic pattern, but more often than not it is precisely not the effect that had been intended. Applying the idea of the 'jo-ha-kyu'-wave once again, a pause can only gain its rhythmic quality as 'kyu'. In other words, it needs to come at the right moment. It needs to be earned, as I once heard an English dialogue coach put it ('earn a pause'). The Russian notion of the 'good pause', the *horoshaya pauza*, also expresses this idea clearly. Only if the rhythm builds up and coagulates at the point of the pause, is it perceived as a proper, 'good pause' (similar to the release point of the 'kyu'). The pause gains its energetic momentum as a result of the intensified acceleration that preceded it, and simultaneously holds the potential for any action in the next build-up of the wave. For the spectator, this creates an atmosphere of suspense, thereby also affording to the pause the quality of an Eisensteinian 'attraction'.

Finally, what has become my standard framing structure for a production, can also be related to the 'jo-ha-kyu' principle. In most of my productions, there is an overture of sorts, before the first line of the text is spoken and the play begins. The idea of a transitory moment that carefully prepares the ground and gradually leads in to the all-important dramatic situation at the outset of the play, is again Meyerhold's. He often used proper preludes; little pieces that opened the evening's performance before the 'actual' play. The British director Simon McBurney applies the same principle in many of his shows, too. Such preludes can break the ice and get the initial embarrassment out of the way, creating a positive atmosphere in the space. They accumulate an affective credit, as it were, which then benefits the 'actual' play. My own thinking in this respect is rather pragmatic: people will have just about made it to the theatre in time, after having quickly rushed home from work to get changed. They come in from the crowded underground train where there was a delay, or they have had to drive around looking for a parking space. No doubt that when the performance begins, not a single member of the audience will be sitting in the auditorium at ease, with an open mind, ready to engage with what is coming up. For me, the prelude therefore has an almost meditative purpose, of calming everyone down, allowing everyone's senses to settle, enabling them to do nothing for a few moments, while I am already showing a few first impressions before the play's action gradually sets in motion. Having said that – in *Hamlet*, the long funeral sequence, with video projections, loud music, slapstick, and the rain hose, opens up many aspects of the play, more like a Shakespearean prologue that outlines what is going to happen. Equally, there may then also be an 'epilogue', a time in which the last line of the text may continue to resonate, to be listened to, for some more moments before the final blackout. In *Hedda Gabler*, the revolving stage keeps turning and turning, Hedda who has just shot herself lying on it, while Tesman on the other side of the wall keeps sorting his notes. Or in *Richard III*, Richard's corpse is hanging from the ceiling like a slaughtered animal in an abbattoir. But this principle is not a strict rule, and depends on the play. Sometimes there is a sudden black-out immediately after the final word, as in *Measure for Measure* or in *Hamlet*, which ends with, 'the rest is silence'.

'The rest is ...': some final words of advice

The tools for the director that we have explored here are principles, ideas and observations which do not focus on being creative, but on being communicative. Directing – and equally, acting – is not in the first instance about *producing*, but about *responding* and being open and attentive to the impulses generated by the material (*Stoff*) as well as by the actors, the space, the scenic rhythm, and the ideas of all the artists assembled in the room. Ingenuity cannot be taught, but communication is something a director can work on, practise and develop further. A related indispensable skill and principal responsibility of the director is therefore to create an atmosphere of openness, of discovery, and of safety and trust, where things can happen that we could never have imagined or conceived of in advance. Being prepared to venture into the unknown, to discover the other – the other person, but also 'otherness', everything you have not been or done before – is important to me, and for my work. The starting questions – about the circumstances defining the situation, the main circumstance prompting the action, and about dramatic processes, character relations and their shifts and changes – offer a shared point of departure for this journey. They do not, however, dictate the exact direction a scene must take. With these exploratory questions, you won't ever fall into the trap of thinking that somewhere out there, there's the one 'right way' of doing a scene, but that you simply can't find it. This big misunderstanding can dry up any creative energy.

Instead, keep going back to these fundamental questions, and keep observing, attentively, and critically, the scenic solutions you have found together. Time and again, directors – students with less stage experience are not at all alone here – get corrupted by falling for the moment and for the quick effect. Perhaps because they get so carried away by the rehearsal process, or because they are stressed by a tight production schedule and/or budget, directors seem to pass a certain point in rehearsals after which they all of a sudden lose any ability to perceive the discrepancy between what they *wish* to see in front of them on the rehearsal stage, and what *really happens* on stage. I always give my students the advice to look at the processes and scenes they are staging as if they were watching a production by a director they actively dislike, in order to maintain a critical perception of what is happening on stage, without kidding themselves and finding everything they direct simply amazing, and entirely captivating, even if it is anything but. So, never stop asking whether you really got the situation right, and continue to listen very carefully to the scenic rhythm of your production, as it emerges. If you realise that something you have found and rehearsed no longer works, and maybe never did, try something else. One of the biggest traps of directing is to stick with the initial idea and merely continue tinkering with small details and marginal minutiae of this first draft, even long after it has dawned on you that the entire draft is in fact skewed. The scene won't get better if you continue to tread down the same path, just adding some more or less pretentious fads here and there, or just tweaking single gestures or the emphasis of a word. If you have tried one path and it does not work, you must try something else. This may even mean going back to the drawing board after days, maybe even weeks, of labouring on this first draft. But have the courage to approach the scene in an entirely new way and to look, together with your actors and your team, for something else, for something better. You will find that, at least in the long term, you won't create conflicts by getting rid of something that does not work, but on the contrary, you will lose the actors' trust if you obsessively continue running down the wrong track and coming up against a brick wall for the hundredth time. Getting stuck is the real problem. Always dare and have the courage to play, and play on.

To conclude, I should stress that all the techniques and methods outlined in this chapter won't come to fruition without the one core quality of a director: your human, social and personal skills. I fully realise that I sometimes completely shoot myself in the foot because of my own deficits in exactly this area. In fact, you might compensate for shortfalls in your directorial technique and method simply by interacting positively with everyone in the team, and by behaving in an open, caring, and empathic way. One of the director's most important qualities might be simply showing magnanimity and being humble in her or his dealings with those who go out there on stage and who open up their innermost soul to the public.

6.2 A POSTSCRIPT ON DIRECTING POSTDRAMATIC THEATRE. AND SHAKESPEARE

The beauty of Shakespeare's language is that the dramatic figures still speak to each other; it is a 'texture' in the truest sense of the word. The dialogue of Richard with Lady Anne is a perfect example: they take a word the other character has just said, turn it around and give it a different sense. Then, the first one takes up the same word and its new meaning, and retorts with yet another meaning. Shakespeare's characters still believe in language. Yet, in the course of the twentieth century, somewhere between Naturalism and Beckett (and in Germany much reinforced by the manipulation of speech by the Nazi propaganda machinery), we have lost language as an uncorrupted, direct and efficacious means of communication. In drama, the power of language took its first blow in bourgeois drama. Its characters began communicating on two levels, displaying the communicative behaviour of the 'double bind': I say one thing, but I mean something else. *What's wrong with you? – Nothing*. This often gets mixed up with the idea of 'character psychology' or of 'subtext'. In the age of Shakespeare, every man carried a weapon; if words were not enough, they drew their daggers. In Ibsen's pacified bourgeois living rooms, different and more nuanced mechanisms of manipulating and dominating the other had to be developed; women, in particular, who were as intelligent and rational as men but did not get their fair share, could not simply draw a sword and duel with Torvald Helmer. Instead, language that works as camouflage began to spread terror in this world and destroy it. In this use of language, there is no congruency between what is said and what is meant. Of course, some sub-genres of commercial Hollywood and television drama, as well as some off-the-peg well-made playwriting, still claim the authenticity, transparency and immediate impact of language. In properly contemporary dramatic literature, however, we have long lost this belief.

Sarah Kane, Elfriede Jelinek, Martin Crimp, Herbert Achternbusch – this is the 'state of the art' in playwriting, which for some decades now has presented a very different challenge to the director. You cannot approach their texts solely through the dramatic situation, and you cannot therefore apply my method straight away. But even less is character psychology a viable approach to these plays. Today, one can no longer return behind the postdramatic horizon. But neither is one able to take it further. The postdramatic work of these authors has as much a place in contemporary theatre as my own theatre; it is absolutely no dogma that you can only direct in the situational and dramatic way. One can, in fact, learn a lot for one's encounter with postdramatic texts by attending closer to some not too dissimilar problems in Shakespeare. If you take a look at the first act of *Richard III*, the contemporary director who applies very strictly the approach via the 'dramatic situation' is presented with at least two massive challenges: first, there is Richard's monologue, and shortly after Lady Anne's monologue before Richard enters in I.2. In both cases, it will not suffice to simply clarify the dramatic situation, as suggested in the previous chapter. Instead, one must open up the attention from the dramatic situation alone to the wider theatrical situation: the presence of the spectators is indeed a constituting factor of Shakespeare's theatre. Unless you want to portray Richard as a weird fellow who walks through the streets talking loudly to himself, the occasion for Richard to begin his monologue – *'Now is the winter of our discontent ...'* – and therefore the main circumstance that defines his situation is the very fact that there is an audience. He turns to us, the spectators, and lets us in on his secret play. From the very beginning, he takes the spectators by the hand and leads them through the play, inviting them to see it through his eyes and share his reactions – *'was ever woman in this humour woo'd? ...'*

One cannot direct Shakespeare without understanding that the spectators' presence is part and parcel of the character's situation. This, of course, is inconceivable in an intimate bourgeois realist play. We thereby discover an important link between Elizabethan theatre and postdramatic theatre. Put somewhat polemically: the famous 'fourth wall', and everything that happened in dramatic literature between Shakespeare and Beckett or Kane has only been an aberration of bourgeois theatre. As I understand the central tenet of Hans-Thies Lehmann's analysis of postdramatic theatre, the dominant dramatic situation is replaced by the dominance of the performance situation. It becomes my main circumstance that I am a performer, sharing a space with an audience. The circle from Shakespeare to postdramatic theatre is closed. Richard speaks as a performer who breaks through the dramatic 'as if'-situation of the play, and instead he situates himself within the theatrical situation. He becomes a narrator who invites the audience to become his accomplice. What happens is energised by the theatrical, performative process, and no longer primarily by the dramatic process.

In addition, there is a further similarity between Elizabethan and postdramatic theatre: the principles of the 'mash-up' and the 'remix'. The principal form of narrating is not the linear, closed series of events. Instead, the same central theme is discussed on several levels of the plot. For the same purpose, today's postdramatic theatre often draws on multiple layers of media, which are used to circumnavigate and debate a certain topic from different perspectives. Paradigmatically, Falk Richter's plays, which he has been producing at the Schaubühne for many years, combine physical movement, dance, video, text, dialogue, acting and music. All these media are used and combined on equal terms, in order to approach the topic and give shape to the material. In this very sense, Shakespeare is a postdramatic mash-up artist, too. He borrows from the style of high poetry, while equally presenting the 'low', popular tone of the clowns, the mechanics, the porter, and other 'low folk' who make an entrance in his plays. Here, he gives a voice to the people, not in rhymed verse, but in a structured 'street language'. He further has sword fights and similar popular acrobatic-artistic entertainment to offer, and he freely mixes genres and traditions: this is outright collage. The most vital lesson of Shakespeare – and there are very few (if any) other examples that have found their way into our Western dramatic canon – is not to be afraid of popular culture for discussing a topic in a nevertheless very serious way. There have been very few other playwrights and theatre-makers who managed to move as effortlessly between high art and popular entertainment.

All these are important lessons Shakespeare holds in stock for the director dealing with postdramatic theatre – from René Pollesch, the Sarah Kane of *Crave* and *4.48 Psychosis*, to Bavarian playwright Herbert Achternbusch and Belgian theatre-maker Alain Platel, whose work has been my own most revealing introduction into the opportunities that the so-called postdramatic form can offer. One might also think of Heiner Müller's affinity to Shakespeare. Directing the later works of Sarah Kane, whom I regard as a major contemporary playwright in her too short career, and equally

Achternbusch's *Susn*, written already in the 1970s, yet still a postdramatic play to its bones, I made the experience that our toolkit of dramatic situations, circumstances, and processes, as explained in the earlier chapter, will still prove useful for the director. I would even dare to say that one is in fact able to break down their plays in much the same way, as long as one bears in mind that postdramatic writing offers a far more complex, fragmented, and mosaic-like picture. At its heart, Kane's *Crave* is a rather conventional play about abuse, written from the perspective of the daughter, the victim of the abuse, who is situated within a dramatic cosmos of father, mother and brother. But then, Sarah Kane took a big stone and threw it right at this 'well made play'; it broke up into a thousand pieces. She then took the shards and pieces and re-arranged them according to the musical principle of the fugue, with its repeated motifs. Therefore, a director won't be on the entirely wrong track if he or she reads and locates every single sentence of the play as reflecting the fundamental dramatic situation of an abused child – starting from the very first sentence, 'You're dead to me', which introduces the double meaning of 'dad' and 'dead'. For me, Kane's playtext is like a field recording. For many years, someone recorded the conversations that took place within the dysfunctional family's apartment. Each sentence is absolutely realistic, located in a situation, but then the 'field recorder' cut them out and produced a postdramatic collage.

In order to put this material on stage, I do not consider it an effective directorial approach to put Kane's abstract musical score on stage by deliberately devising the *mise en scène* as similarly abstract composition. The director will, of course, need to analyse and understand the abstract compositional principles and strategies of postdramatic texts, but this is not what is put on stage. Instead, one has to find the deeper, often brutal narration that is conveyed by these formal principles. Let us consider the analogy to music more fully, as I think it helps clarifying the point. At least for me, even abstract music tells a story: The semiquaver notes and triplets are not the story, but they narrate something, each musical phrase conveys an emotional situation. The director's task is then to engage with this story the author tells, and to narrate it like a musical voice. That was my approach to *Crave*, and an important aspect of my production: each and every single sentence was spoken realistically. Each sentence sounded situational and gestural. If a director attends to and arranges these gestural qualities, the abstract fragments will turn into music. The initial approach, therefore, is the very same one we have discussed: find the dominant circumstance in the situation as a result of which 'it talks'. In *Crave* and *Susn*, I played with this emotional core.

Susn tells the story of a half-Jewish girl who presumably has lost her parents in the holocaust (it is never explicitly mentioned in the play), and who grows up with her grandmother in the Bavarian province. There, within the confined mental climate, she tries to survive, emotionally, as an outsider. This is the plot, the material (*Stoff*), the narrative – yet it meanders, it is disparate, multilateral and multidimensional; the idea of a play as *Stoff* can again help us to get our head around it. For me, analogies with music always help, and I actively drew on them in the second part of this production, where I mixed spoken word poetry with a punk singer's attitude. Neither of these musical genres is considered as 'realistic', but they are ultimately 'real' because they are anchored in an attitude towards the world – typically, an attitude of anger and frustration which grounds these texts and serves as their emotional impetus, revealing the 'main circumstance' in the situation that prompts the process with the intent to change the situation. You find the same grounding in postdramatic texts. At their heart, they are compositions of multiple splinters of situations, and the best postdramatic authors manage to open up an entire world with only a few of these fragmented sentences – Kane, Achternbusch, or equally Elfriede Jelinek, for instance in her *Merchant's Contracts*: everything revolves around the family who speculated and lost all their money, and where the father then decides to kill the entire family. You are hitting a wall of language, which works a lot with incredibly playful redundancies, substantivisation and other strategies typical for a very South-German writing tradition of Ödön von Horvath, Thomas Bernhard, Werner Schwab and others, but behind it is a realistic, situational world. It expresses a world that is as grotesquely inflated, beyond all proportions, as the language; a world lost to the petit bourgeoisie, its values and world-view, where language is either a grotesquely bubbling train of thought, or the mere reiteration of empty and hollow borrowed phrases. It takes to its extreme the disconnect of the identity between language and speaker/character: language has entirely ceased to be an individual's expression. In the work of the best playwrights, those who do not merely copy an artistic form, postdramatic theatre reveals itself as the ultimate realist theatre.

Notes

1 See Bertolt Brecht, 'The Attitude of the Rehearsal Director (in the Inductive Process)', in *Brecht on Theatre*. Ed. Marc Silberman, Steve Giles and Tom Kuhn. London: Bloomsbury Methuen, 2014, 211–12.
2 Jan Kott, *Shakespeare Our Contemporary*. Trans. Boleslaw Taborski. London: Methuen, 1965, pp. 53, 47, 48.
3 I prefer the Brechtian term of a 'dramatic figure' (*Figur*) which emphasises that a character in a play is a dramatic construct that stands exemplarily for human beings in a certain societal and historical context. In German, there is no direct equivalent that carries the same 'psychological' connotations of the English term 'character'. One either speaks of a *Figur* or of the *Rolle*, the role one plays, and hardly ever of the 'person'. As the term 'figure' is far more marked as something extraordinary in an English text, we here use the terms 'figure' and 'character' interchangeably, but always bearing the non-psychological model-character in mind.
4 See 'The Street Scene', in *Brecht on Theatre*. Ed. by Marc Silberman, Steve Giles and Tom Kuhn. Third Ed. London: Bloomsbury Methuen, 2014, pp. 176–83.
5 Keith Johnstone, 'Status', in *Impro: Improvisation and the Theatre*. London: Methuen, 1989, pp. 33–74.

6 A welcome exception is David Roesner's study *Musicality in Theatre: Music as Model, Method, and Metaphor in Theatre-Making* (Farnham: Ashgate, 2014). Anchoring his exploration of theatre-making in Appia, Meyerhold and Artaud, he analyses the contemporary theatre-work of directors such as Robert Wilson, Christoph Marthaler and Heiner Goebbels, as well as the postdramatic writing of Elfriede Jelinek and others, in terms of principles of musical composition.

7 Sergei Eisenstein, 'Montage of Attractions', transl. Daniel Gerould, in *The Drama Review* 18(1), 1974, pp. 77–85.

8 The principle was introduced by Peter Brook's actor Yoshi Oida in *The Invisible Actor.* London and New York: Routledge, 1997, pp. 30–35. See also Lorna Marshall, *The Body Speaks: Performance and Physical Expression*. 2nd Ed. London: Methuen, 2008, pp. 222–7.

Plates 21–24 Scenes from *Hamlet* (2008), with Lars Eidinger in the title role, with Stefan Stern and Urs Jucker (bottom left), and with Sebastian Schwarz (bottom right). Photographs © Arno Declair.

Plates 25–27 *An Enemy of the People* with Eva Meckbach (Katharina Stockmann) and Stefan Stern (Thomas Stockmann), and Christoph Gawenda (Hovstad) with Eva Meckbach in the original 2012 cast (top), and in the second cast 2014 with Christoph Gawenda as Thomas Stockmann, with Eva Meckbach, Andreas Schröders and Moritz Gottwald. Photographs © Arno Declair.

Plates 28–30 Thomas Stockmann's speech, and the aftermath, with Stefan Stern in the original 2012 production (top), and Christoph Gawenda in the second cast of 2014. Photographs © Arno Declair.

Plates 31–33 Shakespeare in the golden cage: *Measure for Measure* (2011), with the late Gert Voss as Duke Vincentio (top right), the same with Erhard Marggraf (Escalus) and Lars Eidinger (Angelo, top left), and Jenny König as Isabella (bottom). Photographs © Arno Declair.

Plates 34 and 35 *Tod in Venedig/Kindertotenlieder* (2012) with Josef Bierbichler (front) and live musician Timo Kreuser, and Lillian Hellman's *Little Foxes* (2014), with Jenny König, David Ruland, Moritz Gottwald, Mark Waschke and Nina Hoss. Photographs ©Arno Declair.

Plates 36 and 37 A 'Globe' at the Schaubühne: the first scene of *Richard III*. Below: Richard (Lars Eidinger) welcoming the princes (with Thomas Bading, Laurenz Laufenberg, Jenny König, Eva Meckbach and Christoph Gawenda as puppeteers). Photographs © Arno Declair.

Plates 38 and 39 Scenes from *Richard III* (2015): Hastings's last council (Sebastian Schwarz, with Robert Beyer, Thomas Bading, and Christoph Gawenda, above). Below: Richard on the throne. Photographs © Arno Declair.

Plates 40–42 Richard (Lars Eidinger) with Lady Anne (Jenny König, top left) and Elizabeth (Eva Meckbach, top right), and in his sleep before the final battle. Photographs © Arno Declair.

Chapter 7

Ostermeier at work [2]

Richard III (2015)

Figure 7.1 The initial scene of *Richard III*, in the 'Schaubühne Globe' in February 2015. Photograph © Jan Pappelbaum.

Rehearsals: (rehearsal studio) 10 November 2014–16 January 2015; (stage rehearsals) 19 January 2015–6 February 2015
Premiere: 7 February 2015, Schaubühne Saal C
Running time: *ca.* 150 minutes, no interval

Translation and adaptation by Marius von Mayenburg

(Continued)

(Continued)

Cast:

Richard III: Lars Eidinger
Buckingham: Moritz Gottwald
Elizabeth: Eva Meckbach
Lady Anne: Jenny König
Hastings, Brakenbury, Ratcliff: Sebastian Schwarz
Catesby, Margaret, First Murderer: Robert Beyer
Edward, Mayor, Second Murderer: Thomas Bading
Clarence, Dorset, Stanley, Prince of Wales (puppet): Christoph Gawenda
Rivers, York (puppet): Laurenz Laufenberg
Musician: Thomas Witte

Creative team

Assistant director: Claudia Marks; Stage design: Jan Pappelbaum; Stage design assistant: Céline Demars; Costume design: Florence von Gerkan; Costume assistant: Ralf Tristan Scezsny; Music: Nils Ostendorf; Video: Sébastien Dupouey; Dramaturgy: Florian Borchmeyer; Light design: Erich Schneider; Puppets: Ingo Mewes, Karin Tiefensee; Puppet training: Susanne Claus, Dorothee Metz; Fight choreography: René Lay; Stage managers: Stefan Dümmler, Frank Mencke; Prompters: Heike Kroemer, Christine Schönfeld; Direction interns: Laura Laufenberg, Greta Lippauer; Stage design intern: Noemi Baldelli; Costume interns: Anna Kurz, Donghwan Kim.

Technical team

Technical director: Daniel Kaiser; Production manager: Lothar Klein; Technical inspector: Helmut Müller; Make-up: Renate Wetzel-Wagner, Christel Thieme; Propmasters: Wolfgang Reuter, Pablo Jadot; Sound: Sven Poser, Stefan Pinkernell; Video: Benni Hartlöhner; Light: Hans-Jürgen Simoncelli; Costumes: Dagmar Fabisch, Johanna Ballhausen; Wardrobe mistress (Ladies): Anne-Katrin Haubold; Wardrobe master (Men): Günter Welz; Stage inspector: Max Schirmer; Stage master: Felix Rohde; Construction: Katrin Omlor; Head of stage machinery: Stephan Staehle; Head of workshops: Helmut von Arentsschild; Paintshop: Andreas Geißel; Set building: Joana Meyer-Föllen; Decoration: Thomas Mielenz; Carpenter: Peter Janke; Metalwork: Katja Kentenich

7.1 *TOTUS MUNDUS AGIT HISTRIONEM*: READING AND STAGING SHAKESPEARE (2014)

> 'Who's there?'
>
> (*Hamlet*, I.1.1)

The first line of *Hamlet* offers a useful starting point to try and attempt a discussion of some Shakespearean scenes. I propose to ask this very question on several levels. One might even take it as a headline to my approach to Shakespeare's work; and even further, to my understanding of why we make theatre at all. *'Who's there?'* Who is the person in front of us? Who is the other? Who is talking to us? Who are we? What is a human being? If you begin to think about possible answers to these questions that arise within the play of *Hamlet*, things quickly get very complicated. Let us take a small example. One can easily imagine a situation where the light goes out, as you climb a stairwell in the middle of the night, and somebody who has heard the sound of your footsteps approaching, asks from above: 'Who's there?' What would be your answer? Simply your name? Would it be an answer to that question, at all? What lies behind the mask of your physical appearance? What lies behind your name? Who are you? Who are we? My point in reading and staging Shakespeare and approaching this author and his universe, my point in making theatre in the first place, is that I myself do not know who I am.

'Who's there?' What is my identity? What is my 'I' and my 'me'? Being confronted with these questions is even more difficult when you are, as is the case in the first scene of *Hamlet*, a ghost who has to answer. If you respond, as the ghost later does, *'I am thy father's spirit'* (I.5.13) – why is the ghost of the father not actually the father? What makes the difference between our inner conception of ourselves and our outside appearance, our social mask, the role we have to play, and what we represent? The laws of civilisation make our lives with each other easier, but at the same time, they prevent us from expressing ourselves without limitation. Therefore, there must be a difference between what we want to be, what we would like or prefer to be, and what we are allowed to be. There have to be limits to what we are allowed to be, because otherwise we would be entirely unable to live together as a civilised community. This gap between what we want to be, and what we have to be in order to be able to get along and live together, is a necessary aspect of human civilisation. Maybe, therefore, our 'I' is the very distance between what and who we are, and what and who we would like to be. *'Full of longing, the "I" that I am looks at the "I" that I could be.'* This is how Dostoevsky put it in *The Brothers Karamazov*. We are, as human beings, continuously trying to perfect our 'I', and to optimise our 'self'. Is this constant process of becoming somebody else our identity? Or the 'I' who wants to be somebody else? Or is it the 'I' that we are longing to be?

This uncertainty about identity and the conception of our 'I' or 'me' is certainly one of the central problems modern man is facing. Elizabethan playwrights, and most of all Shakespeare, were particularly aware of this problem. I have the impression that the force driving the characters in Shakespeare's plays is their urge to find out who the other is, to discover what lies behind their physical appearance, and what their true motives are. At times, it seems to me that this is also the very force that drives the playwright, Shakespeare, himself: to find out more about what human beings are. Luckily, and in marked contrast to many other playwrights and screen-writers of the present, Shakespeare has no answer. But he has many questions. In order to find out more about these, he does not simply put characters on stage; he rather puts characters on stage who then put themselves on stage. Understanding this basic point will make a director's work on Shakespeare much easier. When you discuss with the actors how to play a certain scene, you will not need to talk about how you can, in this very moment, be truthful to the situation, or to the character. Instead, you can talk about what you are *playing* in this moment, as a character. The actor will be playing a character who is playing a situation. Many Shakespearean plays begin with a character coming on stage and informing the audience that he or she is now going to be somebody else: 'from now on, I am not the one I was before'. This is one of the most important Shakespearean *topoi*. In these cases, the theatre event as such begins by explicitly stating the fundamental act of theatre: becoming somebody else. For an actor in a rehearsal space who has to find his or her way into the dramatic situation, and who feels blocked and restrained by the pressure to be truthful to this situation, it will be an act of liberation when the director is able to reassure them: do not even think about being truthful to the situation. Just play the moment the character is *playing*. This means that there is no more right or wrong. As a result, anything you do as an actor, even very bad acting, cannot be but truthful, because it is, for instance, Iago who is simply *playing* the role of Othello's best friend. The very fact of not successfully, of not entirely 'truthfully' acting, therefore might even become the very beauty of portraying Iago, or similarly Richard Gloucester, as he performs being the most lovable lover, not at all interested in power, and posing as pious.

Many of Shakespeare's characters hide their true identity, and they are playing all the time. For the actor playing Richard, and for our portrayal of Richard in a production, it could thus become a very interesting point to show that he himself is overwhelmed by the fact that his acting works so well and produces such good results, and that it has this strong an effect on the people around him. Is there not proof of this in the famous lines after he has met Lady Anne, *'Was ever woman in this humour woo'd …?'* (I.2.241). So, when staging *Richard III*, we equally should not be concerned with how to put on the play in the best way, but instead be prepared to accept all the moments where the actor does not entirely succeed. They can be part and parcel of, and in fact something very positive for, acting Richard. We should keep a sense of the surprise that something really works out well, rather than just expecting it as a given. It seems almost banal to state that none of the characters in a play have lived through the situation they are confronted with before; they do not know what is going to happen next. Still, this needs to be explicitly mentioned, and I have to constantly remind actors of this fact. Too often do we make decisions or arrive at certain ways of playing a scene because of our knowledge of the play as a whole. The character, however, does not know the scene; the character only ever makes an attempt to adapt to the situation, and to respond to the problem he or she is confronted with. Shakespeare invites an actor to enjoy approaching the dramatic situation in just such a virgin-like way, and he therefore casts some doubt on any kind of virtuosity, and on any attempt or even demand to be completely convincing all of the time. I believe that if we saw a Richard Gloucester on stage in front of us who was completely convincing, he would be very boring from the start. We should see him having problems being Richard himself – problems being somebody else.

This doubled theatrical situation is, for me, one of the most important keys to unlock Shakespeare, and that helps me to approach and understand how to stage his plays. The double, or sometimes even triple, theatrical situation suggests an answer to many of the questions I have raised, about who we are, or could be: we are multiple 'I's who try to adapt to the situations we are confronted with by playing, by pretending to be somebody else. This is not only true for theatre, but perhaps even for every moment in our lives. I am forced by the situation that you want to read a book about my theatre to write a text, in which I am pretending to be able to tell you something about Shakespeare. I am playing the role of somebody who knows how to talk to you, but in fact I am not one hundred per cent the 'I' who is able to talk to you, and to write this text. I am therefore performing myself, which is certainly no longer big news today. Long before Hans-Thies Lehmann and his *Postdramatic Theatre*, Shakespeare was probably the first postdramatic writer and theatre maker creating performance art. If we look at some of the ingredients of Shakespeare's writing, a lot of things are involved that qualify as postdramatic theatre according to Lehmann. Not least, we are presented with a melange of different genres and different media, and already in Shakespeare, we find the use of different registers of speech: highly elaborated, very poetic verse, and a completely different language that addresses the groundlings in the pit. Shakespeare was greatly fascinated by popular culture, which is another aspect of postdramatic theatre. He mixed popular culture with high culture; comical scenes follow tragic scenes. When he introduces allusions to the political context of his time into the grave-digger scene, *Hamlet* becomes stand-up comedy for a moment, already within Shakespeare's writing. There are also the battle scenes and spectacular fighting stunts performed by well-trained actors, which were a very important part of entertainment at the time. Furthermore, scholars provide us with insight on how he put his plays together by sampling different, well-known sources. We all know that *Hamlet*, for instance, is an old text which Shakespeare put in a new context. There is the old legend of Hamlet, the poor prince of Denmark, a medieval Scandinavian story dating back to the twelfth century; and there is the genre of revenge tragedy that was so popular in Shakespeare's time. There were also other *Hamlet* plays before, in particular the so-called *Ur-Hamlet*, which have not survived but we know existed. And then comes a writer, or to put it better: a *theatre maker* who brings all of this together in a completely new and different way. And not stopping there, he even presents us with the hero of a revenge tragedy who refuses to take revenge – the major twist Shakespeare gives to the tradition of revenge tragedy in his play. This is postmodern eclecticism *avant la lettre*.

But let me now turn in greater detail to the headline of this section: *Totus mundus agit histrionem*. Although there is no direct evidence, we assume that this is the motto that was actually written on the stage of the Globe theatre. Even if this was not true, it is a beautiful sentence which offers another very interesting lesson for playing and directing Shakespeare. Having been raised in Bavaria, I learnt my Latin at school, and I therefore have a different version of how this sentence could be translated. The somewhat 'official' version, 'All the world's a stage', suggests that we are acting in our lives like characters of a play on stage. But the sentence also implies that we are driven to act by the situations that we are confronted with in our life. *Totus mundus agit histrionem* can also be translated as *totus* – all, *mundus* – world, *agit* can also be an active word, and *histrionem* is not the story, as some might think, but it means 'actor'. The sentence might therefore not only be read as 'the whole world acts like an actor', but also 'the whole world acts the actor' – the whole world forces the actor to act. And by extension: we are forced by the world to act like an actor. We are constantly forced to pretend to be somebody else. We are driven to change identities, to put on a mask, in order to find out, through playing, who we are and who the other might be.

In one of my favourite examples from Shakespeare, at the beginning of *Measure for Measure*, the Duke announces that he has to leave the corrupt city of Vienna, and he passes his power on to Angelo. But as soon as he has left, he disguises himself as a monk and returns. He pretends to be someone else, he puts on a mask and plays a character, not only for reasons of political intrigue, but in order to find out more about himself. He puts himself into the position that everyone has wished for at some point: of being able to listen to your friends when they think you are not present. In my production of the play, Vincentio tries to understand who he is and how it came about that the state of Vienna, for which he is responsible, is so rotten. What he sees in his mirror, which is Angelo, is not flattering at all. The beauty of Shakespeare's writing is, of course, that his opponent, the puritan Angelo, the character who seems to know the truth and messes everything up, is even worse. Vincentio is forced to find out that the most politically correct being is capable of the most horrible deeds – of raping a virgin, who is a novice in a nunnery, and of killing her brother in order to hide the truth. For me, *Measure for Measure* is not a play that critiques the older generation who hands over their responsibility. In fact, the only character, in my production, who has my complete sympathy is Vincentio: because he knows that human beings are not perfect. The young generation of Angelo represents my own generation with its stupid idea of political correctness, and its self-righteous puritanism that makes us believe that we can make everything right. Once I was at this point, too, but now I am leaning more towards Vincentio's position. *Totus mundus agit histrionem*. This becomes a true *poetics*, a kind of manual, not only for the characters in the play, not only for the writer, but also of course for the theatre maker: we play in order to understand better.

As I noted earlier, a first realisation on reading and staging Shakespeare is that when we are acting in a situation, we are trying to solve the problems of this very situation, often even by pretending to be somebody else. Let us return to *Hamlet* to make this point clearer. Hamlet is forced to act by the world around him and its circumstances. These are: 'The time is out of joint' (I.5.215); 'Something is rotten in the state of Denmark' (I.4.100); and the fact that his uncle has murdered his father – that is, if Hamlet can believe the ghost, and he really contemplates whether the ghost is right. How can he be sure? He says it might be the Devil talking to him and tempting him. How could anybody amongst us be sure if all of a sudden a ghost appeared and said, 'your uncle killed your father'? We can't. Today, of course, we believe that we can be sure because we know the play, and therefore we are more intelligent than the moment of the play: we already know that Claudius will later sit down and tell the audience that the ghost is right. But it is only from this very point onwards that we really know this truth, and not before. Therefore, in order to understand the situation of the play, we must try and forget everything we know about the play, and instead focus on the very moment in the play, and on all these circumstances by which Hamlet is forced 'to put an antic disposition on' (I.4.197). Hamlet responds to the threat that the murderer of his father, Claudius, is still alive, by playing the fool, the madman. It was a beautiful discovery when I researched the mythology of the *Hamlet* story that Hamlet at this point was a twelve year old child who had to hide because Claudius wanted to kill him, since he perceived him as a threat to his claim on the throne. Much in my production of *Hamlet* was inspired by this discovery, and by the fact that in the original myth Claudius actually pronounces his intention to kill Hamlet, who therefore goes into hiding in a pigsty and covers his body in shit so he would smell embarrassingly, in order to give the impression that he is mad. Claudius finds him out and indeed believes that this pig-like Hamlet cannot but be mad, and he therefore does not kill him as he no longer considers him a threat. Hamlet thus not only puts a mask on his face, but on his whole body, pretending to be somebody else. He is driven to do so by the circumstances around him: *The world acts Hamlet to act*. The world forces him to react, and it then becomes the core of the drama that he constantly refuses to act. All the circumstances around him want to make him act, yet he doesn't;

this is the beauty and the dialectic contradiction of the play. 'I would prefer not to', as Melville's Bartleby would famously express it much later.

But Hamlet plays the madman not only in order to survive in this 'warlike state' (I.1.9). He also 'puts an antic disposition on' in order to find out the truth about the murder of his father. Sometimes, this strategy is even successful. Therefore, every step he takes after revealing to Horatio that he will 'put an antic disposition on', is for Hamlet a theatrical situation. He is constantly 'put on stage', unable to act in the way his 'I' would demand him to act. He has to pretend to act, he has to pretend to be somebody else, as for example in the scene with Polonius, where he says strange things about people selling fish, girls getting pregnant, and corpses on the pavement being penetrated by flies (II.2). Playing the complete madman, he provokes Polonius to reveal *himself*, i.e. to show the Polonius he is behind his mask. Hamlet's attempts to find out the truth in the politically rotten society that is the state of Denmark assume their most beautiful shape in the 'mouse trap' scene (III.2). The play he has performed is called *The Murder of Gonzago*, and Hamlet spontaneously renames it *The Mousetrap*: he thereby states in the very title what it is about, and it therefore becomes a mousetrap for the rotten political power. It is the beauty of Shakespeare's play that it reasserts the belief that by this play-within-a-play, by making theatre, Hamlet is able to unmask Claudius, the murderer. He finds out with the help of the actors that the claim of his father's ghost is probably true. But he also finds out the truth about himself by doing theatre, by playing, by acting. Something appears as a ghost and has no corporeality; something which seems to be only an illusion, just like the shadows in Plato's cave allegory (and, another very beautiful realisation: 'shadow' was of course also another early modern English synonym for 'actor'). And Hamlet is able to find out what is behind these shadows by playing. By acting out a performance before the eyes of the king. Far beyond a tactic for revealing the truth in a politically rotten society, this is a deeply philosophical idea of answering the existential question of who we are by means of the given circumstances under which we perform and play. And we find out that the shadow of this ghost is saying the right thing.

In the third act, as the mousetrap is sprung, we have hope for a brief moment that Hamlet will thus be able to fulfil his mission. But Shakespeare is more dialectic: Even though he believes in the power of theatre, he is realistic enough to tell the story of Hamlet so that in the end Hamlet does not succeed. The political game of manipulation is stronger than theatre; this, by the way, is also my response to anyone who believes that theatre can change the world. In the scene right after the mousetrap, when he is full of this newly found knowledge of the truth, and the anger and rage that this discovery has caused, he, by accident, believes his uncle to be behind the curtain – again, a form of mask. In the one single moment in which Hamlet is ready to act and to complete the mission, in which he is not the odd hesitating hero of this revenge tragedy, he gives a *wrong* answer to the question 'Who's there?' – because he fails to ask it. If he had,

Polonius may have been able to respond: 'It's me, Ophelia's father, don't kill me!' And Hamlet would not have murdered the father of the woman he loves. Hamlet believes that the truth hidden behind the curtain's physical, visible appearance is the King; or, as he puts it, 'a rat'. Which is probably the same in Hamlet's eyes: a king must be a rat if he has killed his brother to become king. For me, this is the crucial point in the play: after having murdered Polonius, there is no more hope for Hamlet. Even though he was so thoughtful and cautious before, Hamlet acts too fast here. He is driven by the circumstances of the situation, but he does not take the time to ask. For once, Hamlet is not hesitating; and what he does is completely wrong. So let us cheer Hamlet's hesitation. That is what Brecht did, as he described it as a major step for humanism, against a tradition that read the hesitation as Hamlet's fatal flaw. According to Brecht, we should all step back and think first. It is my view, too, that most of the catastrophes of the twentieth century arose out of a similar situation, of not allowing time to hesitate in order to be able to think and reflect. People felt the need to act before having a deeper understanding and knowledge of the situation, and they were therefore misinterpreting the circumstances. They felt that they were forced to act like Hamlet, when he feels he is forced to act and kill the king behind the curtain, but it turns out not to be the king. Even though Hamlet has been able to find out the truth through playing, he is unable to deal with it – and we end up with, or Hamlet ends up with, a lot of dead bodies on stage. With eight or nine bodies (depending on whether one counts the Ghost, which brings us back to the interesting question we started from), *Hamlet* has the third highest body count of Shakespeare's major tragedies, surprisingly even more than *Macbeth*.

Hamlet has led us back into questions of appearance and truth or essence, which seem to me to be one of the main topics in Shakespeare's writing. Before we move to another example of these situations, let me add an idea from Stephen Greenblatt's biography *Will in the World*. Greenblatt develops the theory that Shakespeare's whole family might have been Catholic in the Protestant world of Elizabethan England, where Catholics were threatened with death when they were discovered. If this is true, and even if it was not true, I really like the idea that Shakespeare was a Catholic – sharing this terrible destiny with myself – and that he was therefore used to hiding his true identity (as a Catholic) from very early on in his life. This would mean that even before he became a writer for the theatre, he was used to pretending to be somebody else. He might himself have been driven by the world – *totus mundus agit histrionem*, all the world forces us to behave like an actor – to act as if he was somebody else in order to save his life at a time when several attempts were made by Catholic revolutionaries to overcome Protestantism in England, such as the Gunpowder plot of 1605. The Catholic resistance constituted a manifest threat to Elizabethan power, and consequently everybody involved in the Gunpowder plot was sentenced to death. The world within which we have to imagine the writer William Shakespeare is thus not a playful, romantic world of child-like enjoyment in switching identities and playing (as some movies about Shakespeare falling in love may suggest), but much rather a world of conspiracy, suspicion, spying, and violence. The mere fact that anyone entering London in those days saw the heads of conspirators impaled on sticks and displayed on London Bridge illustrates the climate of this time. It was a world of terror, and a world of prosperity at the same time. A world in which you could never be sure who you were talking to – a friend, or a spy? You therefore needed to set up pretty complex situations in order to find out *'Who's there?'*.

This is one of the reasons why we still put Shakespeare on stage today – another time of terror and prosperity, and of the search to find out who is there, which is what drives, for instance, a lot of people on the internet. We can find all these elements present in the play's central scene (III.1), with Hamlet's famous 'to be or not to be' monologue, and the following dialogue between Ophelia and Hamlet. It is to this scene that I wish to turn now. I first would like to revert once more to the very first, elemental question – *'Who's there?'* As a matter of fact, Claudius and Polonius are both hiding and watching the scene, and the meeting between Ophelia and Hamlet. The strategic need to find out what is right and what is wrong not only applies to the 'good guys' in Shakespeare, but equally to the 'bad guys', in this case Polonius and Claudius: they have set up the whole situation in order to find out the truth about Hamlet's madness. Polonius claims that the reason for Hamlet's madness is rejected love; Claudius meanwhile suspects that his behaviour has different reasons, and that it may be connected with his murdering his brother, Hamlet's father. Claudius needs to find out what Hamlet has found out. To do so, he accepts Polonius' suggestion to make Hamlet act under given circumstances (and it is interesting that before Polonius became a political adviser, he was an actor in his previous career, and this is thus an actor's suggestion). Polonius stages a play with participants who do not know that they are on stage (or, does Hamlet know? We will find out, we cannot know yet). We are confronted here with a double or even triple theatrical situation: there is the audience, there are Hamlet and Ophelia, and there are Claudius and Polonius behind watching them. We thus have the hidden on-stage audience watching Hamlet and Ophelia, and at the same time there's us, the theatre audience, watching this audience watching Hamlet and Ophelia. The main given circumstance for Hamlet is a meeting with the woman he loves. But is he allowed to show his love in this situation? Is he aware that the King and Polonius are watching him? Is he aware of the double theatrical situation?

We know for sure that he finds out in the course of the scene, by hearing a sound that reveals Polonius. Interestingly, scholarship draws our attention to the fact that Hamlet had entered during an earlier scene (II.2), precisely at the moment when Polonius suggests to spy on him by means of a staged encounter with Ophelia, and he might thus have been able to listen in. If Hamlet knows from the beginning about the circumstances framing his encounter with Ophelia, he would have to act under these circumstances by pretending to be somebody else. He would have to pretend to be someone who never loved Ophelia – but at the same time, he is sending hidden messages to her, to save her life. At least this is my reading of the famous, much debated line, 'Get thee to a nunnery' (III.1.131, 147). Let us analyse the situation between Ophelia and Hamlet further through a deeper analysis, which for me implies two major questions:

- What are the circumstances for Ophelia at the beginning, when she meets Hamlet?
- And, on how many different levels does she have to act?

Some of the circumstances for Ophelia are:

1 She listened in on Hamlet giving his *To be or not to be*-monologue, a moment ago.
2 She loves him, but her father asked her not to see him anymore; probably also driven by political considerations.
3 As a consequence, this is the only possibility for her to meet with the person she loves.
4 Her father and the King are watching her. She cannot act whatever way she likes.
5 She fears herself that the reason for Hamlet's madness is the fact that she refuses to see him any longer. (At the very moment Hamlet is no longer heir of the political power in the state of Denmark, his girlfriend all of a sudden decides to not see him anymore. What would you as Hamlet believe about such a woman? That she's only interested in marrying the next king?)
6 And finally, the most dominant circumstance for me: She is put on stage without knowing her text. It is every actor's worst nightmare coming to haunt him from time to time: He is taking over a role, he is pushed out of the wings – but he doesn't know the lines. This happens to Ophelia here. She does not know how to play in this situation; her father is saying 'go' and before she can say 'no', she finds herself in the limelight. And, very importantly, she is spying on Hamlet. She thereby becomes, in this very scene, a stooge of the corrupted, rotten power of King Claudius. She knows that the King is watching; but she doesn't know that Hamlet also knows. Consequently, she is driven by the world, the circumstances, to act as an actress (*histrionem*).

Ophelia cannot act as she wants to, in accordance with who she is (whatever that may mean), because she plays several roles, and she is several things in this situation:

1 She is a spy, spying on Hamlet; for her father and the King, in order to help her father preserve his position as first adviser of the King.
2 She is a lover; she loves Hamlet, but is not allowed to show it; and she does not know how to respond to his misogyny.
3 She is an actress who is on stage for the first time. A debutante, completely overwhelmed by the fact that she does not know which role to play, how to act out which identity.

She is torn apart because the only possibility for her to meet the person she loves is by agreeing to spy on him with the King and Polonius watching at the back. In this scene, Ophelia probably gains awareness that her participation in this political play and plot corrupts her love to Hamlet and destroys her purity, her virginity: she becomes as rotten as the rest of Denmark. This might then be the reason for Hamlet's misogynist attacks.

We could now go on and examine many more situations in *Hamlet*. I could discuss some of my favourite quotes from the play. We could, for instance, have a deeper look and make an attempt to grasp what Hamlet is actually saying when he says, 'the readiness is all' (V.2.221); or: 'there is nothing either good/or bad but thinking makes it so' (II.2.265–6). But I would like instead to move to one further, more general thought about why the characters in Shakespeare's plays act the way they do. I have always been intrigued by the idea that Renaissance and Elizabethan times, or as we call it now, the Early Modern period, were a historical threshold for mankind at which knights, after the medieval era, had to face a new battlefield. Throughout the middle ages, the winner of a conflict had been the one who was better at sword-fight, the one who was better at riding or at inventing elaborate strategies for the army on the battleground. Now, cities began to develop, sheltered by fortresses. All of a sudden, the subjects surrounding the king, who up to this point had been able to prove their love and loyalty by fighting for him and defending him, were confronted with the new circumstances of courtly life. It was no longer the warrior who had the best cards in his hands, but the one who knew how to act with words, how to beat the enemy rhetorically, and how to pursue certain aims and strategies by pretending to be somebody else, just like Iago as he pretends to be Othello's best friend.

Until the very end of the play, Othello does not understand that Iago is his worst enemy. This is the nucleus of the conflict between a warrior, Othello, and a *man of letters*, of words, of language, Iago. His name, a reference to Jacob from the Old Testament (Genesis 25:27–27:45), is not at all accidental. Jacob intends to betray his elder brother Esau, and to seize his right as the first-born to receive the fatherly blessing. In order to do so, Jacob hides under a fur, pretending to be his much hairier brother Esau before the blind Isaac, who has to rely on his sense of touch, and therefore believes to have Esau in front of him while speaking the blessing. Not only does Jacob cooperate with his mother in the betrayal, he is also portrayed with female qualities, such as a gift for language. What people in the Renaissance had to face was the fact that all of a sudden, the male qualities of speedy movement, adroit fighting, and other skills of the warrior were becoming less and less relevant; it was now the one who knew how to utilise language – Iago – who was suddenly able to overcome the strongest warrior of the Venetian army, Othello. Language was able to defeat physical power. Iago and also Richard Gloucester, another character in the tradition of the Vice figure, both announce at the outset of the play that they will put on a mask to hide their vicious motives. What strikes me about the Vice character from the personnel of the medieval Morality plays, is a detail about the staging practice. The Virtues all had their entry from the left or right on stage, but the Vice character appeared from the audience. The Vice figure, in my reading of this historical hypothesis, was therefore a representative of the spectators: Vice can both mean a bad moral habit, but it also means the stand-in, the replacement. For this reason, this figure also spoke a very different language to the Virtues: he expressed himself in a popular, low-key register, in the language of the people.

This idea has always been very appealing to me: the idea of a kind of theatre in which one of us, from amongst the audience, is sent on stage in order to act out all evils which we, civilised as we are, usually and luckily, are not able to act out in our everyday lives. In this sense, theatre becomes an institution that rids, or even cleanses, you of feelings and inner drives that would make a civilized society entirely uncivilized. Theatre transfers our violent, excessive fantasies to a virtual space, in order to get rid of them. This might also be a riposte to those who suggest that nowadays computer games and horror movies make young people violent. I believe that in most cases, the opposite is true.

The world of Shakespeare thus is a world where language is a beautiful and incredibly powerful weapon. But it is a weapon which can be used in both ways: to tell the truth, and to lie, to portray the world in a completely different way from what it is, in order to manipulate one's interlocutors, and to pursue one's own evil interests. Both types of characters exist in Shakespeare's plays: the ones who manipulate the truth, like Iago or Richard III, but also the ones who want to find out about the truth, like Hamlet and Duke Vincentio. This might, then, be the only answer to the question, *'Who's there?'*: it's me, playing a role, to find out the truth. And the truth is: we human beings are capable of everything. Of the best, and the worst.

7.2 PREPARING *RICHARD III*: THE LONGING FOR THE DISAVOWED ABYSS (SEPTEMBER 2014)

I cannot say exactly when and how I began considering the idea of putting on *Richard III*. There were several related aspects that had fascinated me for quite some time, not least the idea of the 'Vice figure'. Robert Weimann, in particular, offers a captivating exploration of the popular tradition of medieval allegories and morality plays. He demonstrates that the virtues and 'good' allegories gradually stood back while the Vice figure became ever more prominent on stage.[1] There also seems to have been a peculiar hierarchy of entering the stage: the virtues entered in the usual way from the wings or the back, yet the Vice figure came directly from the audience. This idea of a character who is sent from amongst the audience in order to embody all our dark desires on stage, and to enact in a play everything we are not permitted to do in our civilised world, is most intriguing. It influenced my initial approach towards *Richard*, and was one of my main motivations for directing the play: Richard, vicariously, acts out everything we would love to do but must never do. I also always try to find strong emotions in my response to a play, and that is why my frustration with all the politically correct theatre I have seen on German stages over recent years became a further reason to produce the play. I am deeply disturbed by this mushy generation of people of my age with their mushy world-view. They seriously think that some well-meant, engaged play will be able to change the system we live in, which brings forth dead bodies on a daily basis, very much like Richard does. This is a ridiculous attitude which makes me seriously angry. All around, artists and audiences merely reaffirm each other in their belief that we all stand on the right and safe side together.

I do not believe at all that this is the purpose of theatre. It is not a 'moral institution', as Schiller suggested, but precisely a carnivalesque space where we have the jester's licence to get away with anything – in particular with actually enacting and giving in to all the disavowed aspects of being human that we must not permit ourselves to follow anywhere else. In addition, I also had numerous discussions with Lars Eidinger about how to continue our work, in particular after *Hamlet*, and he had been developing his own enthusiasm for playing Richard for some time. Right now, two months before starting rehearsals, I envisage Richard as a very likable and appealing character. The production is going to fully exploit Eidinger's charm and his huge popularity, in particular with a young audience. I feel that it is very important that the spectators honestly trust and admire Richard, and that they are ready to follow him. I do not think that Richard should ever lose his credit with the audience, so that eventually the full dimension of his crimes and our readiness to fall for him become even more available to our experience. I am not at all convinced by all these productions that show Richard as a Hitler-parable, or that create a diffuse fascist, totalitarian world. There is no need at all to put *Richard III* on stage in order to demonstrate the evil of fascism. What is interesting is that his amoral excess triggers our own lust, our own desire, and a production should therefore tease the spectators so much that they, too, wish they were Richard for a day, able to let go of any barrier that our civilised world imposes on our behaviour, and able to ignore any feeling of shame and embarrassment. We all have a longing for this disavowed abyss of the civilised human society in us, as is revealed in our fascination with people like Charles Manson or Luka Magnotta. The true horror of watching *Richard III* should be the recognition that what we see is actually a visit to our very own innermost abyss. But we will need to see whether such an approach will be tenable at all in the context of the play.

Finally, the idea to recreate the unique theatre experience of a Globe-type theatre space in the Schaubühne played a further crucial role in my decision to stage this play. Richard is, of course, in constant, direct contact with the audience; he virtually leads the spectators by the hand, and guides them through this spectacle of the human abyss. Jan Pappelbaum began exploring the possibilities of building such a space soon after our work on *Measure for Measure*. This choice of space has then of course become the first huge decision that concretely shapes and influences the future. Many colleagues at the Schaubühne were enthusiastic about the prospect of creating such a special space, and they encouraged us to indulge in more of such luxuries. Yet, we instead have the rather luxurious problem of being victims of our international success, in that it reduces rather than fosters the opportunities to afford such luxury. In fact, we do have to consider, to a degree, the end result. The production might go on tour at some point, and we probably won't be able to take the *Globe* space with us, as much as I would like to do this. And even though I have directed other Shakespeare plays since, this production will be perceived as a follow-up to *Hamlet*; expectations are therefore very high, which can be intimidating and stressful. I will have to keep these thoughts at bay, so that they won't gain the upper hand and infringe on creative decisions.

The second major step in concretely preparing the ground for the production was to commission the translation by Marius von Mayenburg. We met a few times to discuss the dramaturgic emphasis and direction we envisioned for the production, and we debated some cuts. It was this abridged version which he then translated. As in our previous work, Marius' translation aims at making Shakespeare intelligible. It is impossible to transpose the rhymed blank verse from the original English into German: you have the same number of syllables, between ten and eleven, to express the same sense, yet German words have a much higher syllable count than English words. For this purely mathematical reason, you have to condense or reduce the sense and meaning of every single line. If you additionally aim, like the famous Schlegel-Tieck translations of German Romanticism, to preserve the rhyme pattern, you will inevitably end up inventing some most bizarre linguistic constructions just to make the rhyme fit. This makes any translation of Shakespeare into German, which tries to retain the form and be true to the verse, outright incomprehensible. There are then two alternatives: either you serve the form and invent your own poetry; you will get Shakespeare-inspired poetry, at least. Or you let go of the verse and the rhyme altogether and instead try to capture the meaning. Marius' talent is to go the latter way, while still creating a very rhythmic language. He primarily concentrates on the sense and uses free, variable rhythm, and quite often he does in fact arrive at a close approximation of blank verse and its iambic pattern.

Some of the decisions we made for his translation concern pragmatic aspects, such as the choice to keep the cast to the minimum number of actors possible. This was not at all motivated, however, by making a saving in our budget, but much rather to give every actor involved an important share in the production, ideally even to make all of them equal protagonists. I simply cannot imagine that an actor who comes on stage to play Tyrrell for barely ten lines in a four hour evening will develop any big motivation and enthusiasm about the production, so I want to avoid this by all means. I want all the actors to be busy and feeling central to the play – and they will, as some actors may have four roles to play. I want everyone to equally contribute to the production's narration so that no one has the feeling of standing in Richard's, or Lars Eidinger's, shadow. For this reason, Marius and I are currently trying to solve what seems like a huge and complex jigsaw. It also includes one major question that we have not answered yet: What do we do with the female characters? At the moment, we are toying with the idea of an all-male ensemble, but there are alternative options floating around that involve casting one actress, or two. If we were to go for a mixed cast, only Lady Anne and Elizabeth would be played by actresses. I could not, for instance, imagine casting Margaret and the Duchess of York with older actresses, who would then have to play the evil avenging angel. If we cast these characters with male actors, however, there will be something strange about them, which will make them appear more real on stage. As it stands, the creative team is divided about this issue. Florence von Gerkan, the costume designer, said at our last meeting that she finds the idea of an all-male cast very problematic; yesterday, she sent me a text message, saying that she has now totally bought into the idea. But by now, Marius and I are not so sure anymore whether it would be a good choice.

At this moment in time, we are also in a phase where we reconsider our previous decisions about what goes into the text. We eventually found the scene where the little Prince asks Richard for his sword quite appealing, and so it came back in. But we still do not agree on some scenes, like the one where Richard mucks about with Clarence and Brakenbury, which Marius has cut, but I like. At the same time, I do not see the need for Lady Anne's long lament before Richard enters. We both agree, though, that the encounter between Elizabeth, Margaret and the Duchess in Act IV is, if not unnecessary, then at least very difficult to put on stage in an interesting, meaningful way; we will very likely change this into two encounters of Richard, first with Elizabeth, then with his mother. But my biggest concern at the moment is the question of casting and who will play alongside Lars Eidinger. Each decision is going to shape in a decisive way the narrative of the production, and will lead it into very different directions. To give an example that I am passionately debating and contemplating at the moment: I might cast Buckingham as a senior, older court figure who never really got his share in power, or as a young, clever and highly ambitious 'upstart' – both are very different stories, and they reflect back on many other aspects of the play. I want to be clear about the story we eventually tell, and therefore I am taking my time before making any final decision. At the moment, in our planning and scheduling for the theatre, ten actors have an option on the production, and their schedules are kept clear for the rehearsal period. Yet, of these ten, only six or maybe seven are going to be cast eventually. Of course, all ten are desperately waiting to hear back, and all assume that they will play the second most important role in the play. It is almost inevitable that some will feel set back by the ultimate decision. Casting thus requires as much diplomacy as ruling a country – in the play, Edward destroyed the equilibrium at his court by failing to include his brother Richard in his government, and instead even bringing the non-aristocratic family of Elizabeth, whom he has married, into his innermost circle. One can read this as a wider metaphor of social mechanisms and interpersonal dynamics, where the feeling of being set back can create resentment and negative energies that may destroy entirely a functioning social order; something similar can happen in any company, and certainly also at the Schaubühne.

One decision has been firmly made, however: The children will be played by puppets that are animated by the actors, who will also lend them their voices. Every single production of *Richard III* has this dreadful moment in it, when real, innocent children are pushed on stage by the director because she or he is unable to express and represent Richard's brutality otherwise. It is my ambition to convey his monstrosity through the means of theatre and *mise en scène*, and not through casting. Potentially, King Edward will be a puppet, too. We are currently experimenting with a gigantic body for him, with only the head of an actor sticking out on top. For the role of the messenger, if it remains in the play at all, we envisage using a stick puppet the actors will hold up whenever new messages come in. These are, of course, irreversible preliminary decisions we have made by now, and they determine to a degree the direction the production will take.

Both Marius and I have also proposed quite different, radical cuts to end the play. Marius still has some form of battle in his version. I am positively certain, however, that I won't have actors in camouflage uniform and field knapsacks running across the stage acting 'battle'. This cannot be but embarrassing. We further both agreed to cut the sections in Richard's nightmare where the spirits of the dead, in Shakespeare's text, appear to Richmond, too, and wish him well for the impending battle. In our version, there are only going to be 'evil spirits', at least from Richard's perspective. For me, his nightmare already tells the whole story of the battle. I envisage Richard waking up from this nightmare, and like in a movie, we cut directly into a sword-fight between Richard and Richmond, Richard loses, and that's the end. But this idea is no dogma whatsoever, and this may not be how our production is going to end after all. In fact, I am most intrigued by *not* showing Richard's death, and instead leaving it open. For Shakespeare, it was of course imperative to show his utter destruction. The play was, after all, a piece of political propaganda, and it therefore had to paint the picture of Richard in the most colourful and most terrifying colours, in order to justify and back up the Tudor dynasty of Elizabeth I which was not at all built on solid ground. The play's message was to show to those dissatisfied with her reign what the alternative was – chaos and turmoil, a 'tottering state', as Hastings calls it. It was thus decisive that Richard dies eventually, and that the play ends with Richmond founding the Tudor dynasty that still reigned in Shakespeare's days. But none of this is meaningful any longer to a twenty-first-century audience, even less so in Germany. I could therefore equally well imagine to have the ghost scene, Richard wakes up from his nightmare, says his famous line, 'a kingdom for a horse' – and black. From today's perspective, such an ambiguity about the ending might be far more interesting.

Before Marius and I embarked on our recent, intense discussions of the play and the details of its translation, it had not been clear to me how important the aspect of playing, and of a play within a play, is in *Richard III*, too. We will try to emphasise this aspect, which I find most interesting. Not only does Richard come to the front to speak directly to the audience and comment on his every action and its results. Far more than a Machiavellian ruler, I see in him the theatre director: Witnessing his own success in winning Lady Anne, he decides to stage everything. Every single moment that follows this moment is a performance he directs – take his magnificent line with which he destroys the reconciliation that Edward had arranged: *'Who knows not that the noble duke is dead?'* (II.1). Richard is aptly supported by his assistant director Buckingham who contributes with quite a few ideas for the *mise en scène* himself; it is Buckingham who eventually instructs Richard to reject every offer of the crown, and he puts on a gigantic spectacle performed in front of the mayor and the citizen – this is one of my favourite scenes in the play. What we see here is even more perfidious than our real political performances – one can be glad that today's politicians do not read their Shakespeare too well for inspiration!

I initially thought of *Richard* as a history play, but preparing more thoroughly has now revealed how much explicit theatre there is in the play – and for me, Shakespeare is at his very best when he has his characters putting on a dazzling, diabolical play within the play. Take, for instance, the final act of *Measure for Measure*, with the veritable masque that the Duke directs, which must be my favourite Shakespeare moment of all. He shows us characters who use language in such a powerful way that it manipulates and refigures reality – and thereby Shakespeare's use of language directly points to a current issue of our own reality: not actual events as such are the message, but the way they are reported and represented in the media. Now that I have discovered more of the same Shakespearean theatricality in *Richard III* as well, the same typical tragi-comedy which I cherished in *Hamlet* and *Measure for Measure*, I am looking forward to beginning rehearsals in rather calm and relaxed anticipation – even though the twelve weeks of rehearsals I had originally envisaged have already shrunk to ten weeks, as they will be interrupted by performances of other productions abroad. And only three days after the scheduled premiere, we will depart for a three week tour to India with *An Enemy of the People*, so there is no room for any manoeuvre. If I was able to arrange my ideal rehearsals, applying all the tools from storytelling to repetition exercises, to the training of sword-fighting skills and puppetry, I would at least schedule four months of rehearsal. I have no idea, of course, whether the actors would be on board with that, too.

7.3 REHEARSING *RICHARD III*: A DIARY (SEPTEMBER 2014 TO FEBRUARY 2015)

Bauprobe (design rehearsal), 11 September 2014

At the day-long *Bauprobe*, a mock-up of the set and of the 'Globe' auditorium in their original dimensions were built up in the Schaubühne's Saal C, where the production will open in five months' time. The mock-up consisted of a simple wooden framework and brown paper, with rostra lifted to the heights of the two upper tiers of the set to indicate their position. It soon transpired that because of sight-lines, the thrust stage space needed to be brought up by almost twenty centimetres. Jan Pappelbaum and Thomas Ostermeier (T.O.) experimented with different compositions of sand and clay in order to find a mix to cover the stage floor that does not create too much dust when used in performance. Pappelbaum also presented samples of different colour schemes for painting the backwall, which were tried out in various lighting situations. He and T.O. further experimented with different ways of making the central rostrum movable, and various options for the back doors were discussed. Video designer Sébastien Dupouey tested different options of adding video elements, while chief light designer Erich Schneider determined the number, type and positions of lights, also using a couple of moving head LED spots to light the semi-circular forestage. With the sound- and lighting team, the specifications for the special microphone with its in-built light were discussed, and requirements for the elastic band to which it is fixed were tested so it does not snap against the backwall.

Lars Eidinger, the sole actor whose lead role in the production is already confirmed at this stage, and some other ensemble members who hope to be in the production had turned up to get an impression of the stage and auditorium space, test the spatial dynamics of the thrust stage, the different tiers on the backwall, and the effect in the auditorium with T.O. At the end of the day, the exact measurements, colour schemes and materials for the set and the 'Globe' auditorium as well as other technical specifications for the productions were confirmed, and all will now be built in the Schaubühne workshops for the start of rehearsals in November.

Figures 7.2 and 7.3 Building a 'Globe' at the Schaubühne: Jan Pappelbaum's model box for the Schaubühne Globe and the set of *Richard III*. Photographs © Jan Pappelbaum, Peter M. Boenisch.

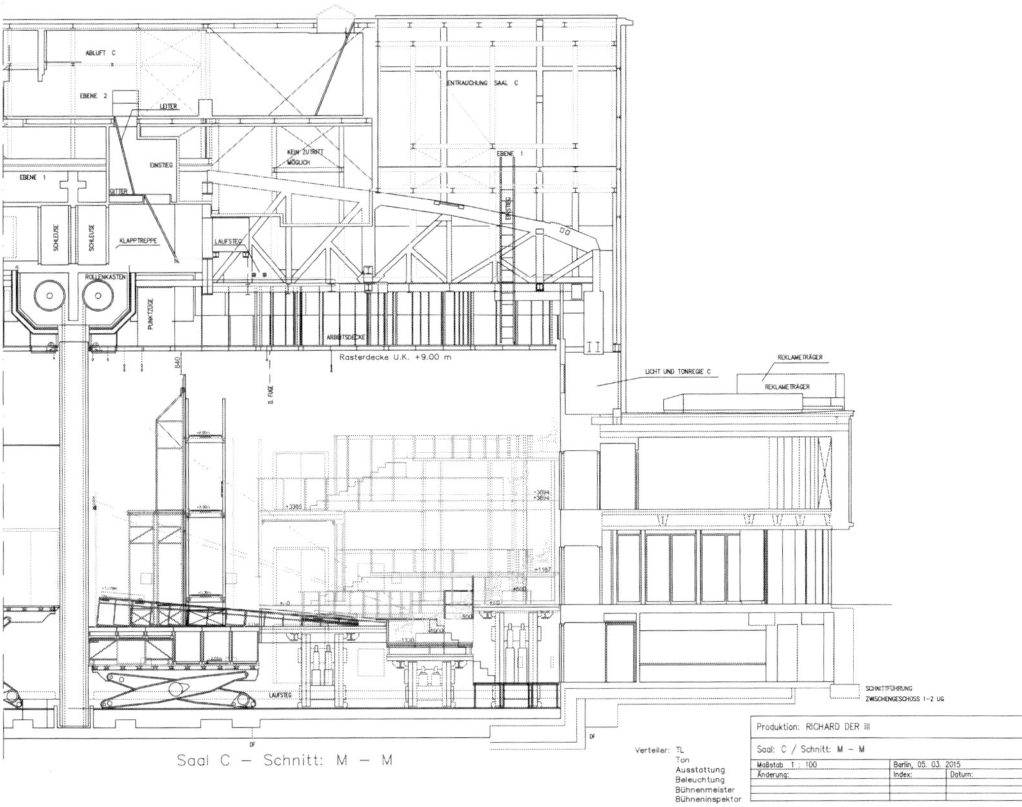

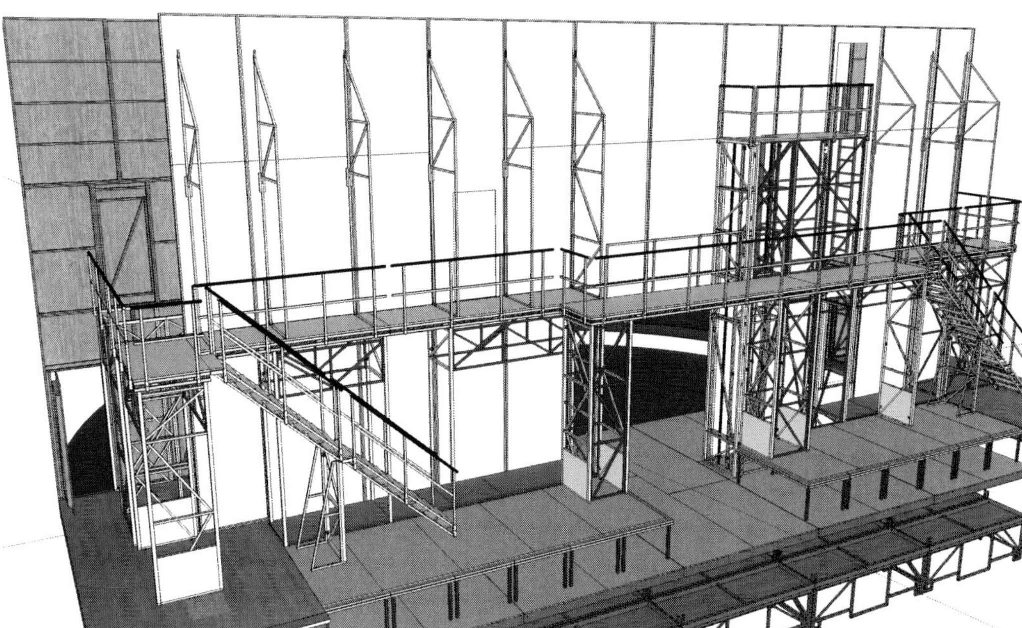

Figures 7.4 and 7.5 An architectural sectional view of the Schaubühne Globe, and a 3-D model of the *Richard* set, showing the backstage side of the set. © Schaubühne.

Konzeptionsprobe (concept rehearsal), 10 November 2014

A tradition in German theatre, the *Konzeptionsprobe* marks the beginning of the formal rehearsal period. The final decision about casting and the allocation of roles for the production had only been announced on the Friday. The *Konzeptionsprobe* is the first occasion for the entire artistic, creative and technical team to come together; moreover, it is an event every employee of the theatre is invited to in order to find out about the forthcoming production. Just short of seventy people have thus gathered in the Schaubühne's rehearsal space, an old factory building in North Berlin, to listen to the director, dramaturg, designer, costume designer, and also the composer and the two puppeteers who all give brief introductions, sharing their thoughts and ideas on *Richard III*. From the first day, the original set is available in the rehearsal space, where, for the majority of the time, all actors and the full creative team attend all rehearsals. Costume designer Florence von Gerkan has set up a 'mood wall' with visual ideas for each performer, five of whom are going to play multiple roles.

Week 1, 10 November 2014

Following the morning's 'concept rehearsal', the first rehearsal 'proper' began with a read-through of Marius von Mayenburg's translation. Most of the first

Figure 7.6 The initial read through in the Schaubühne rehearsal studio. Photograph © Florence von Gerkan.

afternoon was taken up by a long discussion of the Richard–Lady Anne scene (I.2). Day 2 then introduced the first of many 'family photo' exercises this week. They were mainly used to work through the back history of the War of the Roses, in particular the episodes covered in Shakespeare's *Henry VI* plays that concern the figures reappearing in *Richard III*. Realising, for instance, Clarence's previous betrayal in the feud between the houses of York and Lancaster, the background of Margaret's bitter revenge as well as the cruel murders she committed herself on the brothers' father and their youngest sibling, and not least the circumstances of Edward's secret marriage to the widow Elizabeth Woodville, instead of the French king's sister-in-law, a deal that had been brokered by Warwick, introduced important background knowledge. In the course of the week, T.O. then invited the actors to create a family photo from the perspective of their character.

Further discussions explored the plot of the play, and the motifs of the main characters, in particular Richard. Dramaturg Florian Borchmeyer asserted his perspective that the resentment of the old nobility (such as Hastings and Buckingham) against the newly promoted members of Elizabeth's non-aristocratic family contributes in an important way to the play's dynamics. Reading and trying out I.5 for the first time, T.O. concluded: 'I need to see more of Elizabeth's gang on stage'; the character of Dorset, cut from the first draft translation, was reintroduced, to be played by Christoph Gawenda, who was previously on stage as Clarence; a lot of the multi-roling parts were still very fluid at this stage, and many lines would continue to be re-attributed in the further course of rehearsals, mostly for pragmatic reasons. By the end of Week 1, the team had read through Act I, and tried out some of the scenes, including Margaret's curse. 'The rhythm of the production may demand an entirely different dynamics. All we do at this stage is to approach scenes, and to stimulate our imagination of the scenes' (T.O.).

Week 2, 17 November 2014

Fight director René Lay, who had already worked on *Hamlet*, began his work to develop the final fencing scene between Richmond and Richard, which was to involve Stanley and Buckingham as well. Meanwhile, puppet players Dorothee Metz and Susanne Claus started their work training the actors in animating the puppets of the two young princes. Two scenes were planned at this stage: the princes' encounter with Richard on their arrival in London, and a dumb show scene showing the murder of the princes in the tower, with Sebastian Schwarz as murderer. From then on, the first hour in the morning of each rehearsal day was dedicated to puppet training on Mondays, Wednesdays, and Fridays, and fight training on Tuesdays and Thursdays. The scenic rehearsal with T.O. then took place daily from 11am to 4pm, including a lunch-break between 1 and 2. Most if not all of the actors would perform in another play at the Schaubühne in the evening, with standard union regulations prescribing a mandatory rest period of three hours in between rehearsal and performance.

Figures 7.7 An early puppetry training session, with Eva Meckbach and Lars Eidinger. Photo © Peter M. Boenisch.

The scenic work continued with Act II, reading and arranging the reconciliation-scene with Edward. As Christoph Gawenda was now on stage as Dorset, the lines of Stanley were reassigned to Catesby (Robert Beyer). T.O. introduced the first storytelling exercises on the topic of reconciliation after a big quarrel, on persuading someone to do something that is to their own disadvantage, and on admitting that you have failed in an important matter. Meanwhile, costume designer Florence von Gerkan began trying out some concrete costume ideas, especially for the actors who would be multi-roling. When working on Act II Scene 2, it was discovered that Buckingham takes a lead in the scheme to get hold of the princes, and is very eager to do the dirty work for Richard:

> 'The most interesting discovery after ten days of rehearsals, and something that had not been that clear to me before either, is that the murders almost happen by themselves: Richard triggers the prejudices and hatred of others in such a way that they commit them for him. *Richard* thus reveals a lot about the psychology of power. His genius is to allow Buckingham to take the reins in the plotting, and making him feel as if Richard was part of *his* intrigue rather than the other way around; he never realises that Richard has given the reins into his hands in the first place. Therefore, Richard does not come to power because he is evil, but because he knows how to

manage and respond to others, and how to spur them into action. And that makes it quite uninteresting to show Richard on stage as nothing but an evil villain. In fact, his behaviour and his reactions must be so convincing that both characters and spectators are absolutely convinced by his sincerity, and that, just like Buckingham, the last thing the audience would imagine at this moment is that he really gave the order to kill Clarence.' (T.O.)

Playing with this insight, Buckingham (Moritz Gottwald) and Richard (Lars Eidinger) create a musical interlude with composer Nils Ostendorf and on stage musician Thomas Witte, where Buckingham grabs the microphone (that was previously reserved for Richard's monologues) for a rap-song interlude, prior to their departure for Pomfret to bring the princes to London. Also, there was a small change in the stage design: as actors keep running into Witte, who sits stage-left behind his drums and electronic music kit, the stairs leading to the upper level of the set were reversed.

Week 3, 24 November 2014

A popular rehearsal game in T.O.'s work to consolidate lines and expand the actors' concentration came in: for the first hour in the morning, the actors played badminton while running through their lines with prompter Heike Kroemer. In his scenic rehearsal, T.O. then tried out two alternative arrangements for the very beginning of the performance that leads into Richard's monologue. In one version, everyone was sitting or standing at the back and then stepped into the scene; in the second version (which was then developed further and became the opening of the production) the 'glorious summer' with its 'merry meetings' is shown as a party, the actors bringing on beer cans and champagne. Meanwhile, Lars Eidinger brings some braces and dentures to rehearsals which he had done by his dentist.

Figures 7.8 and 7.9 Props in the rehearsal room. Photographs © Peter M. Boenisch.

Reading Act III with the executions of Rivers and Dorset as well as Hastings prompted a wider discussion about the play and its context:

> 'It is important to bear in mind that the play's message to its contemporary audience was to be content with Elizabeth's reign, as else the world would turn into the turmoil which the play portrays. It is an almost apocalyptic scenario of a time that is truly out of joint. There is permanent war, also in the minds of these characters. You are permanently under threat and under suspicion. You never really know who is on your side, who is your friend, and who is your enemy. You suspect everyone else of playing false and betraying you, and at the same time, you try not to show your true face, as you constantly have to fear that you could end up on the gallows next. Whenever you think the situation is bad, it will still get worse. An atmosphere of death has been omnipresent in this world, long before Clarence, Rivers and Hastings died. There are many "failed states" in today's world whose situation resonates with this scenario.' (T.O.)

As Hastings is played by Sebastian Schwarz, the lines of his character Ratcliff in III.3 (where he acts as executioner of Rivers and Dorset) are reassigned to Catesby. Tuesday's rehearsal took the team to the end of Act III. The actors and T.O. then left directly from the rehearsal studio to the airport for performances of *An Enemy of the People* in Romania, and of *Tartuffe* and *Lungs* in Moscow.

Week 4, 1 December 2014

Following Sunday night's performance of *Lungs* in Moscow (with Jenny König and Christoph Gawenda), rehearsals for *Richard* resumed with an evening rehearsal on Monday night. T.O. began to introduce the Meisner repetition exercises, emphasising the importance of the 'mirroring' principle. The detailed observation of the partner on stage, and the synchronisation of a shared rhythm are most relevant principles that are directly applicable to the plot, too: Richard's skill and strategy is precisely his ability to observe and respond to the needs of those around him. Rather than continuing where the work was left off in the previous week, the scenic work started again from the beginning, applying the mirroring exercises in particular in detailed work on I.5, and on other scenes from the first act.

Video as well as music are now fully integrated into the rehearsal process, with composer Nils Ostendorf and video designer Sébastien Dupouey now attending the daily rehearsals. They proposed alternative compositions and images for scenes, and for some of the transitions. T.O. stressed that it is important that the music does not sound 'evil' or 'dramatic', but rather expresses the pleasure and joy of following Richard along his way, as he enacts some of our most evil fantasies and immoral impulses. The audience must relish in giving in to this temptation, rather than morally condemning Richard from the outset. After trying out ideas from her costume stock, costume designer Florence von

Figure 7.10 The cast of *Richard III* doing repetition exercises with Thomas Ostermeier during rehearsals. Photograph © Peter M. Boenisch.

Figure 7.11 Discovering Richard: Lars Eidinger and Thomas Ostermeier in the rehearsal studio. Photograph © Arno Declair.

Gerkan now has some of her drafts tailored in the theatre's costume workshop. With Lars Eidinger, she also works on designing a shoe for Richard.

Week 5, 8 December 2014

Scenic work continued with more detailed work on Act II, sketching out the scenes, determining positions and refining stage action. More detailed storytelling work was done on topics of reconciliation, and in particular on death and dying. After some weeks of working with 'dummies', the actual puppets built for the production arrived, albeit still without costume and hair, which costume designer Florence von Gerkan and make-up artist Christel Thieme now began to work on. The puppets added their own, uncanny energy, in a strange mixture of innocence and strangeness, and will permit the showing on stage of the brutal murder in the Tower, in the pantomime scene that continued being rehearsed.

While still trying out different alternative costume options, T.O. and Florence von Gerkan settled on a rather sober, almost colour-less black and white scheme for most of the costumes that – alongside the sombre tones of the set – emphasises a shadow-like plasticity of the scene. T.O. began to call individual late afternoon rehearsals (4.00–5.30): with 'Richard' Lars Eidinger, he worked on his monologues, and on his dialogue scenes with Lady Anne (Jenny König) and Elizabeth (Eva Meckbach), which are rehearsed privately in the studio, with only T.O. and the respective actors present. Later that week, the microphone with the built-in light was delivered from the technical workshop. It turned out, though, that the light, used as sole lighting source in the monologue scenes, blinded Eidinger; if it was dimmed down, it would become difficult to see the actor. Video designer Sébastien Dupouey therefore suggested integrating a small camera as well into the microphone, as further work would need to be done on this technical device.

Week 6, 15 December 2014

T.O. called a first run-through of the scenes rehearsed so far (Acts I–III). He worked further on the arrangement of the scenes, focusing on timing and scenic details, shaping sequences of action, and trying out the transitions between the scenes, testing various musical options for these interludes with composer Nils Ostendorf and musician Thomas Witte. T.O. spoke of 'laying down the tracks' on which these scenes will eventually run: 'I have no set idea. I just want to try out what works best.' In his notes, he put an emphasis on the clarity of dramatic stakes, timings, the direction of gazes, on adding depth and layers to the acting, for instance by raising the actor's awareness of parallels and oppositions in the text, trying to get them away as much as possible from 'reeling off' text.

T.O. also attended the fight rehearsals, directed by René Lay, and began to work on the 'ghost scene' (V.4) and its transition into the concluding sword fight with Richmond, Stanley, and Buckingham, which will replace the full-blown battle scenes from the play:

Figures 7.12 'Richmond' Laurenz Laufenberg and 'Richard' Lars Eidinger with fight trainer René Lay rehearsing the final battle scene. Photograph © Peter M. Boenisch.

> 'It is less important that Richard is killed by revenants of his own deeds but that he has come to a point where he is conquered by a group of people even though he seemed invincible: at the crucial moment, he lacks a horse. The fencing scene will convey on stage what the many messenger reports verbally tell in the playtext.' (T.O.)

The executions of Hastings, Rivers and Dorset, are going to happen on stage, too: they will be hanged and, back stage, thrown off the scaffolding so that the audience would see their bodies through the opened doors. T.O. showed some footage of executions of Nazi criminals by the allied forces in post-War Germany, while fight director René Lay suggested practicalities and was tasked with preparing a suitable harness. A dedicated 'hanging rehearsal' with a stuntman was called, and T.O. discussed the soundtrack to these hanging scenes with the composer and musician.

There were also more storytelling exercises, in particular to mine Richard's crucial encounter with the Mayor and the citizen, where he three times rejects the crown (III.7). Topics included asking a big favour, admitting failure, rejecting a request, and encounters with priests. T.O. paid particular attention to the aspect of the (played) status relations which the characters adopt. He suggested that there was no need to act Richard's acting in this scene – if the audience, alongside Buckingham and the Lord Mayor, find believable what Richard does, the effect would be far more staggering and upsetting. Also, Buckingham must not know how the scene would work out eventually, especially as the mayor and the citizen leave, and he needs to be nervous whether his plan will succeed at all, after already having failed previously, as he discussed in his initial conversation with Richard. T.O. reminds the performers that, in contrast to our own very public world, everyone here was very cautious in expressing any reaction, as no one knew the other – we saw how Hastings' candid response, offering his personal opinion about Richard sent him to the gallows.

Rehearsals continued with the coronation scene. Richard's throne would be placed on the movable 'discovery space', and he would wear some form of corset. By the end of Friday, the team had worked its way through to Buckingham's fall in IV.3. Rehearsals now broke for Christmas.

Week 7, 29 December 2014

Rehearsals resumed, the morning set aside for the concluding fencing scene, and the scenic rehearsal with T.O. then picking up from Scene IV.4. The characters of Tyrell, the murderer of the princes, and Ratcliff are merged, played by Sebastian Schwarz as 'Ratcliff', who will take over as Richard's confidant after Buckingham's humiliation and flight. Further storytelling ('a moment when events came thick and fast, and you completely lost the plot') revealed a feeling of loneliness, the inability to speak coherently, the extreme physicality that immediately shows the emotional overload, and a visceral feeling of pain as central aspects of the storytelling situations that applied to a number of the scenes in the later stretch of the play – in particular the encounter Richard–Elizabeth, and equally Richard's increasingly erratic behaviour towards the end of the play.

Figure 7.13 Thomas Ostermeier rehearsing with Robert Beyer (Catesby) and Lars Eidinger (Richard). Photograph © Peter M. Boenisch.

In the afternoon, from 4pm, the work on these scenes was again continued in individual, private rehearsals for Richard, Lady Anne and Elizabeth. T.O. worked with the actors in close detail on exploring the metaphors and arguments of the dialogues. Meanwhile, with the puppetry coaches and T.O., the actors began to integrate their work on the princes' arrival in London (III.1), and the rehearsed Tower-murder pantomime, into the flow of the scenes.

After New Year's Day, rehearsals once more resumed at the very beginning of the play. T.O. again stressed that Richard's villainy works by pushing the right buttons in the others:

> 'He triggers and exploits their resentments, their malevolence and their eagerness to come into power and get their share of the 'glorious summer' in every respect. Like a cunning politician or business leader, he does not so much follow a singular, deliberate strategy, but he constantly shows his skills in adaptive behaviour: his major talent is to react to people's needs and to tell them what they want to hear. It is through this skill that he makes them do what he wants them to do, whereas they believe it was their own idea. In particular, he invites, encourages and enables them to act out their desires, just as his monologue after the Lady Anne scene extends this wager to the audience: "The world is rotten, so stop idealising it. What you have just seen shows you that if you only have the courage, the world can belong to you, too!"' (T.O.)

The audience must be seduced by this invitation to power, rather than feeling morally superior. Rather than knowing from the start, they must only gradually become aware of Richard's manipulation of others, and of themselves, while watching. By emphasising this in the actors' portrayal of the characters surrounding and serving Richard, his character would become clearer, stronger, and less one-dimensional, with no need to play personified evil. Similarly, his inappropriate behaviour and breaking of conventions (in Scenes I.5 and II.1 in particular) would be more enjoyable to watch if it cuts straight through a façade of overemphasised 'royal behaviour', which in particular the newly promoted aristocrats around Elizabeth, Rivers and Dorset display and try to maintain.

The conflicts between them and the 'old aristocracy' of Hastings and Buckingham should not be played as irrelevant minor quarrels: especially with Edward's ill health, this conflict is existential for Elizabeth and her clan, which is why the reconciliation in II.1 is so important for them. Richard then frustrates all their attempts, and further attacks them by accusing them of his own deeds (above all, the murder of Clarence). Richard is not at all the only one to wear a mask and hide his true intentions; in fact, everyone does in these scenes. Buckingham, in particular, expresses the class difference, and through his erudite way of speaking, in particular in Richard's presence, he seeks to distinguish himself from the 'nouveaux riches'. For Shakespeare's audience, it was great fun to see great kings quarrelling and fighting – those who, like the British Queen today, are never allowed to show emotions in public.

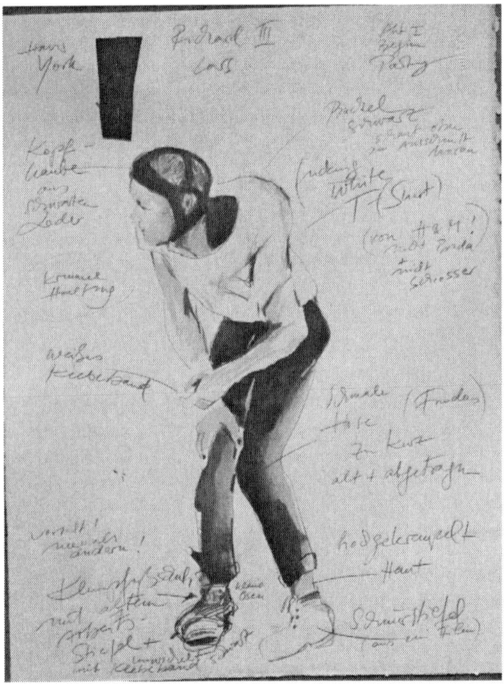

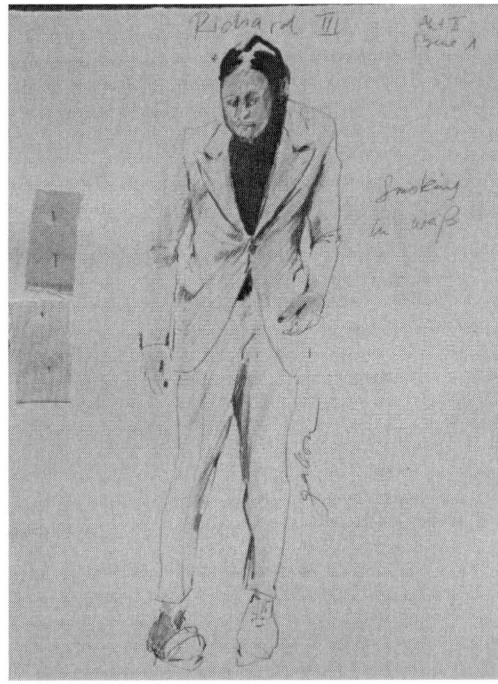

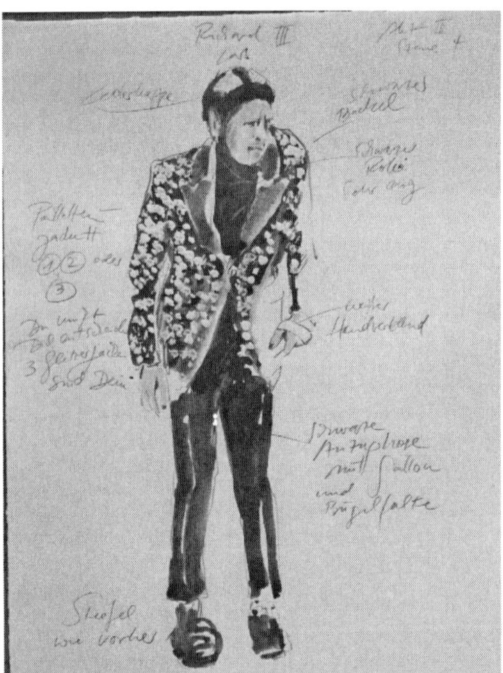

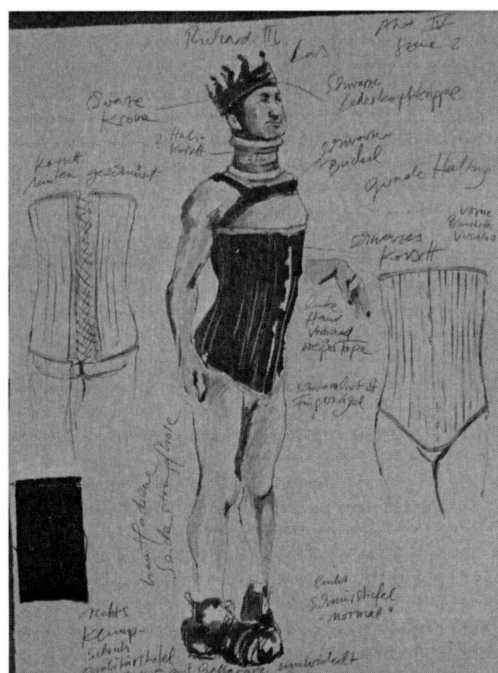

Figures 7.14–7.17 Original figurines for Richard's costumes. © Florence von Gerkan.

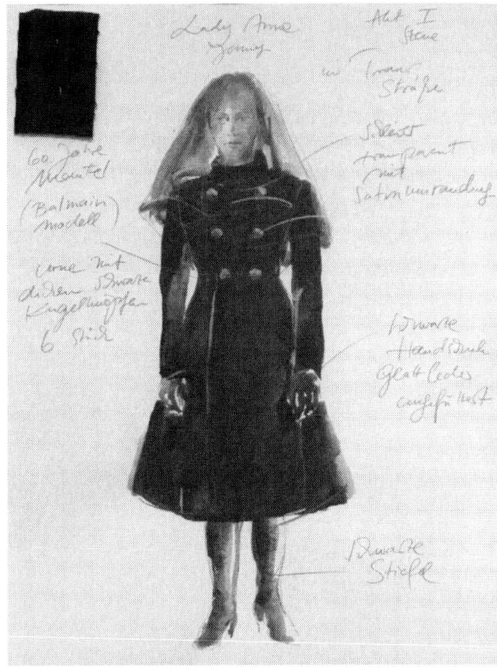

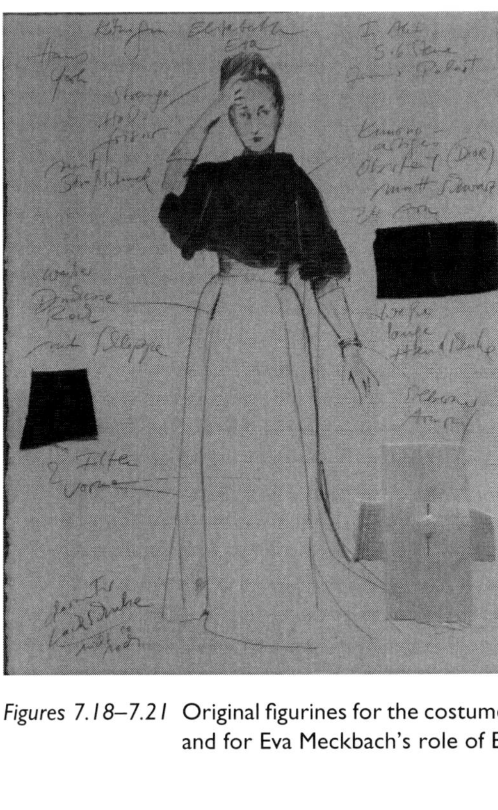

Figures 7.18–7.21 Original figurines for the costumes for Jenny König as party guest and Lady Anne (above), and for Eva Meckbach's role of Elizabeth. © Florence von Gerkan.

Week 8, 5 January 2015

The scenic work continued with Act II, and T.O. once more led extensive repetition training, emphasising the need to be aware of the partner, to listen to what they are saying, and to perceive and respond to the full energy the stage partner emanates. Bearing in mind the context of the play and its apocaplyptic atmosphere where everyone is threatened, he suggested to rather react (to the partner, also to the audience), instead of 'actively acting'. Further storytelling then explored, once more, the topic of receiving the news of the death of a loved person.

In the scenic work, T.O. worked on transitions, aspiring to immediate, filmic 'cuts', on finding positions in space (preventing actors from lining up in straight lines), and on creating precise physical actions to express the characters' emotion, trying to get actors away from 'emoting' in the way they speak lines. During the run, T.O. often prompted the 'subtext'. At the same time, he directed through visual cues, timings and pauses, putting great emphasis on the development of the scenic tempo-rhythm, pauses, and accents. Further, the clarity of the scenic narration as well as the spoken text were important aspects. 'I don't insist on my version of things, but I sense when you play something half-heartedly' (T.O.).

Alongside the scenic rehearsals, T.O. worked with costumer designer Florence von Gerkan and the head of the make-up department Christel Thieme on supporting the multi-roling by showing the distinct characters through different costume, wigs and other accessories, from fatsuits to false teeth and glasses. Numerous propositions were dismissed, as they looked funny and bizarre. With Dupouey, T.O. continued the work on the video imagery, which should offer counterpoints to both scenic action and music; the images should work allegorically, and not show immediately recognisable landscapes, or immediately identifiable objects.

Week 9, 12 January 2015

Another week, another run from the beginning. More tests with wigs, costumes, and accessories; more rejections. T.O. now predominantly orchestrated the interplay of scenic play, light, music and video. The precise timing of musical interludes and samples was cued. In his notes, he discussed any unclear and ambiguous scenic processes he had identified in the actor's play, and he attempted to intensify circumstances and to raise stakes where needed. Rehearsal work concentrated on Acts IV and V, in particular, with detailed rehearsals of Elizabeth and Anne's encounter, the following coronation, and the later Richard–Elizabeth scene. Richard's encounter with the Duchess, his mother, was separated from the Elizabeth scene and will follow later in Act V, before the ghost scene. Following the coronation, Shakespeare shows Richard's inner conflict, the play becomes his psychic profile, exposing his paranoia. Richard's constant eating of potatoes with quark and linseed oil (Hitler's favourite dish), which Lars Eidinger suggested early on in rehearsal, evolved into the facial mask in the silent 'Superman'-scene, which – alongside a change in the music, introducing a repetitive sample accent – now acoustically marks this shift in Richard's character. In a minor incident, Sebastian Schwarz as Ratcliff had not been told about the white facial mask-idea, and used to the food on Richard's plate accidentally nibbled white face paint rather than quark. This concluded the final week in the North Berlin rehearsal space; the atmosphere already noticeably intense.

Week 10, 19 January 2015

Rehearsals moved into Schaubühne. The set was now mounted in Saal C where the production would premier in less than three weeks. After a technical induction, the first scenic rehearsal in the actual space took place. In his notes, T.O. reiterated the importance of ensemble play and communicating with the partner, and he warned against a mode of acting that already knows what would happen next and that communicates a commentary of the scene and the play to the audience.

> 'In order to make the spectators witnesses of the horror and the brutality, you do not need to reiterate it theatrically, through gestures, theatrical emotions, or your way of speaking. Serving the play on a platter prevents the audience from discovering and finding out themselves. Instead, just play the process, and find your play in the processes, the stakes, and your partners. The main find of this production could be to rediscover the power of language.' (T.O.)

Much work was done making the latter part of the production tighter. There was also further technical work on the set; the position of the speakers was

Figure 7.22 Tightening and pacing the show: Christoph Gawenda (here in his Stanley costume), Jenny König (Queen Anne), Thomas Ostermeier, and prompter Heike Krömer working on cuts in one of the final rehearsals before the production opened. Photograph © Arno Declair.

changed, and there was work on the lighting arrangements. Furthermore, the technicalities and practicalities of the hanging scenes were finalised; they would now be performed by a trained stunt-double, not by the actors themselves.

Week 11, 26 January 2015

The first non-stop run of the full production clocked at three hours forty minutes. T.O. went through the text, suggesting some cuts, and he asked each actor to propose five minutes worth of cuts for their own character. The appearance of the Duchess of York, mother of Richard, Clarence and Edward, played by Thomas Bading (who also plays Edward) in Act V was now entirely cut, as was the interlude 'rap'-scene with Richard and Buckingham. The dumb show scene that showed Ratcliff's murder of the two princes in the Tower was also cut.

Throughout the week, in the morning rehearsal, T.O. rehearsed selected scenes, in particular the scenes of Richard and Buckingham, and Richard and Elizabeth. His notes concentrated on pace and clarity, while also correcting technical aspects with lighting. In the evening rehearsal, from 7pm, scenic runs of the full play took place. On Friday, a first full run in front of an audience was scheduled, which was published at short notice via the theatre's 'Friends'

Figures 7.23 and 7.24 Deleted scenes from the 'director's cut': Originally, the murder of Hastings (right), and of Rivers and Dorset (left) was shown on stage, yet the scenes were cut shortly before the premiere. Photographs © Florence von Gerkan and Arno Declair.

association and on social media. It counted in at three hours ten minutes. The target for the premiere is two hours thirty.

Week 12, 2 February 2015

A bombshell to start the final rehearsal week: T.O. decided to drop Richard's final sword-fight scene with Richmond, Buckingham and Stanley, which had been rehearsed for the past ten weeks. In an afternoon rehearsal with Lars Eidinger, working privately on Richard's monologues, Eidinger had continued to play after waking up from his dream, which was to cut directly into the fight scene with Richmond. He indicated all his moves and actions, as the other actors had already left. T.O. encouraged Eidinger to keep going on. He would now similarly perform the fight scene in the production exactly as choreographed, but on his own, fighting with himself. Richmond (a further role assigned to Laurenz Laufenberg) hence no longer featured in the production. Further, the 'hangings' were cut as well and replaced by short silent scenes with music and landscape-video visuals. Also, Richard's (largely silent) solo scene after his coronation (to a sample from Laurie Anderson's 'Oh Superman') was tightened, and now focused mainly on his putting on the white mask.

After a long conversation with the actors, another run with an invited audience. In his notes, T.O. kept concentrating on pacing, on including the audience and capitalising on their proximity. On the final rehearsal days, he returned to extensive repetition exercises, now combined with running lines.

Final changes were made after the dress rehearsal: a video prelude about the War of the Roses and the play's historical context that was initially shown prior to the 'party' sequence in the beginning was dropped, and the appearance of Young Elizabeth (another puppet) alongside her mother for the dialogue with Richard was cut.

Saturday 7 February 2015: premiere at Schaubühne

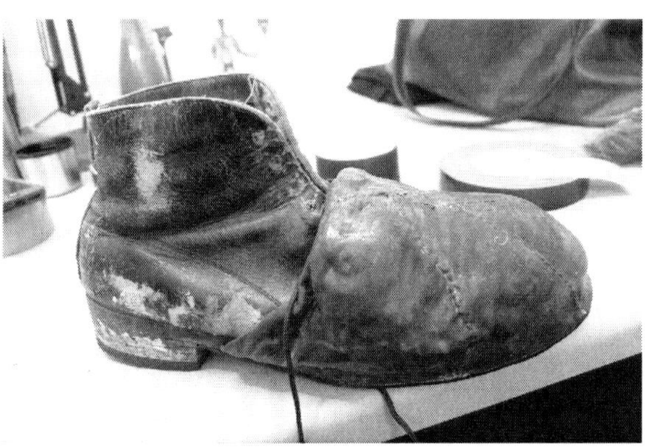

Figure 7.25 Richard's boot. Photograph © Florence von Gerkan.

Figures 7.26–7.29 Richard with Clarence (Lars Eidinger, Christoph Gawenda), and Sebastian Schwarz as Brakenbury, Margaret's curse (Robert Beyer), Buckingham (Moritz Gottwald) and Richard, and Clarence's murder (Christoph Gawenda and Robert Beyer). Photographs © Arno Declair.

Figures 7.30–7.32 Richard's monologue (above), Hastings on the way to the gallows (Sebastian Schwarz), Catesby, Richard and Buckingham (Robert Beyer, Lars Eidinger, Moritz Gottwald). Photographs © Arno Declair.

Figures 7.33–7.35 Richard and the priests meeting the mayor (clockwise from top left Laurenz Laufenberg, Lars Eidinger, Sebastian Schwarz, Robert Beyer, Christoph Gawenda and Moritz Gottwald), Elizabeth and Anne on the way to the Tower (Eva Meckbach and Jenny König), and Richard on the throne (Lars Eidinger, with Robert Beyer and Moritz Gottwald). Photographs © Arno Declair.

7.4 AFTER *RICHARD*: MISSION 'ENSEMBLE ACTING' (JUNE 2015)

The main aspect from which I once started – the 'Vice figure', the one who acts out everything the spectators cannot permit themselves to do in their own lives – is still there: in the microphone, the direct address to the audience, and also the spatial configuration of the production as such. But our intense engagement with the play and its *Stoff* brought up another aspect that eventually became much stronger, and more relevant. It started from an important discovery we made early on, in particular in our 'family portraits', where in the course of several days each actor put on the family constellation from his or her characters' perspective. Here we began to realise how deeply Richard must be hurt and injured by what he had previously experienced in his life: he is an outsider, he never got rewarded for being the strongest warrior during all the Wars of the Roses. He sorted out the bloodiest jobs, but his older brother Edward then prefers his new wife Elizabeth and her kinfolk instead of him. This also causes resentment amongst the old, established aristocracy at court. A related, major finding of the storytelling, the family portraits and then our scenic work on the play was to realise how much Richard exploits this resentment, the prejudice and hatred of these others who also feel disadvantaged, for his intrigues. This was something that had not been that clear to me before. It became the major motor for Lars' portrayal of Richard, and to a large degree also for our overall approach to the play. Such a reading of the play is not political on the surface, but, I would argue, it is so on a deeper level: the outsider who has done all the dirty work in the Wars of the Roses but who never received his reward suddenly sees the opportunity to take power by exploiting his brother's mistake – Edward's mésalliance with Elizabeth and his implantation of her family. As a play, not about evil as such, but about participation in power, the exclusion of an outsider, and the manipulation of others' antipathies, the play does in fact touch some eminent political aspects.

The other aspect that became important as we worked on the production concerned the final act, once Richard has come to power: he becomes a victim of the so-called 'number one phenomenon'. The very moment he has achieved everything, he becomes his own worst enemy. His paranoia provokes him to commit ever crasser murders – Anne, the Princes – and he himself now does not reward his own most loyal vassals such as Buckingham. In his eccentricity, he overreacts and thereby creates his own enemies who perpetuate exactly what they have learnt from Richard: if you are disadvantaged but have a strong enough will and are insidious enough, you can get rid of the tyrant. They repeat the exact pattern that has led Richard to power. Richard grows extremely lonely as the play goes on, and when, towards the end, he lies there under his blanket, you might even feel pity for him – and, judging from what spectators tell me, we may indeed achieve this with our production, which I would consider a major accomplishment. As a result of this insight,

I also feel that in the way we go about the play, it has become possible to tell its full narrative even without all the ado of the battle that make up the play's final twenty or so pages. Prior to starting rehearsals, my biggest concern was how we would manage this part of the play; we had already much reduced the battle scenes in our translation, and they got cut even further in rehearsals – up to the decision to have Lars fight entirely on his own. It was by accident that I watched Lars going through the fight choreography all by himself, and discovered that the scene becomes much stronger, and much more conclusive with our idea of Richard and the 'number one phenomenon', if he fights and loses a battle against himself. This accidental development shows that chance observations and things that fortuitously emerge in rehearsal can be much more powerful than anything you previously masterminded. It was of course a tough decision for the colleagues who had worked really hard to develop the fight scene over eight weeks, and I was fortunate that Christoph Gawenda, Moritz Gottwald and Laurenz Laufenberg were sensitive and modest enough to realise the power of this solution.

Overall, directing *Richard III* has confronted me with a Shakespeare play that is clearly not as powerful and great a work as *Measure for Measure* and *Hamlet*. It is, for sure, an early play whose dramaturgy is in parts rather scrubby; not least the profiling of the main character and the antagonists is very uneven. Nevertheless, Richard is incredibly strong as a dramatic figure, and maybe even more fascinating than Hamlet; he is such a dark and disturbing character who goes against any moral codex of our human civilisation. So, from another perspective, this play, precisely because it does not present another masterful Shakespeare in all its virtuosity, poses an even more exciting task for the director since it confronts you with so many big challenges. Working on the play, the methodologies of storytelling, repetition exercises, and the family portraits all have proven their value, and the puppetry training also had a momentous impact: there, the actors were responsible for a single character in groups of three, which strengthened their teamwork, and their ensemble play. This was an extremely positive experience. What I regret is that in the end we were lacking two weeks to properly make the transition from storytelling and the playful exploration of the material to fixing the scenic arrangements. We had to somewhat abruptly focus on producing results, which was a pity, and was detrimental to the spirit of the entire team in the final couple of weeks before the premiere.

I also feel that we have not yet entirely cracked the space. It is a magic space which creates an incredible power – you even feel its effect in the empty theatre; it feels as if standing in a womb. We should still be able to expand and develop our use of this space a lot, not least our interplay with the audience, and our constant awareness of the spectators' very close presence. This is something I want to try in my next Shakespeare in this space, which will very likely be *Twelfth Night*. But there is no rush, as we are in the exceptionally fortunate situation that both productions playing in this space so far have become extremely successful, and this means that we are able to consistently use our 'Globe'. Usually, it requires five or more repertoire productions to fill one theatre space across any month, but we manage to continually fill this space with sell-out performances of only these two productions. This, I think, is also a result of the special magic this space creates. It is a pity therefore that it seems to be too expensive to take our entire 'Globe' space on tour. At the moment, we are trying to find sponsorship for some of the future performances that are envisaged abroad, for instance in Paris. We will have to see how this may work out.

The one clear mandate that has presented itself to me as a direct outcome of this production is to continue to work on the ensemble, and to work on the ability to create productions where each performance, on every night, and in every single minute, is an effort and achievement of the entire ensemble. The production has not been fully successful in this respect, and hence it will be my mission to keep working on the ensemble spirit, as well as on my own shortcomings that I realise stand in the way of this ambition: to let go of being the boss and instead being confident enough to be an encouraging and enabling leader at all times. With 'ensemble', I do not just mean the available cast of permanently employed actors; I mean ensemble as a process, as a state of mind: a closely knit group of people who are experienced in playing together, and who on the basis of this experience and their mutual trust are able to push their interaction and their collective play to the next level. Ideal ensemble actors immerse themselves fully and without reservation for the two or three months during which you come together to create a new project with each other. For them, acting is not a walk in the park, they won't enter a production somewhat careless, but they will come prepared, knowing, and focused on what is at stake. Ideally, then, a feeling of 'being together', of 'being an ensemble' will emerge from their play, which is something we have seen in the past in the work of Brook, Mnouchkine and Stein, and more recently in some modified form in productions by Simon McBurney, or work at the Volksbühne. Yet, at least within the theatre in the German-speaking countries, this form of ensemble culture, and acting culture, barely exists anymore. This has become my current mission at the Schaubühne.[2] I see the purpose of theatre as presenting an alternative draft of society, and the idea of ensemble happens to run counter to our present-day society that idolises individuality. Maybe this explains why our theatre, at this point in time, is so exceptionally successful with the public.

Notes

1 Robert Weimann, *Shakespeare and the Popular Tradition in the Theater: Studies in the Social Dimension of Dramatic Form and Function*. Transl. Robert Schwartz. Baltimore, MD. Johns Hopkins University Press, 1978.

2 Thomas Ostermeier here refers to 'The Mission', a programmatic statement co-authored by the, at the time, four incoming Artistic Directors as they took their office in 2000. Ostermeier's contribution to this manifesto uses sections from his text 'Theatre in the age of acceleration', included in this volume. An excerpt is published at http://www.schaubuehne.de/uploads/Der-Auftrag.pdf.

Chapter 8

Ostermeier writings [3]

The politics of contemporary theatre

8.1 'THE MORE POLITICAL WE ARE, THE BETTER WE SELL': A CONVERSATION ABOUT THE POLITICAL POTENTIAL OF DIRECTING CLASSICAL DRAMA AND THE NASTY TRAPS OF TODAY'S CULTURAL INDUSTRY (2014)

This conversation took place at the Schaubühne Berlin in May 2014. It was first published as a preview for this present volume in Performance Paradigm *Vol. 10 (2014).*

PETER M. BOENISCH: Thinking about political, radical and resistant contemporary theatre work, the first thing that comes to mind is usually experimental performance art, and not necessarily the staging of dramatic works from the bourgeois classical Western canon, as you produce them at the Schaubühne. Still, the political gestus of your work is eminently important to you.

THOMAS OSTERMEIER: Before we even begin talking about political theatre, I find it very important to challenge the underlying opposition in your question: that between performative, non-narrative and progressive work on the one hand, and narrative, linear, allegedly outdated dramatic theatre on the other. Such binary thinking goes against the very core of postmodern thought, which tells us that everything is possible. It therefore appears extremely peculiar to me to find, time and again, apologists of postmodern contemporary performance art rejecting institutionalised, dramatic theatre as outright evil. In fact, this is a disastrous position. For one, because it is purely ideological, but also because it entirely avoids facing the fact that there exists, in the fields of both dramatic theatre and of performance art, genuinely progressive work as well as not so progressive work. I find that those who in their work today merely repeat the non-narrative formal games of performance art for the hundredth time are much greater conservative epigones than those who start from scratch with a dramatic text, or in whatever form. For years now, I have been warning against the unreflected partisanship for performance forms that affirm what I have described already fifteen years ago at the Baracke as 'capitalist realism': if you attempt to critique today's world by suggesting that everything is so complex and such an impenetrable rhizome that we can only articulate little fragments of reality in our work – then that's nothing but grist to the mills of those in power who must relish such 'critique' which doesn't even attempt to name and tell stories about the big, urgent problems in our society. Of course, the form of classical drama has a long time ago become part of the commodified Hollywood realism that dominates our ways of seeing the world. But I find it very important that we don't ignore the fact that – not for the wider public, but in our own theatre-internal discourse, and in our own theoretical debates – we have arrived at a no less dominant, even dogmatic aesthetic horizon, and that is postdramatic theatre. Performance art has become a hermetically sealed world just as much as dramatic theatre. As soon as it became the majority discourse, performance and postdramatic theatre lost their power to be emancipatory. I therefore very deliberately call for a provocative battle on this crucial point.

PMB: But can the drama of Ibsen or Shakespeare still, or again, be political, radical, resistant, or subversive today, in the age of what Antonio Negri – whom you interview in the Schaubühne's current Spring 2014 season programme brochure – calls 'Empire' and 'multitude'?

TO: This is such a complex topic! I feel we need to start zooming in from the bigger picture before we can start discussing Ibsen or Shakespeare. What comes immediately to my mind are two key questions: what is politics at all in today's world, and how does today's cultural industry function? I see an important connection here, which we have referred to in our *Enemy of the People* production in the text we introduced into the fourth act – the 'Coming Insurrection', arguably one of the most radical political manifestos of the past decade. It says there that it has become fashionable to critique our society in the vain hope to save it, in the theatre, and through art more generally. This points us to a notable desire for political relevance in today's cultural sector, which I see as a phenomenon of the past decade. Many institutionalised, but also many independent culture producers have begun to feel a longing for relevance, and they discovered politics.

Yet, the old idea of the independent artist who functions outside of the institutions as the avant-garde of a future, and who offers from this standpoint a radical critique of our society, no longer works today. Instead, it has become the ultimate selling point for artists that they *seem* to stand outside of the institutions, and I would suggest many artists have become aware of this. So, on the one hand, making critical and political art affords you credibility and authenticity as an artist, but on the other hand this very authenticity is exactly what today's art market wants to buy. As artists we therefore find ourselves stuck in an extreme contradiction: The more we position ourselves outside of the dominant cultural industry and the more we articulate our radical independence – the more we become interesting for that very cultural industry. One of the most salient examples of recent years must be Tino Sehgal who is explicitly politically minded, who attempts to be un-marketable by not giving interviews, by not producing any documents, or any recordings, anything that could become sellable, who thereby seeks to prevent his art from becoming a cultural commodity – and precisely for this very reason his own market value has risen exponentially. I would not for a moment suggest that this has been his strategic speculation, but still, his art was unable to escape from these mechanisms: he who can most credibly argue for standing outside the system achieves the highest market value within the system.

I therefore think our reality has become far more complex than the, again, strictly binary idea suggests – that there exists, on the one hand, the affirmative, institutional world, and on the other hand there is the world of resistance outside of these institutions. Such a concept is no longer adequate, and that's the crux when you discuss ideas of political theatre and its potential to be subversive, radical and resistant. Both worlds rather function as communicating pipes, as Luhmann might express it. The institutions of our society can only survive if they replenish and refresh themselves from time to time with people who have stood outside the system, who have been in fact extremely critical of the system. I am a very good example for this. This is quite a nasty position if you want to resist, subvert and do political work.

PMB: When a Canadian theatre, as it recently happened, purchases your *Enemy of the People* wholesale to stage an exact copy, not unlike the Disney shows or musical productions which you can see in identical copies all around the globe, and also Broadway producers approach you about this option, you must find yourself confronted with exactly this tension or even trap.

TO: I would say the writing has been on the wall much earlier. We are not supported by the city of Berlin to do Augusto Boal-type invisible theatre in underground stations. Our *Enemy of the People* has been shown at probably eighty per cent of the world's most influential theatre festivals. Financially, in addition to the money we get from the city, we need international touring in order to survive. And indeed, in exact analogy to the phenomenon I have attempted to describe, the more we articulate ourselves politically, the better we sell. But, this does not mean that I sit down and think about how I could now create the next political piece. When I work on a play such as *An Enemy of the People* or *Hamlet*, I find during rehearsals, and during my own preparatory reading of the play, traces of topics that reveal resistance and subversion, and as a director, I then try to carve out these topics and to bring them to the foreground. These are topics we debate and negotiate in our productions. I would however not for a moment suggest that theatre itself is an act of resistance.

Hamlet, for instance, is a resistance fighter, but that's the topic of the play. He is called upon to offer resistance in a political situation: 'Something is rotten in the state of Denmark!' Hamlet realises that something isn't right. Isn't that the feeling of every adolescent, at whatever time, in whatever society? You can have the same feeling growing up in China today, but equally you feel that something is rotten as you are growing up in New York, and you feel something isn't right at all as you grow up in Lower Bavaria as I did. It's the topic of *Hamlet*, and Old-School-Shakespeare scholarship would suggest that it is the classical tragedy of revenge. But Shakespeare introduces a truly interesting question for Hamlet: shall I – within the fiction of the plot, but also as a recognisable figure in a specific tradition of this genre, where the audience in Elizabethan London certainly expects me to take up my arms and to take revenge – shall I take on the fight against a politically corrupt, entirely degenerated system, or shall I break through the cycle of revenge? And here I see the genuinely political achievement and the emancipatory process of Hamlet: given the opportunity to murder Claudius, he does not do what Laertes and Fortinbras do, he does not go out and kill, but he breaks through the circle of violence and counter-violence. Isn't this the far more radical emancipation? A guy suddenly asks, shall I take up my arms – or rather do nothing, and sleep? 'I would prefer not to', as Bartleby says. Performing this, as we did, in Ramallah – a play which starts asking the question whether you should take up your weapons and resist – you publicly voice a question that eighty per cent of your audience are confronted with on a daily basis. Performing this play in such a place, or performing in Moscow or China, a different set of political interferences comes into play.

But the longing to get rid of the mission is also exactly what I would describe as the Hamlet-sentiment of my own generation: We have a clear mission, but we also have the desire to shrug off this mission, because it is much too big. We know we simply won't be able to succeed in the mission to save the world, the world where the rule of the market has become absolute. It's the call we all clearly hear – we all have our own ghost of Hamlet's father in our minds because in the course of the twentieth century there were people like Gandhi, Rudi Dutschke in the German 1968 radical left, our own parents who started the Green party, or who on the contrary have been conservative and against all that. These are our own 'Old Hamlets' who call on us and say, something is rotten, you need to take revenge, you need to change the world to save it, and we know perfectly well that the only way to save our planet is a truly radical change. I talk about such questions merely through existing stories, and at times we are able to bring these stories into a context where it transcends the fictional drama and directly touches the political reality, like when a young Palestinian comes to me after seeing our *Hamlet* and says, 'this is not theatre, this is real life.'

PMB: In *An Enemy of the People*, you lift the fourth wall during the assembly scene in the fourth act, and you instigate a discussion with the audience after your Doctor Stockmann has read out the text of 'The Coming Insurrection'. Has this been an attempt then to find a form where your theatre manages to similarly transcend the fiction also for a Western audience, who comfortably lives far away from a war and conflict zone: by creating theatre moments where the boundaries between fiction and reality become porous and fluent?

TO: In *An Enemy of the People*, we have found in the play itself a moment – the public assembly Stockmann organises in the fourth act, and where Ibsen in the original text represents an audience on stage through actors who act the audience – which offered itself to transgress the frame of the theatre of representation, which I usually create, and to thereby trigger exciting and interesting phenomena for each spectator. A friend of mine recently saw the show and he was in absolute disbelief that the audience really takes this moment seriously. He had expected them to say, stop pretending, we don't believe you, we know you are actors, but they engage with them as characters in this discussion.

But I think I need to reiterate one important point. As an Old-School-Marxist, I don't believe for a second that this is a political event, or that any political event could take place in the theatre, or in art, in the first place. Resistance, emancipation, revolution, and true, active politics happen when social movements unite and begin to shake up and change the existing conditions and power relations in a society. In our pacified Western societies in the capitalist centres, we live in entirely apolitical times. We have globalised and exported social and political struggle, and except for the news images of African refugees who drown in the Mediterranean, we don't even see or hear anything. Of course some form of 'politics' happens, but not the radical emancipatory politics where everyone develops their political conscience, and equal participation and co-determination for all is realised: a society without domination, without rule and hegemony. As for every engaged artist, this is my utopia, too. But I am not so naïve as to believe for a moment that we would ever get there solely through art, or that we live, today, in times where there is even a faint chance of moving towards such a different society, even though our own societies are more and more split by an ever more extreme gap between the poor and the rich. But still, the situation has not become sufficiently tenuous that people would get involved in politics beyond their engaged slogans or the stupid talk shows on TV. For Western critical hipsters, the idea of actually involving themselves in party politics is short of revolting – so I have no hope for any revolution soon.

That much about my analysis of our times, and of the political potential of art. I have drawn the consequence to create what I once described as 'sociological theatre': theatre as a laboratory in order to observe human behaviour in our society. Of course, politics is part of society, but I don't think this theatre can then become emancipatory, let alone an act of resistance. It does become interesting, though, in those moments where boundaries start to blur and playful irritation sets in, and where as a result moments of an emerging political consciousness suddenly appear. But again, in *An Enemy of the People*, this is a straightforward dramaturgic manoeuvre. Stockmann is a narcissist, a grumbler, a querulous fellow and smart-arse who suddenly gets stubbornly resistant, and we set it up that the audience at some point says, shit, if all of our political leaders are corrupted by notorious self-importance and narcissism, if we cannot be sure whether their motive really is to bring the truth to light, and not much rather to finally get one over his brother who has looked down on him all his life – aren't our emancipatory movements perhaps all undermined in their very foundations? For me, we have in our recent German history of the 1968 protests two political leaders who exactly illustrate this crucial question – Rudi Dutschke and Andreas Baader: the former managed to pacify his narcissism, the other drove it into militant radicality.

This is the debate I attempt to stimulate through *An Enemy of the People*, but once again I want to ask: Is this already political performance then, or even subversion? Even if, as it happened during our performance of the production at Buenos Aires, the scene triggers a tumultuous riot in the theatre – I am sitting in the back row and rejoice, but more like a schoolboy who has managed to play a clever prank that sets his parents against his teachers. But this is the joy of playing with fire, of kindling conflicts which already exist beneath the surface, and to watch them blow up and escalate. I wouldn't say it is political – because there is no consequence to it.

PMB: But isn't this the very purpose of art, of theatre – to create such spaces of the 'as if', spaces without consequence? If we adopt Jacques Rancière's distinction of 'the police' as the administration of the political, of the party politics of our neoliberal democracies, and of 'the political' as the moments where the configurations and the 'partition of the sensible', as he calls it, are modified – could we not argue that theatre today becomes political precisely where it offers us such new configurations and allows us to make different experiences? Of course, such an idea of 'political performance' falls way behind the Marxist idea of politics as you just described them, as actual change of the conditions of dominance, power and hegemony. Is Rancière's suggestion – and he of course also comes from a Marxist tradition, via his teacher Louis Althusser – nevertheless an attempt to save political theatre in what you just described as apolitical times, where no revolution is anywhere on the horizon?

TO: His idea of organising experience is certainly interesting. It might be an apt description of the experience of *An Enemy of the People*, where spectators get so emotional and so upset that they forget that the actual reason for their emotions, for their rage has been a theatre performance, and not a real political scandal. It is every director's dream to create such moments. The question whether the redistribution of experiences is political is plausible and right – yet I would want to ask: *Cui bono?* For whom or for what? That's what I would really like to find out about a lot of current political thinkers, especially when they start discussing and analysing art works: What is their utopia? Behind every concept for political art, there has to be an answer to this one question: what for? Is it the vision of a radically different society? Or is it, as 'The Coming Insurrection' hints at, to provide another crutch to keep our postdemocratic society going, or another anaesthetic infusion into the veins of a dying society? Where do you want to go with your political art?

PMB: What for – on that question, I would like to return to a point you made earlier. You spoke of the 'Hamlet mentality', our desire to reject the burden of this urgent mission to really do something in order to secure the future and the survival of our planet. I recognise this description for our own generation, for those who have grown up in the 1970s and 1980s. Yet, with the next generation, with our students for example, it often seems to me that the mere discovery that such a mission may exist, that it is possible at all to follow such a mission – the discovery of 'old Hamlet' and his ghost, if you like – is already a rather massive 'political' discovery for them: the fact that there exists something beyond the circulation of goods, of media and information, beyond the marketplace of creativity and innovation, in which theatre to a very large degree is fully integrated nowadays. Talking to this generation about your *Hamlet*-production, for instance, I heard less about the 'I'd rather not to'-position, but far more about the discovery that you can stage *Hamlet* as something different than the reproduction of a classical text one 'does' and one has to know at school, but in a way that opens a space for thinking, as something that actually asks relevant and very personal questions. This seems to be quite an experience for that generation.

TO: And giving them this experience, you make them even more capable of surviving in our global capitalism, because they can think more creatively, and are then able to offer this creativity for sale on the marketplace. Capitalism desires nothing more than people who think differently, and thereby perhaps invent the next iPhone. Here we return to the very reason why critical art and political theatre have become so popular recently: contemporary capitalism has realised that it won't be able to survive if it drowns and kills off the ability to think differently in its economy of numbers, of zeroes and ones, of profits.

PMB: So we're back to the trap in which critical art is stuck. What then is for you the impulse and the appeal to respond to this situation by staging dramatic classics?

TO: They are Trojan horses. It's as simple as that. You write on the tin *An Enemy of the People*, *Hedda Gabler* or *Hamlet*, and you cater to the audience, the same audience who also fill our museums from MOMA in New York to the Tate Modern in London, or the Gropius-Bau here in Berlin. Our bourgeois class, confronted with a loss of meaning and driven by a desire to make sense of the world, seeks to satisfy this desire by turning to the classical canon. That is why after the era of postmodernism we have recently seen the return of culture and of *Bildung*. I have the feeling that once again it is expected that you know what a symphony is, that you know your stuff about art history and also about the literary classics. And so people come to pick up this knowledge in the theatre; they say, I won't manage to read *Hamlet*, but if Ostermeier does it at the Schaubühne, then I go and watch it, so I know what it is about because I might need to know at some point. So I imply people get their dose of the classical literary canon to fill their knowledge gaps, and I then show them the classics as if they were a contemporary play.

PMB: So, you don't see the classics as offering another perspective, a timeless view on the conflicts of the present?

TO: No, I wouldn't make that case. My own huge fondness for Ibsen results from the pure fact that our own society has retreated to fundamental bourgeois values. The biggest desire for many Germans today is to be able to make ends meet financially. For them, the utopia is being a couple who earn well, who live in a decent flat, furnished in today's entirely trivial general style, with the kids attending the best possible schools, ideally an international school, learning the violin and playing classical music, going with them to the theatre, and training them from as early on as possible how to survive in globalised capitalism. Culture, and a big part of it is the classical bourgeois canon of works, is their ultimate attempt to be able to survive in global capitalism, to acquire certain weapons and a certain shell which helps you to stay sane. This brings you pretty close to the problems, and to the ideas of happiness which you find in Ibsen's characters, while being very far from, say, Goethe.

PMB: Based on a similar analysis of our current society and of the problems of global neoliberal capitalism, other artists would still, as a consequence, do the opposite, and turn away from the classics and the established theatre institutions, towards the off-scene and experimental performance.

TO: But as I said in the beginning, I don't think at all it is a question of form, but of modes of organisation. If I were to do experimental theatre in the off-scene, I would need to be aesthetically even more conventional in order to survive – and remember that I find that much of what you call 'experimental performance' has in fact become no more than a convention itself. I find that I am able to work in much greater liberty than in the so-called independent theatre right here, in this institutionalised theatre bunker of the Schaubühne. To start with, I can be sure that my employees get paid every month.

PMB: So it is about exploiting ...

TO: Exactly. You exploit the freedom which spaces like this offer. But again, the all-important question is – *cui bono?* These spaces of play, of freedom – that's all fine, but as an artist working within this space of liberty you must have a certain utopia you want to present to your audience. Otherwise your theatre is no different from a theme park of classical culture.

PMB: So what is your personal utopia, then?

TO: Again, a lot goes through my mind on this question. I think it has already become quite an utopian thought today to insist that art and theatre should belong to the things – like streets, hospitals, education, personal safety – for which our society redistributes its wealth, and to insist that theatre art should be more than an entertainment commodity, but that in fact it helps our society to survive. It offers spaces where we attempt to make sense of ourselves by playing, by doing things that have no place in our every-day life – and not having these spaces would result in alienation, in a spiritual coma, in utter idiocy. Art therefore immunises our society, and for this reason it is right to say we need art. There is no need or obligation whatsoever to defend art in economic or in any other terms. The utopian moment here is to insist on positive terms, and not to consider the public financing of art – and I reject the terms subvention, subsidy, or investment entirely – as a burden and as a problematic legacy which we cannot afford anymore and have to get rid of.

PMB: So your political utopia is to insist on theatre art as public common good, in the same way as others currently defend, for instance, water, health and education as 'commons' against neoliberal marketisation and commodification?

TO: This is my approach to my role and to my function within this industry, and why I am doing it. But no, my true utopia is of course to overcome the material and political realities and to live in a society without domination and suppression. Everything else is day-to-day pragmatism.

PMB: Jodi Dean would argue here that by producing theatre art, by making spectators engage with and articulate their political energies in your *Enemy of the People*, you absorb their political energies and prevent them from actually striving for such a radical utopia.

TO: And Julien Coupat, who is thought to be one of the leading authors of the anonymous 'Coming Insurrection'-manifesto would agree; their arguments are in many points very similar. It is certainly correct to suggest that we pacify radical energies and channel them into art, away from direct action, and that we therefore appear like the henchmen of the dominant affirmative political doctrine. I can absolutely see what Dean is suggesting, and I sympathise with the point she makes. But take the concrete example, our *Enemy of the People*. In the performance just two days ago, I once again had this feeling that there are many young people in the audience – those young people you described earlier rather accurately. A young girl in her early twenties said in the discussion about why she had raised her hand to support Stockmann, 'I believe it is important today to say no in the first place, to raise your voice and say, I am against it.'

This brings us back to emancipation and to core enlightenment values: can such a theatre experience trigger a process of developing political consciousness, where you say – man, shit, why don't I get as upset and swept along as I did in the *Enemy of the People* on a daily basis, when I watch the news, when I hear, to take just a very small local problem, about the privatisation of the water supply in Berlin? I can very well imagine that such a process of making an experience in the theatre helps these people to gather the courage to say no in their real life too, and to get more active and involved in everyday politics. That is my riposte to Dean's position. But perhaps it is only wishful thinking.

8.2 THE FUTURE OF THEATRE (2013)

This essay was originally commissioned for the 50th anniversary special edition of the German literary magazine text + kritik *(Munich 2013, p. 42–50), which brought together commissioned statements by artists about the future of their respective art forms. Thomas Ostermeier was invited to comment on the future of theatre. An abridged version of this text subsequently appeared in* Le Monde Diplomatique, Nachtkritik, *and the Argentinian theatre journal* Funambulos. *The full, original version is here published for the first time in English, translated by Peter M. Boenisch and authorised by Thomas Ostermeier. By kind permission of Edition Text + Kritik.*

The material conditions

Our so-called Western democracies share a simple fact: in order to sustain the commonwealth of society, each state raises taxes. The society skims off some of its wealth so that its democratic institutions, parliaments and local assemblies are able to redistribute it – in accordance with what these institutions deem right and important. This sounds to all intentions completely plausible, even somewhat banal. Nevertheless, I find it worth reminding ourselves that to a large degree our civic societies are based on the fundamental agreement that there are certain 'public duties' which enable both individuals and businesses – to do what, actually? To be happy? To be successful? To learn? To be open to other ideas and other people? A business's location most certainly needs an infrastructure, streets, airports, trains, a sewage system, and more, in order to enable companies to make profits. No less obvious appears to be the indispensable role of the education sector, from primary schools to universities and research institutes, in nurturing the next, well qualified generation. It gets somewhat more complicated when the question of public finances for cultural institutions is raised ...

More and more, we lose our understanding of how to organise a civic society. In the 1980s, Chicago neoliberalism set off on its path to global triumph. The most important achievement of this ideology was the deregulation of the financial markets, under which we have really been suffering in recent years. But the ideas of the 'Chicago Boys' had other effects, too, such as the privatisation of what used to be perceived as 'public duties': the privatisation of universities, hospitals, and public transport, for example – within Europe, these developments are probably most advanced in the United Kingdom. This new ideology, particularly propelled by the collapse of the 'real existing socialism' in the former Eastern European countries, is based on a simple equation: the more the taxes a state levies from its citizens and companies are reduced, the larger is the sum of money that remains in their pockets and that they can therefore consume or invest (the unfortunate fact that many do not invest their spare cash in their own national economy is a different topic). I reiterate these well-known developments in the economic history of the past three decades because I firmly believe that to a large degree, the crisis of legitimacy we experience in theatre today has its roots precisely in this paradigm shift, as far as the economic crisis of justifying the existence of theatre is concerned (I will turn to the crisis of its intellectual legitimacy in the second part of this essay). At their core, the battles between the neoliberals on the one hand and the – well, what should we call them at all? – let us say 'those who protect our civic polity's social function' concern the question of primacy within the state: should there be a primacy of politics or the economy? The triumphant advance of neoliberalism has pushed the state back ever further, and nowadays the idea is widespread that nothing can claim any value unless it creates profit in the markets. Tragically, the established Western European Left has traditionally been sceptical of public institutions, not to say hostile towards the state. For this very reason, the Left finds itself in the painful situation where it has got to defend the state against those who solely believe in the market – the very state of which the Left traditionally, and with some good reason, did not think very highly. And still, personally, the idealist notion that the wealth of a society should be justly distributed among the populace certainly has a resonance for me. I would even go so far as to describe this understanding of the very purpose of a community as utopian because at the back of my mind I have the dream that all goods and the entire wealth of a society is shared and owned equally by all members of this society: the dream of a society without private property. Yet, right now, we are not just miles away from such a utopia – the situation is far worse: the ideology of the market has put any thought in this direction under the suspicion of advocating totalitarianism.

But let us concentrate on the civic, middle-class version of the distribution of our wealth, based on raising taxes from the people and corporations. Even this more modest principle – originally invented by the prospering bourgeoisie as it rose to power in the eighteenth and nineteenth centuries – is being substantially threatened today, as noted earlier. Transport, schools, universities, libraries, parks and recreation areas, and of course cultural institutions, too – all these civic ideas and public institutions that have come under attack today were, in the German context, invented, or at least institutionalised, and put under public responsibility shortly after the foundation of the German Reich in 1870/71, and the subsequent era of prosperity (and crisis), the so-called *Gründerzeit* or 'founders' era'. The bourgeoisie, exercising its newly acquired power and influence, wanted to assert its dominance through these representative institutions that fostered the public good. Back then, the attitude towards the state was far less cynical than today. It was seen as an expression of this same bourgeois ideal of citizenship and as a mode of organising opportunities to attain (material as well as intellectual) wealth. Today's neoliberal discourse, meanwhile, discounts the state as nothing but an obstacle of economic prosperity. In such a political climate, the very same publicly financed cultural institutions that were once the pride of the emerging bourgeois citizen have arrived in a situation where they constantly need to justify and legitimise their existence. Many debates about budget cuts create the impression that cutting back the cultural budget would take a significant burden off the squeezed budgets of local authorities and federal states. Yet, public budgets have come under pressure as a result of globalisation and of changing economic realities. During the 1990s, quite a few local authorities all over Germany sold their publicly owned waterworks, their roads, their local transport system to internationally operating funds, and they thus lost a lot of money and income. Businesses or even entire industries, think of coal mining, are no longer able to compete with low-cost producers in other countries in the global market. The result is a slump in tax-income, leading to considerable pressure on the public purse and creating the so-called 'need for savings'.

Those working in the cultural sector and its institutions are not the cause of the present contraction of public budgets, even though this impression is blithely being circulated. On the contrary: since the early 1990s, Germany has already seen a massive depletion of its cultural resources. Between 1992 and 2012, eighteen theatres in Germany have been closed or merged. The debate is nevertheless persistently fuelled by the implicit suggestion promulgated in many public statements that cultural spending would devour an enormous part of overall budgets. The sober reality, meanwhile, tells a very different story. After World War II, the responsibility for culture in Germany was put into the hands of the federal states. In contrast to, for instance, France, federal states, their cities and local authorities finance all of the nation's cultural spending. Let us bring in some illuminating figures: in Berlin, spending on culture amounts to no more than two per cent of the city's overall budget – and this is the city which seeks to promote itself as the 'city of young artists and contemporary art' internationally; it is the same city which is also very well aware that in today's global economy, art is its only capital, since in its recent history as insular city stuck between East and West, Berlin has lost almost all of its manufacturing industry. Should this not be the reason to spend *more* on culture? If you also bear in mind that the money spent on theatre arts – including opera – amounts to no more than 1.1 per cent of this budget – theatre itself accounting for barely 0.5 per cent – the discussion about cuts to cultural funding in order to make savings in the budget becomes even more absurd. Hamburg, Germany's second largest city, offers a similar picture. The share of the city's budget for culture within the overall budget is 2.1 per cent, of which 0.9 per cent is dedicated to theatre and opera. The situation in neighbouring countries is not much different either. In Vienna, a city renowned for its support of cultural institutions, the actual cultural budget equally amounts to a mere 2.1 per cent of the overall budget. In France, in 2013, the share of the cultural budget has gone down by 3.2 per cent to 2.53 per cent of the country's overall spending, with the performing arts (theatre, dance, music) getting a meagre 0.24 per cent share of the country's overall public expenditure. It thus becomes immediately clear what little effect any budget cuts in the cultural sector will have in balancing the overall budget.

Yet in spite of these figures, public financial support for culture and the arts is time and again called into question, under the cover of the 'need to make savings'. The very idea of publicly representative institutions that emerged from the new values of the bourgeoisie – which in its original intention aims not for profit but for benefits to the public good – has now been thrown overboard. The primacy of the economy has long triumphed over politics. Ordinary people's long-standing suspicion of these temples of bourgeois representation, while certainly justified in part, is on the rise and is in perfect step with the dominant *Zeitgeist*. During a taxi ride in Amsterdam, shortly after the change of government in 2010, my taxi driver, on hearing that I work in theatre, gleefully retorted: 'Now it's payback time'. At the time, the Dutch government had just begun its historically unprecedented destruction of the country's cultural landscape. The taxi driver was smirking about the fact that virtually all public financial support had been cut from this left-wing artistic elite that for decades had been fed and pampered. Some time before, I took part in a panel debate (on an entirely unrelated topic) with, amongst others, a German MP from the liberal FDP party, who was exactly my age. As I arrived, he welcomed me with the words: 'How are you, you champagne-guzzling subsidy scrounger?' This is the climate that is spreading all over Europe today. In countries such as the Netherlands, Italy, and in particular Hungary, cultural funding has already been drastically reduced. The situation in Hungary is particularly devastating, as anti-intellectualism goes hand in hand with open antisemitism and homophobia. This atmosphere led to the dismissal of the artistic director of Budapest's National Theatre, and his replacement with a 'safe pair of hands' from the governing, right-wing nationalist Fidesz party. A very bad climate, indeed. Yet it is important to keep in focus, as I have tried here, the historical dimension: in the current cultural battles (which are mainly a battle *against* culture), the middle-class 'centre' of society has forsaken its own original instrument – the celebration of its economic as well as intellectual hegemony. By opposing the financing of cultural (and other) institutions, the bourgeoisie has begun to eradicate its own roots.

In the field of theatre, a specific development of the past decade has been particularly fatal: under the garb of defending 'free', independent structures, different parts of the sector are turning against each other. Those advocating what is known in Germany as the 'free' (off-) theatre claim that they would be able to spend the millions of Euros swallowed up by the large subsidised theatres in a much more efficient way. It does not even occur to them that this argument turns them into advocates of the neoliberal *Zeitgeist*. Are they not suggesting what could be paraphrased, somewhat bluntly, as: 'We will give you more art for less money'? It won't be a surprise that quite a few politicians in charge of budgets and/or culture have held the door wide open for them. 'Free theatre' sounds, at first sight, fresher, wilder, more romantic, in short: more attractive. But if, as a politician, I give money to a project, a company or a fixed-term initiative, instead of permanently funding an institution, I can also very simply divert the money to another artist as soon as the project has come to an end, or use it for something entirely different within my budget. My opportunities to distribute money thus become far more flexible. This core neoliberal ideal of flexibility means, however, that all the supported projects have got to be successful in the short term. Meanwhile, the long-term artistic development of artists, directors or ensembles, which is so important in the field of theatre, becomes impossible as every single production is now under great pressure to be a success. At the same time, the employment generated by such project-based work can only be short-term and precarious, in contrast to an engagement within an ensemble theatre. Contributions towards social security or pensions are rarely paid, and – in Germany – the status of such precarious cultural employment in the health insurance system is still unclear. As a result, artistic work suffers because one has to make money in the first place and thus take on other jobs, too. Abandoning the institution of publicly financed municipal and state theatres would also lead to the disappearance of whole specialist vocational professions such as the stage builder, the theatre sculptor, the theatre make-up artist, the stage painter, and many others. Johan Simons, who used to lead Hollandia, one of the most important 'free' companies of the 1980s and 1990s in the Netherlands, had to look on as the entire funding for the company was cut following his departure, while the money did not go to another theatre company, either. It was as if Berlin had axed the Schaubühne's funding after Peter Stein resigned as Artistic Director.

Public theatre institutions present us artists with a permanent, major challenge: to give these institutions a new meaning, year upon year, and generation upon generation. If these venues' right to exist is now fundamentally called into question, it is not us, the artists, who are called into question, but much rather the very roots of enlightened citizenship which fashioned these venues in order to express its values. If today's middle class 'centre' of our society wants to bid farewell to these achievements, it also leaves behind a significant part of its cultural identity. Even a great many artists do not realise the unique opportunity offered by the fact that these venues are permanently public-funded, across generations and as a matter of principle. Like me, many of them come from a background whose attitude is hostile towards the state and its institutions, and of course they look at these bourgeois temples with great scepticism. But these bourgeois institutions offer us opportunities to work, and means to produce and to disseminate our own, different narratives of this society. Obviously, the bourgeoisie pays us to be modern jesters: to make fun of them, and thereby to sustain their smug idea that the middle class can take any criticism and that it even laughs at itself. And still it would be fatal to give up these spaces from our side, because then we will become ever more vulnerable to all the economic crises yet to come. Without permanent institutions, one can cut all our funding from one day to the next. This happened in the US after the 2008 financial crisis. Many corporations withdrew from cultural sponsorship, which is the sole financial basis of US theatre. As a result, theatre artists had to bear the brunt of casino capitalism, despite not having contributed at all to the crisis.

So much for the material conditions of making theatre today. It becomes even more difficult if in such a situation, where the very material basis of our work has come under constant threat, theatre finds itself, at the very same time, in an intellectual and aesthetic crisis, too.

The intellectual conditions

In recent years, theatre-making has been dominated by the aesthetic discourse of postdramatic theatre. There is talk about 'making theatre after the performative turn'. Curiously, these new theatre forms, which have emerged in the 1970s and 1980s, have become the aesthetic credo of many municipal theatres and festivals. One should note, though, that today's epigones and imitators of this genre are a far cry from living up to the standards of their role models; they merely cook up an aesthetic mish-mash of ingredients taken from the 1980s avant-garde and a misunderstood idea of *Regietheater*. Yet, across Germany, this is then celebrated as a paragon of modern theatre. The poetics of this genre assumes that a dramatic narrative is no longer relevant; that human beings can no longer be portrayed as subjects with agency; that there are as many subjective realities in the auditorium as there are audience members, and that there is no objective truth behind the events on stage that would affect everyone equally; and that our experience of reality is entirely fragmented and that this experience should be reflected on stage, too. A complex world with its multi-layered experiences leads to the use of numerous media: bodies, dance, images, video, music, projection, documentation, autobiography, text. This sampling of fragments implies that the experience of reality as impenetrably complex must be correct, and that it is therefore futile to raise questions about political responsibility, let alone guilt. A few years ago, I described this attitude as 'capitalist realism', deliberately evoking the notion of 'socialist realism', which had been the affirmative aesthetics within real-existing socialism. I still cannot help but find the new aesthetics similarly affirmative. In a world dominated by neoliberal doctrine, those who profit from this ideology can be nothing but pleased by the suggestion that there are no culprits anymore, that everything has become so complex and convoluted that those responsible can no longer be named.

I do not suggest at all that this describes all the representatives of postdramatic theatre; on the contrary. In documentary theatre, in particular, in the works of artists such as Milo Rau and Rimini Protokoll, one can find the opposite. Their documentary work, on the borderline of journalistic reportage and its critical interrogations, results in theatre productions that are far more enlightening and illuminating than the majority of productions on the playbills of our municipal theatres. I want to bring in another thought here: I see in the flourishing of these forms of documentary theatre-making with its 'experts of the everyday' (as Rimini Protokoll refer to their amateur performers, the 'real people' they put on stage) an indicator of the crisis of traditional theatre. The established art of acting and the cultivation of a canonical repertoire have, to a large degree, lost touch with our social reality. Those in the auditorium are no longer able to recognise their own everyday lives on stage. This is a direct result of the aestheticism that has dominated German theatre for the past three decades, where productions of the classics only defined themselves through references to previous productions. As a result of this closed circle (or perhaps better: this downward spiral) theatre has inexorably lost any link to social and political realities. In the field of acting, too, one may observe that many performers no longer draw inspiration from their own lives and experiences, but exclusively from the role models they so admire. This situation of an intellectual crisis in contemporary theatre has resulted in the peculiar fact that the 'experts of the everyday' reveal much more about our reality, and much more competently, than professional actors – whereas that ought to be one of the principal tasks of the actor!

This problem is at the very core of the crisis of theatre today, a crisis which may be addressed by the experiments of postdramatic theatre I have already referred to. Yet, traditional theatre should confront this challenge, too. It should start with the actors' training and their continuous professional development. When Brecht was the Berliner Ensemble's artistic director, he made his actors go out into the real world, to attend court trials, or volunteer for factory work, so that they could competently report about the behaviour of real people on stage. In this spirit, I try to get my own actors to refer to and tell stories about their own biographies and about their observations and experiences outside the theatre. How does the fear of social decline in our time shape human behaviour? How does the pressure to perform and to succeed in our society impact on our emotional relations and desires? How do we subordinate our private lives to this imperative? How often do relationships fall apart because of the social reality of the 'flexible individual'? Why do we have a highly elaborated terminology to describe the relationships with our partners? Why do we think that we have developed a high proficiency in analysing the psychology of everyday life? Why do we regurgitate this same terminology during our social evening events, when we are out for dinner or out at the pub? Why do we passionately debate the latest gossip about relationships and one-night-stands? Yet why do we only have an underdeveloped vocabulary to describe our political realities (the 'shit system' Billing talks about in *An Enemy of the People*)? Why do we never discuss the catastrophic social and political developments of the past few decades with equal passion and fervour – even though they are shaping almost every single aspect of all our relationships and psychologies? Flexible working hours, the digitisation of everyday life, our permanent availability (even late at night we check our business emails), the duty to identify one-hundred per cent with the company we work for, as if we are married to it. And all this in a world of flexible contracts, where we can never be sure that we will not be unemployed tomorrow, and that our overambitious commitment to our employer may thus not pay off after all. These are the realities of contemporary life that, all around us, inscribe themselves right into human physical behaviour. How else can we explain the boom of newspaper articles about illness, fatigue, depression, burnout? How else can we explain the fact that these problems are all on the increase? All these physical and psychological deformations that affect people today are a direct indicator that a purely economic way of thinking has been built into even the tiniest arteries of our society.

This is what theatre ought to talk about – and it can do so in a competent way if only we feed our imagination with the things that happen in the world around us every day. An ideal theatre offers the secret promise: to engage with the problems of our reality I have just described. First of all, the institutionalised theatres should actually be free from any economic pressure, because they are publicly financed. Even if considerations of audience numbers and box office income have begun to dominate, public theatre should be a space which expresses itself free from any economic pressure to justify and legitimate its existence. Isn't this a beautiful dream: a society that asserts its own ideals and values by affording some fools and jesters, borrowed from the tradition of the aristocratic court theatre of yore. They have all the liberty to hold a mirror up to this society, to challenge it, to mock it. Theatre could therefore be a space that has a purifying, cathartic power. One must think: 'It can't be that bad if our society still believes that it is right and worthwhile to playfully challenge itself'(isn't the lack of playful challenge, of ridicule, play and reflection the very indicator of the fundamentalism that is variously spreading all over the world?). In other narrative media, the pressures of audience figures and economic success are much bigger, and consequently the freedom of artistic expression is much curtailed. The quality of what is offered in mainstream television is a direct reflection of this lack of freedom.

The monopolisation of the newspaper industry has likewise resulted in us being ever less informed by competent, independent journalists. In my experience, this dissatisfaction with mainstream television and news media causes many, predominantly young, spectators at the Schaubühne to perceive our theatre as a space where you are able to express yourself, to play, and to reflect freely and independently; a space where nevertheless all the deformations of our 'flexible human bodies' I noted are not disavowed, but find their expression on stage. Add to this the simple reality of every theatre event: it happens right now, in the very moment, and in three-dimensional space, created by the live actors and their bodies. There is no second take, and no 'postproduction' afterwards, as in the editing suites of the film industry. The actor seeks to express him- or herself, in the here and now, in the presence of the spectators, who decide as experts of their perception whether they believe the actor, or not. In our digitised world, where we spend most of our time in front of two-dimensional screens, this immediate moment, when a virtual act invokes all the reality of the world, has become the very mission and the challenge of theatre today.

Appendix

A.1 THOMAS OSTERMEIER: WORKS 1994–2015

1994

Trommeln in der Nacht (Drums in the Night)

By Bertolt Brecht. Stage design: Jan Pappelbaum. Costumes by Gisela Hillmann. Music: Lars Rudolph. Perf.: Martin Engler, Anja Marlene Korpiun, Ferdinand Dörfler, Anke Schüler, Tilo Werner, Victor Calero, Thomas Gerber, Lars Rudolph, Andreas Petri, Eugen Krößner, Katja Jung, Ruth Spichtig, Christian Tschirner, Max Hopp. bat studio theatre of Ernst-Busch-Theatre Academy at Schoko-Laden, 15 October 1994.

1995

Die Unbekannte (The Unknown Woman)

By Alexander Blok. Stage design: Jan Pappelbaum. Costumes: Gisela Hillmann. Music: Jason Kahn. Dramaturgy: Antje Borchardt. Puppetry: Suse Wächter. Meyerhold Training: Gennadi Bogdanov. Perf.: Anke Schüler, Eugen Krößner, Robert Beyer, Suse Wächter, Ursina Lardi, Martin Engler, Christoph Tomanek, Erik Brünner, Christian Nickel, Mathias Noell, Boris Lehmann, Anja Werner, Christian Weise. bat studio theatre, 16 September 1995.

1996/97

Recherche Faust/Artaud

By Jens Hillje and Thomas Ostermeier, with texts by Georg Heym, Antonin Artaud, Arthur Rimbaud and Johann Wolfgang Goethe. Stage design: Stéphane Laimé. Costumes: Johanna Pfau. Music: Stefan Ziethen. Dramaturgy: Jens Hillje. Film: Marc Heinz. Perf. Wolfgang Kociesa, Hugo de Carvalho, Pierre Dubey, Martin Engler, Andrea Heil, Stéphan Pastor, Andreas Petri, Dominique Frot. Degree diploma production, bat studio theatre, 19 September 1996.

Fette Männer im Rock **(Fat Men in Skirts)**

By Nicky Silver. Stage design: Volker Thiele. Costumes: Johanna Pfau. Perf.: Bernd Stempel, Astrid Meyerfeldt, Michael Schweighöfer, Cathlen Gawlich. Baracke am Deutschen Theater, 5 December 1996.

Messer in Hennen **(Knives in Hens)**

By David Harrower. Transl. Felicitas Große. Stage design: Johanna Pfau. Costumes: Marion Münch. Music: Jörg Gollasch. Dramaturgy: Jens Hillje. Perf.: Petra Hartung, Daniel Morgenroth, Tilo Werner. Counter tenor: Jens Arndt. Clarinet: Antje Gloede. Baracke am Deutschen Theater, 2 March 1997.

Mann ist Mann **(Man Equals Man)**

By Bertolt Brecht. Actor Training/Biomechanics: Gennadi Bogdanov. Stage design: Jan Pappelbaum. Costumes: Marion Münch. Music: Jörg Gollasch. Musical Director: Ute Falkenau. Dramaturgy: Jens Hillje. Perf.: Martin Engler, Ronald Kukulies, André Szymanski, Mark Waschke, Falk Rockstroh, Tilo Werner, Linda Olsansky, Martin Brauer, Roger Jahnke, Anna Schudt. Piano: Ute Werner. Baracke am Deutschen Theater, 1 July 1997.

1997/98

Suzuki

By Alexej Schipenko. With Sükriye Dönmez, Tuncay Gary, Aykut Kayacik, Adnan Maral, Falk Rockstroh, André Szymanski, Metin Teki, Cem Sultan Ungan. Baracke am Deutsches Theater, 25 September 1997.

Shoppen und Ficken **(Shopping and Fucking)**

By Mark Ravenhill. Transl. Jakob Kraut. Stage design: Rufus Didwiszus. Costumes: Marion Münch. Music: Jörg Gollasch. Dramaturgy: Jens Hillje. Perf.: Jule Böwe, Bernd Stempel, Bruno Cathomas, André Szymanski and Thomas Bading. Baracke am Deutschen Theater, 17 January 1998.

1998/99

Unter der Gürtellinie **(Below the Belt)**

By Richard Dresser. Transl. Peter Stephan Jungk. Stage design: Rufus Didwiszus. Costumes: Marion Münch. Music: Jörg Gollasch. Dramaturgy: Jens Hillje. Perf. Tilo Werner, Bernd Stempel, Falk Rockstroh. Musicians: Haney Quartett (Wolfram Korr, Franziska Blumers, Hans Dohm, Stephan Loew). Baracke am Deutschen Theater, 3 September 1998.

Disco Pigs

By Enda Walsh. Transl. Ian Galbraith. Perf.: Bibiana Beglau, Marc Hosemann. Live music: Thomas Witte, Jörg Gollasch. Deutsches Schauspielhaus Hamburg, Malersaal, 14 October 1998.

Der blaue Vogel (The blue bird)

By Maurice Maeterlinck. Stage design: Jan Pappelbaum. Costumes: Rufus Didwiszus and Bernd Skodzig. Music: Jörg Gollasch. Vocals and choreography: Ute Falkenau. Perf.: Anja-Marlene Korpiun, Tilo Werner, Udo Kroschwald, Nina Hoss, Bernd Stempel, André Szymanski, Kay Bartholomäus Schulze, Ronald Kukulies, Falk Rockstroh, Thomas Bading, Horst Lebinsky, Gudrun Ritter and Gabriele Heinz. Deutsches Theater Berlin, 12 January 1999.

Feuergesicht (Fireface)

By Marius von Mayenburg. Stage design: Rufus Didwiszus. Costumes: Almut Eppinger. Music: Jörg Gollasch. Dramaturgy: Marius von Mayenburg, Tilman Raabke; Perf.: Wolf Aniol, Gundi Ellert, Judith Engel, Robert Beyer, Mark Waschke. Deutsches Schauspielhaus Hamburg, 15 April 1999. Transfer to Schaubühne am Lehniner Platz, 22 October 2000.

Suzuki 2

By Alexej Schipenko. With Sükriye Dönmez, Tuncay Gary, Aykut Kayacik, Adnan Maral, Falk Rockstroh, André Szymanski, Metin Tekin, Cem Sultan Ungan. Baracke am Deutschen Theater, 9 June 1999.

1999/2000

Personenkreis 3.1 (Category 3.1)

By Lars Norén. Transl. Angelika Grundlach. Stage design: Jan Pappelbaum. Costumes: Almut Eppinger. Music: Jörg Gollasch. Dramaturgy: Roland Schimmelpfennig. Perf.: Anna Schudt, André Szymanski, Falk Rockstroh, Thomas Bading, Mark Waschke, Hans Diehl, Julika Jenkins, Stephanie Eidt, Adnan Maral, Kay Bartholomäus Schulze, Robert Beyer, Martin Brambach, Jule Böwe, Marina Galic, Christine Harbort. Piano: Ute Werner. Schaubühne am Lehniner Platz, 24 January 2000.

Gier (Crave)

By Sarah Kane. Transl. Marius von Mayenburg. Stage design: Rufus Didwiszus. Costumes: Bernd Skodzig. Music: Jörg Gollasch. Dramaturgy: Marius von Mayenburg. Video: Jörg Felden, Rufus Didwiszus. Puppetry: Hans Thiemann.

Perf.: Falk Rockstroh, Thomas Dannemann, Cristin König, Michaela Steiger. Schaubühne am Lehniner Platz, 23 March 2000.

***Parasiten* (Parasites)**

By Marius von Mayenburg. Stage design: Stephan Fernau. Costumes: Almut Eppinger. Music: Jörg Gollasch. Dramaturgy: Marius von Mayenburg, Marion Hirte. Perf.: Karin Pfammatter, Tilo Werner, Cristin König, Mark Waschke, Werner Rehm. Coproduction with Deutsches Schauspielhaus Hamburg, 18 May 2000. Premiere at Schaubühne 14 October 2000.

2000/1

***Der Name* (The Name)**

By Jon Fosse. Transl. Hinrich Schmidt-Henkel. Stage design: Rufus Didwiszus. Costumes: Almut Eppinger. Music: Jörg Gollasch. Dramaturgy: Roland Schimmelpfennig, Maja Zade. Perf.: Anja-Marlene Korpiun, Jens Harzer, Jule Böwe, Stephanie Eidt, Hans Fleischmann, Tilo Werner. Co-production with Salazburger Festspiele, 6 August 2000. Premiere at Schaubühne, 2 October 2000.

***Das ist ein Stuhl* (This is a chair)**

By Caryl Churchill. Transl. Bernd Samland. Stage design: Ralf Käselau. Costumes: Almut Eppinger. Dramaturgy: Roland Schimmelpfennig. Perf.: Mark Waschke, Jule Böwe, Martin Brambach, Anna Schudt, Linda Olsansky, André Szymanski, Cristin König, Adnan Maral, Stephanie Eidt, Marina Galic, Robert Beyer, Thomas Bading, Jörg Hartmann. Schaubühne am Lehniner Platz, 19 January 2001.

***Dantons Tod* (Danton's Death)**

By Georg Büchner. Stage design: Jan Pappelbaum. Costumes: Almut Eppinger. Music: Jörg Gollasch. Dramaturgy: Roland Schimmelpfennig, Marius von Mayenburg. Perf.: Kay Bartholomäus Schulze, Ronald Kukulies, Julika Jenkins, Thomas Bading, Mark Waschke, Lars Eidinger, Hans Diehl, Tilo Werner, André Szymanski, Werner Rehm, Falk Rockstroh, Cristin König. Musicians: Silke Eberhard, Christian Gerber, Matthias Trippner. Schaubühne am Lehniner Platz, 31 March 2001.

2001/2

Supermarket

By Biljana Srbljanović. Transl. Alexander Urosevic. Stage design: Jan Pappelbaum. Costumes: Almut Eppinger. Music: Jörg Gollasch. Video: Julian

Rosefeldt. Dramaturgy: Roland Schimmelpfennig. Perf.: Falk Rockstroh, Linda Olsansky, Mark Waschke, Gerd Wameling, Jörg Hartmann, Cristin König. Musicians: Jörg Gollasch, Fabian Kalbitzer, Martin Klingeberg, Matthias Trippner. Coproduktion with Vienna Festwochen, 15 June 2001. Premiere at Schaubühne 23 September 2001.

Push Up 1–3

By Roland Schimmelpfennig. Stage design: Ulrich Frommhold. Costumes: Nele Fleischmann. Music: Elektroblitz Mitte. Dramaturgy: Eva-Maria Vogtländer. Perf.: Falk Rockstroh, Tina Engel, Linda Olsansky, Mark Waschke, Julika Jenkins, Tilo Prückner, Lars Eidinger, Martina Krauel. Schaubühne am Lehniner Platz, 10 November 2001.

***Der starke Stamm* (The strong tribe)**

By Marieluise Fleisser. Stage design: Rufus Didwiszus. Costumes: Ann Poppel. Music: Jörg Gollasch. Dramaturgy: Marion Tiedtke. Perf.: Martin Schwab, Paul Herwig, Hildegard Schmahl, Walter Hess, Katharina Marie Schubert, Jochen Striebeck, Buddy Elias, Jochen Noch, Heidy Forster, René Dumont, Michael Tregor, Stephan Zinner, Dorothea Lata. Children: Marie-Therese von Buttlar, Alexander Göppert, Leopold van Buttlar, Florian Göppert. Kammerspiele Munich, 22 January 2002.

***Goldene Zeiten* (Better Days)**

By Richard Dresser. Transl. Brigitte Landes. Stage design: Jan Pappelbaum. Costumes: Almut Eppinger. Music: Stefan Ziethen. Dramaturgy: Marius von Mayenburg. Video: Julian Rosefeldt. Perf.: Mark Waschke, Bruno Cathomas, Anne Tismer, Matthias Matschke, Jule Böwe, Lars Eidinger, Robert Beyer. Schaubühne am Lehniner Platz, 26 April 2002.

2002/3

The Girl on the Sofa

By Jon Fosse. Transl. David Harrower. Stage design: Rufus Didwiszus. Costumes: Almut Eppinger. Music: Matteo Fargion. Dramaturgy: Maja Zade. Perf.: Abby Ford, Ruth Lass, Leah Muller, Julie Legrand, Paul M. Meston, Daniel Cerqueira, Liz Kettle, Michael Mellinger, Bill Pollock. Musician: Joanna Dudley. Edinburgh International Festival, Royal Lyceum, 12 August 2002.

***Nora – Ein Puppenheim* (A Doll's House)**

By Henrik Ibsen. Transl. Hinrich Schmidt-Henkel. Stage design: Jan Pappelbaum. Costumes: Almut Eppinger. Music: Lars Eidinger. Dramaturgy:

Beate Heine, Maja Zade. Perf.: Jörg Hartmann, Anne Tismer, Lars Eidinger, Jenny Schily, Kay Bartholomäus Schulze, Agnes Lampkin, Enrico Stolzenburg. Children: Milena Bühring/Sophia Bühring, Constantin Fischer/Sören Hinnenthal, Robin Meisner/Eric Neumann. Schaubühne am Lehniner Platz, 26 November 2002.

Wunschkonzert (Request Show)

By Franz Xaver Kroetz. Stage design: Jan Pappelbaum. Costumes: Almut Eppinger. Vocals: Ulrike Paula Bindert. Music: Niclas Ramdohr. Radio production: Karsten Adam. Dramaturgy: Marius von Mayenburg. Perf.: Anne Tismer. Schaubühne am Lehniner Platz, 7 February 2003.

Woyzeck

By Georg Büchner. Adapted by Schaubühne. Stage design: Jan Pappelbaum. Costumes: Almut Eppinger. Music: Niclas Ramdohr. Dramaturgy: Marius von Mayenburg. Stage fight: Klaus Figge. Dance training: Ralf Habicht. Folk dance choreography: Şükran Ezgimen. Perf.: Bruno Cathomas, Christina Geiße, Felix Römer, Kay Bartholomäus Schulze, Ronald Kukulies, Ruud Gielens, Lars Eidinger, Linda Olsansky, Udo Kroschwald, Detlev Schmitt, Erwin Bröderbauer, André Szymanski, Josef Hoffmann, Paul Matzke, Niklas Polhans, Martin Winkel, David Gieselmann, Mark Waschke. Children: Mai-Nam Scharapenko/Romy Maaß, Mai-Ly Scharapenko/Anastasia Maaß. Rap: Freaky Floe, Rebel. Dance: 'Micky' Axel Schiffler, 'Telle' Michael Tetzlaff, Jerome Granzow, Neves Arabe, 'Patrock' Patrick Schulze, 'Jackspin' Jakob Seydel, 'Sancho' Christian Garmatter, 'Hawk' Ralf Habicht. Schaubühne am Lehniner Platz, 20 May 2003.

2003/4

Risiko (Suburban Motel, Part 6)

By George F. Walker. Transl. Frank Heibert. Stage design: Jan Pappelbaum. Costumes: Heike Keinath. Dramaturgy: Anita Kerzmann, Maja Zade. Perf.: Kay Bartholomäus Schulze, Jule Böwe, Ursula Staack, Gunnar Teuber. Schaubühne Studio, 23 August 2003.

Der Würgeengel (The Exterminating Angel)

By Karst Woudstra, after the movie *El ángel exterminador* by Luis Buñuel and Luis Alcoriza. Transl. Barbara Buri and Maria von Loe. Stage design: Jan Pappelbaum. Costumes: Almut Eppinger. Music: Lars Eidinger. Dramaturgy: Beate Heine. Perf.: Wolf Aniol, Anne Tismer, Jule Böwe, Kay Bartholomäus Schulze, Markus Gertken, Jörg Hartmann, Jenny Schily, Falk Rockstroh,

Christina Geiße, Felix Römer, David Ruland, Linda Olsansky, Robert Beyer, Cristin König, Stephanie Eidt, Lars Eidinger, Zaw Lin Shwe. Schaubühne am Lehniner Platz, 1 November 2003.

Lulu. Eine Monstertragödie (1894) (Lulu, A Monster Tragedy, 1894)

By Frank Wedekind. Stage design: Jan Pappelbaum. Costumes: Almut Eppinger. Music: Matthias Trippner. Dramaturgy: Beate Heine. Perf.: Falk Rockstroh, Anne Tismer, Wolf Aniol, Gerd Böckmann, Lars Eidinger, Thomas Bading, Ursina Lardi, David Ruland, Jörg Hartmann, Pascale Schiller, Marina Lubrich, Anna Schmutz-Lacroix, Katharina Hauck, Mark Waschke, Christina Geiße, Robert Beyer. Schaubühne am Lehniner Platz, 24 March 2004.

Baumeister Solness (The Master Builder)

By Henrik Ibsen. Transl. Hinrich Schmidt-Henkel. Stage design: Jan Pappelbaum. Costumes: Anja Maier. Music: Matthias Trippner. Perf.: Gert Voss, Kirsten Dene, Branko Samarovski, Markus Gertken, Sabine Haupt, Urs Hefti, Dorothee Hartinger. Burgtheater Vienna, 10 June 2004.

2004/5

Eldorado

By Marius von Mayenburg. Stage design: Jan Pappelbaum. Costumes: Almut Eppinger. Music: Matthias Trippner, Christine Söring. Dramaturgy: Maja Zade. Perf.: Dieter Mann, Stephanie Eidt, Matthias Matschke, Ingrid Andree, André Szymanski, Judith Engel. Schaubühne am Lehniner Platz, 11 December 2004.

Zerbombt (Blasted)

By Sarah Kane. Transl. Nils Tabert. Stage design: Jan Pappelbaum, Costumes: Almut Eppinger. Music: Malte Beckenbach. Dramaturgy: Marius von Mayenburg. Perf.: Ulrich Mühe, Katharina Schüttler, Thomas Thieme. Schaubühne am Lehniner Platz, 16 March 2005.

Vor Sonnenaufgang (Before Sunrise)

By Gerhart Hauptmann. Stage design: Rufus Didwiszus. Costumes: Nina Wetzel. Music: Mark Polscher. Video: Sébastien Dupouey. Dramaturgy: Marion Tiedtke. Perf.: Peter Brombacher, Hildegard Schmahl, Julia Jentsch, Michael Neuenschwander, Murali Perumal, Stephan Bissmeier, Paul Herwig, Narudee Sriprasertkul. Kammerspiele Munich, 29 May 2005.

2005/6

Hedda Gabler

By Henrik Ibsen. Transl. Hinrich Schmidt-Henkel. Stage design: Jan Pappelbaum. Costumes: Nina Wetzel. Music: Malte Beckenbach. Dramaturgy: Marius von Mayenburg. Video: Sébastian Dupouey. Perf.: Lars Eidinger, Katharina Schüttler, Lore Stefanek, Annedore Bauer, Jörg Hartmann, Kay Bartholomäus Schulze. Schaubühne am Lehniner Platz, 26 October 2005.

Trauer muss Elektra tragen (Death becomes Electra)

By Eugene O'Neill. Transl. Michael Walter, adaptation Schaubühne. Stage design: Jan Pappelbaum. Costumes: Bernd Skodzig. Music: Lars Eidinger. Dramaturgy: Marius von Mayenburg. Perf.: Thomas Thieme, Susanne Lothar, Axel Wandtke, Katharina Schüttler, Rafael Stachowiak, André Szymanski, Daniela Holtz. Schaubühne am Lehniner Platz, 4 March 2006.

Ein Sommernachtstraum (A Midsummer Night's Dream)

After William Shakespeare. Transl. Frank Günther. Choreography Constanza Macras. Stage design: Jan Pappelbaum. Costumes: Ulrike Gutbrod. Music: R. Chris Dahlgren, Maurice de Martin, Alex Nowitz. Dramaturgy: Marius von Mayenburg. Perf.: Nabih Amaraoui, Robert Beyer, Lars Eidinger, Markus Gertken, Jörg Hartmann, Bettina Hoppe, Hyoung-Min Kim, Florencia Lamarca, Eva Meckbach, Alex Nowitz, Gail Sharrol Skrela, Rafael Stachowiak. Coproduction with the Hellenic Festival Athens, 28 June 2006. Premiere at Schaubühne 2 September 2006.

2006/7

Liebe ist nur eine Möglichkeit (Love is only a possibility)

By Christoph Nussbaumeder after Christian Ehrhardt. Stage design: Jan Pappelbaum, Magda Willi. Costumes: Almut Eppinger. Music: Maurice de Martin. Photography: Corinne Rose, Benjamin Krieg. Dramaturgy: Marius von Mayenburg. Perf.: David Ruland, Nicola Gründel, Christoph Gareisen, Katrin Heller, Gerdy Zint, Murali Perumal, Cathlen Gawlich, Uwe Fischer, Felix Römer, Eva Meckbach, Bettina Hoppe. Schaubühne am Lehniner Platz, 17 October 2006.

Das Produkt (Product)

By Mark Ravenhill. Transl. Nils Tabert. Stage design: Jan Pappelbaum. Costumes: Almut Eppinger. Music: Malte Beckenbach. Dramaturgy: Irina

Szodruch. Perf.: Jörg Hartmann, Simone Kabst. Schaubühne am Lehniner Platz, 23 November 2006.

***Die Ehe der Maria Braun* (The Marriage of Maria Braun)**

After the movie by Rainer Werner Fassbinder. Script: Peter Märthesheimer, Pea Fröhlich. Stage design: Nina Wetzel. Costumes: Ulrike Gutbrod. Music: Nils Ostendorf. Video: Sébastien Dupouey. Dramaturgy: Julia Lochte. Perf.: Brigitte Hobmeier, Steven Scharf, Jean-Pierre Cornu, Hans Kremer, Bernd Moss. Kammerspiele Munich, 1 January 2007, transfer to Schaubühne 23 November 2009.

***Die Katze auf dem heißen Blechdach* (Cat on a hot tin roof)**

By Tennessee Williams. Transl. Jörn van Dyk. Stage design: Jan Pappelbaum. Costumes: Ulrike Gutbrod. Music: Maurice de Martin. Dramaturgy: Ralph Hammerthaler. Video: Sébastien Dupouey. Perf.: Jule Böwe, Mark Waschke, Bettina Hoppe, Kirsten Dene, Josef Bierbichler, Christoph Gareisen, David Ruland. Children: Annika Frommholz, Leon Kessler, Paulina Noak, Helena Siegmund-Schultze, Carlo Vollert, Constantin Fischer, Hannah Klaes, Lotte Thierbach, Darvin Werland, Sarah Werland. On video: André Szymanski. Schaubühne am Lehniner Platz, 30 January 2007.

2007/8

Room Service

By John Murray and Allen Boretz. Transl. Helmar Harald Fischer. Stage design: Jan Pappelbaum. Costumes: Ann Poppel. Dramaturgy: Marius von Mayenburg. Music: Maurice de Martin. Perf.: Felix Römer, Kurt Krömer, Thomas Bading, Robert Beyer, David Ruland, Eva Meckbach, Rafael Stachowiak, Elzemarieke de Vos, Jörg Hartmann, Ulrich Hoppe, Christoph Gareisen, Kay Bartholomäus Schulze, Gerdy Zint. Musicians: Musiker: Maurice de Martin, Antonio Palesano. Schaubühne am Lehniner Platz, 31 October 2007.

***Die Stadt/Der Schnitt* (Double Bill)**

Stage design: Jan Pappelbaum, Magda Willi. Composition: Alex Nowitz. Film installation: Julian Rosefeldt. Costumes: Almut Eppinger. Dramaturgy: Marius von Mayenburg. Dance: Florencia Lamarca, Gail Sharrol Skrela.

Die Stadt (The City). By Martin Crimp. Transl. Marius von Mayenburg. Perf. Bettina Hoppe, Jörg Hartmann, Lea Draeger, Children: Helena Siegmund-Schulze, Hannah Klaes.

Der Schnitt (The Cut). By Mark Ravenhill. Transl. Nils Tabert. Perf.: Thomas Bading, Judith Rosmair, David Ruland, Sebastian Schwarz, Judith Strössenreuter.

Schaubühne am Lehniner Platz, 21 March 2008.

Hamlet

By William Shakespeare. Transl. Marius von Mayenburg. Stage design: Jan Pappelbaum. Costumes: Nina Wetzel. Music: Nils Ostendorf. Dramaturgy: Marius von Mayenburg. Video: Sébastien Dupouey. Fight training: René Lay. Perf.: Urs Jucker, Lars Eidinger, Judith Rosmair, Robert Beyer, Sebastian Schwarz, Stefan Stern. Coproduction with the Hellenic Festival Athens, 7 July 2008, and the Festival d'Avignon, 16 July 2008. Premiere at Schaubühne 17 September 2008.

2008/9

John Gabriel Borkmann

By Henrik Ibsen. Transl. Marius von Mayenburg after the translation by Sigurd Ibsen. Stage design: Jan Pappelbaum. Costumes: Nina Wetzel. Music: Nils Ostendorf. Dramaturgy: Marius von Mayenburg. Perf.: Josef Bierbichler, Kirsten Dene, Sebastian Schwarz, Angela Winkler, Cathlen Gawlich, Felix Römer, Elzemarieke de Vos. Coproduction with Théâtre National de Bretagne Rennes, 10 December 2008, and Ruhrfestspiele Recklinghausen. Premiere at Schaubühne 14 January 2009.

Susn

By Herbert Achternbusch. Stage design and costumes: Nina Wetzel. Music: Nils Ostendorf. Video: Sébastien Dupouey. Dramaturgy: Julia Lochte. Perf.: Brigitte Hobmeier, Edmund Telgenkämper. Kammerspiele Munich, 24 April 2009.

2009/10

***Dämonen* (Demons)**

By Lars Norén. Transl. Angelika Gundlach. Stage design and costumes: Nina Wetzel. Music: Nils Ostendorf. Video: Sébastien Dupouey. Dramaturgy: Bernd Stegemann. Perf.: Brigitte Hobmeier, Lars Eidinger, Eva Meckbach, Tilman Strauss. Schaubühne am Lehniner Platz, 2 March 2010.

2010/11

Othello

By William Shakespeare. Transl. Marius von Mayenburg. Stage design: Jan Pappelbaum. Costumes: Nina Wetzel. Music: The Polydelic Souls. Musical Director: Nils Ostendorf. Video: Sébastien Dupouey. Dramaturgy: Marius von Mayenburg. Perf.: Sebastian Nakajew, Stefan Stern, Thomas Bading, Tilman Strauß, Niels Bormann, Erhard Marggraf, Ulrich Hoppe, Eva Meckbach, Laura

Tratnik, Luise Wolfram. Coproduction with Hellenic Festival Epidaurus, 6 August 2010. Premiere at Schaubühne 9 October 2010.

Spoken (Ghosts)

By Henrik Ibsen. Transl. Judith Herzberg. Stage design: Jan Pappelbaum. Costumes: Wojciech Dziedzic. Music: Nils Ostendorf. Video: Sébastien Dupouey. Perf.: Eelco Smits, Marieke Heebink, Fred Goessens, Isis Cabolet, Hans Kesting. Toneelgroep Amsterdam, 27 February 2011.

2011/12

Mass für Mass (Measure for Measure)

By William Shakespeare. Transl. Marius von Mayenburg. Stage design: Jan Pappelbaum. Costumes: Ulrike Gutbrod. Music: Nils Ostendorf. Dramaturgy: Peter Kleinert. Musicial Direction: Timo Kreuser. Perf.: Gert Voss, Lars Eidinger, Jenny König, Erhard Marggraf, Stefan Stern, Franz Hartwig, Bernardo Arias Porras. Musicians: Carolina Riaño Gómez, Nils Ostendorf, Kim Efert. Coproduction with Salzburger Festspiele, 17 August 2011, Premiere at Schaubühne 17 September 2011.

Miss Julie

By August Strindberg. Transl. Mikhail Durnenkov. Adapt. Mikhail Durnenkov and Thomas Ostermeier. Stage design: Jan Pappelbaum. Costumes: Gabriele Vöhringer. Music: Nils Ostendorf, Daniel Freitag. Video: Sébastien Dupouey. Dramaturgy: Roman Dolzhanskiy. Perf.: Chulpan Khamatova, Evegny Mironov, Yulia Peresild. Theatre of Nations Moscow, 21 December 2011.

Ein Volksfeind (An Enemy of the People)

By Henrik Ibsen. Transl. Florian Borchmeyer. Stage design: Jan Pappelbaum. Costumes: Nina Wetzel. Music: Malte Beckenbach, Daniel Freitag. Dramaturgy: Florian Borchmeyer. Chalk drawings: Katharina Ziemke. Perf.: Stefan Stern, Ingo Hülsmann, Eva Meckbach, Christoph Gawenda, David Ruland, Moritz Gottwald, Thomas Bading. Coproduction with Festival d'Avignon, 18 July 2012, Premiere at Schaubühne 8 September 2012.

2012/13

Der Tod in Venedig/Kindertotenlieder (Death in Venice/Songs on the Death of Children)

After Thomas Mann and Gustav Mahler by Maja Zade and Thomas Ostermeier. Choreography: Mikel Aristegui. Composition: Timo Kreuser. Stage design: Jan

Pappelbaum. Costumes: Bernd Skodzig. Video: Benjamin Krug. Dramaturgy: Maja Zade. Sound direction: Daniel Plewe, Wilm Thoben. Perf.: Josef Bierbichler, Leon Klose/Maximilian Ostermann, Martina Borroni, Marcella Giesche, Rosabel Huguet, Sabine Hollweck, Felix Römer, Mikel Aristegui, Bernardo Arias Porras, Kay Bartholomäus Schulze. Musician: Timo Kreuser. Coproduction with Théâtre National de Bretagne Rennes, 10 November 2012, Premiere at Schaubühne 12 January 2013.

Les revenants (Ghosts)

By Henrik Ibsen. Transl. and adapt. Olivier Cadiot and Thomas Ostermeier. Stage design: Jan Pappelbaum. Costumes: Nina Wetzel. Music: Nils Ostendorf. Video: Sébastien Dupouey. Dramaturgy: Gianni Schneider. Perf.: Eric Caravaca, Valérie Dréville, Jean-Pierre Gos, Mélodie Richard, François Loriquet. Théâtre Vidy Lausanne, 15 March 2013.

De Meeuw (The Seagull)

By Anton Chekhov. Transl. Janine Brogt. Stage design: Jan Pappelbaum. Costumes: Sabine Greunig. Music: Nils Ostendorf. Paintings: Katharina Ziemke. Dramaturgy: Florian Hellwig, Peter Kleinert. Perf.: Chris Nietvelt, Eelco Smits, Hans Kesting; Hélène Devos, Alwin Pulinckx, Bart Slegers, Hugo Koolschijn, Janni Goslinga. Live Painter: Bas Pepperkorn, Rupa Charan van Teylingen. Toneelgroep Amsterdam, 16 June 2013.

2013/14

Die kleinen Füchse (The Little Foxes)

By Lillian Hellman. Transl. Bernd Samland, adapted by Thomas Ostermeier and Florian Borchmeyer. Stage design: Jan Pappelbaum. Costumes: Dagmar Fabisch. Music: Malte Beckenbach. Dramaturgy: Florian Borchmeyer. Perf.: Nina Hoss, Thomas Bading, Ursina Lardi, David Ruland, Moritz Gottwald, Andreas Schröders, Mark Waschke, Iris Becher, Jenny König. Schaubühne am Lehniner Platz, 18 January 2014.

Die Ehe der Maria Braun (The Marriage of Maria Braun) – New Version

After the movie by Rainer Werner Fassbinder. Script: Peter Märthesheimer, Pea Fröhlich. Stage design: Nina Wetzel. Costumes: Ulrike Gutbrod, Nina Wetzel. Music: Nils Ostendorf. Video: Sébastien Dupouey. Dramaturgy: Florian Borchmeyer. Perf.: Ursina Lardi, Sebastian Schwarz, Thomas Bading, Robert Beyer, Moritz Gottwald. Coproduction with Festival d'Avignon, 23 July 2014. Premiere at Schaubühne, 6 September 2014.

2014/15

Richard III

By William Shakespeare. Transl. Marius von Mayenburg. Stage Design: Jan Pappelbaum. Costumes: Florence von Gerkan with Ralf Tristan Scezsny. Music: Nils Ostendorf. Video: Sébastien Dupouey. Dramaturgy: Florian Borchmeyer. Puppets: Ingo Mewes, Karin Tiefensee. Puppet training: Susanne Claus, Dorothee Metz. Fight training: René Lay. Perf.: Lars Eidinger, Moritz Gottwald, Eva Meckbach, Jenny König, Sebastian Schwarz, Robert Beyer, Thomas Bading, Christoph Gawenda, Laurenz Laufenberg. Musician: Thomas Witte. Schaubühne am Lehniner Platz, 7 February 2015.

Bella Figura

By Yasmina Reza. Transl. Thomas Ostermeier and Florian Borchmeyer. Stage Design: Jan Pappelbaum. Costumes: Florence von Gerkan. Music: Malte Beckenbach. Video: Guillaume Cailleau, Benjamin Krieg. Dramaturgy: Florian Borchmeyer. Perf.: Nina Hoss, Mark Waschke, Stephanie Eidt, Renato Schuch, Lore Stefanek. Schaubühne am Lehniner Platz, 16 May 2015.

A.2 SOURCES OF THE TEXTS IN THIS VOLUME

Chapter 1 is an original contribution by Peter M. Boenisch.

Section 2.1 is translated from Thomas Ostermeier's 1999 lecture script by Peter M. Boenisch, authorised and edited by Thomas Ostermeier.

Section 2.2 is translated from the book *Kräfte messen* (Hamburg: Edition Körber Stiftung 2009) by Peter M. Boenisch, and authorised and edited by Thomas Ostermeier. By permission of Edition Körber Stiftung.

Section 3.1 is based on conversations by Peter M. Boenisch with Jan Pappelbaum in March 2014 and June 2015, and has been authorised and edited by Jan Pappelbaum for this volume.

Section 3.2 is based on a conversation by Peter M. Boenisch with Lars Eidinger in May 2014, and has been authorised and edited by Lars Eidinger for this volume.

Section 3.3 is based on a conversation by Peter M. Boenisch with Sébastien Dupouey in June 2015, and has been authorised and edited by Sébastien Dupouey for this volume.

Section 4.1 is reprinted from *Contemporary Theatre Review* Vol. 16(2), 2006, pp. 235–50, by permission of Taylor & Francis Ltd.

Section 4.2 is reprinted from *Ibsen Studies* Vol. X(2), 2010, pp. 68–74 by permission of Taylor & Francis Ltd.

Section 5.1 is based on a conversation by Peter M. Boenisch with Florian Borchmeyer in May 2014, and has been authorised and edited by Florian Borchmeyer for this volume.

Sections 5.2 and 5.3 are based on conversations by Peter M. Boenisch with the cast members between January 2014 and May 2015.

Section 5.4 is based on a conversation by Peter M. Boenisch with Katharina Ziemke in July 2014, and has been authorised and edited by Katharina Ziemke for this volume.

Section 5.5 is based on a conversation by Peter M. Boenisch with Christoph Schletz in June 2015, and has been authorised and edited by Christoph Schletz for this volume.

Chapter 6 is an original contribution by Thomas Ostermeier and Peter M. Boenisch.

Section 7.1 is an original contribution by Thomas Ostermeier.

Sections 7.2 and 7.4 are based on conversations by Peter M. Boenisch with Thomas Ostermeier, and have been authorised and edited by Thomas Ostermeier for this volume.

Chapter 7.3 has been compiled by Peter M. Boenisch with assistance by Greta Lippauer.

Section 8.1 is an original contribution by Thomas Ostermeier and Peter M. Boenisch.

Section 8.2 is translated from *text + kritik,* special issue 'Die Zukunft der Literatur', Munich 2013, pp. 42–50, by Peter M. Boenisch, and authorised and edited by Thomas Ostermeier. By permission of Edition Text + Kritik.

Index

'Almost the only question we ask of any piece of theatre is: Is it alive? Thomas Ostermeier's theatre absolutely is. Alongside his "social vision" of the exterior world is also a profound musicality, which leaps past logic to another deeper human truth. The wordless, the un-sayable, the unreasonable and the instinctive and incidental is always there in his work. There is a poetic dimension which, by definition, cannot be defined by any book. So don't look for answers. Here, perhaps, in this book is a description of a journey that is as much a kind of self-interrogation as the revelation of a "method"'.
Simon McBurney *OBE, founder and artistic director, Complicite*

With *The Theatre of Thomas Ostermeier*, the German director presents his directorial method for the first time. The book provides a toolkit for understanding and enacting the strategies of his advanced contemporary approach to staging dramatic texts. In addition, the book also includes:

- Ostermeier's seminal essays, lectures and manifestos translated into English for the first time.
- Over 140 photos from the archive of Arno Declair, who has documented Ostermeier's work at the Schaubühne Berlin for many years, and by others.
- In-depth 'casebook' studies of two of his productions: Ibsen's *An Enemy of the People* (2012) and Shakespeare's *Richard III* (2015).
- Contributions from Ostermeier's actors and his closest collaborators to show how his principles are put into practice.

An extraordinary, richly illustrated insight into Ostermeier's working methods, this volume will be of interest to practitioners and scholars of contemporary European theatre alike.

Peter M. Boenisch is Professor of European Theatre at the University of Kent, and a Fellow at the International Research Centre 'Interweaving Performance Cultures' at Berlin. He is the author of *Directing Scenes and Senses: The Thinking of Regie* (2015).

Thomas Ostermeier is the most internationally recognised German theatre director of the present. He is best known for his acclaimed productions of *Hedda Gabler*, *Shopping and Fucking*, and *Hamlet*. Since 1999, he has been Artistic Director of the Schaubühne Berlin, and since 2005, he has also been Professor for *Regie* at Ernst-Busch-Theatre Academy Berlin. He became the youngest ever recipient of the Golden Lion award for his life's work at the 2011 Venice Biennial.

DRAMA AND THEATRE STUDIES

Front cover image: Scenes from *Richard III* (2015): Richard (Lars Eidinger) with Lady Anne (Jenny König). Photograph © Arno Declair.
Back cover image: Thomas Ostermeier. © Ute Mahler & Werner Mahler/OSTKREUZ.

Routledge
Taylor & Francis Group
www.routledge.com

an **informa** business
ISBN 978-1-138-91447-6
9 781138 914476